CREATE, PROMOTE AND DIS[...]
STATIONS AND SHOWS O[...]

ONLINE BROADCASTING
POWER!

BEN SAWYER & DAVE GREELY

Online Broadcasting Power!

Library of Congress Catalog Number 99-068487

ISBN: 0-966288-98-X

5 4 3 2 1

MUSKA&LIPMAN

Muska & Lipman Publishing
2645 Erie Avenue, Suite 41
Cincinnati, Ohio 45208
www.muskalipman.com
publisher@muskalipman.com

This book is composed in Melior, Columbia, Helvetica, and Courier typefaces using QuarkXpress 4.1.1, Adobe PhotoShop 5.0.2, and Adobe Illustrator 8.0. Created in Cincinnati, Ohio, in the United States of America.

Credits

Publisher
Andy Shafran

Managing Editor
Hope Stephan

Development Editor
Ben Milstead

Copy Editor
Chuck Hutchinson

Technical Editor
Jon Campbell

Proofreader
Molly Flynn

Cover Designer
Michael Williams

Production Manager
Cathie Tibbetts

Production Team
DOV Graphics
  Michelle Frey
  John Windhorst

Indexer
Kevin Broccoli

About the Authors

Ben Sawyer

Ben Sawyer has authored or co-authored more than ten computer trade books, including *MP3 Power With Winamp* and *Creating GeoCities Websites* for Muska & Lipman. Sawyer is the co-founder of Digitalmill and has written numerous articles on a wide range of technology areas including e-commerce, interactive game development, software marketing, and computer graphics. He is also a regular speaker on the topics of e-commerce and other emerging Internet trends.

Dave Greely

Dave Greely is the co-founder of Digitalmill and has co-authored several computer trade books, including *MP3 Power With Winamp* and *Creating GeoCities Websites* for Muska & Lipman.

Dedication

Ben Sawyer: This book is for Doug Briggs, who has taught me, among other things, how to sail. Good luck in Colorado and thanks for the house!

Dave Greely: For Gary Hawkins, a brilliant sportswriter who gave me my first job, helped me become a better writer, and set a great example of how to enjoy work and life.

Acknowledgments

In addition to all of the wonderful people listed on the Credits page, the authors would like to thank the following:

David Rogelberg and Sherry Rogelberg and everyone else at Studio B, our book agency.

We'd also like to offer special thanks to Publisher Andy Shafran and Managing Editor Hope Stephan at Muska & Lipman Publishing and to Elizabeth Agostinelli—Andy for again giving us the opportunity to work with Muska & Lipman and Hope and Elizabeth for cracking their friendly whips.

We'd also like to thank everyone else at Muska & Lipman, including editors Ben Milstead, Chuck Hutchinson, and Jon Campbell.

Special thanks to our "Beta Readers" Bryan Payne of Audiorealm, Joly (aka WWWhatsup), and Steve Wolf of Wolf FM. We also want to acknowledge the members of the SHOUTcast mailing list, who contributed many ideas and cheerleading for this book.

Among those in the Internet radio industry, we would like to thank Louis and, again, Bryan Payne of Audiorealm; Mark Surfas, David Wright, and Chris of GameSpy Industries (creators of RadioSpy), Jason Kay of myCaster; Peter Rothman and Jeremy of Live365; Jack Moffit of icecast, Marty Roberts and Lisa Amore at RealNetworks, Nancy Gardner from DDB-Seattle; Danielle Kreinbrink of Telos Systems; Joshua Marks of Voquette; and the gang at MusicDish.

Last, but certainly not least, special thanks to our friends at Nullsoft—Justin Frankel, Rob Lord, Tom Pepper, Steve Gedikian, and Ian Rogers, who turned this whole industry on its head with the creation of SHOUTcast.

Contents

3—Learning From Today's Internet Radio

4—Getting Everything you Need—From Hardware to Software, Microphones to ISDN Lines 69

Part II Radio Station Software Step-by-Step

6—Broadcasting with RealServer 7.0 127

7—MyCaster and Windows Media Audio 167

Part III Preparing Content for Your Station

Part IV Managing Your Internet Radio Station

D—Streaming Audio Master 439

Introduction

Welcome to *Online Broadcasting Power!* This book explores broadcasting audio online in several formats, everything from the tools you need to the step-by-step processes of building your station and managing it.

This introduction briefly outlines what you'll find in the various chapters and describes conventions that will be used throughout the book.

What You'll Find in This Book

This book will provide you with an in-depth look at Internet broadcasting. It begins with some background about radio in general and Internet broadcasting in particular. It also covers the tools and processes involved in building an Internet radio station in a number of formats and goes on to discuss the management of that station. Much of the book is technical in nature, but it also covers promotion, legal issues, and commercializing your station.

Who This Book Is For

This book is for anyone interested in broadcasting over the Internet, whether your intended listeners are a handful of friends or a wide commercial audience. It assumes that you are connected to the Internet and are comfortable working with technology. You might also want to read Muska & Lipman's *MP3 Power with Winamp,* by Justin Frankel, Ben Sawyer, and Dave Greely.

How This Book Is Organized

This book includes seventeen chapters and four appendices:

▶ **Chapter 1, "What is Internet Radio?"**—A look back at the history of radio from its invention in the early 1900s to the Internet's current impact on broadcasting.

▶ **Chapter 2, "The Internet Radio Landscape: Players, Stations, Shows, Streaming, and Remotes"**—An overview of Internet radio types and technologies that will help you decide which work best for you.

▶ **Chapter 3, "Learning From Today's Internet Radio"**—A look at some interesting Internet radio stations of various styles and sizes.

▶ **Chapter 4, "Getting Everything You Need—From Hardware to Software, Microphones to ISDN Lines"**—If the rest of this book is a recipe for creating an Internet radio station, this chapter is the list of ingredients.

▶ **Chapter 5, "Building a SHOUTcast Station Step-by-Step"**—Covers all aspects of creating an Internet radio station using SHOUTcast.

▶ **Chapter 6, "Broadcasting with RealServer 7.0"**—Covers all aspects of creating an Internet radio station using icecast.

▶ **Chapter 7, "MyCaster and Windows Media Audio"**—Covers all aspects of creating an Internet radio station using MyCaster and Windows Media.

▶ **Chapter 8, "Alternative Server and Radio Station Solutions"**—Shows the reader the basics of obtaining, installing, and using these servers.

▶ **Chapter 9, "Outsourcing and Station Hosting"**—If you don't want to serve your station yourself, you can turn to a number of services. This chapter covers many of these.

▶ **Chapter 10, "Building a Web Site for Your Station"**—Covers what your station's Web site should include, such as dynamic playlists, ICQ request forms, chat rooms, and more.

▶ **Chapter 11, "Digitizing and Formats"**—Covers recording options, how to get good sound signals, and using a digitizing programs.

▶ **Chapter 12, "Encoding Step-by-Step"**—Discusses encoding to MP3 format, ripping from CDs, creating RealAudio content, and creating Windows Media audio.

▶ **Chapter 13, "Programming: Doing Talk, Booking Guests, Making Playlists, and Setting Up A Show"**—Covers music and talk programming and other items, such as pacing your show and obtaining content.

▶ **Chapter 14, "Doing Remotes and Live Broadcasts"**—Covers the special issues involved in remotes and live broadcasts and how they relate to the various servers.

▶ **Chapter 15, "Promoting Your Station and Broadcast"**—Covers the basics of Web and traditional promotion.

▶ **Chapter 16, "The Legalities of Running Your Station"**—Covers the rules that govern online broadcasting and how to obtain statutory licenses from the various agencies.

▶ **Chapter 17, "Commercializing Your Station"**—Covers techniques involved in commercializing your station, such as advertising and selling records, banner ads, and audio time.

▶ **Appendix A, "Multicasting Your Broadcast"**

▶ **Appendix B, "DJ Tools for Live Mixing"**

▶ **Appendix C, "Using RadioSpy"**

▶ **Appendix D, "Streaming Audio Master"**

Conventions Used in This Book

The following conventions are used in this book:

▶ For convenience, we'll usually refer to operations involving the primary mouse button with phrases such as "the left mouse button" and "left-clicking." For operations involving the secondary mouse button, we'll usually use phrases such as "the right mouse button" and "right-clicking." Please keep this in mind if you have your mouse set up as a left-hand mouse.

▶ All URLs mentioned in the book appear in **boldface.**

Besides these terminological and typographic conventions, the book also features the following special displays for different types of important text:

TIP
Text formatted like this will provide a helpful tip relevant to the topic being discussed in the main text.

NOTE
Notes highlight other information that is interesting or useful and that relates to the topic under discussion in the main text.

CAUTION
Warnings about actions or operations that could make irreversible changes to your image or that might lead to consequences that are potentially confusing will be displayed as a Caution. Be sure to read Caution text—it could help you to avoid some very troublesome pitfalls!

Keeping the Book's Content Current

For updates, corrections, and other information related to the content of the book, head out to **http://www.stationbuilder.com/.**

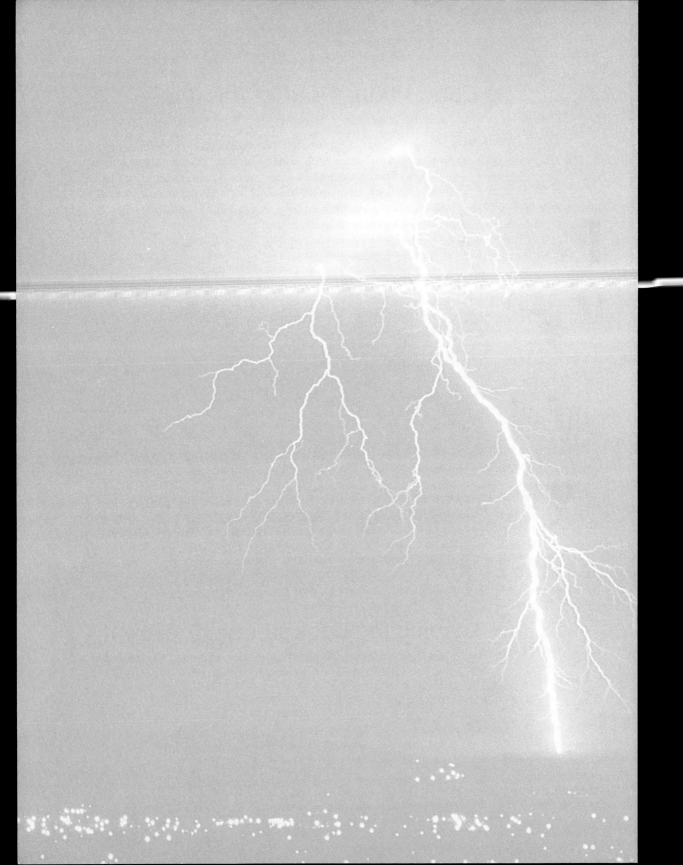

Part I

Understanding the Basics

1

What is Internet Radio?

After reading this book, you should have a good understanding of what Internet radio is about. We want you to understand the subtleties of Internet broadcasting and be the best broadcaster possible. To do so, we need to go back—way back—and explore the history of radio, the Internet, the World Wide Web, and Internet radio. You also need to understand the role of Internet radio, both in terms of its functional purpose and its place in the history of broadcasting. Then we can help you understand the true power, purpose, and unique features of Internet radio.

Internet radio in its purest form is the broadcasting of audio via Internet technology. This process is also known as Webcasting. However, Webcasting can also include sending video and other information, such as streaming text or a slideshow, in a broadcast form (i.e. pushed out toward users). Internet radio is a subset of Webcasting that is focused on audio. Internet radio takes the form of traditional radio broadcasts in terms of content, style, and program format, but it uses a completely different form of transportation.

What is the Place of Internet Radio?

Traditional radio began as a communications medium, used to send messages back and forth from one place to another. From there it became much more of a one-to-many medium, which created the field of broadcasting. Radio as we know it today built from that and is essentially the third major mass-market medium, behind television and ahead of print.

With Internet radio, you have the redefinition of radio as a medium and as a technology. Internet radio obviously doesn't use the wave-based technology of traditional radio nor does it necessarily work with a mass-market model, due to the niche-nature of the Internet. Internet radio, because it uses the Internet as the means of distribution, is a world-wide medium that can reach someone in Kenya almost as easily as it can reach someone in New York City or Kuala Lumpur.

Despite the major differences, Internet radio and traditional radio do share one common purpose—to inform and/or entertain people through audio content such as music, talk, or a mix of the two. While it is true that through the same technology of Internet radio we can deliver video and pictures, Internet radio isn't about taking radio into the video age (that's an entirely different beast). Internet radio will always remain focused on music, talk, and discussion, and only occasionally will it include a Web site picture or in-studio Webcam as an enhancement to a broadcast.

The role of radio has been both as a pure communications medium and as a medium of entertainment and enlightenment. In that way, radio has taken on a meaning less tied to its technological foundation and more attached to its purpose. Understanding how radio has gone from a technological breakthrough to defining a more functional style of broadcasting is important. It will ground you as an Internet radio pioneer, giving you a sense of place in the history of all radio and not just as some whiz bang user of a neat new Internet trend.

Many broadcast pioneers felt an immense social and personal responsibility in their work. Understanding how that carries over to broadcasting today can also help you as a provider of Internet radio. Many traditional radio stations are beacons in a society's worst times, whether they are natural disasters or man-made ones. Radio stations are among the first targets in coups and other military actions and are also used as critical countermeasures to totalitarianism. That role, too, has carried over to Internet radio, where, during the troubles in the former Yugoslavia, many radio stations that were knocked off the air used the Internet to continue broadcasting.

Thus, one can be left with the question, what is the place of Internet radio? And what is your place as a purveyor of it? To answer that, we think it makes sense to look at the history of radio, radio broadcasting, the rise of the Internet, and specifically Internet radio. This will help you gain some insight into the role, responsibilities, and purposes of what you'll do as a station or show operator.

From Marconi to Me: The History of Broadcasting to Narrowcasting

A little background can be a good thing. Even though we are now entering a new age of radio—and a totally new way of broadcasting audio to the masses—it's important to know how we get from a man named Marconi, who many credit with inventing radio back in the early 1900s, and end up today with Me (that is, You). By this, we mean that, with Internet radio, you (and potentially everyone in the world) are the broadcaster. In less than one hundred years, audio broadcasting has gone from Marconi to Me, and you can learn many lessons from this journey that will make you a great radio station operator. So, sit back and enjoy the story.

Radio: What It Is and How It Works

Radio is the wireless transmission or reception of electromagnetic radiation in the radio frequency range from one place to another. A typical radio communication system has two main components: a *transmitter* and a *receiver*. A radio wave carries information-bearing signals; the information may be encoded directly on the wave by periodically interrupting its transmission, or it may be impressed on the carrier frequency by a process called *modulation*.

Because of their varying characteristics, radio waves of different lengths are employed for different purposes and are usually identified by their frequency. The shortest waves have the highest frequency, or number of cycles per second; the longest waves have the lowest frequency, or fewest cycles per second.

Modulation

There are two types of modulation: amplitude modulation (AM) or frequency modulation (FM). An amplitude-modulated signal consists of the carrier frequency plus two sidebands resulting from the modulation. Frequency modulation produces more than one pair of sidebands for each modulation frequency. These sidebands produce the complex variations that emerge as speech or other sound in radio broadcasting, and in the alterations of light and darkness in television broadcasting.

Transmission

A radio transmitter includes an oscillation generator for converting commercial electric power into oscillations of a predetermined radio frequency; amplifiers for increasing the intensity of these oscillations; and a transducer for converting the information to be transmitted into a varying electrical voltage. For sound transmission, a microphone is the transducer. For picture transmission, the transducer is a photoelectric device.

The modulator controls the variations in the oscillation intensity, and an antenna radiates a similarly modulated carrier wave. The particular method of designing and arranging the various components depends on the effects desired.

Receivers

A radio receiver includes an antenna for receiving the electromagnetic waves and converting them into electrical oscillations, amplifiers for increasing the intensity of these oscillations, detection equipment for demodulating, a speaker for converting the impulses into sound waves audible by the human ear, and oscillators to generate radio-frequency waves that can be "mixed" with the incoming waves.

A radio has no moving parts except the *speaker cone*, which vibrates within a range of a few thousandths of a centimeter, so the only power required to operate the radio is electrical power to force electrons through the various circuits. When radios first came into general use in the 1920s, most were operated by batteries. Although batteries are used widely in portable sets today, a power supply from a power line has major advantages because it permits the designer more freedom in selecting circuit components.

A Brief History of Radio Broadcasting

The idea of radio broadcasting began in 1873 when British physicist James Clerk Maxwell published his theory of electromagnetic waves, which applied primarily to light waves. Around 1888, German physicist Heinrich Hertz actually generated such waves electrically, proving the existence and transmitting capability of Maxwell's waves by showing that a spark created in a specially designed device could produce a smaller spark in an identical device a few feet away.

Guglielmo Marconi, an Italian electrical engineer and inventor, is generally credited with being the inventor of radio, although some maintain that Serbian inventor Nikola Tesla deserves at least as much credit.

Starting in 1895, Marconi developed an improved coherer and connected it to a rudimentary form of antenna. He also developed improved spark oscillators. In 1896, he transmitted signals for a distance of more than one mile and applied for his first British patent. In 1899, he established commercial communication between England and France. By 1901, he had transmitted a radio signal from Cornwall, England, across the Atlantic Ocean to a receiver in Newfoundland, Canada.

Marconi soon received financial support, and the Wireless Telegraph and Signal Company, Ltd., was formed in 1897. Marconi received £15,000 in cash and half the company stock. Two years later, the company's name was changed to Marconi's Wireless Telegraph Company, Ltd.

For his work in the field of wireless telegraphy, Marconi shared the 1909 Nobel Prize in physics with German physicist Karl Braun. At around the same time, various technical improvements were being made, including the development of the modern vacuum tube, which proved invaluable as an amplifier and oscillator.

Although Marconi made the first radio voice broadcast in 1895, the patent for radio belongs to Nikola Tesla. Tesla moved from Lika, Croatia, to the United States in 1884 to work with Alexander Graham Bell, Thomas Edison, and George Westinghouse. Tesla's radio was invented in Europe in 1893, and a U.S. patent for the electronic transmission of signals and data was filed on September 2, 1897. The patent was allowed on March 20, 1900, and became Tesla's second radio patent, the first having been granted in 1898. Marconi's patent for voice transmission alone was filed on November 10, 1900, and was rejected as a duplicate of Tesla's.

In later years, the Marconi Company attempted to strip Tesla of his patent. After years of litigation and thousands of pages of testimony from the world's great scientists, the U.S. Supreme Court ruled Tesla's to be the sole valid patent in June 1943.

A critical point to understand about Marconi is that he saw radio more as a communication tool rather than an entertainment tool. However, David Sarnoff, who took a job as an office boy in 1907 at New York's American Marconi, had entertainment in mind. In 1916, Sarnoff proposed a "radio music box" that he envisioned becoming a fixture in every home. It would allow people to listen to radio broadcasts—broadcasts that would constitute entertainment—and not just information provided from ships at sea or military units.

In 1917, Sarnoff became manager of a reorganized commercial department at the Marconi Company. He administered a business that thrived on contracts with the U. S. Navy during World War I and helped persuade the government not to monopolize radio communications. President Woodrow Wilson and the U.S. Navy allowed the General Electric Company (GE) to buy the American branch of the Marconi Company and pool its radio patents in what became the Radio Corporation of America (RCA). Sarnoff, who had lead this crusade, became the man in charge of the RCA division of GE.

Following its development, sales of Sarnoff's "radio music box" exceeded expectations, and he prodded the company to develop a portable radio. Sarnoff was promoted to executive vice president at the end of December 1922. The sales of home radio comprised 75 percent of RCA's revenues that year.

Sarnoff looked ahead to a merger of radio with the phonograph, non-commercial networked broadcasting, and the movie industry. However, the American Telephone and Telegraph Company (AT&T) had plans of its own for broadcasting.

In 1926, Sarnoff bought out the telephone company's network and merged it with RCA's to create the National Broadcasting Company (NBC). NBC would broadcast content via the radio, but it would include sponsors and commercials. Despite the complaints of some, most people were willing to accept commercial interruptions in radio entertainment because it would be free content to begin with.

In 1929, RCA bought the Victor Talking Machine Company. In 1930, Sarnoff became president of RCA/Victor and in 1932, RCA gained the right to make its own radios under its patent pool. Now RCA was completely vertically integrated—making radios and content. This development came at the end of an anti-trust suit by the U. S. Attorney General initiated in 1930. The suit had threatened to end RCA's patent licensing rights and force it into direct competition with its parent companies. It also would have closed down NBC's 50,000-watt superstations.

RCA's victory gained it the independence that Sarnoff had sought. RCA employed a major group of the nation's top radio engineers, the largest factory in the world for making radios, and an extensive retail and distribution network, as well as the leading radio station network (NBC) and a movie studio (RKO Pictures). And Sarnoff was atop it all.

So, Hertz may have pioneered the theory, but Marconi made it actually useful, while Tesla got the first patent for radio. However, although all these men created the foundation for radio, it was David Sarnoff who envisioned a common world, entertained and informed by broadcasting radio to the masses. This point is important because, as someone interested in Internet radio, you need to draw a distinction between the technology that gives the capability to stream audio and the skills and techniques that turn that technology into what constitutes an actual Internet radio station or show.

Early Broadcasters

After World War I, the Westinghouse Electric Corporation established what is widely considered to be the first commercially owned radio station to offer programming to the general public: KDKA in Pittsburgh. It aired various forms of entertainment.

Another early broadcaster was AT&T. As early as 1922, AT&T began considering "toll broadcasting" in which it would charge fees in return for airing advertisements on its stations. In Britain (and many countries that followed its lead), broadcasting was developing differently. Radio owners paid yearly licensing fees that were collected by the government and turned over to an independent state enterprise—the British Broadcasting Corporation (BBC). The BBC produced programming for its network of stations.

Radio broadcasting reached new heights during World War II (1939–1945), carrying war news directly from the front. American President Franklin Delano Roosevelt often used radio to directly address the American people with his fireside chats. Eventually, radio's success spurred technology companies to develop visual roadcasting—which is, of course, television.

The earliest U.S. patent for an all-electronic television system was granted in 1927. As early as 1935, the BBC initiated experimental television broadcasts in London for several hours each day. RCA unveiled television to the American public at the 1939 New York World's Fair, with live coverage of opening ceremonies featuring a speech by President Roosevelt.

The early years of television offered little news coverage. In 1956, NBC introduced *The Huntley-Brinkley Report*, a half-hour national news telecast. The other networks soon followed. From this, the standard network newscast has become a staple—and an important part of American history.

In the early days of television, advertising agencies actually produced nearly all American network radio shows and most early television programming as well. Stations often sold agencies full sponsorship, which included placing a product name in a show's title. Interestingly, this intertwining of content and commercialism eventually began to fall out of favor as broadcasting matured and regulations kicked in barring certain advertising practices or products from the air. Ironically, today on the Internet, the intertwining of content and commerce is more blatant than ever in recent history. And in the last decade, TV, movies, and other media have also returned to a more interwoven relationship between content and commercialism.

This evolution shows that, throughout the history of radio and broadcasting, the symbiotic relationship between what is produced and what is advertised or sold has been in flux; sometimes the two are nearly one and the same (like an infomercial or a show or movie that spawns a toy line), or they are sometimes more opposed or well regulated (for example, a newscast or a program such as *60 Minutes*). At no point, however, is the relationship ever completely broken; the two go hand in hand. If not, then content would have to be charged for (as in the movies or pay-per-view), and charging limits the audience that can afford to pay outright for all available content.

Television's Effect

Television's growing popularity eventually relegated radio to a secondary entertainment medium. Radio advertising revenues fell as the American public turned more heavily to television in the 1950s. Radio was down, but it wasn't out. Many forms of media adapt when new types create shifts in audience levels or attitudes, as did radio.

Radio's rebirth seems to have coincided with the birth of car culture, suburbia (which spawned the commute), and rock-n-roll, which created a whole new culture of people who wanted to consume music in a major way. When cars began to be equipped with radios in the early Fifties as the suburbs expanded, the medium underwent a resurgence. That resurgence was soon followed by the breakout of rock-n-roll in the late Fifties.

As America grew, and more and more people commuted, radio began to grow again. Stations also had a growing music base to listen to, and with many different forms of music now (jazz, classical, rock, pop), plus news and eventually talk radio, competing stations could differentiate themselves in many ways. Several independent stations appeared, providing a more local angle to broadcasting in every nook and cranny of the country. Although not every station flourished, the industry as a whole was far from wiped out by the spread of television.

Broadcasting Gains Competition and Consolidation

In the United States, the communications industry was brought under control by the creation of the Federal Communications Commission (FCC). (In a prior life, the FCC had been the Federal Radio Commission, or FRC, before the advent of TV.) The FCC licensed broadcasters in various regions to ensure they used the airwaves correctly and didn't end up blocking out each other's signals. In other countries, governments owned the radio and TV stations. What also brought the growing communications industry under control in the United States was the creation of giant networks of stations. Today, most radio stations are owned by one of several enormous networks that have pushed independent stations largely out of the mix. TV, too, originally started as lots of local stations that sprang up all over the country.

In the radio world, networks created programming for local stations, which took that programming and aired it for their viewers. In return, the networks got specific blocks of advertising time on those shows, which they then sold to profit from their programming. NBC and CBS, two of the early radio network kings, transferred this system over to TV. They were joined later by ABC, and for a long time, these "Big Three," as they were known, ruled the TV airwaves in the United States When cable came along, it provided a new way of transmitting broadcasts through direct connections to the households. This new technology created more channels and improved the signal for many people in the United States, but it fractured the audience for TV. Cable today has become big competition for the major TV networks.

The Big Three became the Big Four when Rupert Murdoch and his News Corporation finally made a success out of the Fox network in the late eighties and early nineties. In the late nineties, two upstart networks, UPN and The WB, further grabbed slivers of the audience available to broadcasters. With so many new ways to access TV channels and content, the audience splintered as it gravitated to many different types of shows and networks. Today, even the broadest broadcaster may barely deliver an audience greater than 20 million for a single show.

With radio out of favor, many of the original big radio networks faltered, as those companies turned their attention toward TV. The result was that radio itself actually flourished as radio-focused companies and independent stations took the mantel from the original pioneers. However, as media became big business in the Eighties, some of the pioneers of the new radio began consolidating stations. This way, they could offer advertisers the best of both worlds—small, targeted audiences, tailored to their needs; and the ability to buy many different groups at once.

Radio, which before the Internet was perhaps the most niche media going, has seen unbelievable consolidation, with Infinity Broadcasting (now a division of CBS Corp.) and AMFM Inc. making up huge networks of hundreds of stations owned by a single group. Advertisers, therefore, have a one-stop shop to reach an array of listeners who are divided geographically and demographically among the hundreds of stations that exist in the United States

These networks came into being because, despite the individual number of stations and types of shows, advertisers needed an easy way to reach customers without having to deal with hundreds of individual companies. In addition, networks also came about so that smaller companies could pool together and attract audiences, share costs, and share resources.

Now radio may be about to face another challenge—this time from music on the Internet. When TV came along, people thought radio would die, but instead it reinvented itself into a medium for cars, commuters, and office workers. With the Internet, however, radio is meeting a new broadcasting technology, one that can deliver far more choices and can even reach cars via wireless Internet. With the proliferation of appliances that let you access streaming audio easily and cheaply and as radio shifts to the Web, radio is again changing quite a bit. That's why it's important to see the history of radio through the history of the Internet and the Web. Although Internet radio is just in the beginning stages of development, it will eventually be the next chapter in the history of radio.

The Internet

The Internet was originally invented as a notion; not a wire was built at its inception. Instead, it started as a project at the Rand Corporation, a highly respected think-tank related to the Department of Defense based in Washington, D.C. As the Cold War raged in the Sixties, America began trying to figure out how it would maintain command and control of the nation in the event of nuclear war. Researchers at Rand—particularly, Paul Baran—began envisioning a decentralized messaging system, a decentralized network, that would route messages through different nodes ultimately to their destination. The idea known as *The Rand Proposal* became public in 1964.

The Rand Proposal was amazing in both its simplicity and its strategy. Essentially, Baran and his colleagues proposed that a new computer communication network be built from the ground up. It would be totally decentralized and designed to work even if parts of it didn't survive. All the nodes on the network would be of equal stature, with each one able to send, receive, and forward messages. The messages themselves would be divided into small components (called *packets*) that would all shoot out over the network separately and then be reassembled at their destination. If any one node was destroyed, the message would bounce around seeking alternative pathways until it ultimately could reach the destination point. In addition, the message would still be available even if the end node was destroyed because the packets would still be in the system somewhere.

The Rand Proposal quickly became more than just a piece of paper. For several years after its 1964 debut, several major universities built test networks and experimented with Baran's original ideas. The military took notice of this work and began funding a national network in 1969. It became the origins of the plan for something known as ARPAnet.

ARPA is the Advanced Research Projects Agency. A division of the U.S. Department of Defense now known as DARPA (Defense Advanced Research Projects Agency), ARPA undertook the big picture research and design, plus coordination with outside contractors, to invent the next generation of weapons and technologies that the U.S. felt were needed to maintain its national security. The idea of a highly decentralized (and thus reliable) communications network that could survive a nuclear war was deemed an extremely important project, and ARPA immediately began building it. The result was ARPAnet, which began by linking computers at major government and university research labs around the country. This new network helped scientists share critical data about next-generation weapons and tested the decentralized network ideas of the Rand Proposal. By 1972, ARPAnet was already up to thirty-seven nodes.

Who Just Wants to Work...?

An interesting aspect about technology is the way it repeats itself; people find new ways to apply technology to things they care about or things they just have to do. Just as Sarnoff envisioned people using Marconi's wireless radio technology for something other than just communications—namely entertainment—the people crunching numbers for the government, big corporations, and rocket scientists began using their huge computers and the ARPAnet for more than just research. In the Sixties, for example, a group of computer programmers invented a game called SpaceWar (the first computer game) while their co-workers thought they were just working late.

Instead of using the network to share computing time, most of the people with ARPAnet access were sending personal messages and news—in other words, electronic mail (e-mail). As you might guess, many of the messages were decidedly not about military or research topics; in fact, one of the first electronic mailing lists was used by its subscribers to keep up on the latest releases of science fiction books. And so, like radio, the Internet, even in its earliest days, caused people to want to broaden its roots and use it to entertain and inform them.

The Internet Explodes

The original language of ARPAnet was known as Network Control Protocol (NCP). NCP wasn't capable of handling many nodes, so a more complex network protocol was needed to handle the rapid growth of this new national network. This protocol still needed to represent the origins of the network, allowing for decentralized and equal footing. In January 1983, ARPAnet switched over to a new protocol known as Transmission Control Protocol/Internet Protocol (TCP/IP). With this change, the groundwork for what we now call the Internet was complete.

As more organizations began to understand the power of a national (and even worldwide) computer network, other networks began springing up—all connected by or using the same basic technologies put forward by ARPAnet.

As ARPAnet began taking on a separate life, the U.S. military broke away to set up its own shop with MILNET. The computer science community created CSNET, and BITNET (the first three letters were an acronym for "Because It's Time") was created by the college community. Soon, all these separate networks created gateways to let them interconnect as one big network—hence, the origin of the word *Internet.*

This activity was joined by the National Science Foundation (NSF), which saw the power of the emerging Internet. It joined in with NSFnet, which connected five big NSF supercomputing centers across the country. This and other high-speed networks—more commonly known as *backbones*—helped provide the capacity needed to support further growth of the Internet.

In 1989, with NSFnet and a dozen other networks operating together, the U.S. government closed down the network that started it all. ARPAnet has become just a memory, and in its place now is the Internet—an amalgamation of far-flung networks and computers, all working on the original principles of decentralization, open systems, and equal opportunity that had been the foundation of the 1964 Rand Proposal.

Enter the World Wide Web

As more networks and nodes began populating the Internet, its growth demanded better organization and systems. As more and more people began using the Net (as it's called) from colleges and other locations, the demand for better e-mail and communication systems brought forth new rounds of features.

Users, programmers, and computer science departments created entities such as Usenet, which was used to post and distribute information via bulletin boards across the Net. To improve organization, a domain naming system was created. Nodes on the Internet were divided by country, and six fundamental Internet domains in the U.S. (with the extensions *.com, .edu, .gov, .mil, .net,* and *.org*) were established for naming areas. Nevertheless, the amount of data on the Internet and the number of computers attached to it were still growing enormously.

People responded to this growth with more solutions. Researchers at McGill University in Canada created Archie, a program that helped users explore the Net and catalog information found there. Programmers at the University of Minnesota created an Internet database retrieval system called Gopher (in reference to both the "go-for" metaphor and the name of the school's sport teams, the Golden Gophers). A File Transfer Protocol (FTP) had already been in existence for a while, and FTP sites began organizing their information for easier downloading.

Despite all this refinement, more organization and user-friendliness were needed before the Internet could reach its full potential. At the same time, the Internet was devoid of multimedia, and graphics were occasional but scarce. Most consumers were still using slow modems to access local bulletin board systems or emerging online services such as CompuServe, America Online (AOL), or Prodigy. Then an unknown computer developer at a world-renowned physics research center in Europe created what is now called the *World Wide Web.*

Tim Berners-Lee Spins a Web and Changes Everything

Most people think of the Internet as an entirely American creation, yet its most important modern-day incarnation—the World Wide Web—was born in Europe, developed by an English computer programmer named Tim Berners-Lee.

The original version of the Web came to life at the European Laboratory for Particle Physics (CERN), where Tim Berners-Lee worked. He came up with the idea as a way to help track all the different projects and people working at CERN, but it moved into bigger and better things as it became a way for him, via an online "Web" of documents, to link together all the various documents and databases at CERN. CERN and Berners-Lee developed this idea privately, building on the core tenets that had made the Internet a success. The embryonic Web was decentralized, was simple to use, and focused on openness and equality. It also ran on top of the TCP/IP protocols used by the Internet, and it was "platform agnostic" (because so many different types of computers were in use at CERN, Berners-Lee couldn't afford to create a platform-centric Web). By focusing on the data rather than any specific software or hardware, Berners-Lee created a file structure for Web documents that could be read by virtually any computer. All a computer user needed was a program that could interpret the underlying language of the Web: Hypertext Markup Language, or HTML. Virtually any computer in 1990 could handle the earliest versions of HTML.

Then Berners-Lee released his ideas, code, and file structures—for free— to the world.

From Humble Beginnings to New World

People immediately began working to build upon Berners-Lee's work on creating the Web. The next watershed moment came when students at the National Center for Supercomputing Applications (NCSA), led by Marc Andreesen, created Mosaic, the first major graphical Web browsing tool. Incorporating a graphical user interface and providing great ease of use, this new piece of software had almost as powerful an impact as the debut of the Web.

After Mosaic appeared and the Web began to take shape, the commercialization of the Web and the maturing of Internet and Web technology began screaming forward. Andreesen and many of his programmers left school to form one of the pioneering companies of the Web—Netscape. Berners-Lee left CERN to head up the World Wide Web Consortium (W3C), a think tank and standards creator/arbitrator that helps create the next generation of standardized and open Web technologies. Microsoft, AOL, and hundreds of companies began embracing the Internet and creating tools, browsers, and new Web services for people to log on to and use.

Within six years after the debut of Mosaic, and more than thirty years since the original Rand Proposal, the Web had become a global phenomenon. As it grew, many innovations emerged that would change the world. One of those new technologies was the idea of streaming audio over the Internet. With this technology, people, instead of just reading a page or looking at a photo, could actually hear sounds, speeches, and music as if they had just turned on their radio.

The Beginnings of Internet Radio

In 1993, a former Microsoft manager, Rob Glaser, founded Progressive Networks with his friend David Halperin, a well-known political advisor and writer. The original idea was to create a company that would teach progressive causes or issues via some new medium. Cable and CD-ROM were considered, but both, upon closer inspection, seemed tough routes. Then a friend showed Glaser how to use Mosaic and the Web, and Glaser knew then and there that this was the medium for Progressive Networks. He had been a major vice president at Microsoft and had the money to chase wide-open ideas during the emergence of the World Wide Web.

Before Glaser left Microsoft, he had been heading up Microsoft's multimedia development efforts, and he remembered a demonstration of low-bit-rate audio distributed over an internal network from those days. He thought that if he could get some programmers to duplicate that idea but make it work on the Internet and Web, he would have a way of breaking through the media distribution problems inherent in the way TV, radio, and even CD-ROM media work. It could be a way to get the progressive ideas that he originally imagined his company championing out to the masses.

Hiring programmers and dipping into his Microsoft savings, Glaser and the original cast of Progressive developed RealAudio. RealAudio 1.0 was a highly compressed audio format that could enable streaming audio over the Internet. With streaming audio, people wouldn't have to wait for an entire audio file to download before they could listen to it. Instead, with RealAudio, after a few seconds of *buffering* (that is, pre-storing) the audio file, music, or speech, whatever was recorded into the file would start playing. The first version, which was targeted to work on 486-powered PCs with a 14.4Kbps modem, left a lot to be desired in terms of fidelity, but it did work. After a few seconds of buffering, a spoken voice of low-AM quality (but still listenable) could be heard and would stream fine as long as the connection held and the file sent forth data.

In early 1995, the first prototype was shown. The first version didn't handle music well. Progressive developed a special format (RealAudio), a server to broadcast it, and a player for people to install on their end to listen to files broadcast by that server. With some deft agreements with major browser companies to include the RealPlayer in their downloads and a good technology at its launch, RealAudio instantly became a hit. Other technologies for streaming audio over the Web existed or joined RealAudio at its launch. Products such as Streamworks from Xing, TrueSpeech from the DSP Group, and Shockwave Audio from Macromedia found limited audiences as Real—from its first mover status and excellent distribution—captured the consumers and developers interested in getting audio content on and from the Web. With quick user adoption and good marketing, Real quickly emerged as *the* way to distribute audio on the Internet, and thus many pioneering radio stations began with RealAudio as their technology of choice.

Building on its success, Progressive has re-engineered its format and technology nearly six times since version 1.0. Today, Progressive, which has changed its name to RealNetworks, is up to a totally re-engineered audio, video, and multimedia playing platform called G2 that supports a variety of media formats. Its RealServer product powers thousands of radio stations around the world, and its RealPlayer has more than 50 million installations.

Other makers of products for streaming audio and Internet radio more or less fell by the wayside as Real ascended to the top of the heap. In fact, its best competitor, Xing, is now a subsidiary of Real that concentrates on MPEG audio-based (MP3) products and services. Only Microsoft, with its Windows Media Audio (WMA) format, and a group of MP3-related companies such as Nullsoft (makers of Winamp) and the open source icecast product seem to have come along to provide any competition (albeit cool competition) to Real in the streaming audio space.

Broadcast.com and the Aggregators

With Real building the technology, servers, and players, others had to take that technology and build new services and sites with it. As the story goes, two Indiana University graduates (Mark Cuban and Todd Wagener) were in Dallas, Texas, but wanted to listen to their Hoosier basketball instead of the local offerings. Their answer was to use the Web and RealAudio technology to capture those local sports radio broadcasts and transmit them onto the Internet for everyone to hear. That initial notion gave way to Audionet.com, which, after its skyrocketing growth and before its mega-billion-dollar IPO, was renamed Broadcast.com (see Figure 1.1).

Figure 1.1
Broadcast.com, which was acquired by Yahoo! in 1999, is now known as Yahoo! Broadcast. Its pages are packed with Internet radio stations and shows to tune into.

The company quickly grew by gathering up contracts and rights to rebroadcast dozens of radio stations and sports venues via the Web. It also started placing entire CDs on the site (with permission, of course) and broadcasting tons of unseen events, such as company quarterly earnings calls, press briefings, and more. The Internet, with its diverse niche audiences and lower cost of broadcasting, made it easier to broadcast many smaller topics and content. Broadcast.com succeeded in a big way, collecting up to 350 different college and professional sports teams within a couple of years. Today, the company broadcasts hundreds of different stations, shows, briefings, and sports programs as a division of Yahoo!, now known as Yahoo! Broadcast.

Broadcast.com may have been the first big Web radio aggregator, but it is by no means alone. Others have joined in—for example, Netradio.com, Spinner.com, and WWW.com. These companies represent what Internet analysts call *aggregators*. Because the Internet is a decentralized system, providing a means of centralization to help people find the things they are looking for is a good idea. Just like malls bring together a collection of stores to provide a meaningful way for shoppers to gather and shop easily, aggregators on the Web help create simpler one-stop shopping for Web surfers trying to find a specific type of radio station or show on the Web. Some aggregators work via the Web, whereas others, such as EarthTuner (see Figure 1.2), are entirely separate browsers that people run to help them find Internet radio stations.

Figure 1.2
Although some sites like Broadcast.com use Web sites to direct people to a plethora of stations and shows, EarthTuner is a specific browser program that helps surfers tune in to a variety of Internet broadcasts.

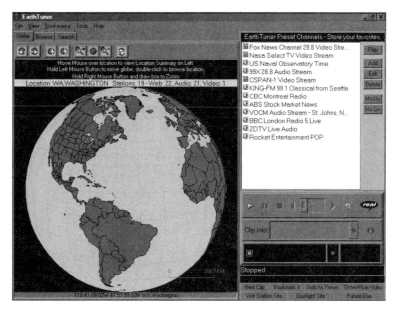

Part I Understanding the Basics

Here Comes SHOUTcast and Personal Radio

Justin Frankel, a gifted programmer, is one of the great success stories of the Internet. While attending his first year of college at the University of Utah, he stumbled across an upstart technology called MP3, an audio format that compresses high-fidelity audio ten to twelve times. Using this format, a near-CD quality file can be stored in a 3MB to 5MB file. Frankel's interest in creating a program that could play back these files resulted in the development of Winamp, the most successful MP3 player to date. While Real focused on its RealAudio format, Winamp and other MP3 players focused on just the high fidelity of the MP3 format, which many flocked to from 1996 to 1998.

Not content with his local radio in Phoenix and missing his favorite radio program, *Lovelines*, which wasn't played on the stations near his home, Frankel decided to create an extension to his Winamp player that would allow any file or sound playing for it to be converted into a version of the MP3 format that could be streamed onto the Internet. The first effort, known by its code name I Can Yell (or ICY), was a small success. Frankel and partner Tom Pepper were able to create a broadcast mechanism out of any audio stream passing through Winamp and out through a simple server application they created. To test it, the two created their own version of *Lovelines*. Hooked on the idea, they developed the software into a finished form and renamed it SHOUTcast.

The big difference between SHOUTcast and other forms of Internet radio is that it is much more conducive to the personal broadcaster. In addition, the product works seamlessly with MP3 files, which have become the de facto file format for high-fidelity digital audio. With its simple setup, compatibility with the ultra-popular Winamp, and extendable architecture, SHOUTcast has become a hit in the burgeoning Internet radio movement. By November 1999, more than 1,000 public SHOUTcast servers were operating on the Web, and perhaps just as many were operating in a private fashion. SHOUTcast was soon joined by icecast, an open source program that duplicated SHOUTcast's main MP3/personal Internet radio, if not every one of its features. More than 150 servers were operating it publicly in the fall of 1999.

With the advent of SHOUTcast and a recent move by Real to give away a twenty-five-user version of its Basic RealServer, radio had come full circle. The Web has ushered in the capability for everyone to be not only a listener but also a broadcaster. With tools and services now sprouting up everywhere, broadcasters can be large companies trying to reach millions of listeners or just a single person broadcasting a show for friends to hear their favorite music.

Traditional Radio Responds with Digital Audio Radio

Some think (us included) that traditional radio will be finally destroyed by Internet radio. Just as it morphed when TV came along, traditional radio is trying to respond to the Internet and digital broadcasting world with what is known as Digital Audio Radio (DAR). DAR is a newer type of technology that lets radio stations encode their broadcasts in a digital format and send them out over the airwaves. With stations encoding data representing the audio information rather than using a frequency, radio sound can be much better; AM stations will sound as good as FM stations, and FM stations will have near-CD quality audio. In this format, the stations can broadcast other digital information, such as text describing the station format or songs playing, even graphics and e-mail. Certainly, this capability will be a big technological improvement over current day radio, but is it enough?

Will Internet Radio Kill Traditional Radio?

In the short term (say, the next ten years), before wireless Internet and wireless Internet broadcasting become prevalent, DAR should be a big step forward in the capability of current-day radio to compete with TV and the Internet. However, as the Web becomes wireless and bandwidth increases, tuning in to an Internet-based broadcast should be just as easy as tuning into a DAR broadcast. At that point, the world of traditional radio broadcasting could very well see its end.

By then, however, many traditional radio stations will have made the jump to broadcasting over the Internet. In addition, in areas of the country and world where wireless Internet isn't available or is too expensive, traditional radio/DAR will remain the cheapest and easiest way to tune in a broadcast. Finally, the notion of radio will always live on; whether the Internet kills the method of transmission is irrelevant in that radio broadcasting will always have a future.

What Can We Learn? What Is The Future?

After a brief tour through the history of radio, the Internet, the Web, and Internet radio, what lessons and insights can we gain? Well, for starters, we know that radio has had a rich history and that the Internet has extended radio in a whole new way.

We can also see that two types of companies and people have been involved in the history of radio—people like Marconi, Tesla, Rob Glaser, and Justin Frankel, who helped build the technologies that enabled it; and people like Sarnoff, Mark Cuban, and Todd Wagener (of Broadcast.com), who used the technology to create new ways of entertaining and informing people. Even on the Net, companies and people involved in Internet radio have tended to be either more content oriented or more into enabling the technology.

Perhaps most important is understanding that, in moving radio broadcasting from a more centralized, frequency-based system to a decentralized system based on the Internet, some fundamental shifts are taking place in what radio is now becoming. First and foremost, radio is changing from representing the name of the technology (broadcasting audio via radio waves) to representing a style of Web broadcasting, namely streaming audio that takes the form of a traditional radio broadcast or radio show. Internet radio has adopted many facets of traditional radio broadcasting, including using a disc jockey, playlists, call-in shows, advertising interruptions, and more. Radio is losing its technological meaning and taking on a definition of purpose; that's an incredible transformation because, as the technology changes, the capabilities and the nature of what it means to create a radio station or show will change with it.

As similar in purpose as Internet radio and traditional radio are, we must look at the history of the Web and the Internet and realize that Internet radio is an entirely new form of audio broadcasting—one that is very different from what Sarnoff and the others invented in the middle of the twentieth century. The key to that difference is held in the roots of the Internet and the Web itself—those roots being decentralizing control, enabling interoperability of communications, connecting disparate communities of users and information, and providing a global capability to connect to each other. What does this mean for the future of Internet radio and what we will consider the New Radio? Consider the following:

▶ Traditional radio is based on broadcasting to an audience based in a specific geographic region, whereas Internet broadcasting goes global the second it's started.

▶ Traditional radio is overseen by the FCC and other governmental agencies that police how the airwaves are divided and used (because they are a licensed right and not wholly owned), whereas no one oversees Internet radio broadcasts, save for violations of copyrights.

▶ Traditional radio, even in niche formats, targets a much broader audience, whereas Internet radio thrives on the decentralized format of the Net itself. Internet radio is much more about one-to-one communications than the one-to-many format of traditional radio broadcasting.

▶ Internet radio tends to combine itself with other media and communications found on the Web, including Web pages, graphics, chat, e-mail, and immediate messaging. The same technology that enables your audio broadcast also enables many other forms of communication.

▶ Traditional radio is more or less an audio experience only. Anyone can start an Internet radio station as long as he or she has a computer, a connection to the Internet, and the right software. Traditional radio requires a license and large capital investment in equipment and rights fees.

The future of radio—as it pertains to the Internet and to you—is that entirely new content types and radio formats will be enabled because of its relatively inexpensive nature and capability to reach even smaller communities of interest. This growth will create a blossoming of interesting topics and uses for broadcast audio. The power of broadcasting (even in its narrowest schemes) will reach more people who will be able to start their own stations and shows; in the truest sense, everyone can be both a listener and a broadcaster.

To understand Internet radio, you have to start by identifying the various parts of the Internet radio landscape. This landscape includes the styles of stations that can be set up, the technologies that enable Internet streaming audio, and the various types of situations and tools that enable you to create a fully working radio station on the Internet. In this chapter, we will provide an overview and comparisons of Internet radio types and technologies that will help you best decide which technologies work for your station, and we'll provide more details about Internet radio in general.

What Type of Station (or Show) Will You Offer?

Before you can begin dissecting the landscape that is current-day Internet radio, you have to establish up front what type of station you're building. As we discussed in the preceding chapter, Net broadcasters fall into two categories: those casting about for the largest possible audience they can muster and those who are building radio stations uniquely for themselves or a small group of listeners.

Determining what type of station you want is an important first step in building an Internet radio station. Although most of the available streaming audio servers and software packages support broadcasters big and small, often a specific server or technology is more useful for one of the two major types of radio stations found on the Web.

Besides aiming for a wide or narrow audience, you can broadcast either a station or a show using Internet radio. If you broadcast for an extended, set period of time, at regular intervals, with a specific purpose, then you have more of a show than a station. If, on the other hand, you broadcast twenty-four hours a day, seven days a week, or for long periods of time, or you do a variety of things, then you operate more like a station.

The Styles of Internet Radio

To define the Internet radio landscape, let's look at some of the types of stations people are building and some of the terms we'll use in this book to define various styles of Internet radio.

Personal Internet Radio

Personal Internet radio stations are those stations set up mostly for non-commercial personal interest. These stations tend to be small and are run on a shoestring budget as a hobby by their operator(s). Sometimes they might accept some small amount of advertising (if they can get it) or sponsorship for their broadcasting activities, but the main motivation is that the operator enjoys broadcasting and building the site.

Professional Internet Radio

Professional Internet radio stations are mostly formed for a specific commercial purpose, either as a for-profit venture or as part of a corporate communications plan (for example, broadcasting shareholder meetings or a company-wide radio station), and not as a personal hobby or non-commercial venture.

Live, Remote, Pre-Recorded, On Demand, and In-Progress

The style of show you have can also depend on the circumstances you use to create the content and how you make it available to your listeners.

2

The Internet Radio Landscape: Players, Stations, Shows, Streaming, and Remotes

In terms of content, you can create it on the fly via a *live* broadcast, or you can pre-record and encode the content. For a *remote* broadcast, the source of the content is not in the same facility that the station is actually housed in.

In terms of how the station is made available, the broadcast can either be *on-demand* or provided *in-progress*. The difference is what the users hear when they select the broadcast. If your station is provided on-demand, the users will start listening to the audio at the beginning of the playlist or show. On the other hand, if the station is provided in progress, the users will hear whatever audio is being played out from the server at the moment they tune in.

Most Internet radio stations and shows are *pre-recorded*, playing music, interviews, or other audio content already developed, digitized, encoded, and stored on a server. Many shows, however, lean toward a live or remote broadcast because they record interviews or broadcast events more so than set musical playlists. In terms of whether stations or shows are served on-demand or in-progress, most shows are usually served on-demand (unless they are part of a station that broadcasts around the clock), whereas most stations, especially music-oriented stations, are provided in-progress.

In Chapter 4, we'll describe the specific issues and tools involved with pulling off each type of broadcast.

Commercial Versus Non-Commercial

Just because you build a big station doesn't mean it's commercial, and just because you build a personal Internet radio station doesn't mean you can't accept advertising. The only true defining characteristic of a commercial Internet radio station is whether it is designed on purpose to accept advertising or promote a commercial venture. If that is the case, then your station is *not* a not-for-profit station. Commercial stations don't have any outright restrictions on them per se, but most of the major Internet audio serving packages require you to pay or at least pay extra to use their software for commercial purposes.

TIP

Sometimes, in describing stations with small audiences, the term *narrowcaster* is used. This term is a misnomer that needs clarification. A narrowcaster is a station or show that appeals to a specific audience on a very narrow subject. That audience could be large or small, regardless of the topic. For example, a radio show devoted to Nintendo's Pokemon game might get millions of listeners, but on a topic, it is far more narrow than, say, an NBA game or the nightly news. Narrowcasting is very popular on the Web because attracting audiences devoted to a specific topic is easy. In many cases, those audiences are small, and the Net makes it economical to broadcast to a narrow interest group.

The Main Types of Commercial Internet Radio Sites and Stations

Commercial Internet radio has taken on several forms as it has grown from its humble origins. Aside from stations or shows that promote specific commercial causes or purposes, most commercial Internet radio Web sites are aggregators of content, not single broadcasters.

Because it's hard to scale a broadcast up to millions of users, and because most Internet radio tends to be more narrowly focused, the true commercial stake in Internet radio is tilted toward Web sites or broadcast services that can create large audiences by collecting several small audiences under one umbrella. That being the case, you will find several types of aggregators working the Internet radio landscape:

▶ **Original content creators**—These sites create original Internet radio stations or shows, using original content they create themselves. Their premise is that the lower cost of Internet radio broadcasting enables them to attract a large audience by creating a plethora of Internet radio stations and shows that focus on narrow but attractive topics (such as the all-videogame news channel or a show all about Web design) that, in total, attract a large audience. Leaders in this category include Talk.com and Pseudo.com, which are creating original on-air talk shows and news broadcasts for users to listen to. They hope to make money via associated advertising for their Internet broadcasts, or they charge a fee to listen to it.

▶ **Rebroadcasters**—These companies gather Internet broadcast rights to existing content (versus producing it themselves) and then rebroadcast it on the Internet. They hope to make money via associated advertising for their Internet broadcasts, or they charge a fee either to listen to it or to transmit it to their audience. A leader in this category is Broadcast.com, which carries a number of major existing radio stations, financial meetings, and sports broadcasts. Another major rebroadcaster is Broadcast America (**www.broadcastamerica.com**) which is located in Portland, Maine, and rebroadcasts a number of radio stations and shows from around the world.

▶ **Theme channel providers**—Theme channel providers are an important variation of the Rebroadcaster type. Instead of rebroadcasting an amalgamation of content, they tend to concentrate on one type of audio content (mostly music or talk seems to be the choice) and then create themed channels within that area. NetRadio (**www.netradio.com**) and Spinner (**www.spinner.com**) are two of the most popular sites hosting these types of stations. Both concentrate on music and offer channels for fans of jazz, techno, rock, classical, and many more styles. They hope to make money via associated advertising or, in the case of music, from associated sales of music played on their stations.

▶ **Bazaar or homestead enablers**—With the personal broadcasting rovolution now in full bloom, several companies are trying to create specific commercial services that aggregate personally produced stations. This is the model being used by SHOUTcast.com and Live365.com. SHOUTcast.com is the companion site to the SHOUTcast server system. Users of SHOUTcast have the option of having their stations publicly listed on SHOUTcast.com, which acts as sort of a bazaar to all the available SHOUTcast stations. SHOUTcast thus becomes a top destination for listeners and can charge advertising for that audience. Live365 is an audio homesteading service. It repeats the signal sent from a single broadcaster, so more people can listen to it. It can also host stations. In exchange for this free service, Live365 and others like it may (eventually) embed advertising in the outgoing streams or offer extended services to its broadcasters.

▶ **Pointer services**—These sites don't necessarily host stations, but they do provide a central place for people to find links to stations that are broadcasting on the Internet. By listing many stations and organizing them by content and other characteristics, these pointer sites become a central exchange for listeners and stations trying to reach them. Services like this can be Web-based or can take the form of specialized clients such as MP3Spy or DigiBand Radio. Most pointer services hope the large amount of listener traffic they generate will create advertising and e-commerce revenue.

Mixing It Up

The styles described in the preceding sections outline the most basic breakdowns for the various forms Internet radio tends to take on. By no means are these types exclusive to each other. For example, you might run a personal station that broadcasts remotely and for commercial purposes, or you might run a large-scale professional station that is nothing more than a pre-recorded loop of shows about your company's products or interviews with its executives. Before you jump into a more specific style of radio (that is, a format such as talk, music, or sports), you should identify which of these styles you will be closest to. From there, you need to understand which tools and techniques will fit best that style of station. In most cases, your choice will be a mixture of styles and formats that create something that is uniquely successful for your interests or needs.

In the Internet radio space, aggregators are sites that help listeners find content or stations to listen to. Essentially, three different types of aggregators are used in the Internet radio space. Some sites act like malls; for example, Broadcast.com links to or rebroadcasts major audio content on the Web. Others are merely pointers, like RadioSpy, an application by GameSpy Industries which points users to currently active radio stations but doesn't host them itself. Finally there are companies like Live365.com or AudioRealm.com, which give people free streaming stations in hopes of aggregating the individual station audiences into one huge audience that will attract advertisers.

The Basic Technologies of Internet Radio

Five components of technology make up Internet radio. Although entire sections of this book cover some of them in great detail, the rest of this chapter is devoted to a quick overview of each of these components:

► **Enabling technologies**—These fundamental technologies, such as Internet protocols and digitized audio formats, define how you store and then send audio over the Internet.

► **Connections, servers, and hosts**—These specific Internet connections, streaming audio servers, and hosts are used to physically do the work of moving audio out to listeners.

► **Production and broadcast utilities**—Just a streaming audio server does not an Internet radio station or show make. To enable broadcasting on the Web, you need several other types of software, such as audio editors and encoders. You'll also optionally make use of plug-ins that enable automated playlist publishing, monitor listener activity, or enable sound effects on cue.

▶ **Related hardware**—This computer and audio hardware is used to enable a broadcast or enable a listener to hear a broadcast. This hardware includes sound cards, microphones, mixers, specialized encoding systems, and networking equipment that stations use.

▶ **Playback software and add-ons**—On the other end of a broadcast are listeners, and they need special software such as the RealPlayer to be able to listen to your broadcasts. Furthermore, listeners can install other software that boosts the sound of incoming broadcasts or that enables them to chat or page DJs live on the air from their PCs.

Having identified the major components that are assembled to create an Internet radio show or broadcast, let's look at each one more closely to further understand the Internet radio landscape.

Enabling Technologies: Audio Formats and Transmission Protocols

In the radio biz, a *format* is the style of content aired over a station—for example, album-oriented rock (also known as AOR) or talk radio. However, when we refer to formats for streaming audio, we're referring to the technical format for storing digital audio in a file for sending it over the Internet.

Internet radio transmits audio after it has been stored in some sort of format that is conducive to transmission over the Internet or that can be converted into a format for transmission easily by the server. Even in cases in which a live stream is being transmitted, a server or plug-in to a server first renders the data into a format for transmission. In most cases, you pre-render the audio into a format your server can handle. Streaming audio servers accept two types of audio formats: ones they can directly transmit and ones they accept for incoming audio and then convert to whatever format they transmit with on the outgoing side. So, although you might feed a streaming audio server several different types of audio formats, on the outgoing side, you end up with one format of audio.

The four formats used on the outgoing side in Internet radio are RealAudio, MPEG/MP3, QuickTime, and Windows Media Audio (WMA). RealAudio is the most often used, due mostly to the dominance of RealNetworks' format and the number of people using it since its debut. MPEG/MP3 broadcasting is quickly catching up and is the outgoing format for SHOUTcast, icecast, and the Destiny server, whereas QuickTime audio, a format not used often, is employed by those people streaming QuickTime-oriented broadcasts to the Net. WMA is the format used to broadcast Internet radio using Microsoft's Windows Media Service.

At the most basic level in terms of digital audio, two file formats are in use: raw audio formats, which store a perfect replication of the digitized audio; and specialized formats, which store audio in a compressed form. These compressed forms of audio usually result in some loss of quality in order to create either smaller files overall or to make the file small enough to enable it to stream out over the Net even in low bandwidth settings.

Raw Audio Formats

In Internet radio, raw audio formats such as .WAV and .AIFF are sometimes used to initially store digitized audio before it is encoded into a specialized format for transmission. In addition, some servers (such as SHOUTcast) let you feed them these types of files that are encoded on the fly into an outgoing format.

Encoded Formats That Directly Transmit

MPEG/MP3, RealAudio, WMA, and QuickTime are specially encoded file formats used by servers to transmit their broadcasts directly to listeners. The MP3 format is especially enjoyed as a storage format for audio because it combines near-CD quality with a small file size.

Alternative Encoded Formats

To say that MP3, QuickTime, and RealAudio are the only encoded formats that are used in Internet radio is a mistake. Some servers such as SHOUTcast also support transmitting audio stored in other formats like VQF (Vector Quantization Format) and AAC (Advanced Audio Coding). And although the formats mentioned previously are the dominant encoded formats for Internet radio today, a newer format may emerge in a few years to replace them, so it's good to keep informed about other formats that may be useful.

Lossy Versus Lossless Format

In technical terms, any file format that drops out quality to create a compressed version of a file is known as a *lossy format*. Those formats that don't compress content and never lose the quality of the original are known as *lossless formats*. For example, .WAV files (Windows) and .AIFF files (Macintosh) are lossless formats that store digital audio in its rawest forms. The problem with these formats is that the files aren't very streamable due to their size and the speed at which most users access the Internet today. One second of even low-quality audio might be larger than 40KB, and high-quality audio transmits at 170KB per second. Only the fastest connections could handle that type of streaming. For that reason, streaming servers must use specialized formats to transmit data.

You'll find more details about audio file formats in Chapter 11, but for now you have a basic understanding of the formats you're most likely to encounter and the styles of formats and their roles in the Internet audio landscape.

Protocols

Another foundation-level technology you need to know something about is Internet transmission protocols. Whereas file formats form the foundation of how audio is stored or formatted for broadcasting, Internet transmission protocols define how your audio information travels from your server over the Internet to the listeners. Although knowing the absolute details of a transmission protocol is not necessary, having an understanding of the fundamentals does help you to understand more about how your station will operate over the Web. It's also helpful to be familiar enough with the technologies to understand why they are used and what their features and limits are.

Unicast Versus Multicast

Before jumping into a discussion of various protocols, you need to understand the biggest structural split in how you can transmit streaming audio over the Internet. There are big differences between a product that uses a unicast method and one that allows for a multicasting method of streaming audio.

Unicasting is a system in which you are initiating, sending, and maintaining a single point-to-point stream of audio from your server to the server of each listener on your station. This method is used by 95 percent of broadcasters on the Web today.

Multicasting is a promising technology for all Webcasters because it potentially provides a way to reach more listeners with less bandwidth than other ways of currently reaching them. With multicasting, the idea is that, as your audio streams are sent out, they can be split and repeated to many more users as they head toward each endpoint in a listening stream.

However, there are catches with multicasting. For example, if two people using the same Internet service provider (ISP) are connecting to your broadcast, the first person gets the stream in much the same way he or she does today. However, if a second person from that same location requests your stream, the stream is split only at the last point; the ISP just duplicates the information from it to the two simultaneous requesters. Instead of having two distinct high-band connections to your broadcast, you now have just one stream headed out to a common point and then split in time for delivery to the two unique requesters. Figure 2.1 illustrates this multicasting topology. The problem with this is measuring your audience. If the stream is split down the line, then somehow the client needs to communicate back to the original source to let it know it's listening. Some servers, therefore, will initiate another message-only channel to a listener that helps log information about their listening.

Figure 2.1
In this topology illustration of multicasting audio, you can see how the stream reaches multiple users without broadcasting separately to each user as the unicast method does.

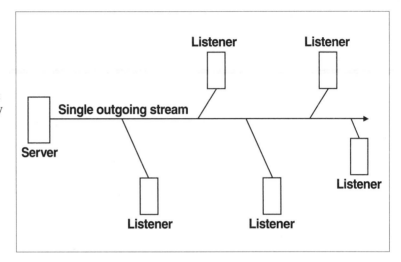

For this type of Webcasting to take place, though, the entire network between you and your listeners has to become *multicast-compliant.* The first of the multicast-compliant networks is a special layer of the Internet known as the *mBone.* Today, you can use products such as Live.com's Livecaster to enable mBone broadcasts. In the future, when new technologies such as TCP/IPv6 and specialized hardware that is multicast-compliant become prevalent, more and more people will be able to broadcast and receive multicast-capable broadcasts.

Until multicasting becomes an inherent Internet technology, you—as well as listeners—will have to jump through special hoops to send out and listen to multicasted stations. These hoops involve special configurations to your server to work with the few networks on the Internet that are multicast enabled and the potential need for listeners to run specialized clients or configurations to tune in multicasted content. When this technology is prevalent, though, you can expect to be able to scale your radio stations up to more users for very little expense in outgoing bandwidth. You will find more details on multicasting in Appendix A of this book. This appendix also lists a number of sites and books available on the topic.

How Information is Transmitted via the Internet

Information travels over the Internet in small bits and pieces known as *packets*. A file of information, no matter the size, is divided into very small pieces. In turn, each piece of information is coded so that it knows where it's going. When it gets to the other side, the computer there knows where in the reassembled file that piece of information is located. Packets fly across the Internet at great speed, bouncing around in some cases, as they seek their ultimate destination.

The big difference between using streaming audio and just transferring a full file is that, as packets go out and are received on the other end, the computer immediately assembles the data. On-demand files must completely download once the final packet is sent, then the entire batch is reassembled into the file. With streaming media, once enough packets are captured to assemble some fragment of listenable audio, the packet data is assembled and played. If packets arrive fast enough, then the result is a continuous stream of audio until the listener stops listening or the station or show is no longer streaming out data.

When the computer has even the smallest amount needed to generate audio, it does so continuously until no more data is available. When not transmitting data as a stream, the computer waits until it receives the final packets and then perfectly reassembles the file.

Most of the packets on the Internet are sent out in a protocol format known as Transmission Control Protocol/Internet Protocol (TCP/IP). TCP/IP not only ensures that data gets where it's supposed to be going, but it also ensures that it gets there correctly and uncorrupted. That's why your e-mail shows up without dropped characters, and that document you sent is exactly how it appeared when you sent it. However, faults with TCP/IP in general prevent it from being perfect for streaming audio. One is that all the error checking bogs down the system. With streaming audio, you don't necessarily need the information to be perfect, so dropping some of the inherent error handling in TCP/IP is necessary. Second, TCP/IP (specifically the IP part) treats all data the same; therefore, it's hard to set a priority on data like streaming audio so that it can get preferential treatment over the Internet or to enable other specialized features that could improve quality or provide more features. Thus, when it comes to Internet radio and streaming audio, some alternative transmission protocols are used in place of TCP or run on top of TCP/IP to improve the capability to stream audio or provide extended functionality to streamers.

Part I Understanding the Basics

UDP (User Datagram Protocol)

User Datagram Protocol (UDP) is a communication protocol that is similar to TCP in that it runs in tandem with IP. The big difference between it and TCP is that UDP is a much more stripped-down protocol than TCP is. UDP has very little error checking and doesn't even guarantee that an entire set of data will reach its destination. It is, however, smaller and quicker to use as a method of broadcasting data. For these reasons, UDP is used by Real and other streaming audio technologies as a basic level of transport for data.

NOTE

Datagram is essentially another word for *packet*. To read more details about UDP, check out **www.freesoft.org/CIE/RFC/768/index.htm.**

Because UDP doesn't provide sequencing of the packets it sends, when that data arrives, the receiving application doesn't know how to reassemble it if the data are out of order. This doesn't really mean much for audio broadcasting. An audio streaming application using UDP simply plays back the data as it arrives. If a packet is out of order or never arrives, the application doesn't destroy the integrity of the file—save perhaps for a dropped bit of noise, a pop or hiss in the broadcast, or a second of silence.

RTP (Real-time Transport Protocol)

The Real-time Transport Protocol (RTP) usually runs on top of UDP (although it can run on top of other protocols) and, as such, does not guarantee real-time delivery of data. However, it provides extra mechanisms to applications for streaming data over the Net. This protocol was developed at Columbia University and is supported by Real, Microsoft, and Netscape, among others.

RTP consists of a data part and a control part much like TCP; in fact, it's called RTCP. The data part of RTP provides support for applications with real-time needs such as broadcasting (in which the data has to be there as soon as possible, as opposed to e-mail, which can take its relative time). Packets conforming to RTP include special information that helps with timing issues, loss of data detection, security, and identification of the type of content in its packets. Furthermore, RTCP offers multicasting support as well as the capability to synchronize different media streams.

RTP works in conjunction with UDP/IP but is *transport-independent*, meaning it can run on top of other transmission protocols.

> **TIP**
>
> The RTP FAQ is located at **http://www.cs.columbia.edu/~hgs/rtp/faq.html**, and the RTP Web site is located at **http://www.cs.columbia.edu/~hgs/rtp/**.

RTSP (Real-Time Streaming Protocol)

Real-Time Streaming Protocol (RTSP) is an extension to RTP that was developed by Netscape and RealNetworks. It has been submitted to the Internet Engineering Task Force (IETF) for adoption as a standard. It uses RTP but is optimized in way that efficiently streams audio-visual data to large groups on the Web. RTSP also allows for more precise placement of elements within a stream, such as messages to pop up graphical elements or trigger other events during broadcast.

> **TIP**
>
> You can read more details on RTSP at:
> **www.cis.ohio-state.edu/htbin/rfc/rfc2326.html**.

IP Multicast and IPv6

IP is the basic Internet protocol and the backbone protocol for all packets of data sent over the Internet. Currently, the Internet uses IPv4, and a standard known as IPv6 is being developed. This new version, while co-existing with IPv4, will eventually replace IPv4 as the standard version of IP and enable the Internet to grow. With IPv6, more room (that is, more addresses and sites) will be available. This protocol also will enable new features, one of which is more robust multicasting capabilities.

In the meantime, because IPv4 only optionally supports mBone, IP Multicast helps make mBone broadcast-capable. This extended form of the IP protocol enables transmissions using it to go out over mBone.

UMTP (UDP Multicast Tunneling Protocol)

As we stated earlier, to multicast and for others to listen to a multicasted show, specialized protocols that enable multicasting have to be used. UDP Multicast Tunneling Protocol (UMTP) is one such protocol that enables a program to stream information through the mBone by tunneling multicast UDP data inside unicast UDP data packets. This protocol method is used by some programs instead of a more direct multicast-compatible protocol because it requires little change in users' operating systems or setups to enable mBone-compatible broadcasts. It is, therefore, used in some special situations in which traditional multicast protocols would be tough to use.

TIP
You can read more details about UMTP at **http://www.live.com/umtp.txt**.

Overall, a new protocol proposal seems to pop up on the Internet every month. As people involved with streaming audio (and other content types) over the Internet continue to build the technologies, we can expect even more as the industry tries to add more capabilities and ensure even better sounding broadcasts. The biggest difference in the future will be the growth in multicasting. With IPv6 eventually making it out of the standards committees that design and adopt major protocols, and with more software packages supporting multicasting, even a small personal station will be able to reach an audience into the thousands.

Connections, Servers, and Hosts

By now, you have some basic idea of how Internet radio works: You store audio in a format that can be read by your computer, and a server program that uses specialized protocols sends that information in tiny packets to users connected to the Internet. Those users' computers reassemble the packets as they come in, and by using specialized software that converts those packets to audio, they hear your broadcast. At this point in the game, you understand some basics about the various audio formats used and the protocols used to transmit audio. The software that takes that audio, converts it into data that can be transmitted, and then transmits it is a server—specifically a streaming audio server.

Several major audio servers and Internet radio packages are prevalent, or at least promising, in terms of being used for building an Internet radio station. Each one of the five we've decided to use or cover in this book has a specific strength or purpose in the realm of Internet radio, so it pays to understand the main place each holds. In addition, you need some way to host that server and enable it to connect to the Internet to send out its streams. Several hosting styles related to Internet audio are also important to how the industry works; we'll describe them after identifying the major server products.

RealServer

www.real.com

RealAudio from RealNetworks is probably the most prevalent technology used for Internet radio today. At the same time, it isn't necessarily the most conducive technology for narrowcasters because it requires more work to set up, and broadcasting to more than twenty-five to fifty people requires an investment in higher-end and higher-priced servers. In addition, if you're going to build a radio station around audio-based broadcasting, in our opinion, RealAudio isn't as good as what you can achieve with SHOUTcast or other MP3-focused technologies. With RealNetworks' Basic Server, you need to convert your audio feed to the RealAudio format, which requires an additional encoding step, whereas with SHOUTcast and icecast, your files can stay in the MP3 format or other formats in which they were originally created or encoded.

Despite the drawbacks, however, RealAudio and RealServer provide a good system for building an Internet radio station. First and foremost, RealNetworks provides excellent support. Millions of users have installed RealNetworks' client, RealPlayer, on their machines. RealNetworks also provides excellent documentation for broadcasters, and its capability to stream to thousands of simultaneous users at the high end of the listening spectrum is good. RealServer running on a Sun Solaris UNIX workstation is an especially effective workhorse.

Another key to using RealNetworks' technology for a radio station is its capability to be the interface for your station. By using the RealPlayer's capability to display multimedia and Macromedia Flash-styled content directly in its players, you can create dynamic shows that mix multimedia with your station's audio broadcast.

SHOUTcast

www.shoutcast.com

Developed by the braintrust behind Winamp, SHOUTcast is the leading narrowcaster solution for personal Internet radio stations. With SHOUTcast, any audio blasting through Winamp is transferred into a compressed MP3 format and then sent out via the SHOUTcast server component, which people connect to your machine to hear.

SHOUTcast is uniquely designed for personal Internet radio broadcasters and contains many features and tools geared toward this group.

Icecast

www.icecast.org

When SHOUTcast hit the Net, a group of enterprising software developers decided to create an open source competitor to the SHOUTcast system. The result is icecast, a favorite SHOUTcast substitute for UNIX and, especially, Linux users. It works in much the same fashion as SHOUTcast but isn't an exact clone, and it provides some different features of its own not found in SHOUTcast.

RadioDestiny Broadcast

www.radiodestiny.com

Another MPEG-based radio server package, RadioDestiny is a Windows 98/NT product that enables live and pre-recorded audio to be broadcast over the Net. The package isn't as robust as other broadcasting options, but it is an option some people may choose to investigate and use.

Windows Media Technologies

www.microsoft.com/windows/windowsmedia/

Microsoft seems to have had more iterations of its media technology than Shirley MacLaine claims past lives. Originally, Microsoft Windows spawned the .WAV file format, which essentially is a simple format for raw audio much like .AIFF is for the Macintosh or .MU is for UNIX. As streaming media made headway because of Real, Microsoft began snapping up various companies involved in the space, including Vxtreme and others. It also cross-licensed with Real, using version 5.0 of its format, and turned out the Windows Media Player and the NetShow server.

NetShow spawned its own audio format, known as Active Streaming Format (ASF). NetShow was a server component that worked in conjunction with Internet Information Server (IIS) and NT Server to deliver streaming audio and video via the Internet. That was a bit short-lived, at least as audio went, with the creation of Windows Media, a new audio format that is claimed to have twice the power of the MP3 format.

Re-dubbed the Windows Media Technologies, this format enables near-CD quality at half the bit rate (64kbps) when compared to the MP3 format. Several products, including Winamp, now support .WMA (Windows Media Audio) files, and serving is possible by downloading the WMT service for NT Server and Internet Information Server.

How Stations Are Hosted on the Internet

Just as with Web sites, Internet radio stations can be served out to the Internet in several ways. Your station originates from some machine connected to the Internet that acts as the originating server. That server is either under your own control or hosted by a third party. If you are in control of your own server and manage it and the connection, it is known as an *in-house server*. Servers managed or housed by an outside company are known as *hosted servers*.

With the exception of personal radio stations, most people connect to Internet radio stations through hosted servers. Managing a server, its connections, and security in-house is expensive and time-consuming when compared to just leasing servers or space on a server at the hundreds of hosting services around the world that specialize in Internet hosting.

Many different types of hosting situations are used for Internet radio, and it's important to have an overview of all them. Host solutions fall into six major types of possibilities or scenarios:

▶ **Dedicated server**—A dedicated server, which includes the outgoing connection to the Internet, is owned or leased entirely by its broadcaster. In this capacity, a server system is configured by the hosting company to your specifications and then connected to a network, which is connected to the Internet. You remotely connect to the back end of the server, and aside from some minor responsibilities, the hosting company does nothing to manage the server; instead, the server is entirely managed by you, the customer. Dedicated servers are popular for the flexibility they provide to companies.

▶ **Co-location server**—This type of server is a completely dedicated server with a twist; in a dedicated situation, the hosting company provides the hardware setup to your specification from an array of offerings it has. However, if you need a really specialized system, you might want to build it yourself and then locate it at the hosting company's site, (a process known commonly as *co-location)* so the company can monitor it and connect it to its fast connections to the Internet.

▶ **Shared server**—A shared server is a server on the Web that hosts broadcasts you create but does not give you specific control of the entire service. In this case, you are given a specific directory on the server to locate your data, and a Web-based interface gives you a connection to the server to manipulate streaming settings. In this regard, you are probably sharing space and resources of the server with other people and their broadcasts. With less space and more restrictions than a completely hosted server, the cost of this type of server is usually cheaper than that solution.

▶ **On-demand stream**—An on-demand stream is simply a stored broadcast that is hosted by a service and then broadcast upon request to users. Almost any normal Web hosting service can provide an on-demand stream unless the expected requests for it will be large at any given time (as can be the case with popular continuous streams or live events).

▶ **Hosted, live simulcast**—A live simulcast isn't much different from a service that lets you send out a continuous stream of audio for listeners. The slight difference is that not every hosting service is prepared to accept live streams that may come in via the Web, a direct ISDN link, satellite, or other medium. Several companies, including Vstream, Yahoo! Broadcast Services, and RealBroadcast, will help you prepare and then send out such broadcasts through their networks.

Part I Understanding the Basics

▶ **Repeater**—A repeater enables more people to hear a stream from your dedicated server by rebroadcasting it using the repeater's access to a larger amount of bandwidth. Live365 and AudioRealm are two examples of pioneering repeater services. They are popular with personal broadcasters who have slow connections to the Internet. With a repeater service, personal broadcasters can broadcast a single stream to the repeater facility, which then duplicates the stream on its system and, with its sizable bandwidth, can give many more people the chance to listen to that broadcast than possible if the broadcaster had used only his or her personal available bandwidth.

Connections

If you are using a hosting service to serve your audio out to the Internet, you are already connected to the Internet through that service's presumably high-bandwidth connections. However, if you're using your personal machine or an in-house server, you need to obtain a direct connection to the Internet yourself. You also might need a direct connection if you want to do a live broadcast or provide an original stream from your facilities to a hosting service for repeating out to the Internet through its systems.

Streaming audio requires a lot of bandwidth. You can stream audio in a reduced form over a 28.8k, 33.3k, or 56k modem connection, and that connection is fine if you're listening to a single stream. However, if you're going to broadcast to twenty to thirty or even hundreds of simultaneous users, you need a connection with more bandwidth than just a normal modem. Thus, part of understanding the basics of Internet radio is understanding some basics about the types of high-bandwidth connections used by today's Internet radio broadcasters to connect their stations to the Internet.

Five types of common high-bandwidth connections are in use today on the Internet. The following list explains what they are and how they are used in relation to Internet radio. Chapter 4 goes into much more detail about how to enable each type of connection as needed for your station.

▶ **T1/Fractional T1**—Higher-speed connections than a T1 can be used by high-end Web hosts, but they are not in the reach of most individuals. A T1 line, however, is used by many in-house stations to enable a high-capacity Web connection for broadcasting. If bandwidth needs are high, you can use multiple T1s, and if you don't need all the capacity of a T1, you can lease just a fraction of its bandwidth. For the most part, though, companies that need this level of bandwidth are better off not dealing with the headaches of installing and managing such a connection and should turn to a hosting service that can provide this kind of bandwidth and more.

▶ **ISDN**—ISDN lines are not used very much for outgoing broadcasts except by some personal broadcasters running stations feeding four to five users. However, they are used extensively to feed repeaters or live broadcasts back to a facility for encoding and simulcasting. ISDN lines provide not only higher-speed Internet connections, but they also can transmit audio in a higher-fidelity manner than plain old telephone service (POTS) lines.

▶ **DSL**—Digital Subscriber Lines are high-speed data lines that run over regular phone lines. Although they are not available everywhere, where they are available, they are becoming very popular with personal broadcasters. These lines enable you to send broadcasts directly from your personal machines out to the Internet. A strong DSL connection can enable you to stream via unicast methods to twenty to thirty people or more, depending on the audio quality setting you use.

▶ **Cable modem**—Like Digital Subscriber Lines, cable modems are high-speed services that enable connections to the Internet via the same cable system that provides you with your cable TV service. Cable modems are very popular with personal broadcasters as well, because, as with DSL lines, they offer large bandwidth capable of hosting fifty, one hundred, or more listeners via unicast methods, depending on the audio quality settings used for the station. However, as will be discussed in further detail, many cable modem services aren't necessarily happy with this use of their services. They may require extra fees or bar you from using a cable modem line to host your station.

▶ **Wireless connections**—You should be aware of two types of wireless connections. First and foremost are new wireless local area network (LAN) products that enable you to connect machines together via wireless networking. Wireless LAN connections are sometimes used by remote broadcasters at trade shows and other events to connect their on-site systems to each other and eventually to a system near a phone line that can transmit a signal back to the server facility.

The other type of wireless connection is a wireless Internet service. As of today, two-way wireless and satellite Internet service is very much in its infancy. However, if certain projects and products come out in the next few years as planned, some excellent high-speed wireless Internet access services could very well be of use to Internet radio broadcasters.

Production and Broadcast Utilities

The software used to enable a broadcast doesn't just begin or end with the streaming audio server you install. That may be the most important piece of software in Internet radio, but many different types of products can contribute to your station or show. We'll cover many of them in this book to some degree. The categories and main products for each are as follows:

► **Content creation tools**—As we mentioned earlier, you need software that can help you capture audio and then encode it for broadcast. Examples include popular software such as Sound Forge—which is a top-rated digitized audio capture and editing product from Sonic Foundry—as well as specific encoding products such as Xing's AudioCatalyst from MP3 Production, or Real's RealProducer product for encoding content into the RealAudio format. You also might want to get a content management tool to help you organize all your audio content as it builds up. You can find packages that make it easier to organize playlists and manage audio files than what most server systems offer.

► **Server-side plug-ins**—Some server systems such as SHOUTcast enable extended features for their broadcasters through the use of specialized plug-in modules. Plug-ins can be used to help with server management, to enable live on-air mixing, or to enable automatic publishing of playlists to the Web, and more.

► **On-air utilities**—Aside from specific server software, several popular tools are available for enabling quick access to sound effects. You can also find software for enabling chats and instant DJ requests such as ICQ, as well as software for monitoring listener activity and enabling commercials and voice-over.

► **Web site production software**—Not every station or show has a companion Web site, but many do. Thus, most stations need to have some semblance of traditional Web site production tools, which, for the most part, means a Web page editor and a graphics package.

Related Hardware

Internet radio requires not only computer hardware to run the associated software, but also can include several types of audio hardware and specialized equipment that help with your broadcast capabilities.

In terms of computers, the main piece of hardware is the system that runs the server. For large-scale broadcasters, this system must be a powerful machine capable of handling a large load of listeners or an array of machines that, as a group (known technically as a *cluster*), enable the broadcast. Most personal broadcasters use a single machine, and for the most part, it is an Intel/AMD-based system running either Windows or Linux or a Macintosh. Most professional broadcasters, on the other end of the spectrum, lean toward Sun Solaris/UNIX systems or an array of higher-end NT systems.

The hardware does not end with the computer system used to run the server. Many broadcasters also use audio mixers that help clean, boost, and tweak audio signals passing through them before going into their systems (especially if they are combining several audio streams into one before it heads to the server for broadcast). For live broadcasts or for extra speed during content production, some broadcasters use hardware-based encoding products. Separate content production machines or machines set up for remote broadcasting may be needed as well.

You also can't forget hardware such as microphones or headsets for interviews and on-air chatter or specialized hardware that enables people to join your broadcast via phone. Some broadcasters may also want to purchase DAT machines for recording offsite as well. In Chapter 4, we will cover more specifics about the types of system configurations and hardware you will need to have or consider for enabling your broadcast.

From Broadcasters to Listeners: The Main Playback Products

At last count, more than one hundred different players were available for MP3 files. The RealPlayer (for playing RealAudio) is now in its seventh generation, and both the QuickTime Player and Microsoft's Media Player support MP3 as well as their own native formats (QuickTime and Windows Media Audio, respectively).

However, not every player can listen to the four most streamed audio types. Table 2.1 at the end of this section outlines which players can listen to which streamable formats.

Real Player 7/7+

www.real.com

RealPlayer is the most popular product for listening to streaming audio or watching streaming video. It has millions of installations, and in version 7, it has added support for MPEG streaming in addition to its own RealAudio format. Therefore, it can listen to both RealServer-based stations as well as those created with SHOUTcast, icecast, and other MPEG/MP3-oriented server systems.

Versions of RealPlayer are available for both the Macintosh and Windows platforms. Figure 2.2 shows the RealPlayer 7 program.

Figure 2.2
The RealPlayer 7 is the most installed audio/video player program around.

Winamp

www.winamp.com

Winamp is *the* MP3 player (see Figure 2.3). In fact, it is possibly the king of all audio players because it does so much more than just play back MP3 files.

Winamp is a Windows-only product, although two versions of Winamp are available. One version supports Windows 95, 98, and NT for Intel processors. The other version exists specifically for Windows NT for Alpha processors. In terms of Windows players, none of the others comes close to the level of support, add-ons, and features of Winamp.

Figure 2.3
The Winamp Player for Windows is the most popular MP3 player used.

Windows Media Player

www.microsoft.com

Although the true fans use Winamp, Microsoft gave MP3 files a huge boost when it released the latest version of the Windows Media Player, because it included support for MP3 files. While other media-playing giants, most notably RealNetworks, were slower to support MP3 files, Microsoft charged forward and added this capability to its player (see Figure 2.4). The latest version, version 7.0, now includes support for skins and other advanced features.

Figure 2.4
The Windows Media Player, now available in version 7, supports MP3, Windows Media Audio, and more. Due to Microsoft's formidable distribution it is gaining in popularity versus RealPlayer.

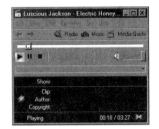

QuickTime

www.quicktime.com

The QuickTime Player, shown in Figure 2.5, is a cross-platform player, running on PCs and Macintoshes. Although most PC users don't use it to receive audio, many Mac users do. It also can be used to receive QuickTime audio-based broadcasts.

Figure 2.5
The QuickTime player shown here for Windows is a staple on the Mac platform.

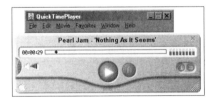

Sonique

www.sonique.com

If there is a real challenger to Winamp for popular and cool MP3 player for the PC, it is Sonique. This well-liked MP3 player supports a variety of audio formats (including Windows Media Audio) and supports streaming audio as well. When AOL purchased Winamp, Sonique, clearly a favorite among the remaining players, was quickly snapped up by Lycos. Figure 2.6 shows the Sonique player in action.

Figure 2.6
Sonique is an MP3 player that supports a wide variety of audio formats.

UltraPlayer

www.ultraplayer.com

The UltraPlayer is a relatively new MP3 and Windows Media Player but one that is quickly making waves, especially among online radio fans. The player features an all-new MP3 decoding engine that its creators say is optimized for online MP3 Internet radio—and some regular online DJs swear by it. In addition, the latest version features recording controls so listeners can record your broadcasts for playback later. See Figure 2.7.

Figure 2.7
Watch out for the rising star of UltraPlayer, which sports a new decoding engine for MP3 files and allows people to record incoming streams.

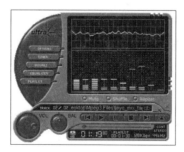

Macast

www.macast.com

Formerly known as MacAMP, the Macast product was created at about the same time as Winamp. It supports Layer II and III formats as well as connectivity to SHOUTcast and icecast streams. Macast supports skins and plug-ins as well. If you own a Mac, this is the player to get. See Figure 2.8.

Figure 2.8
The Macast Player.

FreeAmp (Linux)

www.freeamp.org

FreeAmp, shown in Figure 2.9, is an MP3 player being developed as an "open source" project by three developers. Although a version of FreeAmp is available for the Windows platform, it is overshadowed by Winamp. It also is available for the Linux platform, where it is a leading player. If you own a Linux-based system, FreeAmp is an excellent player. FreeAmp supports connecting to SHOUTcast and icecast stations as well.

Figure 2.9
The FreeAmp Player is an open source player available for a variety of platforms, including Linux and Windows.

Table 2.1
Breakdown of Players.

Player Name	Which Station Types Can the Player Connect To?				
	RealServer	SHOUTcast	icecast	Windows Media Audio	QuickTime
RealPlayer	Yes	Yes, but doesn't show title or other extended information	Yes, but doesn't show title or other extended information	No	No
Winamp	No	Yes	Yes	Yes	No
Microsoft Media Player	Sometimes	No	No	Yes	No
QuickTime	No	No	No	No	Yes
Sonique	No	Yes	Yes	Yes	No
UltraPlayer	No	Yes	Yes	Yes	No
FreeAmp	No	Yes, but doesn't show title or other extended information	Yes, but doesn't show title or other extended information	No	No
Macast	No	Yes, but doesn't show title or other extended information	Yes, but doesn't show title or other extended information	No	No

Pulling It All Together: What Is Internet Radio?

In the beginning, Internet radio started as nothing more than streaming audio. The ability to stream made accessing audio on the Internet easier because long download times associated with raw audio formats such as .WAV or .AIFF went away. Sure, the quality wasn't as good, but it worked, and with the delays gone in downloading (save for a few seconds of pre-buffering before the stream starts), people could now broadcast on the Internet.

For a major period, the only product that you could reach a wide audience with was RealServer. With the advent of MP3 technology and products such as SHOUTcast and icecast, that has changed, and now more people than ever can broadcast streaming audio. Additionally, access to higher levels of bandwidth with which to enable personal broadcasting just weren't available yet.

The protocols such as RTP and RTSP were also not available at the beginning, and production tools and technologies such as the MP3 format and Windows Media Audio didn't really come into being until more recently.

It's hard to imagine, but the big difference today as opposed to just two years ago is that what is now a definable landscape populated with key technologies, forms of broadcast, server software, and playback products didn't exist in the capable form it does today. Much of the technology we've described in this chapter was still just over the horizon then. Only recently have all the pieces outlined in this puzzle really come together to enable a large group of individuals and companies to produce entire Internet radio stations or shows.

As streaming audio has caught on, what began with a few pioneers and a few traditional radio stations retransmitting their broadcasts over the Web has now turned into a full-fledged movement. Now, thousands upon thousands of unique radio stations are broadcasting on the Internet, and over the coming years, this number is expected to reach well into the tens of thousands.

So what is Internet radio? Is it traditional radio? Is it just streaming audio? Is it just a bunch of really cool technologies and protocols? In its fullest sense, Internet radio is the compilation of a lot of incredible software, hardware, and formats that are then melded with the traditional models of radio broadcasting. The goal is to create an audio broadcast, enabled by streaming audio over the Internet, to generate an organized, entertaining, and/or informative form of content that people choose to listen to via technologies enabled by the Internet.

Now that you understand what the basic technologies enable Internet radio and its various incarnations to do on the Internet, it's time to get more specific about building your own show or station. In the next chapter, we will identify some pioneering or interesting stations and shows you can learn from. Then, in Chapter 4, we'll go into much more detail about where you can get and assemble the pieces you need.

Part I Understanding the Basics

3

Learning From Today's Internet Radio

Before sprinting ahead into the how-tos, let's take a look at how some existing stations are using Internet radio. Many Internet stations are succeeding at different levels, depending on their goals. Some are enormous multi-channel stations offering everything from classical to heavy metal music, extensive content, e-commerce, and more. Some have received significant venture capital or have even been bought by enormous corporations. Others fill an extremely focused niche, such as broadcasting music only by a particular artist.

The best aspect of Internet broadcasting is that it offers the opportunity to try everything from the 2 million songs over 130 channels that Spinner broadcasts every day to simply offering a cool SHOUTcast station that only a handful of people with similar interests will enjoy. Whatever you want to try, you can try it on the Internet, unlike the radio waves.

The examples we selected are not the only Internet stations worth listening to or studying. They are examples of varying size and complexity and, in some instances, offer interesting features worth considering.

Underground Radio 3WK

Broadcasts in: RealPlayer
www.3wk.com

Underground Radio 3WK of St. Louis offers the type of alternative music you'll have a hard time finding on over-the-air commercial stations. A quick look at 3WK's Currents Chart reveals such underrated artists as Built To Spill, Gomez, Mark Lanegan, and Wheat, as well as some of the edgier, well-known acts such as Beck, Nine Inch Nails, Rage Against the Machine, and Tori Amos.

3WK also takes requests, not only of current artists but also of new, lesser-known artists. 3WK will request a CD and possibly play a new band if the people there like what you recommend. You can even "derequest" music that you think is being played too much. The Artist Catalogue offers links to the Web pages of artists played on 3WK. 3WK has received some outstanding reviews, including *Rolling Stone* magazine calling it "the FM radio of your dreams."

3WK says its reason for being is simple: "[W]e love music. We hate the corporate state of AM/FM radio today, and know there are hundreds of thousands of people like us all over the world. And we know there are innumerable artists that belong on your stereo that aren't making their way there because you don't know about them. Thus 3WK."

You can also check the daily playlist to see what to expect and what you missed (see Figure 3.1) . And any station that will play a new Beck tune followed by a Neil Young classic and follow that with Modest Mouse is pretty cool as far as we're concerned.

Figure 3.1
3WK offers truly alternative rock that is hard to find on over-the-air commercial radio.

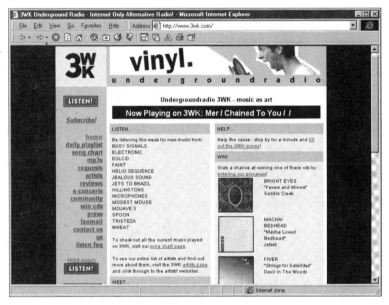

LosDudes Internet Request Radio

Broadcasts in: Windows Media Player
www.losdudes.com

Owned by DedicatedRadio.com, an Internet audio startup, LosDudes.com offers Internet request radio and was even featured in Bill Gates' keynote speech at COMDEX in the fall of 1999.

You must provide an e-mail address to make requests as a registered listener. After you have registered, you can type in a short dedication and request songs. To pick a song, you can search the LosDudes database by selecting an artist from its extensive (AC/DC to ZZ Top) database and then selecting one of the handful of songs by that artist.

As the music continues, you will be told how many requests are in front of yours. When your song comes up, you will hear your dedication, which has been converted into an audio file. Make sure you keep it clean; any foul language will disable your account because LosDudes records users' IP addresses.

Although the ability to request songs and have those requests filled quickly sets LosDudes apart from most Internet stations, you don't have to make a request or be a registered user to listen.

LosDudes also offers a chat room, an e-mail list, and some humorous news stories. In November 1999, the home page even featured Sammy Hagar in the Featured Dude Remembrance section and encouraged users to request some Hagar. The people at LosDudes had just missed Hagar's concert in Las Vegas around the time of COMDEX. Sorry, dudes.

By focusing on requesters and its members, LosDudes, shown in Figure 3.2, is trying to create a critical bond with its listeners using the two-way interactive nature of the Internet.

Figure 3.2
LosDudes.com offers some interesting features such as requests and a computerized DJ that reads dedications you type in.

NetRadio.com

Broadcasts in: Windows Media or RealPlayer
www.netradio.com

NetRadio.com is one of the leading "theme broadcasters." Theme broadcasters try to offer groups of stations that offer specific genres of music or brands of talk. NetRadio offers 120 programmed music channels, offers fairly extensive content, sells advertising and CDs, and integrates content with CD sales. NetRadio's channels are available 24 hours a day, seven days a week.

NetRadio says its goal is to become "the Internet's leading fully integrated entertainment and marketing platform for media and media-related products and services." It has shown a good ability to recommend and deliver music to its users.

NetRadio makes money through advertising and sponsorship as well as by using its content to drive sales at its CDPoint store. CDPoint offers approximately 250,000 titles. It also attracts users with text and audio news content.

To listen to music, you can pick from one of sixteen genres, such as blues, classical, rock, news, and information (see Figure 3.3). Then you can pick one of the specific channels. For example, the rock genre includes Adult Alternative, British Invasion, Industrial, Punk, and more. The resulting page includes links to pages about top artists from that genre (for example, Punk features the Sex Pistols, Dead Kennedys, the Buzzcocks, the Ramones, and New Model Army). The pages also contain links to related channels, brief information about the channels and the channels' programmers, and some of the programmers' favorite CDs. These CDs are, of course, available for purchase and linked to directly at CDPoint.

NetRadio also offers an affiliate program that pays 5 cents for each unique visitor who clicks through from the affiliate site to NetRadio.com. The minimum check is $35.

Finally, NetRadio's Learn area offers information on various types of music and offers recommended CDs and NetRadio channels.

NetRadio shows one of the more interesting aspects of the Internet radio revolution: the capability to provide focused channels of music that appeal to fans of that genre. As you'll see in perusing the channels, the NetRadio site focuses on genres of music that traditional radio never could. By aggregating all these niche channels into one big site, NetRadio is able to grab a large share of audience that can potentially make it a commercially viable Web site.

Figure 3.3
NetRadio offers 120 channels in 16 genres of music.

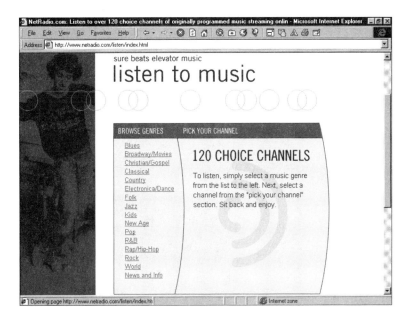

Spinner

Broadcasts in: RealPlayer, Spinner Plus, Spinner Lite
www.spinner.com

Launched in 1996, Spinner has become a top Internet music destination that broadcasts more than 130 channels (and 250,000 digitized songs) of continuous music. In June 1999, AOL acquired Spinner.

Spinner reaches 1.3 million listeners per month and broadcasts a startling 2 million songs per day. Spinner also offers two music players: the standalone Internet application Spinner Plus and the Web-based Spinner Lite. These players for registered users offer song information (artist, song title, album title) and links that allow online purchasing at Amazon.com and real-time listener feedback.

Spinner's site and its players show that, by combining streaming audio with a unique interface, new types of broadcasting and commerce are possible. For example, Spinner uses the RealPlayer's capability to be embedded in a custom-developed Web page. Spinner delivers a player that includes custom information, ads, and commerce links.

You can rate the current song, get artist information, find music news, and enter contests. You can also check any of the numerous channels on the site to see what songs are currently playing.

Although Spinner, shown in Figure 3.4, does not offer on-demand music, it does use experienced music programmers to select the music you hear. In our experience, these "music czars and czarinas," as they are called, do an outstanding job. Spinner stands out not only because of its outstanding technology, but also because it does an outstanding job of selecting quality music.

Figure 3.4
Spinner offers an extensive collection of music and two of its own players: Spinner Lite and Spinner Plus.

Yahoo! Broadcast

Broadcasts in: Windows Media Player, RealAudio
www.broadcast.com

Formerly known as Broadcast.com, Yahoo! Broadcast now looks like everything else that Yahoo! owns. Yahoo! Broadcast is a portal for Web audio that lists and broadcasts both Internet-only radio and webcasts what numerous stations are playing over the air. Yahoo! Broadcast also highlights various music, sports, and other events.

You can either search, browse by location or call letters, or browse by categories such as Alternative, Blues, Sports, Talk, Top 40, Urban, and more. Yahoo! Broadcast also broadcasts video (news and so on) and broadband video.

Yahoo! Broadcast earns money by selling banner and audio ads (placed before a broadcasted stream) and also sells audio books and videos as part of its revenue plans. The other big portion of its business is in selling the services and audience attraction it has to help companies broadcast their content on the Internet via its Yahoo! Broadcast Services arm.

The true lesson to learn about Yahoo! Broadcast, however, is twofold. First is its power of aggregation. Broadcast.com didn't become the huge phenomenon it was by broadcasting a simple rock station. Instead, it focused on unique programming that wasn't being delivered to people on a nationwide basis. It took local sports events, earnings calls, and news stations and gave them out to a national audience. Only Internet radio made this capability possible for a low fee. Second, it focused on services. Companies and other entities hire Yahoo! Broadcast to get them onto the Internet and bring them an audience. As founder Mark Cuban is fond of pointing out, there is a whole other audience to Internet radio—people wanting to get their message out!

TechTalk with Mike and Andy

Broadcasts in: SHOUTcast, Windows Media, RealAudio
www.techtalkradio.com

TechTalk with Mike and Andy is, as you have probably gathered from the program's name, a talk radio show focused on technology. The show has been on the air since 1997 and can be heard over the Internet or on KNWZ-AM in the Palm Springs, California, area on Saturdays. The focus of the show is a fun consumer approach to technology and includes hardware and software product reviews as well as interviews.

The TechTalk Radio site includes computer news from PC World Online, CNET's Computers.com, and the PC World Tip of the Day. A new product review section is on the way, and a Q&A forum, classifieds, statistics from PCData, and links to Web sites are also mentioned during the show.

TechTalk is available in SHOUTcast, Windows Media, and RealAudio. Past shows are archived and available in RealAudio. This is a nice example of a broadcaster not catering to a particular format. Although some of the audio formats are better than others, the people running this TechTalk show realize that their listeners may all choose different technologies to listen to streaming audio. To cast the widest net, they use three of the most popular technologies to broadcast their show.

What TechTalk really shows is the power of the Internet to extend a local show or station to the rest of the world—and in this case, to take a niche radio topic and give itself a worldwide audience. In addition, the show uses its complementary Web site, shown in Figure 3.5, to provide links to products it recommends on the air, guest home pages, and older shows. These features extend the common talk format even more, giving users a place to go and follow up on a broadcast.

Figure 3.5
TechTalk with Mike and Andy is broadcast over the air and on the Web.

Grand Royal Radio

Broadcasts in: SHOUTcast
www.grandroyal.com/grRadio.html

Grand Royal Records is the record label owned by the Beastie Boys, not only one of America's most popular bands but also early users of MP3 and Internet audio technology. Grand Royal is the home of artists such as Ben Lee, Sean Lennon, and Luscious Jackson. The Grand Royal site includes plenty of goodies in addition to Grand Royal Radio.

Grand Royal uses its Web site to promote its bands and sell music and merchandise. Best of all, Grand Royal has an excellent radio station that plays music by Grand Royal artists and others.

Grand Royal Radio is available on SHOUTcast and, for Macintosh users, Macast. The playlist lets listeners know what they're hearing currently and the last ten songs played (this feature is generated by the Music Ticker Plug-In for Winamp). One recent playlist included artists such as Ben Lee, Teenage Fan Club, the Velvet Underground, Elvis Costello, Blur, and the Beatles.

Grand Royal Radio, shown in Figure 3.6, stands out because it shows how a small business can use a personal radio station to hype its business and products. Although using Internet radio is probably a no-brainer for a record label like Grand Royal, other types of companies can use it, too. By broadcasting a talk show about a product, you can create your own Web infomercials. Or, if your product requires further education or discussion, you might create an informative weekly call-in show to support the product's owners. Grand Royal may just play records, but in the end this site shows that Internet radio isn't just for radio stations and personal music broadcasts.

Figure 3.6
Grand Royal Radio plays songs from the label's artists as well as some others.

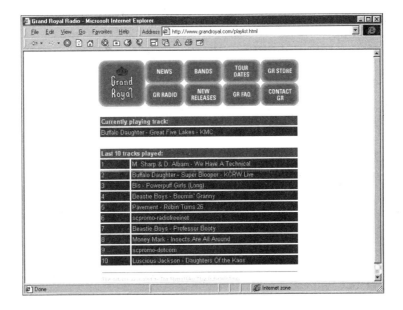

House of Blues Internet Radio

Broadcasts in: Windows Media Player
www.hob.com/internetradio/

The real-world House of Blues was founded in 1992 and has become an entertainment company that includes restaurants and performance venues; radio, television, and Internet programming; and more. The House of Blues Web site aims to be a portal for music lovers.

Despite the name, the House of Blues does not stick only to that genre of music. HOB.com offers cybercasts and pay-per-view of live shows that take place at various House of Blues locations or other arenas. All of HOB.com's audio features can be heard with either a RealPlayer or Windows Media Player except the radio station, which requires the Windows Media Player.

The HOB.com on-demand audio includes digital downloads of individual songs from the House of Blue's live performance archive, sneak previews of CDs about to be released (30-second clips), archived concerts by a wide variety of artists, and artist interviews.

HOB.com also has extensive editorial content, including music news (from other sources such as Spin.com, Vibe Online, *Variety*, and more), an Artist of the Month and Emerging Artist features, artist biographies, and Six Degrees of Blues—a regular feature on important blues performers.

The HOB.com Community area includes ticket giveaways, games, digital postcards, and other contests. An online store offers HOB merchandise.

Not surprisingly, HOB.com also offers a 24-hour-a-day Internet radio station that, according to the site, offers "an eclectic mix of new and old music...rock, pop, R&B, urban, metal, alternative, country, ska, jazz and more."

However, the HOB station, shown in Figure 3.7, doesn't always offer Rage Against the Machine followed by Mary J. Blige followed by Dixie Chicks followed by Miles Davis; its 30-minute Pot Luck show is the most eclectic. The station broadcasts five one-hour programs and two 30-minute programs, all of which air four times during a 24-hour period and offer different types of music.

Figure 3.7
The House of Blues offers seven different programs on its Web radio station.

Some of the programs are as follows:

▶ On Tour is a one-hour show that features music from and interviews with artists currently on tour.

▶ The House of Blues Radio Hour is a weekly syndicated radio show hosted by Elwood Blues (Dan Aykroyd) that is available in more than 180 radio markets as well as on the Web.

▶ Coming to the House of Blues features the music of artists who are on their way to one of the seven House of Blues locations around the U.S.

▶ Noise Reduction is sixty minutes of "the best music no one is listening to"—in other words, quality music (in the opinion of HOB.com) that has yet to receive extensive commercial radio play.

▶ Detour is focused on drum and bass music.

▶ The Putuyamo World Music Hour features music from around the world.

Two of these programs directly and wisely promote the House of Blues either as a brand or by getting people interested in artists who are soon to be performing at the House of Blues. We don't mean to say that visitors won't find quality listening here. The segmenting of music can draw listeners back to the HOB.com site regularly to hear more of their favorite types of music, and the repeating of the programs makes it easier for people to do so all over the world in different time zones. It also allows HOB.com to offer 24-hour programming without having to program 24 hours of music; instead, it has six hours of music, which is probably more than an average listener will be available to hear in a 24-hour period.

SpankRadio

Broadcasts in: RealAudio, Windows Media Player
www.spankradio.com

SpankRadio, based in Dallas, Texas, is another example of the Internet bringing underplayed music such as Stereolab, Spiritualized, Poster Children, Built to Spill, Guided By Voices, and more to the thousands of people who are tired of commercial radio. Hosts Jessica and Angela operate on that seemingly long-forgotten idea of playing what they like (meaning a lot of Guided By Voices and Built to Spill), figuring some people out there have similar tastes.

Personal broadcasters, take note! Internet radio on a small scale can succeed if you use it to share your interests with others. Just as home pages attract visitors because they might be interested in seeing what you have to share, Internet radio works the same way. Music, more than many other types of media, tends to be one that thrives on shared experiences. By building a station around yourself and your tastes and then pushing it as a shared experience, you will find others interested in hearing what you play—especially if they think it comes from your own personal taste, and not some attempt to target a specific listener per se.

SpankRadio, shown in Figure 3.8, also has a handful of archived live shows, some news and reviews, and a message board. The Spank playlist is a long collection of links that allows users to click through and buy at CDNow.com, which, we hope, keeps SpankRadio broadcasting.

Figure 3.8
SpankRadio provides truly alternative rock music.

DiscJockey.com

Broadcasts in: RealAudio, Windows Media
www.discjockey.com

Rather than categorizing music just into genre-specific channels, as many Internet stations do, DiscJockey.com divides its music by decade from the Forties through the Nineties and offers genres within each decade. For example, the Nineties includes Sons of Seattle, Modern Swing, Electronica, and many more. The Sixties includes Surf's Up, Motown Memories, and more.

The RadioActive Zone includes member chats, discussion boards, user profiles, and classified ads. The DiscJockey.com site also offers audio features and news for music fans and an artist search feature that allows you to find an artist currently playing on one of DiscJockey.com's channels. The DiscJockey.com store is an affiliate of The Web's Entertainment Center (**www.twec.com**).

Part I Understanding the Basics

Factory 188

Broadcasts in: SHOUTcast or RealAudio
www.factory188.nu

Factory 188 out of Portland, Maine, specializes in "24/7 automated beats," as they say, playing artists such as DJ Spooky, London Funk Allstars, UNKLE, Peshay, and more. Factory 188 offers music via SHOUTcast (modem or broadband) and RealAudio. It is a great example of a small station that knows its listeners and offers them what they want. Factory 188 also has a chat room and a pair of special shows: Futuresounds (new promotional music) and Skylab05 Afterhours.

This site is sponsored by Black.Light.Media, which offers advertising on its publications and partner sites, Web design, ad design and campaign concepts, and Internet marketing consultation.

Factory 188, shown in Figure 3.9, shows another interesting small business use of Internet radio. Whereas most small businesses use Internet radio to inform people about their products, others may simply use it as a draw to attract people to their brand or Web site and rarely, if ever, mention or focus on their products during the broadcast. Or perhaps they sponsor a station that plays small commercial clips instead of devoting the station to it. In this case, a station might be like much of early radio and TV, where sponsors not only advertised on a program but also created the programs in the first place to build an audience they could eventually advertise to. After all, soap operas got that name for a reason!

Figure 3.9
Factory 188 specializes in "24/7 automated beats."

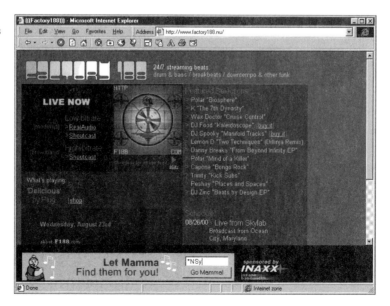

The More You Look, the More You Learn

The stations mentioned in this chapter are not necessarily the absolute best of the Web, nor are they the only stations worth checking out. There are a number of broadcast specific directories, which are covered in Chapter 15. However, as you can see from many of the stations mentioned here, Internet radio already has numerous interesting practitioners and some serious heavy-hitters. The more you surf to new stations (and their complementary Web sites), the more you'll find interesting companies and people doing great things. In this chapter, we intended to point out some stations that you can immediately find and learn from. We hope that these stations will spark some exciting ideas of your own.

4

Getting Everything You Need– From Hardware to Software, Microphones to ISDN Lines

If the rest of this book is a recipe for creating an Internet radio station, then you can think of this chapter as the list of ingredients. As outlined in Chapter 2, a decent amount of hardware and software technology makes up the Internet radio landscape. Although you can launch a station with just a minimal set of products, the point of this book is to cover everything you need to build a great station or show on the Web.

Choosing a Server

No matter what kind of station or show you start—whether it's talk-oriented, music-oriented, call-in, or a live remote—the first place to start when you're assembling the components of your station is to choose the type of server system you want to run. Your choice for server dictates, in some ways, what subsequent products and technologies you can assemble to enable your station or show. For example, if you choose RealServer, then you need content development tools that support encoding audio in the RealAudio format. If you go with SHOUTcast, you should consider downloading some of the various plug-ins—such as SAM or MP3Ticker—that extend its functionality.

Choosing a server system is fairly straightforward; you have five major choices for software. Table 4.1 outlines why you might want to choose one system over another. Features and costs listed are as of this writing and subject to change.

Table 4.1
Major Internet Audio Servers

Product	Choose if you're a:	Choose if you want to:	Choose if your platform is:	Price
RealServer G2 Plus or Professional	Commercial Broadcaster	Have access to a large base of installed players and make use of non-audio streaming options such as RealFlash, RealVideo and RealText.	Windows 95/98, NT, Solaris IRIX Digital UNIX	$1,995 for 60 simultaneous users, and ███████ for more
RealServer G2 Basic	Personal Broadcaster	Use the RealAudio technology without paying $2,000 for a server.	Windows 95/98, NT, Solaris IRIX Digital UNIX	Free for 25 simultaneous users
SHOUTcast 1.6	Personal Broadcaster Commercial Broadcaster	Have an unlimited use license, storing content in the MP3 format, if you're using Winamp.	Windows 95/98, NT, FreeBSD BSDi, Linux, Solaris, AIX	Free
icecast	Personal Broadcaster	Have a system that is OpenSource	Linux	Free
Windows Media Technologies	Commercial Broadcaster	Have specific uses for WMA Codec and technology that include rights management and other advanced commercial features.	NT	Free
SAM - (Streaming Audio Master)	Personal Broadcaster Commercial Broadcaster	Works with WMA and MP3 files as well as in-conjunction with a number of leading servers like icecast and SHOUTcast or as a standalone server. Main claim to fame is excellent on-air broadcast tools, and exquisite stat tracking.	Windows 95/98, NT	Free
Mycaster	Personal Broadcaster	Stream MP3 files but want a very simple program to do so. Mycaster is extremely easy to use but lacks the power of SHOUTcast or icecast.	Windows 95/98, NT	Free

Table 4.1 *(continued)*
Major Internet Audio Servers

Product	Choose if you're a:	Choose if you want to:	Choose if your platform is:	Price
Destiny Radio Server	Personal Broadcaster	Use an alternative MP3 broadcasting product other than icecast or SHOUTcast. Also available in a Macintosh version which makes it the only personal solution (other than outsourcing through MyPlay or Live365) for the Mac.	Windows 98, NT, and Mac	Free
QuickTime Streaming Server	Commercial Broadcaster	Use a Macintosh platform or are specifically interested in broadcasting in the QuickTime format. Apple has also made this product OpenSource as well.	Macintosh	Free, Included with MacOS X server

Having used each system, we recommend the following:

▶ SHOUTcast for small- to medium-sized personal and commercial broadcasting

▶ icecast if you're running Linux and want an OpenSource product

▶ Mycaster if you want to use the easiest solution

▶ Windows Media Technologies if you need a large broadcast and have a heavy NT investment

▶ QuickTime Streaming Server if you're using Macintoshes for Web servers

For the SHOUTcast system, in particular, and other servers, you can download or purchase and install various plug-ins and utilities to add features. We will cover them as they pertain to each radio server platform within their respective chapters because, in some cases, they are too numerous to mention here.

Selecting Hardware

Hardware starts with the main server from which you plan to run your station, but it also includes several additional pieces of hardware, such as microphones, headsets, specialized encoding and stream-enhancing systems, and more.

Computer System

For the most part, we're assuming you have some form of computer that is a capable of running streaming audio server software. Even if you're going to choose a hosting service, you need a machine capable of digitizing audio and encoding it.

When you purchase a system for Internet radio broadcasting, it should be a system capable of handling the load of listeners you expect at peak usage for your station. A system that gets fifty or fewer simultaneous users doesn't need much; a Pentium II 200 (or equivalent) with 32MB of memory should be able to handle that number of users without much effort. However, if you plan to have 500 simultaneous listeners or thousands, you need to consider much more powerful hardware to support the listener load on the server as it pumps out the audio packets to them.

If you're a personal broadcaster, you can figure that, as long as you conform to the system requirements of the server software you choose, you should be able to handle fifty to one hundred users without much more robust hardware than the software indicates it needs.

Going beyond a hundred or several hundred users takes power, though. Most servers that can handle such large loads tend to be UNIX-based systems with loads of memory. Many companies actually use an array of servers operating in unison to handle large loads.

See the specific server how-to chapters in Part II, "Radio Station Software Step-by-Step," for more information on system requirements and scaling issues.

Sound Cards

Sound cards not only enable you to hear audio created on your computer, but they also act as audio inputs to your system, allowing you to digitize it and then send it out over the Web. In addition, they enable you to play sound effects during your broadcast, enable audio chat, and perform other functions.

If you are even semi-serious about starting an Internet radio station or show, you should invest some money in a good sound card. Not all sound cards are created equal. Essentially, three styles of cards are in use: low-end cards that are aimed at the broad base of computer users; higher-end cards aimed at game players and computer audiophiles; and professional cards aimed at musicians and people working extensively with audio on their computers.

For the personal broadcaster, any higher-end card up to a professional card is more than enough to have. A beginner can find a sound card for $100. A good sound card for a beginner is the Sound Blaster Live! MP3+. Some professionals or serious hobbyists might decide to go with a professional card, which, on the low end, can run around $300 to $400 and can get quite pricey depending on features and quality. The more money you spend, the more extensive the features will be and the better the audio-to-digital conversion quality. If you plan to transfer frequently to MP3 from DAT, cassette, or LP, then a higher-end offering with better range and signal-to-noise ratio will produce discernibly better files.

Next, we'll describe some cards you might want to consider and explain how they stack up against each other.

Antex Electronics

If you're looking for the top of the high-end sound cards, Antex Electronics (**www.antex.com**) is the place to go. This company has staked out the market niche, selling sound cards to demanding musicians and computer audio engineers. The Antex StudioCard 2000 and StudioCard A/V Pro sell for about $800 to $1,100 but feature the kind of quality you would expect from a card that costs four to ten times more than mass market cards.

These cards feature 20-bit quality. They also have multiple input capabilities. For example, the StudioCard 2000 can record or play back eight stereo tracks (using four physical ins and outs). The 20-bit A/D and D/A converters allow you to record and play back near perfect sound, and with a high signal-to-noise ratio, there is no background noise or hum whatsoever. The card claims less than 0.003 percent total harmonic distortion and features a sampling range of 6.25 to 50kHz—more than anything you would find on a lower-end card.

GadgetLabs

Another respected card used by musicians and recording hobbyists is the GadgetLabs Wave 8/24 (**www.gadgetlabs.com/wave824.htm**). This card, which has gotten great reviews, features eight distinct inputs, XLR inputs, and excellent quality sampling (24-bits with 128-bit oversampling). If you have a need for a great card that especially gives you the chance to directly hook up a lot of inputs, this might be worth a look.

TurtleBeach

If you want a great sound card that features much less noise and better sampling capability than the SoundBlaster standard but don't need to go to the upper echelon, the TurtleBeach Multisound card (**www.voyetra-turtle-beach.com/site/default.asp**) is an excellent product. The product costs less than $400 and features 20-bit A/D and D/A converters and a 97dB signal-to-noise ratio; total harmonic distortion is claimed at 0.005 percent. The sampling rate for the card ranges from 5.5125 to 48kHz.

SoundBlaster Live!

You can choose from many different varieties of SoundBlaster cards. Millions have been sold or bundled with computers since the late Eighties, when they became the de facto standard for PC sound cards. *Standard* doesn't necessarily mean best in terms of quality. SoundBlasters aren't bad cards. They've just been engineered to sell for low prices, a fact that helped the company pioneer the market and achieve the success it has. However, as prices have come down and more demanding users have pushed for better features, SoundBlaster cards (and compatible cards) have gained better capabilities.

Most people probably use a SoundBlaster 16- or 64-style card. These cards typically have some level of noise associated with them and feature 16-bit A/D and D/A converters with a sampling range between 5 and 48kHz. For most purposes, they're fine cards. Although the cards are noisy and not ideal for creating or capturing audio to convert into MP3 files, unless you're doing some serious conversion for your band or personal listening, you don't need to upgrade to a higher-end card.

Most computer audiophiles who aren't grabbing one of the higher-end cards described earlier, however, are getting SoundBlaster Live! cards. This card packs a lot of punch for under $160. And the SoundBlaster Live! value gives you much of the same functionality as the regular SB Live! for even less. Both cards demonstrate how capable even the low end of the PC sound card market has become.

Among the cool features of the SB Live! product line is the capability to play back multiple audio streams, digital connections to your DVD/CD drives, and several auxiliary ports (not seen on the Value). Having multiple streams makes it easy for you to use a product such as SHOUTcast to mix multiple streams of music into a single mix for broadcasting right on your own system. This capability is cool if, for example, you want to mix .WAV file sound effects with an outgoing CD audio stream or your own voice.

TIP

Linux drivers for the SoundBlaster Live! line have been created. Check them out at **www.sblive.com**, the SoundBlaster Live! homepage.

Mixers

Using mixing consoles, you can combine several channels of audio into a single channel of audio, all the while tweaking the tone and levels of sound of any one stream to make it sound as you like. Mixers also include equalizing effects, faders, pans, and muting effects for each channel. In short, mixers let you manage every individual sound contributing to the mix of sounds you finally output. In Internet radio, you might use a mixer to manage multiple streams of sound coming into the sound card for digitizing, including multiple microphone streams, DAT tape, live performances, and more.

A number of mixers are available, but, for the most part, you shouldn't need anything too high end. Most hobbyists, unless they're mixing talk, tape, CD, and digital audio into their broadcasts, might not even bother with one. However, if you find you're going to mix many media types and want to have a little more control over the entire package of audio you're broadcasting, then a mixer is a good piece of hardware to add to your setup.

When it comes to good mixers for the average person, Mackie's VLZ series is recommended, especially the 1202-VLZ PRO and the 1642-VLZ PRO models. Both offer a number of inputs and good quality; plus, they are very common, meaning you can usually find used and nearly new models for sale at local music shops or on eBay (where we found several auctioneers offering models for auction between $200 and $800). You can check out the Mackie VLZ series on the Web at **www.mackie.com/ Products/VLZ_PRO_Series.asp**.

> **TIP**
>
> Don't know much about operating a mixer? Check out *Mackie Compact Mixers* by Rudy and Ruby Trubitt (Hal Leonard Publishing Company, 1999, ISBN: 0634006703). This book costs about $16 and, while covering slightly earlier models than what Mackie makes today, it's totally applicable to the basics of mixing using Mackie mixers.

Microphones and Headsets

If you're going to talk during your broadcasts, you need a microphone or two. The microphones that come with most sound cards are absolutely terrible. Even for a personal broadcaster, it pays to splurge and get a semi-decent to professional-level microphone. That way, you can avoid sounding like you're on the other end of a tin-can-and-string telephone.

Many companies make microphones, but two that make mics most often used by musicians, broadcasters, and taping enthusiasts are Sennheiser (**www.sennheiserusa.com**) and Shure (**www.shure.com**). Telex is another manufacturer that focuses on computer-oriented microphones and has some interesting USB-based microphones you might consider for certain situations.

Table 4.2 outlines models and prices for Shure and Sennheiser products you might consider using. All information is as of this writing and subject to change.

Table 4.2
Microphones and Headsets

Model	Type	Description	Price
SENNHEISER			
M@B15	Headset with single earphone	Extremely lightweight with omni-directional microphone	$19.95 (SRP)
M@B25	Single headphone headset	Lightweight with omni-directional microphone	$19.95 (SRP)
M@B35	Traditional headset	Two headphones with omni-directional microphone	$124.95 (SRP)
M@B40	Headset with headphones	Very lightweight with noise-canceling cardioid microphone	$59.95 (SRP)
E815S	Traditional microphone	Cardioid microphone with excellent speech and vocal performance	$109.00 (SRP)
HMD 25	Broadcast-style headset	Professional broadcast-style headset with supercardioid dynamic microphone featuring extremely low distortion	$375.00 (SRP)
HMD 45	Broadcast-style headset	Professional broadcast headset similar to HMD 25 but lighter with a slightly larger frequency range	$450.00 (SRP)
SHURE			
SM2	Broadcast-style headset	Professional broadcast headset with microphone and dual-ear headphones for mono or stereo operation	N/A
SM7A	Broadcast-style microphone	Traditional mounted radio microphone, popular for radio and television work (particularly for voice-over recording)	N/A
14A	Traditional performance microphone	Shure's most popular, best-performing, and highest-quality microphone in its price range; designed primarily for vocal artists	N/A

Table 4.2 *(continued)*
Microphones and Headsets

Model	Type	Description	Price
55SH	Vintage-looking microphone	Used by performers and others who want a vintage look and feel to their microphone	N/A
SM10A and 12A	Headset microphone	A head-worn microphone for vocal performers; the SM10A is the same but with one in-ear receiver	N/A
WH20	Headset microphone	Just the microphone and no headphones	N/A

Internet Audio DSP and Encoding Hardware

When it comes to major encoding work, some pros like to turn to specialized DSP (digital signal processing) hardware that can speed up the encoding process with a little extra effort. Two interesting products are available from Telos subsidiaries: AudioActive and Cutting Edge.

AudioActive makes a hardware-based MP3 encoder that can encode files in real-time for live broadcasting or fast encoding. Provide it a sound source, and on the other end, out comes excellent MP3 audio. Many professional-level broadcasters use this product for broadcasting and encoding in general because the components that analyze and compress the audio are superior to those found in most sound cards. In addition, it's far easier to tote one of these systems around as a remote broadcasting tool and feed an MP3 stream directly back to a group of servers than it is to set up a complete computer system on the road.

AudioActive's sister company, Cutting Edge, makes the Omnia.Net preprocessor system. This product sits between your final mix and either your server or hardware encoder; it takes any audio stream that passes through it and lets you add a final set of optimizations over that stream. This product can help boost any dimension of the sound and streamline it for the encoding process before it goes out. The result is superior-sounding Internet audio.

Both products come at a cost, though, and are really only available to commercial- and professional-styled broadcasters.

Connecting Hardware

When it comes to connecting to the Internet, as covered in Chapter 2, you can consider several types of connections. If you're going to use DSL or a cable modem, your local Internet service provider, telephone company, or cable company can supply you with the modem and equipment to enable your connection.

Typically, DSL and cable modem services cost about $40 to $80 a month for individual users and $80 to $500 for commercial users. DSL differs from cable modems in two major ways. First, cable modems operating at peak efficiency (although not all do, since cable modems can bog down as more users subscribe to them) should be faster. Second, DSL services usually guarantee their transfer rates (both upstream and downstream), whereas cable modems can't. The more users who are on your node in a cable modem service, the worse the performance will get. In addition, most cable services limit your upstream capabilities. Running even a 10-stream personal station on a cable modem service 20 hours a day, seven days a week, may incur the wrath of the service. DSL services usually don't have the upstream issues cable services have and thus can be better for most broadcasters. Note also that DSL and cable modems aren't available everywhere yet. DSL also requires that your location be fairly close (i.e. within a couple miles) to a telephone switch in order to use it. Call your local DSL provider to see if your location complies.

> **TIP**
> Be sure to read over a cable modem or DSL user agreement closely, and ask about upstream usage. This agreement more than likely contains rules concerning this usage. The service may completely ban major upstream traffic such as a broadcast, limit you to a certain level, or require extra fees. Before you broadcast even one stream for any length of time, you should know the rules of your high-bandwidth service.

In terms of ISDN or a T1 line, however, you need to acquire the necessary connecting hardware yourself. For T1 lines, you should consult with the local telephone company and ISP that will help you install such a hefty line in your facilities. T1 lines can cost $1,000 to $1,500 a month depending on where you are located in the U.S. and can cost even more in other countries. You also need a T1-compatible router that can interface with the line and provide access to the server. T1-compatible routers are available from most networking catalogs and mail-order Web sites; they run from $800 to $1,500 and much more, depending on manufacturer, features, and model.

Part I Understanding the Basics

ISDN isn't as expensive as T1, but it's slower than a DSL line or cable modem. However, ISDN is great for enabling high-quality outgoing audio to a hosted server and for smaller broadcasters who can't get DSL or cable modems. To enable ISDN, you need to order an ISDN line from your local telephone company. ISDN also requires you to be only a certain distance from a central telephone switching station (as with DSL), which means if you're in the sticks as opposed to being in a populated area of town, you might be out of luck. If you can get ISDN service, you need to get an ISDN modem (also sometimes called an ISDN *router*), which is a specialized modem that enables ISDN data connections. This type of modem can run about $200 to $400, depending on features and manufacturer, and should be available from most major computer catalogs and mail-order Web sites.

TIP

For more details on getting higher-speed services such as T1 and ISDN installed, check out *Getting Connected: The Internet at 56K and Up* by Kevin Dowd (O'Reilly & Associates, 1996, ISBN: 1565921542). This book covers much of the information you will need to know about installing higher-speed connections.

Finding Additional Software

The server isn't the only software you'll ever need. In the following sections, we'll describe by category the specific products worth purchasing or downloading before you begin building your station or show on the Web.

Audio Production Software

The first major piece of software you need after acquiring a server is audio production software. This category includes digitizing software to capture and edit raw audio and encoding software to turn that captured audio into the preferred formats of the servers you want to work with.

Table 4.3 and Table 4.4 describe the major sound capture/editing tools and encoding products you might want to purchase or download. All information is as of this writing and is subject to change.

Table 4.3
Digitization and Audio Capturing Software

Product Name	Manufacturer	Platforms Supported	Price	Comments
Sound Forge	Sonic Foundry (www.sfoundry.com)	Windows	$499.95	The best higher-end editor for Windows 9X/NT systems.
Sound Forge XP	Sonic Foundry (www.sfoundry.com)	Windows	$59.95	A "lite" version of the company's top-line editor, which is good for everyone but the more demanding developer.
Sound Edit 16	Macromedia (www.macromedia.com)	Macintosh	$340.00	Solid Macintosh editor with many higher-end features.
Goldwave		Windows	$40.00	For shareware, this is a good product. The interface is a little clunky, but the system has lots of power and supports MP3 encoding.
CoolEdit	Syntrillium (www.syntrillium.com)	Windows	Shareware/ Version costs $399.00	Well-liked shareware editor with many features.
Peak LE	Bias, Inc.	Macintosh	$99.00	The best of the lower-priced Mac sound editing tools.

Table 4.4
Encoding Software

Product Name	Manufacturer	Platforms Supported	Price	Comments
AudioCatalyst	Xing	Macintosh, PC	$29.99	Best ripper/encoder for converting audio stored on CDs into the MP3 Format.
Xing Encoder	Xing	Windows	$19.99	Standalone encoder for converting audio stored in .WAV or other audio formats into the MP3 format.
RealProducer	RealNetworks	Macintosh, Windows, Linux	Free	Basic encoder software for converting raw audio into the RealAudio format.
RealProducer Plus	RealNetworks	Macintosh, Windows, Linux	$149.99	Upgraded version of the basic encoder.
Sound Forge	Sonic Foundry	Windows	$499.95	Supports encoding files into the WMA, MP3, and RealAudio formats.
Sound Forge XP	Sonic Foundry	Windows	$59.95	Supports encoding files into the WMA, MP3, and RealAudio formats.

Web Site Production Tools

You should consider having a complementary Web site for your Internet radio station or show. It either can be a simple one-page site that explains what the station is, or it can be much more complex, hosting chats, providing a Webcam to the studio, putting up playlists, posting upcoming songs, archiving past shows, and more. To do so, you need to assemble a few key tools, as described in the following sections, for developing Web sites.

Web Page Editors

You can get two types of Web page editors: editors that enable you to design your pages visually and editors that focus on building a page by hand via direct Hypertext Markup Language (HTML) coding. There is no right or wrong way to go, per se; in fact, most people use a combination of both a visual editor and an HTML text editor to get the best of both worlds. Table 4.5 outlines the best editors to use depending on your preferences.

Table 4.5
Web Editing Programs

Platform	Visual (Low-End)	Visual (High-End)	HTML Editor
Windows	FrontPage 2000 (**www.microsoft.com**)	Dreamweaver (**www.macromedia.com**) Fusion (**www.netobjects.com**)	Homesite (**www.allaire.com**)
Macintosh	Pagemill (**www.pagemill.com**)	Dreamweaver (**www.macromedia.com**) GoLive (**www.adobe.com**)	BBEdit (**www.bbedit.com**)

If you just want a good freebie editor, FrontPage Express, part of the full installation of Microsoft Internet Explorer for the PC, is available on the IE download site located at **www.microsoft.com/windows/ie/default.htm**.

And Macintosh fans can find BBEdit Lite, a popular editor located on the Web at **web.barebones.com/free/free.html**.

Graphics Editors

Every good site has some level of graphics. If you're going to build a site, you need a graphics editor. Luckily, some good products are available on the lower end of the pricing spectrum, and on the higher end of the production and cost range is Photoshop 5.5, which is a tool any serious Web site developer has on hand (see Table 4.6).

Table 4.6
Graphics Editors

Platform	Shareware/Lower End	High End
Windows	Paint Shop Pro 6 (**www.jasc.com**)	Photoshop 5.5 (**www.adobe.com**)
Macintosh	GraphicConverter (**www.lemkesoft.de**)	Photoshop 5.5 (**www.adobe.com**)

FTP Programs

To upload files—either content to your server or pages for your Web site—you need an FTP (File Transfer Protocol) program that enables you to transfer files from your PC to the remote server. Table 4.7 lists the two best programs for the Windows and Macintosh platforms.

Table 4.7
Best FTP Programs to Download on the PC and Mac

Platform	Shareware/Lower End
Windows	CuteFTP (**www.cuteftp.com**)
Macintosh	Fetch (**www.dartmouth.edu/pages/softdev/fetch.html**)

Listener Communication Tools

The beauty of the Internet is that it is a two-way communications medium. By using the power of various forms of Web communication, you can communicate directly with your listeners and let them be part of your broadcast. To do that, though, you need the various products that make chatting, immediate messaging, live, on-air phone calls, or even audio chat submissions possible.

Chat Tools

You need two types of chat tools if you're going to go all out on the chat end. First is a chat client that can enable you to enter IRC-based chat rooms. Second is MP3Spy, a program that enables you to easily create your own chat room and to chat with other listeners.

Table 4.8
Leading IRC and Chat Tools.

Platform	Product(s)
Windows	MIRC (**www.mirc.co.uk/get.html**) MP3Spy (**www.radiospy.com/download/**)
Macintosh	Ircle (**www.ircle.houseit.com/download.html**)

Audio Chat

The audio chat revolution is just beginning, but with an audio chat room, the chatter is audio-based, not text-based. With the right sound card or hardware setup, you can broadcast this chatter directly during your show. The best audio chat room software going right now is Hearme.com. There is no real software to download; instead, you install the product directly on your Web page via some HTML code you cut and paste onto a Web page. Hearme.com is covered in much more detail in Chapter 10.

Immediate Messaging

Immediate messaging is a great tool for on-air stations. You can use it to accept requests from listeners as well as communicate with fans. The single best and most popular immediate messaging product is ICQ (**www.icq.com**), which is used by many stations, especially SHOUTcast-created music stations.

ICQ is available for both Windows 95/98 and Macintosh as well as Windows CE, NT, Java, and the PalmPilot. You can find links to download all of them at **www.icq.com/download/**. In Chapter 10, you'll find information on how to embed ICQ forms on your site so that any user listening can send you a message right from your Web page.

Other immediate messaging tools such as Yahoo! Messenger are available, but the sheer size of installed versions of ICQ and its popularity among Internet broadcasters make it the best.

AOL Instant Messenger (AIM) is built into the RealPlayer, so you might want to consider getting it as well if you expect many listeners to tune into your station via the RealPlayer G2/7 or higher. You can download AOL Instant Messenger from **www.aol.com/downloadaol.adp** for the Macintosh, Windows, and Java platforms.

Using Webcams

Some broadcasters like to have a little video feed to go along with their stations or shows. Although they might not specifically use it to create a television show on the Web (that's another entire book!), they might use it to provide a simple way for people to see a shot of the studio, a guest, or one of the station's DJs or show's hosts. Whatever the reason, if you want to have a Webcam, you need to grab a simple piece of hardware and some additional software.

For hardware, you might consider several popular Webcams sold on the market, as outlined in Table 4.9. Table 4.10 outlines come additional software for using with your Webcam.

Table 4.9
Popular Webcams to Use for In-Studio Shots

Product	Manufacturer	Comments	Price
QuickCam Express	Logitech (www.logitech.com)	Very inexpensive camera used by many but features only 352×244 resolution.	$49.95 (SRP)
QuickCam Web	Logitech	Uses USB interface, captures at 640x480 resolution, and features built-in microphone.	$99.95 (SRP)
QuickCam Pro	Logitech	Is available in parallel and USB port versions, has excellent positioning capability, and accepts separate lens packs for wide angle and zoom capability.	$149.95 (SRP)
DVC325	Kodak (www.kodak.com)	Uses USB interface and captures at 640x480 resolution.	$129.95

TIP

Linux users can find software for using the QuickCam Express at **http://www.1000klub.com/~loomer/qcam.html**.

Table 4.10
Webcam Software

Product	Platform	Description and Download URL	Price
Websnapper	Windows	Very simple, easy-to-use package. (**www.demonweb.co.uk/c3sys/websnap.htm**)	Free
Webcam32	Windows	The leading shareware Webcam package for Windows; works with many camera types. (**www.surveyorcorp.com/webcam32_software.html**). Trial version available at **www.surveyorcorp.com/eval.html**.	$49.95
Sitecam 4.0	Macintosh	Very popular Macintosh-based Webcam software. (**http://download.cnet.com/downloads/0-10214-100-916422.html**)	Free

Enabling On-Air Phone Calls

To enable on-air phone calls, you obviously need a device that puts your phone calls on the air. Many professional radio stations use fancy systems, but for the do-it-yourselfer, we recommend that you get a simple telephone recording control device from Radio Shack (Catalog #43-228) and use it in conjunction with a phone system that can handle multiple lines through the same phone.

The device costs around $20. In Chapter 14, we'll describe how to use this device for your station or show.

TIP

If you're going to do a lot of on-air interviews via phone and take calls from listeners, you should consider getting a mixer that can help you adjust the quality of the incoming calls. For example, you might want to better equalize and normalize an incoming call.

If you want better-quality sound from a phone call for interviews or doing a remote broadcast back to the server via phone lines, there are a number of higher-end phone attachments that can be used. See Chapter 14 for a complete list with details.

On-Air Tools and Miscellaneous Goodies

By now, you've probably assembled a master toolbox of production tools, server software, and listener communication software. You also may have decided to purchase a good microphone or two, a mixer, and—if you have the need and the budget—extra processing hardware to help with encoding or enhancing the outgoing audio streams for your broadcast. You're not done, though; you still might consider shopping for or downloading a few more tools.

Kickwave

www.radioearth.com/kickwave.htm

Kickwave from Radio Earth can help you turn .WAV files into queued sound effects for your broadcast. This software version of what is known as a *cart machine* in the radio business lets you press hot keys on your keyboard to trigger any specific .WAV file you set it up for. It's great for setting explosions, drum rolls, laugh tracks, or any other useful spur-of-the-moment effect for your broadcast.

MP3 Explorer

www.trashsoft.com

As your station grows and the number of MP3 files you have climbs, a database system and organizer that helps you track all the files, edit their ID3 tag information, and build playlists can be an important tool. The MP3 Explorer program offers a host of features for managing files stored in the MP3 format. If you intend to run a music-oriented show or station, the MP3 format will most likely be your format of choice; hence, this program could be of use.

Mixing Software

Several companies make DJ mixing software that works entirely with digital audio files. Although we expect most DJs would rather spin using a pair of Technics plugged into a mixer and then into their system for live shows, the digital audio DJ mixing systems such as Mixman (**www.mixman.com**), Virtual Turntables (**carrot.prohosting.com/**), and PC DJ (**www.pcdj.com**) can be interesting tools to use in creating mixed-up radio shows right from your desktop. You can find out more details about these products and using them for Internet radio in Appendix B of this book.

Players and Player Utilities

In Chapter 2, we covered the names of the major players used for listening to streaming audio. While you're busy collecting all the software and hardware you're going to use, you should also collect and install all the major players. You should do so for two reasons. One is to understand how users of each will be able to connect to your station. The other is to collect the links to place on a station's Web page for people to download software with which they can listen to your broadcast.

In addition, from your page, you can link to several player utilities (not counting plug-ins for Winamp or Sonique) and install them for your own listening pleasure. These utilities can help improve the quality of sound that a listener gets from an incoming stream.

SRS Labs makes the Wow Thing! plug-in that enhances incoming streamed audio. It can be used with Winamp, QuickTime Player, and the Windows Media Player. You can download it from **www.wowthing.com/ software/plugin_main.html**.

QSound (**www.qsound.com**) makes another series of plug-ins that enhance incoming streams:

▶ QMP3D is a 3D audio enhancement plug-in for the Winamp player that adds surround-sound and other audio effect capabilities, including Qbass and Qverb, to audio played through Winamp.

▶ iQ automatically converts streaming mono files in stereo and then expands the sound beyond your speakers to add depth to your favorite audio. iQ software is available for the PC and the Mac.

▶ iQms is 3D audio enhancement software for Windows Media Player.

▶ IQFX is a software plug-in for the RealPlayer G2 and RealPlayer Plus G2 that improves the surround-sound and other audio effects of incoming RealAudio streams.

You can download all of them from **www.qsound.com/products/conpc.asp**.

Getting Ready to Build Your Station or Show

Now that you've filled up your shopping cart, you're ready to move on to Part II of this book. The next section will deal step by step with the leading radio station packages available, guiding you through their installation, setup, and management. After that, you can put the rest of the products to use by building an accompanying Web site and setting up ways for listeners to interact with your station or show.

Windows users should download the server, and unzip into an appropriate folder such as "c:\Program Files\SHOUTcast." Once the files are extracted into the folder, create a shortcut for SC_SERV.EXE to the Desktop. Start up the SHOUTcast Server by running the executable, then click on the "Edit config" menu option located at the top. This will start the default text editor, opening the configuration file for SHOUTcast Server. Please follow all the directions that are written into the configuration file.

Once you are done making changes, save the file, close the editor, and restart the SHOUTcast Server application. Windows users should download the server and unzip into an appropriate folder such as "c:\Program Files\SHOUTcast".

Once the files are extracted into the folder, create a shortcut for SC_SERV.EXE to the Desktop. Start up the SHOUTcast Server by running the executable, then click on the "Edit config" menu option located at the top. This will start the default text editor, opening the configuration file for SHOUTcast Server. Please follow all the directions that are written into the configuration file.

Once you are done making changes, save the file, close the editor, and restart the SHOUTcast Server application.

Part II
Radio Station Software Step-by-Step

5

Building a SHOUTcast Station Step-by-Step

RealAudio and RealServer, as well as a few other early products, may have been the origins for the idea of Internet radio, but it was probably SHOUTcast streaming audio, which transformed the popular Winamp player into a tool for personal Internet radio, that jump-started what today is one of the fastest growing Internet phenomena. With SHOUTcast, Nullsoft has created a simple system that enables you to take any song you're listening to via Winamp and send it out over the Internet. Today, SHOUTcast is one of many new Internet radio technologies and is used by thousands of Internet radio pioneers around the world.

In this chapter, you will learn how to install SHOUTcast Server and how to handle various plug-ins to create your own station. Also covered are some additional SHOUTcast-related systems such as SAM and the RadioSpy DJ tools.

The Creation of SHOUTcast

Justin Frankel created SHOUTcast after he decided he wanted to build a way for people to run their own personal radio stations. His motivation was sparked by his interest in having someone stream to him the show *Love Lines* from its Los Angeles home base to Phoenix. The show, while syndicated, isn't carried by local stations in Phoenix. With a little programming and support from Tom Pepper, Nullsoft's network engineer, SHOUTcast was born. Today, after AOL's purchase of Nullsoft, Tom Pepper, who directly heads the SHOUTcast system, has delivered several revisions to the server system and SHOUTcast DSP tools for Winamp.

How SHOUTcast Works

SHOUTcast is a broadcast system made up of two components: a server system and the SHOUTcast source DSP plug-in for Winamp. With Winamp, you can play any number of audio files. The DSP plug-in decodes any source material playing in SHOUTcast to standard raw audio, re-encodes it on the fly into the MP3 format, and then sends it to the server system.

Part II Radio Station Software

The SHOUTcast Server, a standalone application, receives the source stream and then relays it to listeners who are connected to it. The system also includes the site SHOUTcast.com and a directory server known as yp.shoutcast.com. This directory server catalogs all the public SHOUTcast Servers (you can make your server private if you choose) and provides a directory to prospective listeners on the **www.shoutcast.com** Web site. This site also provides links to station home pages, ICQ links, chat rooms, and AOL Instant Messenger (AIM) links.

Overall, SHOUTcast is set up to be a comprehensive server system mostly aimed at personal broadcasters with smaller audiences. However, it is highly scalable and capable of supporting large audiences; with its plug-in architecture, it can be extended beyond its core set of functions in many ways.

Developing Your Own SHOUTcast Station or Show

To develop your own SHOUTcast station, you need some special software, a little ingenuity to create a cool playlist, and a connection capable of supporting enough upstream bandwidth to send your broadcast onto the Net. To make a successful station, you also need to promote your station and experiment with some of the SHOUTcast DJ tools made available by Radiospy.com and others. With everything installed, you can begin broadcasting (see Figure 5.1).

Figure 5.1
Here, you can see the Winamp program with the SHOUTcast Source plug-in, the SHOUTcast Server, and RadioSpy.

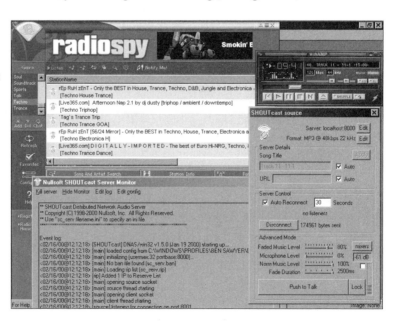

To use SHOUTcast properly, you need to download several pieces of software and configure both a Winamp plug-in and a text file that configures the SHOUTcast Server. This process sounds more complex than it is. When you understand the critical pieces to configure, you shouldn't have much of a problem getting the system up and running. The following step-by-step guide and other information should supply you with ample help in getting your SHOUTcast station operable.

Step 1: Acquire the Necessary Software for SHOUTcast

The first step is to fill up your SHOUTcast toolbox. That means acquiring the software you need, including two major Winamp plug-ins, MP3 codecs (available from Microsoft), and the SHOUTcast Server program found at SHOUTcast.com. You might also want to download RadioSpy from **radiospy.com** and get the DJ plug-in for it as well as SAM, which you can find on **www.audiorealm.com**.

First and foremost, you need the SHOUTcast Server and a copy of the latest version of Winamp installed on your system.

Step 2: If Needed, Install the Windows Media Server MP3 Codecs

To create the MP3 stream that goes to users via SHOUTcast, Winamp needs to have a set of encoding plug-ins that create the specific bit stream of MP3 content. Instead of supplying these codecs, you need to get them from another route. The best way to get them is to install the Windows Media Server Tools, which include a set of MP3 codecs that work perfectly for the SHOUTcast system. The Windows Media Server is actually an NT-only product, but you can install the toolset without consequence on any Windows 95/98/NT system. You may see these tools referred to as the NetShow tools, because NetShow is the old name for what is now known as Windows Media Server.

You can acquire the Windows Media Server Tools from a link on the SHOUTcast documentation page (**http://www.shoutcast.com/support/docs/**). You can also download them directly from the following Web address:

> **http://mskyus.www.conxion.com/msdownload/netshow/3.01/**
> **x86/en/nstools.exe.**

Part II Radio Station Software

After you download the tools, double-click on the NSTOOLS icon; the program then extracts and runs the Setup program (see Figure 5.2). The first option for setup is to install either the complete tools package or just the PowerPoint tools. For now, you should choose the complete setup and then input (or accept) the location where you want to store the programs. The codecs needed for SHOUTcast are installed as part of the installation process. You don't need to do anything more after the installation is done.

Figure 5.2
Installing the Windows Media Server Tools is a critical step in enabling SHOUTcast Radio.

The codecs included with the Windows Media Server Tools don't allow you to broadcast at any better quality than 56bps. That and lower bit rates are fine for almost every broadcaster. If you want to broadcast at higher bit rates, you need to install another set of codecs. However, you must purchase them directly from Opticom (**www.opticom.de**).

Step 3: Install the SHOUTcast DSP Broadcasting Tools into Winamp

SHOUTcast needs to receive a stream of audio from your Winamp player to be able to play. The server can then broadcast over the Internet. This stream is created by the combination of the SHOUTcast DSP plug-in and the aforementioned MP3 codecs supplied via the Windows Media Tools. You can download the SHOUTcast DSP plug-in from **http://scastweb2-qfe0.spinner.com/download/scast/dsp150b2.exe**. After you download it, you need to install it and store it in your Winamp Plugins directory.

You can install some other useful plug-ins if you want to be able to act as a DJ and talk during your SHOUTcast sessions; you'll find more details on these plug-ins a bit later in this chapter.

Step 4: Install the SHOUTcast Server System

Although Winamp itself is a Windows application, the SHOUTcast broadcasting server can be run on a number of platforms: Windows, FreeBSD, BSDi 4.0+, Linux, Irix 6.2, Irix 5.3, Solaris 2.6, AIX 4.1x, and Mac.

You can download various versions of the latest SHOUTcast Server by going to **http://www.shoutcast.com/download/license.phtml** and accepting the license. Then you can proceed to the next screen, where you can choose from the various platforms SHOUTcast is available for.

At this point, you can download the file for your preferred server version. If you're serving from UNIX, you should download the version appropriate for your operating system, unzip the distribution, and untar the archive. You can use a text editor to configure the sc_serv.conf file (see the following section for details, and make sure you use emacs). It doesn't matter what user the server is logged in under as long as the logged-in user has read access to the config file as well as write access for the files you define for file storage and log storage.

Windows users should download the SHOUTcast-version number.exe file and run it to activate the install system, which will let you choose an install type and directory and subsequently unpak and install all the program contents into the directory of your choice.

Please note that it may not overwrite previous instances of SHOUTcast files, including your logs, readme, and sc_serv.ini files, so you may want to install it to a different directory from what you already use for any previous version of SHOUTcast to ensure the full package installs and you can view updated configuration and documentation files.

Step 5: Configure Winamp to Send Content to the SHOUTcast Server

With the server installed, the codecs downloaded, and the SHOUTcast DSP plug-in ready for action, you can begin creating the connections and settings that enable you to broadcast your audio to the world.

Part II Radio Station Software

Start by configuring the SHOUTcast DSP plug-in for Winamp. You do so
by running Winamp and choosing Options > Preferences (Ctrl+P). Then
you choose the DSP/Effect Purpose setting in the Plug-ins section of the
Winamp Preferences dialog (see Figure 5.3).

Figure 5.3

In this dialog, you first
choose the DSP/Effect
Purpose setting.

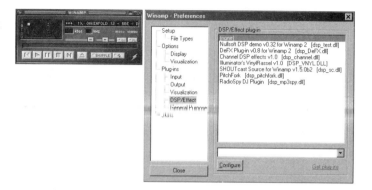

From the list of available plug-ins, choose the one labeled SHOUTcast
Source for Winamp v. 1.5 [dsp_sc.dll] or a later version, as shown in
Figure 5.4.

Figure 5.4

You then choose the
SHOUTcast Source
plug-in.

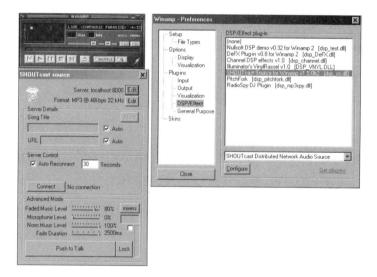

After you select that DSP/Effect plug-in, click on Configure to bring up the Configure SHOUTcast Plug-in dialog box (see Figure 5.5).

Figure 5.5
In the Configure SHOUTcast Plug-in dialog box, you can configure SHOUTcast to work as you want it.

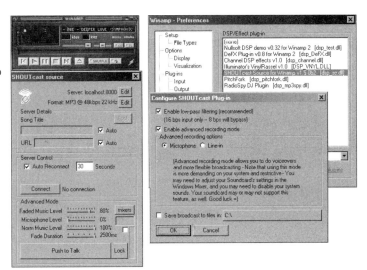

The Configure SHOUTcast Plug-in dialog box contains four major items you need to consider in configuring your SHOUTcast station:

▶ **Enable Low-Pass Filtering**—This recommended setting ensures that SHOUTcast sends out only files that have been created using 16-bit or better sampling (not to be confused with bit rate). This option ensures better quality files.

▶ **Enable Advanced Recording Mode**—If you want to use a microphone or provide a separate line-in source to the SHOUTcast Server, you must enable the advanced recording mode by checking this box and choosing one of the two advanced recording options. See "Using a Microphone with SHOUTcast" later in this chapter for more details on this mode.

▶ **Advanced Recording Options**—You can use these options to add support for line-in and microphone mixing to your SHOUTcast productions. See "Using a Microphone with SHOUTcast" later in this chapter for more information about these settings and using the advanced recording controls.

▶ **Save Broadcast to Files In**—If you check this option and list a filename, you can save your entire broadcast to some area on your disk as an MP3 file. This capability is useful if you want to later provide an archive of past shows via SHOUTcast or make them available for download from your Web site.

After you set up the configuration of the SHOUTcast Source plug-in and return to Winamp, you must configure the plug-in itself so that it knows where to find the SHOUTcast Server and how you want some aspects of your station to run. The main SHOUTcast Source dialog is shown in Figure 5.6. This dialog pops up when you first select the SHOUTcast Source DSP plug-in to begin with. If it doesn't appear (as can sometimes happen), select None for the DSP selection from the Winamp Preferences. Close the Preferences and try selecting it again until it does pop up. Also, look in the system tray, and double-click on the SHOUTcast source icon to pull it back up later when you want to change the configuration.

Figure 5.6
In the main SHOUTcast Source dialog, you can configure the plug-in itself.

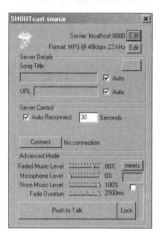

The SHOUTcast Source dialog contains a few sections, including two "sub-dialogs" that are associated with the Server and Format options.

The first section of the SHOUTcast Source dialog is the Server section, which, by default, is set to Server: localhost: 8000. Clicking on the Edit button brings up the SHOUTcast Server Selection dialog box, which is shown in Figure 5.7.

Figure 5.7
You need to fill in the fields in the SHOUTcast Server Selection dialog box.

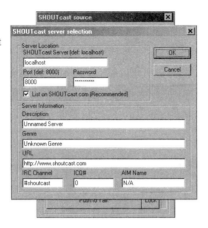

This dialog has a number of fields associated with it that you need to fill in. It's also important that these details match some of the ones you fill out in the scserv.ini file (see more later on this). Most of this information describes your server to the public; you use it to set the location of the server, the password to access it, and more. Here are the specific details of each field in this dialog box:

▶ **SHOUTcast Server (def: localhost)**—In this field, enter the IP number of the machine that is running the SHOUTcast Server. If you're running the server on the same machine as the Winamp program supplying the source audio, then you can just enter **localhost** in the field; this setting is the default.

▶ **Port (def: 8000)**—In this field, enter the port number that the SHOUTcast Server is listening on for the source audio. It should match the number placed in the <u>PortBase</u> attribute of your sc_serv.ini file, or it won't work. The default setting is 8000, but you can change it to any number. Beware, however, that other Internet applications may be using other numbers; therefore, you could create a conflict if you change it. Most people running two servers choose 8000 and 5000 as their port numbers.

▶ **Password**—Place the password for basic administration of the server here. It must match the <u>Password</u> attribute set in the sc_serv.ini file. You optionally can set an administrator-only password as well, but you can set it only via the sc_serv.ini file.

▶ **List on SHOUTcast.com (Recommended)**—This check box, when checked (which is the default setting), instructs SHOUTcast to list your server publicly on SHOUTcast.com. If you want to run a private server, you should uncheck this box.

▶ **Description**—Type the description of your server. Your description can be anything, but the more precisely descriptive it is, the better it will attract interested listeners when it is publicly shown on the SHOUTcast.com listings.

▶ **Genre**—List the genre(s) you are playing, and be precise. You can list multiple genres. A list of popular genres is shown in Table 5.1.

▶ **URL**—Type the http:// URL of a Web page related to your station.

▶ **IRC Channel**—List the IRC channel you want listeners of your station to automatically connect to when they choose the Chat button on SHOUTcast.com's directory listings (see Figure 5.8).

Figure 5.8
Every listing on the SHOUTcast.com directory includes a Chat button link, as well as optional buttons for ICQ and AIM links.

▶ **ICQ#**—List your ICQ number here (for more details on ICQ, see Chapter 10). This number will appear in the SHOUTcast.com directory listings.

▶ **AIM Name**—List your AIM (AOL Instant Messenger) name here. It will appear in the SHOUTcast.com directory listings.

Table 5.1
The Genres

SHOUTcast.com	RadioSpy	Both
R&B	Alt	Talk
Various	Ambient	Comedy
Mixed	Blues	Techno
'80s	Christian	Dance/House
'70s	Disco	Rock/Alternative
	Ethnic	Metal
	Euro	Rap
	Game	Pop
	Gospel	Funk
	Industrial	Jazz
	Oldies	Classical
	Punk	
	Reggae	
	Ska	
	Soul	
	Soundtrack	
	Trance	

The next sub-dialog has to do with the format of the outgoing stream. Here, you set the bit rate of the file, the sample rate, and some other attributes. Just click on the Edit button next to Format in the SHOUTcast Source dialog to bring up the Format Selection (MPEG layer 3 only) dialog box (see Figure 5.9). The available settings should be configured like this:

▶ **Name**—Here, you choose the name for your format.

▶ **Format**—Here, you set the type of format (for now, only MP3 is offered, but others such as Windows Media Audio could be offered in the future).

▶ **Attributes**—From this drop-down list, you choose the quality and bit rate of the resulting SHOUTcast MP3 stream. If you've installed the codecs properly (as outlined earlier), you should have close to 40 specific choices you can employ. (Only 20 or so of those selections are of the stereo variety.)

Part II Radio Station Software

You can choose Save As to create a named setting for your choices. This way, you can choose from the Name list to set the quality attributes for your SHOUTcast station for any future sessions with SHOUTcast.

Figure 5.9
You must choose your MP3 settings before broadcasting. Be sure to choose a codec format that works with your available upstream bandwidth, as well as that of your likely listeners' downstream bandwidth.

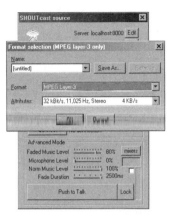

TIP

Choosing the exact attributes in the Format Selection dialog box requires a little bit of planning. Your Internet connection can support only so many simultaneous users at certain bit rates. See the "Selecting Bit Rates and Maximum Number of Users" sidebar later in this chapter.

After you have gone through the Server and Format dialogs, you can return to the main SHOUTcast Source dialog and begin filling out the rest of the options as follows:

▶ **Server Details**—In this section, you set how the SHOUTcast Source plug-in sends the song title and server URL information to the SHOUTcast Server. Selecting the Auto check boxes causes the system to automatically send this information to the server based on the song playing and the URL of the server it autodetects. If you want to override these settings, uncheck the boxes and type the information you want to have the system send otherwise.

▶ **Server Control: Auto Reconnect**—This check box and field combo lets you tell the server whether it should autoreconnect to the server if a disruption occurs in the connection between it and the server. If so, you can place the number of seconds the source plug-in should wait between resets.

▶ **Connect**—Click on this button after the SHOUTcast Server is running and you have filled out the proper information and set the proper configurations in the sc_serv.ini file. If the SHOUTcast Server software is available, and everything is properly configured, the system should connect properly. If not, it will begin a countdown to try again or cancel.

TIP

Passive plug-ins (line input and CD audio, for instance) do not work with the SHOUTcast Source plug-in. If you want to serve these types of audio, you must use the live input plug-in for Winamp (Winamp, Open Location, URL=linerec://) with a sound card that is capable of recording its own output.

When you are finished with the configuration, you can click the close box in the upper-right corner of the dialog to collapse it down to the system tray. The Connect button is useful only if you have the server running and are able to connect to it. This action requires configuring the server itself, and that brings up the next step in building a SHOUTcast-based station or show.

Step 6: Configure the SHOUTcast Server System

You can configure your SHOUTcast Server by editing the sc_serv.ini file located in the directory/folder path you chose when installing the SHOUTcast Server. You can edit this file by using any standard text editor (see Figure 5.10) Most of the file is full of commented text (text preceded by a semicolon is commented). Just type in the values you want to use for each of the variables that are in the file.

NOTE

This chapter contains information on configuring SHOUTcast Server up through Version 1.6X. SHOUTcast version 1.76 DNAS (Distributed Network Audio Server) is the latest version of the server as this book went to press. There are very few changes in features or configurations from what is presented here. The following are the few differences worth noting:

In the config file the following options have been added:

▶ **WebLog** (Yes/No, default No)—This will display http:// requests in the log file.

▶ **TchLog** (Yes/No, default Yes)—This will display yp touches in the log file.

▶ **Sleep** (value)—This is a tweakable parameter for high-traffic SHOUTcast servers which adjusts sleep granularity on the CPU—do not make changes to this unless you really understand your system and SHOUTcast.

▶ **CpuCount** (value)—Another tweakable parameter for high-traffic SHOUTcast servers which lets you adjusts client threads in your system. Again, do not make changes to this variable unless you really understand your system and SHOUTcast.

Part II Radio Station Software

NOTE *(continued)*

According to Nullsoft, as of SHOUTcast 1.6.0, there are two modes of operation. The DNAS's primary function is as a live-broadcast repeater. It receives data from a broadcaster (for example, Winamp), notifies the SHOUTcast directory when it gets information from the client, and then repeats the broadcast audio data from the source to the listeners. The newer second mode of operation is on-demand content streaming. This works by letting you place MP3 files in the content directory, which is found in your SHOUTcast directory. SHOUTcast will send these streams to listeners along with a small amount of protection to prevent people from saving the stream.

To use on-demand streaming, place the content into your content directory, then place a link on your Web page as follows:

```
<A HREF="http://your.shoutcastserver's.address:port/content/
music.pls">Listen Here!</A>
```

The music.pls part of the link is important—it is a cue to the SHOUTcast server to play a file called Music.MP3 stored in your content directory. Substitute "music" with any name of a file you want—but you must use the .pls extension for on-demand streaming and not .mp3.

There is a new XML Statistic feature set now as well. This feature lets you provide statistics to external applications via XML, which can be used to provide live stat information (if you know how to parse the XML) and to create your own stats pages using a scripting language like PHP or Perl. You can find detailed information on this feature in the SHOUTcast 1.7X readme file.

Figure 5.10

To configure your SHOUTcast Server, you need to edit the sc_serv.ini file by using your favorite text editor.

```
SHOUTcast Distributed Network Audio Server configuration file
; Copyright (C) 1998-2000 Nullsoft, Inc.
; All Rights Reserved.
; Last modified Jan 20 2000

; If you want to manage multiple configurations, just copy
; this file to another name, and run sc_serv with that name
; such as:
; sc_serv.exe sc_leet.conf

; *****************************
; Logging configuration
; *****************************

; LogFile: file to use for logging. Can be '/dev/null' or 'none'
; or empty to turn off logging. The default is ./sc_serv.log
; on *nix systems or sc_serv_dir\sc_serv.log on win32.
; Note: on win32 systems if no path is specified the location is
; in the same dir as the executable, on *nix systems it is in the
; current directory.
LogFile=sc_serv.log

; RealTime displays a status line that is updated every second
; with the latest information on the current stream (*nix and win32
; console systems only)
RealTime=1

; ScreenLog controls whether logging is printed to the screen or not
; on *nix and win32 console systems. It is useful to disable this when
; running servers in background without their own terminals. Default is 1
ScreenLog=1
```

The test file contains a number of variables and attributes you can change. They are as follows:

▶ **LogFile**—This attribute lets you set the filename for the file that SHOUTcast Server will use for logging. You can set it to non or leave it empty if you don't want to have a log file. The default setting is sc_serv.log.

> **TIP**
>
> On Win32 systems, if no path is specified, the log file is in the same directory as the executable. On *nix systems, it is in the current directory.

▶ **RealTime**—This attribute lets you decide whether the SHOUTcast Server will display a status line that is updated every second with the latest information on the current stream. The default of on is 1. You can set it to 0 to turn it off.

▶ **ScreenLog**—This attribute lets you set whether the log information that SHOUTcast Server generates is printed onto the screen. Nullsoft recommends disabling this feature when you run your server in the background without Nullsoft's own terminals. The default setting is 1 (on). You can use 0 to turn it off.

▶ **ShowLastSongs**—This attribute lets you set how many songs to list in the /played.html page when people hit your server address. The default is 10, but you can set it between 1 and 20.

> **TIP**
>
> The MusicTicker plug-in for Winamp adds features to listing your last played songs. See Chapter 10 for information on using MusicTicker to list songs played on your station's Web site.

▶ **HistoryLog**—With this attribute, you can set the filename for the HistoryLog file. Use none or leave it empty to turn off this feature. The default setting is HistoryLog=sc_hist.log.

▶ **HistoryTime**—This attribute lets you specify the frequency of updates to the history log. The time is set in number of seconds, and the default is 30.

▶ **PortBase**—This attribute lets you set the portbase of your server on which users listen. The PortBase+1 number must be available as well for the source to stream in on (unless you are running a relay server). Port settings below 1024 may require a root privilege on UNIX-style machines. The default port is 8000, and most people leave it at this setting. If you run more than one server on one machine, you need to assign different port numbers to each server so there is no conflict.

▶ **SrcIP**—This attribute lets you define specifically where a source stream to your SHOUTcast Server can originate from. Setting this attribute is useful if you want to limit who can send content to your server. If you set this attribute to any specific IP address, the server will accept a source stream only from that Web address. If you set it to <u>ANY</u>, it will accept a stream from any other computer. If you set to 127.0.0.1, it will not accept any stream from any machine (this setting is useful if your source files are local).

▶ **DestIP**—This attribute deals with what IP address is used for incoming connections to your stream. The default setting is <u>ANY</u>, but if you are running the server on a machine with multiple IP addresses, you can use this attribute to specify which specific IP should be used for SHOUTcast Server.

▶ **Yport**—When you run a SHOUTcast Server, it communicates with the yp.shoutcast.com server to create a directory listing and provide other server information for SHOUTcast.com. This attribute lets you set the port setting on your system used to connect your server to the yp.shoutcast.com server. For the most part, you should leave it at the default setting of 80. If you are behind a firewall or Web proxy, then you might need to change it, however.

▶ **NameLookups**—This attribute lets you tell the server whether it should do reverse DNS server lookups for your log. In a reverse DNS lookup, an application—in this case, the SHOUTcast Server program—attempts to look for the actual DNS name (for example, maine.rr.com) for any IP address given to it by a connecting computer. This process takes a bit longer and may increase the time required for a listener to connect to your machine; therefore, it is set to 0 (off). You can set it to 1 (on) if you want the server to do a reverse DNS lookup for each new connection.

▶ **RelayPort**—If you plan to use a relay server, you can use this and the <u>RelayServer</u> attributes to specify how your server will work as a relay server. The relay port must be set to the port number of the SHOUTcast Server you want to relay.

▶ **RelayServer**—This attribute works in conjunction with the <u>RelayPort</u> attribute. You need to set this attribute to the IP number of the SHOUTcast Server you want to relay.

▶ **MaxUser**—This attribute lets you set the maximum number of users that your server will allow to connect simultaneously. The default is 32, and the maximum is 1024. Remember, you must have the available bandwidth to support the number of users at your bit rate (you'll learn how to determine bandwidth needs later in this chapter).

▶ **Password**—This attribute lets you set the password the stream source must use to connect to your server. If no <u>AdminPassword</u> is set (see next), then this password also gives access to administrative pages.

▶ **AdminPassword**—This password, when specified, adds a second level of access to your SHOUTcast Server. Essentially, it separates being able to configure the server under a different password than from the main <u>Password</u> attribute, which can be used to limit who can and can't relay or send a source to your server. The password entered here is required to enter the HTTP administration aspect of the SHOUTcast Server. The normal password can still be used to log in and view connected users, but only users logged in under the <u>AdminPassword</u> will be able to kick off users, ban users, and specify reserve hosts.

▶ **AutoDumpUsers**—This attribute controls whether listeners are disconnected if your source stream disconnects from the server. A 0 means that the system doesn't dump users, whereas placing a 1 here causes the server to disconnect users if it loses the source stream.

▶ **AutoDumpSourceTime**—This attribute lets you set how long the source stream can be down before users are disconnected. The time is set in seconds, and the default is 30. A 0 here lets the source stream remain idle indefinitely.

▶ **IntroFile**—This attribute lets you specify an MP3 file that will be streamed to the listeners as soon as they connect and prior to the live stream they will receive when fully connected. This file must have the same sample rate and channels that the live stream is set to for it to work properly. The bit rate, however, can vary. You can use a wildcard setting to specify the bit rate in the filename; the wildcard causes the server to play the intro file that matches the bit rate the server is set to. For example, if you create two intro MP3 files, one titled intro64.mp3 and one titled intro48.mp3, and specify the <u>IntroFile</u> attribute as <u>IntroFile=c:\mp3files\intro%d.mp3</u>, then if you're currently running your server at 64kbps, the system will automatically play the intro64.mp3 file.

▶ **BackupFile**—This attribute lets you specify an MP3 file that will be streamed to listeners over and over again if the source stream disconnects. To do this, the <u>AutoDumpUsers</u> should be set to 0. When the source goes down, this file will play, and when the source stream reconnects, listeners will begin hearing that audio again. As with the <u>IntroFile</u> attribute, you must set the <u>BackupFile</u> attribute to the same sample rate and channels of your broadcast settings, but you can vary the bit rate of the files you use and specify a wildcard using the <u>%d</u> setting, as explained in the description of <u>IntroFile</u>.

▶ **TitleFormat**—This attribute lets you format the string of information the SHOUTcast Server sends to the Winamp player that updates the current song being played on your station. <u>TitleFormat</u> first lets you set any additional text you want for your station title. For example, if you set <u>TitleFormat</u> equal to <u>Day Care Radio</u> (<u>TitleFormat=Day Care Radio</u>), then that title is all that will stream to the Winamp player's

Part II Radio Station Software

title bar. You can also place a code, %s, in that setting to pass through whatever title setting was made in the SHOUTcast Source plug-in earlier.

▶ **URLFormat**—This attribute lets you set the format string for which URL is sent to the listener. It works just like the TitleFormat attribute.

▶ **PublicServer**—This attribute lets you set whether your server is publicly displayed on the SHOUTcast.com Web site and the yp.shoutcast.com directory. Options are always, never, or default. If you want to run a private server, set PublicServer=never.

▶ **MetaInterval**—This attribute lets you specify how often, in bytes, various metadata (for example, URL, Title) should be sent alongside the audio data. Nullsoft recommends you leave this attribute at the default setting of 8192.

Selecting Bit Rates and Maximum Number of Users

When you're selecting a bit rate to stream at and setting an appropriate number for the maximum number of users, you should keep the following points in mind:

▶ You cannot serve more users than you have available bandwidth. If you're running the SHOUTcast Server over a modem link at any speed, the most you can muster is one user at 24 or 32kbps. Attempting to serve more users than you have bandwidth only causes skippage.

▶ Shell system administrators will be unhappy if you consume their available bandwidth and server processes without their consent. SHOUTcast is a highly demanding program of both software processes and bandwidth. A T1 line can theoretically support only about 60 listeners if no other traffic is on that T1. Additionally, each listener takes up a system process on the server operating system, which can crash some operating systems if allowed to expand beyond the limits of the system. If you throw up a SHOUTcast Server unbeknownst to the system administrator with 50+ maximum users, you had better be prepared to face the consequences.

▶ Pick a smart number of maximum users for your server. Calculate by taking the available bandwidth you have, multiplying by 0.9 to account for overhead, and dividing by the bit rate you want to serve at. To create a typical DSL connection, for example, you could use this equation:
@ 768kbps upstream $\times$ 0.9 / 24kbps ~= 29 maximum users

Again, if you set this number too high, when you reach the limit of bandwidth, all the streams will start to skip.

Using Extended Current Log Files

The "status" log reporting in SHOUTcast is fairly simple in that it merely writes plain text to the log. If you want to jazz things up a bit and perhaps format things better, you can create an HTML template to apply to the log information. The result, as shown in Figure 5.11, is a customized current log file when displayed in your favorite Web browser. This capability is also useful when you want to display this sort of information in some customized form to your station's listeners.

Figure 5.11
You can use the extended current log feature of SHOUTcast to create a custom status page for your Radio station-specific Web site.

Ben's Broadcast

This station has :0 listeners out of a possible 32

Our listeners include:

Slot	Host	Connected for

My station is current playing Techno, House music.

We've had 0 total hits as of today!

Visit us on the Web at: http://www.shoutcast.com
What's playing right now: U2 - Achtung Baby - 02 - Even Better Than The Real Thing

TIP

This sort of reporting is different from the traditional log files, the history files, or the status information shown in the Web interface to the SHOUTcast Server. All those reports and formatted information tables are totally unaffected by this customized system.

To create an extended log file, you first need to create an HTML template file. This template file consists of any HTML and other text you want to use, plus some simple "template keywords" that are inserted in the form of HTML comments (HTML comments are any text located between a <!— and a —>). These comment tags insert in SHOUTcast Server supplied information to the template and then output that information as a fully customized HTML file you can display on your Web site.

Part II Radio Station Software

You can build your template and save it as any filename you want (we suggest sctemp.txt or something similar). Table 5.2 shows you the various template keywords supported by version 1.51 of SHOUTcast.

Table 5.2
Template Keywords

Keyword	Description
<!-LISTENERS —>	Number of listeners
<!-MAXLISTENERS —>	Server-configured maximum number of listeners
<!-LISTENERTABLE —>	A simple table of listeners
<!-GENRE —>	Current genre string
<!-DESCRIPTION —>	Current description string
<!-URL —>	Current URL string
<!-HITS —>	Number of hits since server was started
<!-CURRENTSONG —>	Current song name

After you build the template, you need to return to your SHOUTcast Server .INI file and set some additional attributes. You can add these settings:

▶ **CurrentLogIn**—This setting should be set to the path and filename of the template file (for example, CurrentLog=sctemp.txt), By default, this attribute is commented out and set to ; CurrentLog=c:\hi.in.

▶ **CurrentLogOut**—This setting indicates the path and filename you want to output to your server. It is, by default, set to c:\hi.html but can be named anything, and you can also access this file remotely by going to http://[your server's ip:port]/current.html.

▶ **CurrentLogTime**—This setting indicates how often, in seconds, the custom current log system should be updated. It is commented out in the sc_serv.ini file initially and set to a default value of 30 seconds.

Using a Microphone with SHOUTcast

SHOUTcast 1.5x has good support for microphones and line-in mixing. What used to require a bit of a workaround or require third-party tools now is built into the SHOUTcast Source DSP plug-in. You also can use the RadioSpy DJ tools if you prefer an alternative microphone control.

The following sections describe the step-by-step process for using a microphone with SHOUTcast radio using the built-in support with the SHOUTcast Source DSP plug-in.

Step 1: Understand Your Sound Card's Capabilities

You can do voice input with SHOUTcast in two ways: parallel to other sounds and music and in between the music. Which road you follow depends on whether you have a full-duplex sound card. Only full-duplex sound cards allow you to broadcast voice simultaneously with music. If you don't have such a card, you have to stop the music to greet your public. (Full-duplex card owners have the option to go either way.) Most modern cards are full duplex, but consult your hardware manual if you're unsure.

Step 2: Purchase a Microphone

No microphone, no talk. Although the microphones that ship with many PCs and sound systems may seem good enough on a practical scale, they are pretty poor overall. You can get a decent microphone for as little as $25 to $30 at your local Radio Shack or music store. Refer to the list of microphones and headset systems described in Chapter 4.

Step 3: Set Up the SHOUTcast Source DSP Plug-In for Microphone Support

When you have your microphone set up, you need to configure SHOUTcast to support it. You do so by first pulling up the configuration dialog for the SHOUTcast Source plug-in (see Figure 5.12). Select the Enable Advanced Recording Mode check box, and then choose the option you want for advanced recording options: either Microphone or Line-in. Essentially, the choice is between one of two different mixer inputs that exist on most sound cards. If you're using a microphone, then you should choose the Microphone setting.

Figure 5.12
To use a microphone with SHOUTcast, you must enable the advanced recording controls via the configuration dialog of the SHOUTcast Source DSP plug-in.

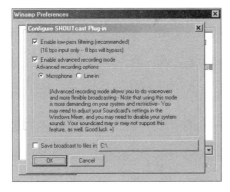

When you're finished here, close the configuration dialog and return to Winamp.

Step 4: Run Your SHOUTcast Server and Connect

For the advanced recording controls to work, you must have your SHOUTcast server up and running.

Step 5: Tweak Advanced Mode Settings

Next, you need to pull up the SHOUTcast Source dialog, which now features the Advanced Mode extension to the normal dialog (see Figure 5.13). Here, you will notice several new buttons and sliders. These various items control one basic aspect of the advanced recording tools: how the music fades down when you decide to talk over it and how low the microphone level is when you do.

Figure 5.13
This SHOUTcast Source dialog has the advanced recording controls activated.

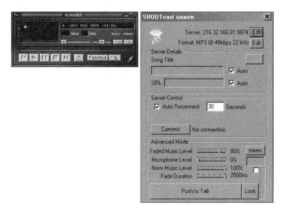

The specifics of each option setting are as follows:

▶ **Faded Music Level**—This slider lets you control the resulting volume level (0 to 100 percent) music will fade to when you click on the Push to Talk button.

▶ **Microphone Level**—This slider lets you control the maximum volume of your microphone level when you click on the Push to Talk button. With most sound cards and microphone setups, it's recommended that you set this level to about 80 percent or less, depending on distortion.

▶ **Norm Music Level**—This slider lets you set the volume level when the Push to Talk button is not active (that is, normally operation volume level).

▶ **Fade Duration**—This button controls the rate (0 to 2500ms) of fade from the normal music level to the faded music level and back.

> ▶ **Mixers**—This button pulls up the default Windows audio mixer control for your sound card.

Check box next to sound levels:

> ▶ **Push to Talk**   After you have configured your levels and fade duration and want to talk over or out on your broadcast, click on this button and hold it down while you speak.

> ▶ **Lock**—If you want to talk for an extended period of time, click on the lock button. With a single click, you turn on the talk mode, and with another single click, you turn off talk mode.

Troubleshooting Microphone Options

You can access the volume controls on your computer through the system tray (see Figure 5.14). Using these controls, you can adjust the volume of all the sound that comes back to you. Check the microphone control here; you can't hear your voice if the volume is very low or the Mute check box is selected. This doesn't mean that your listeners can't hear you, however. Playback affects what you hear, not what they hear. If you don't have a microphone control, select Options/Properties. Then scroll down in the list box until you see Microphone. Click on the check box next to it to enable your microphone.

Part II Radio Station Software

Figure 5.14
Set the recording levels to enable the microphone to work after switching to the recording controls.

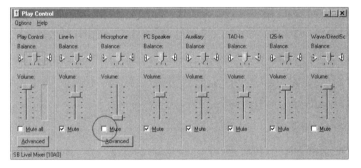

You also can choose Properties from the Options menu to locate an option to switch the volume controls so that you can access the recording controls. Select Recording, and then click on OK to switch to the volume controls for recording levels. These levels control the volume of recordings your card generates (how loud the microphone level is). In many cases, these controls are muted or set to 0 so that you can shut off access to additional noise coming from other audio sources and have sound coming from only one. You need to unmute the microphone and line inputs so that people can hear you.

NOTE

SoundBlaster Live is a special case that doesn't work exactly as other cards do in terms of handling the recording controls. Instead of selecting each individual device in recording controls, you can select only one for the SoundBlaster Live card. However, a control called What U Hear has been added. When selected, this control allows you to record or broadcast everything that you hear through your PC speakers. Instead of selecting only the sources you want in the recording controls, you can go back to playback controls and mute the devices you don't want to broadcast. Everything that is not muted will be broadcast. Needless to say, you should be careful. All your miscellaneous system beeps and ICQ incoming message warnings can be broadcast all over the Net!

Administering SHOUTcast

You can handle most SHOUTcast administration by using a Web-based interface for the SHOUTcast Server or by editing the aforementioned sc_serv.ini files and the SHOUTcast Source dialog. Although not every feature can be administered via the Web interface, you can do most of the major tasks, including banning problematic listeners and setting the maximum listener rate. Because the entire system is Web-based, you can administer it just by opening a Web browser on a local or remote machine.

You can handle further administration of the server by editing and configuring your SHOUTcast DSP Source and the sc_serv.ini files. This process, of course, requires access to the host server. The following process illustrates how you can perform basic administrative tasks via the Web:

Step 1: Open Your Web Browser and Point it to Your SHOUTcast Server

To administer SHOUTcast outside of making set changes to the SHOUTcast Source plug-in or the sc_serv.ini files, you must open your browser and pull up the server's Web-based interface. In your Web browser, type **http://server ip address:8000** (or the port number you assigned in the SHOUTcast Source plug-in or sc_serv.ini file) to bring up the basic Web interface for the SHOUTcast Server. This part of the SHOUTcast Server's built-in Web system is actually made for public consumption. The screen offers links to the server's current status (see Figure 5.15).

Figure 5.15
The SHOUTcast Server includes a built-in Web interface for remote access and administration. The greeting screen shows the server's current status.

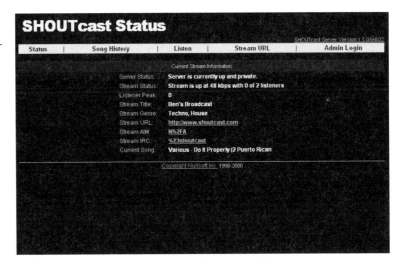

Other screens include the Song History screen (see Figure 5.16), which itself is fairly minimal when compared to plug-ins like MusicTicker (see Chapter 10 for more details on MusicTicker). The top menu includes links for people to click to listen to the current stream and to automatically go to the server's related Web page. You also can access administration functions by clicking on the Admin Login button.

Figure 5.16
The SHOUTcast Server Web interface includes a screen listing the last songs played.

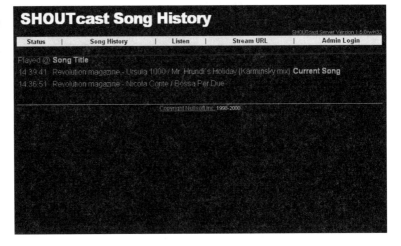

Step 2: Click on the Admin Log Link and Log in to the Administrator Area

After you click on the Admin Log link, you are prompted to supply a password. It is either the default password for the SHOUTcast Server or, if you set an additional administrator-only password, then it is that one instead. After you fill in the correct password, you are sent to the administration pages.

Step 3: Use the Administration Features

When you are logged in to the administrator area, you will see a screen similar to Figure 5.17. Across the top, the options have changed to administrator-oriented links. On the main page, you will see a list of active listeners as well as basic current statistics and information.

Figure 5.17
The basic administrator screen shows the current statistics for your station or show.

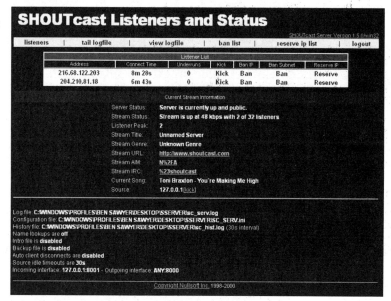

Your options from the top menu are as follows:

▶ **Listeners**—Gives listener information on the main administration screen, as shown in Figure 5.17.

▶ **Tail logfile**—Shows you the last few lines of your log file (see Figure 5.18) so that you can evaluate the latest events that your SHOUTcast Server has encountered.

Figure 5.18
The Log File screen shows lines from your log file.

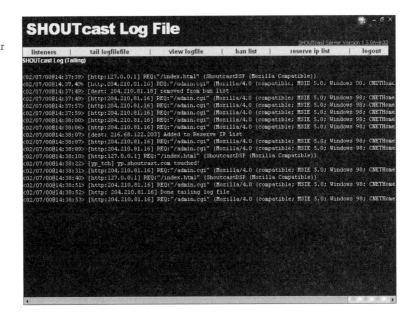

▶ **View logfile**—Gives you access to your entire log file (see Figure 5.19).

Figure 5.19
You can access your entire log file by using the View Log File screen.

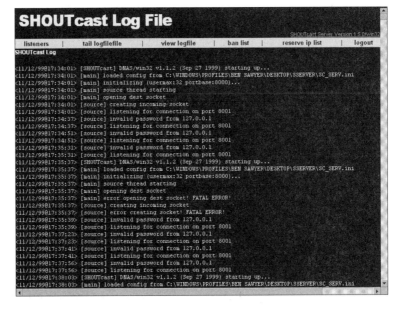

Part II Radio Station Software

▶ **Ban list**—Shows you a list of all the IP addresses and subnets you
have banned (see Figure 5.20) with a link next to each one to remove
the ban on, or "unban," that address or subnet.

Figure 5.20
You can decide who
can and can't hear
your station or show
by using the Ban
List screen.

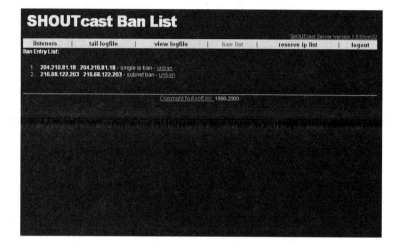

TIP
You can edit the ban list by looking at the .TXT file that SHOUTcast generates
when you build a ban list of any sort.

▶ **Reserve ip list**—Shows a list of IP addresses that are always granted
access to your server (see Figure 5.21), even if the maximum listener
count has been reached.

Figure 5.21
The few, the proud,
the Reserve IP list.

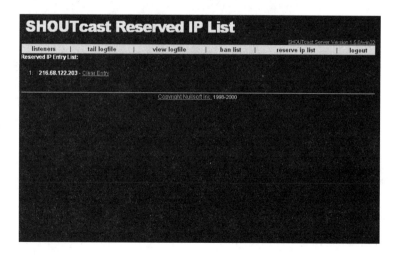

▶ **Logout**—Lets you return to the main screen of the remote access system for SHOUTcast by logging out of the administrator area.

Additionally, you will note the following four active links for each listener; they are actions you can take against any active listener:

▶ **Kick (listener)**—Click on this option to kick off a user from your server. Clicking on this option does not ban the user, however.

▶ **Ban IP (of listener)**—Lets you permanently ban any IP address that you no longer want to give access to your SHOUTcast server.

▶ **Ban Subnet (of listener)**—Lets you permanently ban an entire subnet as opposed to one specific IP address within a subnet. This option is useful for banning people who are trying to stay attached by jumping to different IP addresses within the same subnet.

▶ **Reserve IP (of listener)**—If you want to provide an always-connect pass to certain IP addresses, you can add IP addresses to this list. This option is useful if you want to set a maximum listener rate at a few notches below your capability and then build a reserve list. When a listener (or relay server) on the reserve IP list connects—even if the server is full—that listener will be let in and allowed to connect. Thus, it's smart to make sure for every reserve IP you expect to connect that you set your maximum listener rate equal to the total number of listeners your bandwidth supports—the number of addresses on your reserve IP list.

Finally, notice that next to the Source setting on your current stats and information list below the listener table is the link to kick. If you click on this link, the server disconnects the source stream attached to it.

Additional Remote Administrative Options

As we stated earlier, making major changes to SHOUTcast operations requires access to the sc_serv.ini file, as well as access to the server itself. Assuming you run the SHOUTcast DSP source and Winamp locally and relay to your server, the remaining issue is how to remotely gain access to your server to make these changes.

The easiest way to make changes is to purchase remote control software such as PCAnywhere (**www.symantec.com**) or LapLink 2000 (**www.laplink.com**). This software can make it easy for you to log in to your system via the Internet and make changes to the server, as well as stop and start the program, which is necessary for certain changes to take effect.

Part II Radio Station Software

Troubleshooting SHOUTcast

With any software, things can go wrong. SHOUTcast relies on a number of various parts being installed properly and configured to work together. Thus, problems occur. The following are some of the most common problems that Nullsoft has seen occur and how to deal with them:

Winamp says "Error creating ACM stream" when I try to use SHOUTcast.

This error is displayed if you don't have an MPEG Layer-3 ACM codec installed on your computer. Go back to the beginning of this chapter, and make sure you got the Windows Media Server Tools and installed them properly. You should have the MP3 Layer-3 ACM codecs installed.

After you've installed this codec, restart Winamp and try playing a stream to your SHOUTcast Server. If you already have the Windows Media Server encoding software installed, and this technique isn't working, try restarting Winamp. If it still doesn't work, try reinstalling the Windows Media Server encoder.

Winamp says "Error connecting to server" when I try to use SHOUTcast.

You get this error if your SHOUTcast Server is not running or is not listening on the port on which you are trying to connect. If you have edited sc_serv.ini so that the PortBase=8000 line has changed, the URL must reflect that change. If it says PortBase=31337 in this sc_serv.ini file, then the URL is http://server:31337. If you have not altered sc_serv.ini, the URL should be http://[server address]:8000.

Listeners on the Internet are getting "Error connecting to server" messages when they attempt to connect.

The problem is likely with your connection or ISP. The most common problem in this case is that another program using the port is running. If another program is using that port on the server, you have to change in sc_serv.ini and in the Winamp DSP plug-in configuration, as well as use a different port. This problem also brings about the Error connecting to host message.

My ISP has a firewall that prevents users from connecting to my host. What do I do now?

You need to contact your ISP and ask whether you can run a SHOUTcast Server through the firewall. Good luck.

Winamp says "Invalid password on server" when I try to use SHOUTcast.

The password set in the server in sc_serv.ini and the password you configured in the Winamp SHOUTcast DSP plug-in are not the same. They must be the same. By default, they are both <u>changeme</u> when you start. As we stated earlier, you really should change that password to avoid having people stream with your server when you don't want them to. To stop this error, make sure the passwords are the same in both the server .INI file and in the DSP configuration.

The stream stops at 8KB when prebuffering.

This problem has nothing to do with your Internet connection or your copy of Winamp. This problem occurs when Winamp *was* sending data to the SHOUTcast Server (and is still connected to it) but is no longer sending any data. Get the stream owner to play something in Winamp, and the SHOUTcast Server should resume sending data to clients.

Winamp says "ICY 401 service not available" when I try to connect.

This error happens when the stream owner isn't connected to his or her server. If you are the owner, run through the following checklist. If you aren't the owner, track down the owner and have him or her run through this checklist.

▶ Do you have the SHOUTcast DSP plug-in installed and selected inside Winamp? If not, get it from **http://www.shoutcast.com**.

▶ Do you have the SHOUTcast DSP plug-in configured properly for your SHOUTcast Server's settings?

▶ Are you playing anything in Winamp? You have to play something in order to send it to your listeners.

▶ Are you getting error messages when you first play something in Winamp? If so, check your SHOUTcast DSP plug-in settings.

▶ Try restarting Winamp, ensuring that the DSP plug-in is selected and playing something.

Part II Radio Station Software

My listeners get "Error connecting to host" messages when they try to connect.

Your listeners get these messages if your SHOUTcast Server is not running or is not listening on the port on which they are trying to connect. If you have edited sc_serv.ini so that the PortBase=8000 line has changed, the port in the DSP configuration must reflect that change. If PortBase=31337, then the port in the DSP configuration must be 31337. If you have not altered sc_serv.ini, leave the port as 8000 in both.

If you continue to have this problem, it is possible that another program is using the port you have selected. This is probably the case if you see errors similar to [bind] error running dest socket! FATAL ERROR! in the SHOUTcast Server's error log. Try changing the port number in the SHOUTcast Server and in the DSP plug-in configuration. (Remember, these numbers must be the same.)

Listeners say the audio coming from the SHOUTcast Server is choppy.

This problem occurs when your listeners are not receiving a continuous stream of data. It could happen for one of several reasons:

► **Your Internet connection**—If your Internet link cannot sustain the number of users connected to your server, all listeners will experience broken audio. Follow the guidelines outlined in the "Selecting Bit Rate and Maximum Number of Users" sidebar, which explains how many users your Internet connection can safely serve a stream to. If you are on a low-speed connection (such as a modem), you might want to consider relaying your SHOUTcast stream with a server on a faster connection.

► **Your processor speed**—If your computer is not fast enough to decode in Winamp, encode the stream, and broadcast it out to users, not only will you notice that your computer is slow, but your listeners will too. You could try lowering the decoding quality in Winamp to give the encoder/server more processor time, but this solution isn't very good. Try running SHOUTcast on a faster processor.

► **Your listeners' Internet connection**—Not everyone will be on a fast ISP, which may result in the stream getting broken up. First, make sure you are broadcasting at a speed your listeners can hear. If you are targeting modem users, broadcast at 24kbps and under; for ISDN users, 56kbps and under. Second, if one listener is getting broken audio, but no other listeners are, tell that listener to increase his or her buffer (in the Nitrane preferences) and then restart the stream (by stopping and then playing).

▶ **Your listeners' processor speed**—If your listeners can't play MP3s without them breaking up, chances are they won't be able to play SHOUTcast streams either. (They would have to have a very slow processor—below a 90MHz Pentium I—for this problem to occur.)

Making the Most of SHOUTcast

Assuming you have SHOUTcast up and running, let's move the discussion to making the most of this exciting technology. Most people will probably just slap together a playlist and stick out a server at first. Let's face it: Life would be easy if that's all it took to have a cool SHOUTcast station. With SHOUTcast, like everything else on the Net, you need to go the extra mile if you want to truly stand out. Here's how the better SHOUTcasters stand out from the crowd.

Just throwing up any old playlist for people to hear isn't necessarily the best way to develop a SHOUTcast station. You might want to make use of the following tips:

1. **Stick to your labeled genre.**

   If you're doing country, don't drop in the odd techno song. Make sure your station either sticks to its format or puts songs in the mixed or various category. People want your content to match the advertised format. Because the genres play such an important role in the SHOUTcast.com Web site, it's important you don't disrupt the genre tracking by creating false genre listings.

2. **Use the SHOUTcast promos.**

   They're cool and they promote the technology.

   Nullsoft hired J.J. McKay Productions to create wicked cool SHOUTcast plug-ins. These plug-ins promote SHOUTcast radio to your listeners and provide nice, professional-sounding bumpers between your songs.

3. **Intersperse cool bumpers and sound bites.**

   Create cool bumpers that talk up songs or your station ID; intersperse cool quotes and sound effects to give your station an attitude. If you want to hire the same J.J. McKay Productions that Nullsoft did, you can find it on the Web at **www.jjmckay.com**. We e-mailed J.J. and asked him to give us the ballpark cost of a 6- to 10-second station ID. He said it's about $15 dry (no effects) and $30 fully produced. J.J. McKay Productions accepts American Express, Visa, and MasterCard. You can order the promos directly from the site, and he even will deliver them in MP3 format. His pages even include some suggested phrases to use (see Figure 5.22).

Figure 5.22

Not the type to come up with your own cool station ID tagline? Check out J.J. McKay Productions' list of suggested promos.

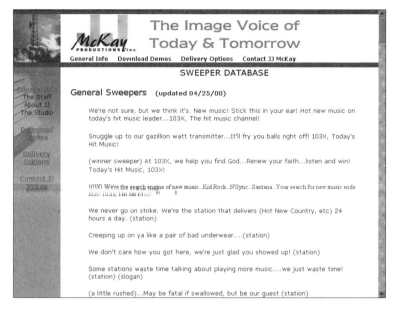

4. **Follow the Statutory License playlist guidelines for Webcasters.**

   Too legit or quit?

   You need to follow some established rules to stay legit in the emerging world of Webcasting. You might otherwise get a nasty letter in the mail from any of the various organizations trying to keep Webcasters legitimate. At the same time, some of the rules actually try to force you to promote some variety in what you Webcast, which brings us to the next tip.

5. **Mix up your playlists to keep repeat visitors listening.**

   One playlist three to four hours long isn't going to cut it after a month. If you want a loyal following, you need to vary that playlist. Give people new stuff to keep coming back to. The biggest complaint about regular radio (which, let's face it, sucks) is that it keeps repeating way too many songs.

6. **Listen to a full playing first, and tweak the flow.**

   Listen all the way through your list. Don't just dump your playlist in, click on Random, and broadcast. Just as you did with the best mix tapes you made before, you need to spend the time to tweak your playlist. Find those rough transitions, and look for opportunities to put in bumpers and station IDs. Make sure you have a playlist that sounds good from beginning to end.

7. **Spice things up.**

   This tip is more biased, but we find that some interspersed comedy is a nice addition to a lot of stations. Even if you just put in a one-liner, adding a joke or two in an hour-long set is a nice way to give your station some attitude.

SHOUT It Out!

SHOUTcast is a great system that is very flexible. Although it's not the easiest thing to set up, it's not that difficult either, and it has a lot of flexibility and power that is conducive to individual broadcasters.

Mastering SHOUTcast really requires experimenting with all its features— even those you don't plan to use. When you've got the hang of it, you can make wonderful things happen with SHOUTcast. Additionally, with its easy support for playlists and support of many major audio formats, SHOUTcast is a server system that will require very little from you to get your audio into a form that you can broadcast easily over the Net.

You can't go wrong with SHOUTcast. What started as a fun side project for a couple of programmers has given birth to the individual broadcaster revolution. As Nullsoft continues to build the server, Winamp, and SHOUTcast.com, we can only expect more great things to come.

Part II Radio Station Software

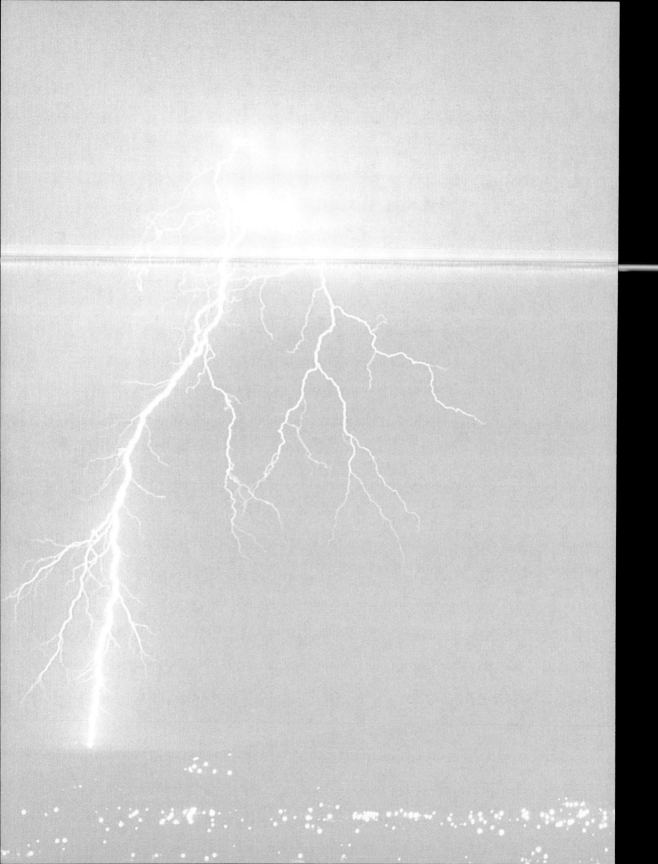

6

Broadcasting with RealServer 7.0

SHOUTcast, MyCaster, icecast, and other newer radio servers may be leading the personal broadcasting revolution on the Web, but the true king of the hill is still RealServer, now in its seventh version since it debuted on the Web in the mid-Nineties.

While aimed mostly at higher-end broadcasters and those doing video, Flash, and other multimedia broadcasting besides just audio, RealServer is a strong server system to use. With its free Basic Server, all users can use RealServer (provided they have compliant operating systems), and for most personal broadcasters, having 25 concurrent streams is more than enough to have a fun time.

In this chapter, we'll go from zero to 60 on RealServer. We'll install it, get it configured correctly, and broadcast on-demand and live content. After that, it's up to you to make the server work as your broadcasting system of choice.

NOTE

This chapter is not meant to be the end-all be-all on RealServer. The RealServer system, especially higher-end versions, includes many more features than could be covered in one chapter. What is contained here, though, are step-by-step instructions on the installation and basic administration of the server—more than enough information to begin broadcasting your radio station or show with RealServer.

At the end of the chapter, you'll find a list of resources for understanding much more about RealServer and its advanced capabilities.

TIP

RealPlayer and the RealAudio format are very popular—even more so than MP3. Although many people are installing alternative audio players such as Winamp, Sonique, and Media Player on their systems, RealPlayer is the number-one installed media player worldwide. Some of the more adventurous personal broadcasters may thus want to install and make their stations and shows available via RealServer as well as SHOUTcast and other alternatives.

Installing RealServer 7.0

The installation of RealServer 7.0 is pretty straightforward. After downloading the server program from Realnetworks.com, you run the program and step through the installation wizard.

The following sections provide a complete step-by-step breakdown of installing RealServer 7.0.

NOTE

RealServer's documentation claims it can be installed and run on Windows 95/98 machines. This claim is not true, nor is installing on such machines recommended. Version 7 runs only on NT or Windows 2000 servers as it relates to the Windows platform. You need to download version 6 (a link is provided on the Basic Server 7 download page) to work with Windows 95/98.

This installation is for Windows NT machines. Most *nix systems follow the same basic installation routine. See the installation Readme file located on the Web at **http://service.real.com/help/library/guides/g270/readme.html** for more information on peculiarities of installing RealServer 7.0 on non-NT machines.

Step 1: Download RealServer 7.0 from Realnetworks.com

RealNetworks offers several versions of its server system:

▶ **RealServer Basic**—A free 25-stream version of the server that is perfect for most low-end or personal radio stations or shows.

▶ **RealServer Plus**—A 60-stream version of the Basic Server. This version also includes a CD-ROM version of the software and a hard copy of the Administrator's guide. It includes support for Flash Animations and one to two years of basic support and upgrades; it costs $1,995.

▶ **RealServer Professional**—Top-of-the-line system that includes many more features and concurrent stream capability over the Basic and Plus versions. Versions with 100 streams cost $5,995, and versions with up to 2,000 simultaneous streams are available at a cost of $79,995. You also can purchase extensions to the system for advertising, authentication, and splitting. See Realnetworks.com for more information.

TIP

If you're very serious about using the Professional version, you can download a 30-day trial version directly from Realnetworks.com.

For purposes of this chapter, we'll concentrate on the Basic version of RealServer 7.0. At this point, download RealServer Basic from the Web at **http://proforma.real.com/rn/servers/basic/index.html.**

You need to fill out a form (see Figure 6.1) and choose the Operating System type from the list (four were available at the time of this writing: NT, Solaris 2.6, Solaris 2.7, and Linux). Then you are taken to a download list. There, you need to select the location from which you want to download and save the application to your desktop.

Figure 6.1
You need to fill out the form to proceed to the Basic Server download page.

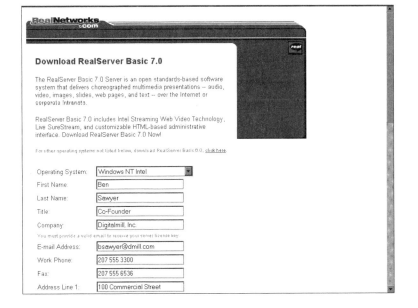

TIP

If you have a different server type than those listed in the Operating System download list, you can click on the link provided above the form to download RealServer 6.0, which supports a wider variety of operating systems, including Windows 95 and 98.

Part II　Radio Station Software

Step 2: Retrieve and Save
License File from RealNetworks

After you have successfully downloaded RealServer Basic, you will receive a customized license file from RealNetworks via e-mail. Attached to that e-mail is a license file. You need to save the license file to your desktop or some other easily accessible folder on your system. You will need this file in the next step of the installation process.

Step 3: Run the Installation Program

After you have downloaded RealServer 7.0 to your desktop, it's time to step through the Installation wizard. This Installation process Installs RealServer 7.0 as a service on your NT system and lets you define some basic configuration issues (most of which you can change later during the administration process).

The wizard is a series of screens that include questions for you to address. When you complete the questions, the system will finish installing and will require you to reboot the server so that the service can finish initiating.

The following sections provide a run-through of all the major screens.

Screen 1: Welcome Screen

The welcome screen (see Figure 6.2) greets you and warns you about copyright and piracy issues. Click the Next button to continue.

Figure 6.2
The welcome screen for the RealServer installation wizard gets you started through the installation process.

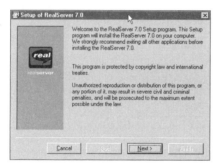

Screen 2: License File Location

The second screen of the installation wizard prompts you to enter the location of the license file (see Figure 6.3) you were sent via e-mail from RealNetworks. If you're unsure of the location, click on the Browse button to bring up a standard file open dialog box in which you can locate the license file and open it.

After you have entered into the text field the path and filename of your license file, you can click on Next to move on with the wizard. The program checks to see whether the license file is valid and, if so, continues to the next step.

Figure 6.3
Here, you can tell the installation wizard where you saved the license file sent to you via e-mail from RealNetworks.

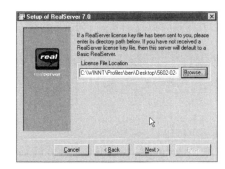

Screen 3: End User License Agreement

Before being allowed to continue with the installation, you must agree with the RealNetworks End User License Agreement (EULA), as shown in Figure 6.4. Read through it, and click on the Accept button to move on with installation.

Figure 6.4
Be sure to accept the RealNetworks End User License Agreement.

Screen 4: E-mail and Program Directory

Screen 4 of the installation wizard prompts you to enter the e-mail contact for the program and to provide the location on your system where you want the RealServer program to be installed (see Figure 6.5). The default directory is Program Files\Real\RealServer. After you've entered the information, click on Next to continue.

Figure 6.5
Here, you give the wizard the directory you want RealServer installed to and your e-mail address.

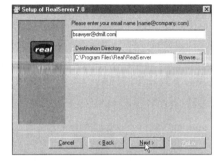

Screen 5: Username and Password

The username and password you enter on the next setup screen (see Figure 6.6) will be what you use to log in to the RealServer administration program. Here, you need to select a username and provide a password. You should write it down until you've successfully logged in to the server administration system (at which point you should be able to remember it and get rid of the written record). Otherwise, you'll have to uninstall and then reinstall the server again. When you're ready, click on Next to continue.

Figure 6.6
Here, you provide a username and password for use later in administering the server.

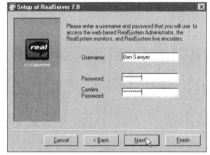

Screen 6: PNA Connection Port

In the sixth screen of the installation wizard, you enter the port number that will handle PNA connections to the server (see Figure 6.7) . It's best to leave the default number of 7070. As usual, click on Next to continue.

Figure 6.7
On this screen, you enter the PNA port number of your choice or (recommended) accept the default.

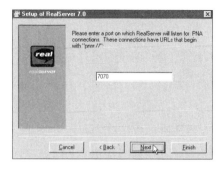

Screen 7: RTSP Connection Port

On the next wizard screen, you enter the port number that will handle Real-Time Streaming Protocol (RTSP) connections to the server. It's best to leave the default number of 554. Then click on Next to continue.

Figure 6.8
On this screen, you enter the RTSP port number of your choice or (recommended) accept the default.

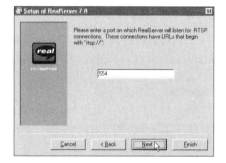

Screen 8: HTTP Connection Port

In the eighth screen of the installation wizard, you enter the port number that will handle HTTP connections to the server (see Figure 6.9). It's best to leave the default number of 8080. Then click on Next to continue.

Figure 6.9
Here, you enter the HTTP port number of your choice or (recommended) accept the default.

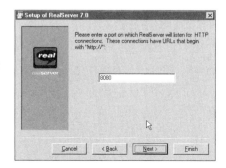

Part II Radio Station Software

Screen 9: Administrator Request Port

RealServer's installation process now gives you a randomly generated port number that is used for logging in (locally and remotely) for administration chores (see Figure 6.10). You can either accept that port number or provide one of your own. When you're ready, click on Next to move to the next installation screen.

Figure 6.10
On this screen, you enter the administrator port number of your choice or (recommended) accept the randomly generated port number.

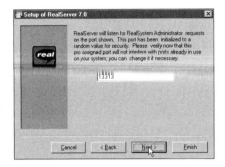

Screen 10: NT Service Yes or No?

When you install RealServer on an NT system, it gives you the choice of having the server set up as a service or standalone program (see Figure 6.11). The default is to set it up as a service. If you accept that option, leave the check box selected, and click on Next to continue.

Figure 6.11
On this installation wizard screen, you must decide whether you want to install RealServer as an NT service or a standalone application. The default setting is to accept it as a service.

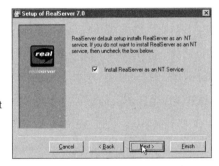

Screen 11: Confirmation of Configuration

Having set the administration name and ports, you are given a summary of those settings (see Figure 6.12). By clicking on Back, you can return to previous screens in the installation wizard and change any previous settings. If you are satisfied, click on Finish to begin the installation.

Figure 6.12
This screen provides one final rundown before you accept the configuration choices you made during installation.

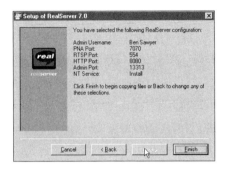

RealServer then begins copying files until it is complete (see Figure 6.13).

Figure 6.13
When you're done with the wizard installation choices, it copies the files to your server.

Screen 12: Finished!

Installation is now complete (see Figure 6.14). Click on OK, and if you left the Launch the RealSystem Administrator option checked, your browser will launch and pull up the administrator system.

Figure 6.14
Your installation is now complete; it's time to move on to further configuration and administration efforts.

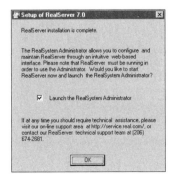

RealServer Configuration

After you have successfully installed RealServer, you need to begin configuring it and provide it with content that can be streamed to listeners. Administration with RealServer is fairly simple, thanks to a Web-based interface that runs in any browser locally or remotely over the Web. Figure 6.15 shows the welcome screen to the RealServer 7.0 administration system.

Figure 6.15
Welcome to the
RealServer 7.0
administration system.

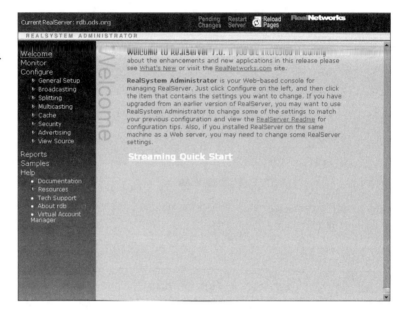

Along the left side of the screen are a number of configuration categories, as well as links to reports, sample content, online documentation, and more.

Truth be told, a solid installation is 50 percent of what you need to do to configure RealServer 7.0. The rest can be handled through the basic configuration screens that are part of the overall RealServer administrator system.

Step 1: General Setup Options

Clicking on the General Setup menu item on the left side of the administration screen reveals seven specific configuration items that you can tweak. Let's step through them one screen at a time.

Ports

On the Ports screen (see Figure 6.16), you will find port number assignments that RealServer sets up to listen for requests by your Web browser or other applications that it will respond to. For example, a request to the Admin port causes the server to request login and, if correctly given, allows access to the administration screens. Most of these port assignments can be set at installation time as well.

Figure 6.16
The Ports
configuration screen.

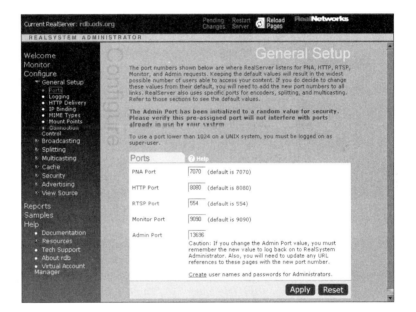

On this screen, you can see the five port types. All but the Admin port have default values that you should not change unless a specific conflict on your system necessitates it. The Admin Port value is randomly generated at installation time (for security reasons) and can be changed at any time by the administrator.

Also, note a link on this page that you can use to jump to another section of the configuration system where you can set up administrator names and passwords.

Logging

The Logging configuration screen (see Figure 6.17) determines how RealServer 7.0 log files look, which boils down to which statistics RealServer will track, how often, and how it will format the files overall.

Figure 6.17
The Logging
configuration screen.

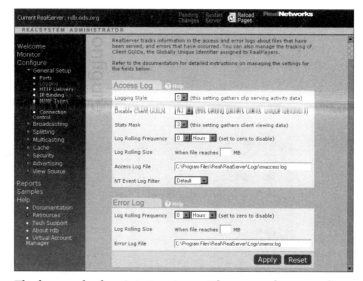

The logs are broken into two types. The *access log* saves data concerning who listened to what, when, and how. The *error log* collects only data related to errors generated by the RealServer system. This log makes it easy for you to find problems without having to sort through the entire access log.

To configure the access log, you can set seven different attributes. The Logging Style attribute accepts a setting of 0 to 5, which lets you quickly set the types of statistics RealServer 7.0 will track and how they will be written out to the log. See Table 6.1 for a description of each style.

Table 6.1
Logging Style Settings

Style Code	Variables Written to the Log
0	IP_address of connecting client I Timestamp I "GET filename protocol/version" I HTTP_status_code I Bytes_sent I Client_info I StatsMask results
1	IP_address of connecting client I Timestamp I "GET filename protocol/version" I HTTP_status_code I bytes_sent I client_info I StatsMask results I file_size I file_time sent_time I resends I failed_resends
2	Same as logging style 1 with the addition of client_GUID.
3	Same as logging style 2 with the addition of stream_components I start_time I server_address
4	Same as logging style 3 with the addition of average_bitrate I packets_sent
5	Same as logging style 3 with the addition of presentation_id

The Disable Client GUIDs attribute lets you decide whether you want the logging system to track the global user IDs of the RealPlayers that attach to your server. Every single RealPlayer shipped includes a unique ID, which you can use to track repeat listeners and other statistics concerning individual listeners. You can turn off this setting if you don't want to track this statistic.

You can adjust the Stats Mask setting (which is a number from 1 to 3), to decide exactly how many types of statistics RealServer 7.0 will track. Setting the Stats Mask to 3 will track everything under the sun and write it to the log file. Because level 2 is the highest level needed to track audio-based information, you can reset this setting to 2. Setting it to 3 instructs the server to write video-oriented statistics to the log file as well. Setting this attribute to 1 instructs the server to collect a small set of statistics concerning audio feeds from your RealServer 7.0 setup. Table 6.2 shows the statistics collected by level 1 and the additional statistics collected by setting the Stats Mask to level 2. If you want to explore level 3 statistics, consult the RealServer 7.0 documentation.

Table 6.2
RealServer Stats Mask Variables for Levels 1 and 2

Field	Description
Level 1 Log Variables	
missing	The number of packets requested by the client but that didn't arrive according to the client.
early	The number of requested packets that arrived out of order by being sent too early to the client.
late	The total number of packets that were received by the client too late.
audio_format (Note: Audio_Format and the Format for Level 2 are nearly the same variable.)	The decoder used to play the clip. Values are written out as follows in the log: sipr for RealAudio 5.0 formats dnet for RealAudio 3.0 formats 28.8 for RealAudio 2.0 28.8 format lpcJ for RealAudio 2.0 14.4 format cook for RealAudio G2 format
Level 2 Log Variables	
Bandwidth	The bandwidth of the clip as encoded in bits per second.
Available	The average bits per second while a user was listening to a clip.
Highest	The highest time in milliseconds for a packet resent request due to a request for such during a broadcast.
Lowest	The lowest time in milliseconds for a packet resent request due to a request for such during a broadcast.

Part II Radio Station Software

Table 6.2 continued on next page

Table 6.2 *(continued)*
RealServer Stats Mask Variables for Levels 1 and 2

Field	Description
Level 2 Log Variables	
Average	The average time in milliseconds for client resent requests and the resent packets' arrival.
Requested	The number of resent packets requested by the client during a session.
Received	The total number of resent packets received by the client.
Late	The total number of packets that arrived too late to the user after a resend request.
Rebuffering	The percentage of rebuffering a clip had.
Transport	The transport type used for the connection written as code: 0 for UDP, 1 for TCP, 2 for IP Multicast, and 3 for PNAviaHTTP.
Startup	Time in milliseconds when the client receives the first clip data. The data may arrive before the clip starts playing.
Format	The decoder that was used to play the clip. Possible values are as follows: sipr for RealAudio 5.0 formats dnet for RealAudio 3.0 formats 28.8 for RealAudio 2.0 28.8 format lpcJ for RealAudio 2.0 14.4 format cook for RealAudio G2 format

By adjusting the Log Rolling Frequency and Log Rolling Size attributes, you can decide whether the access log ever resets back to 0. If the Log Rolling Frequency is set to 0, the log will grow continuously until you otherwise reset it (for example, by copying the file to archives and then deleting it). If you set a value for Log Rolling Frequency, the system will grow the log for a specified time frame and then at every set interval will reset the log to 0. You can also reset the logs by setting a Log Rolling Size instead. Just insert the number of megabytes you want log files to grow to until they are reset. Leave this option blank if you want the Log Rolling Frequency to be the only determinate of log size and log reset control.

The Access Log File attribute identifies the filename and path of the access log file itself.

The NT Event Log Filter attribute determines which events that are specific to Windows NT (if you are running your server on top of NT), if any, are written to the access log.

Unlike the access log, the error log offers only three attributes you can set. Two include the Log Rolling specifications (which work in the same way as their access log counterparts) and the last includes setting the Error Log File path and filename.

HTTP Delivery

RealServer includes the capability to serve out HTML-based pages. It's not a full Web server, but in the case that your server doesn't include HTTP page serving, RealServer 7.0 can step up to the plate. Thus, the attributes under the HTTP Delivery configuration system offer you ways to tweak RealServer's HTML delivery capability. The only thing this amounts to, though, is the ability to list which directories (and, by default, RealServer sets up five already) RealServer can openly serve HTML pages from. For more details on this feature, refer to RealServer's online documentation. For most of you, you can leave this configuration option untouched.

IP Binding

If you install RealServer on a machine that has more than one IP address mapped to it, you will want the option to restrict RealServer's capability to serve from one specific IP address or more. Click on Add New to give it at least one or more addresses from which it can make RealServer accessible. If you want RealServer to support all the IP addresses on a single system, add the IP address 0.0.0.0 and remove all other addresses from the list. By default, the list has no IP addresses listed, and none need be added for a single IP address system.

MIME Types

For the most part, you can leave the MIME Types section untouched. Here, you can add MIME types to a list that RealServer uses to stream content via the HTTP protocol. Refer to RealServer's documentation for more details on this feature.

Mount Points

Mount points are essentially directory paths on your server in which you can store content; RealServer can then access these paths. The Mount Points page shows active mount points and the base path for those directories.

Every mount point begins and ends with a forward slash, with the exception of the main mount point, which is a single / and the only one set during initial installation. The default base path is the subdirectory of content, which itself is linked off the main RealServer directory.

To add a new mount point content subdirectory under your RealServer directory, click on Add New. Then fill out the blank information. When you're done, click on Apply. A new Web page opens, telling you whether it successfully added the new mount point. You have to stop and restart the server for the change to take effect after being set up.

Connection Control

On the Connection Control screen (see Figure 6.18), you can determine how various connection issues are treated by the server. Mostly, you can restrict access to content either by setting the Maximum Client Connections to a set number (0 means no restrictions and is the default setting). If you give it a 0 setting, the maximum number of client connections are restricted only by the license number of connections your version of RealServer supports (which in the case of the Basic Server is 25).

Figure 6.18

The Connection Control configuration screen.

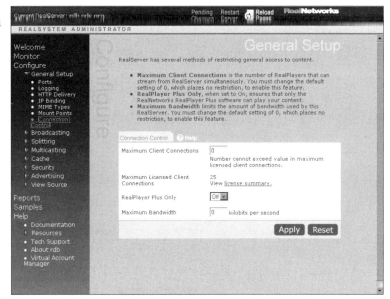

The RealPlayer Plus Only setting locks out all non-RealPlayer Plus clients. There must be a use for this option, although we can't imagine what.

By adjusting the Maximum Bandwidth setting, you can limit connections to the RealServer by limiting the amount of bandwidth it will use when broadcasting. If it is set to the default setting of 0, no restrictions are placed on bandwidth. This capability is useful if you have a large bandwidth available to the server and want to restrict the server from using it all up even for a few connections.

Step 2: Broadcasting Options

You use the broadcasting options to set up how your live encoders interact with the RealServer system. You can choose from two major encoder types: pre-G2 encoders and the G2 encoder. You must configure settings for both of them if you plan to use both. Most people just use the G2 encoder, though.

G2 Encoder

On the G2 Encoder screen (see Figure 6.19), you can configure how RealServer will accept information from people using G2-level encoder tools or better. You can set a mount point (the default is /encoder/), a port number (the default is 4040), and a timeout range (in seconds, with 30 being the default).

Figure 6.19
The G2 Encoder screen.

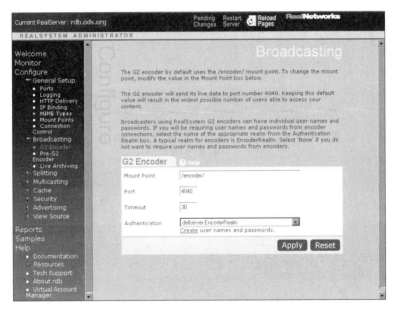

You also can set an authentication level. Choose from any of the available authentications you've created in the Security section of RealServer Administrator. The default setting is the EncoderRealm, but you can create any number of new password/user realms that people must supply if they're going to be able to supply content directly to the server via the RealProducer and Encoder tools.

Pre-G2 Encoder

On the Pre-G2 Encoder screen, you can configure RealServer to accept content from encoders that were developed before the RealSystem G2 or RealServer 7.0. These encoders send data to the /live/ mountpoint and through port 5050 on the server unless you otherwise change them. You handle authentication for encoder content by providing usernames and passwords that are supplied by users of those encoders. Today, most people use G2-level tools or higher.

Live Archiving

On the Live Archiving screen (see Figure 6.20), you can configure how all live broadcasts are handled for archiving purposes. This capability is especially useful for talk shows that generate unique content every time they do a broadcast. RealServer uses a selective system so that you archive only those live streams you want to archive. You do so by building a list of stream names that are monitored by RealServer. If a live stream hits RealServer and matches one in your list, RealServer broadcasts it and writes the file to the /Archive/ path of the RealServer directory. You can optionally have RealServer limit archive files by a maximum megabyte size or by the number of days, hours, and minutes the files should be archived. You can leave these settings at 0 for RealServer to archive until the live stream stops. You can easily start and stop archiving by choosing Disabled or Enabled from the Archiving drop-down box on this screen.

Figure 6.20
On the Live Archiving configuration screen, you can decide which live broadcasts should be archived.

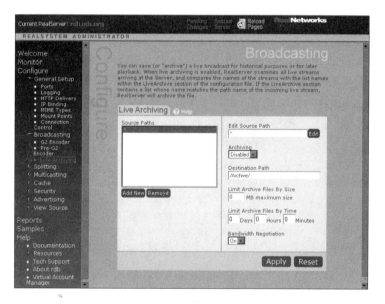

Step 3: Splitting

Splitting streams in RealServer is similar to the concept of relay servers in the world of SHOUTcast. Essentially, you define a port number where a downstream RealServer can offer a stream on its server that it gets from your server. The idea is that the downstream server pulls only one stream from you but then uses its available bandwidth and connections to serve that stream back out to more listeners. With splitting, you need define only the source port for other RealServers to connect to; by default, this port is 3030.

NOTE

Splitting is possible with Basic Server, except you are still limited to 25 connections downstream and cannot pull from someone else's server using Basic Server. Thus, for the most part, splitting is a moot issue with the Basic Server version.

Step 4: Multicasting

RealServer supports robust multicasting capabilities. However, multicasting is an advanced option we can't possibly cover easily here. For more details on multicasting, read Chapter 13 of the RealServer Administrator documentation.

Step 5: Cache

Like other types of caches, the RealServer cache stores popular content in such a way to optimize sending out that content. The RealServer media cache tracks which clips are most requested and stores them in memory as much as possible for quick serving to the next requestor. The Cache Log Path attribute is a path and filename that writes out cache-related events to a log in your logs directory.

Step 6: Security

Security on RealServer is handled through three critical areas; you can set access control issues, set user authentication levels, and even set up custom-developed databases for your access controls. Basic Server supports only a few critical security areas. If you need clip-specific security settings and more, you need to upgrade to a higher level of the server than Basic Server.

Access Control

Although you can already use the Connection Control settings to limit access to a set number of clients, type of client, or to no more listeners after a certain level of bandwidth is reached, you can use the Access Control section (see Figure 6.21) of RealServer Administrator to control specific permissions. You can give any specific IP address or netmask (also called a *subnet*) permission or deny permission to access various ports on your RealServer. For example, by setting the access to Deny and then entering a specific IP address and setting it to port 7070, 8080, 554, or 9090 (defaults for most of the major RealServer ports), you can effectively ban that IP address (and its user) from your broadcast. You can also enter an entire netmask that will block or add a special permission to an entire subnet or range of IP addresses.

Figure 6.21
The Access Control configuration screen.

To set an access control, you click on the Add New button below the Access Rules list. RealServer Administrator assigns a rule number (it tends to automatically assign rule numbers in increments of 100, starting with 100 for the first rule). Then you can decide whether it's an access control or a deny control. You can give it a specific IP address or an entire netmask, and then you can deny it access to a specific server (by supplying that server's IP address) or leave it with the default setting of Any to apply it to all servers. Then you can type in the port(s) you want to give them explicit access or deny access to (use commas to separate multiple ports). When you're done, click on Apply to set the changes. You need to stop and restart RealServer for those changes to take effect.

Authentication

On the Authentication section of RealServer Administrator (see Figure 6.22), you can create specific names and passwords that are grouped into *realms*. Realms are then used to give access to certain functions of the server, such as access to the administrator or the right to send encoded content to the server. For example, on the G2 Encoder configuration described earlier, you can assign access to the capability to send content to the server by choosing which realm (and its users) are allowed to send content.

Figure 6.22
On the Authentication configuration screen, you can set up groups of users, names, and passwords for accessing the RealServer system.

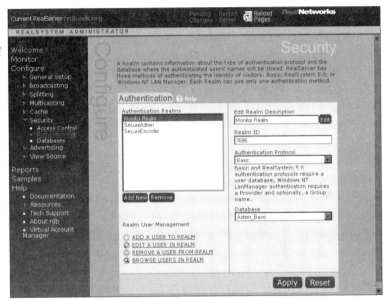

From the large window on the left side of the Authentication form, you can choose an active realm. Below this list are links to add, edit, or remove users from a realm. You can browse users in the realm as well. When you're adding a user to a realm, you must supply a username, add a password, and then confirm the password. When you click on OK, RealServer should update and confirm whether the user was successfully added.

To create an entire new realm, you click on the Add New button at the bottom of the list of authentication realms. (Remove is there as well, which is useful because you often click on Add New when, in fact, you mean to add an actual user, not a new realm.) After you have added a new realm, you must supply the realm description and its ID. (The ID is what is listed in any other area of the RealServer Administrator where you set a realm for security purposes, so be sure to make it something easy to understand.) Then you must choose the authentication protocol and the database style to use to save username and password information to. Most people running RealServer Basic should use the basic authentication protocol and use the Admin_Basic database style. Consult the RealServer manual's Authentication section about the other options listed in those two areas of the Authentication screen.

Databases

In the Databases section of the Security configuration area of RealServer, you can name the actual databases and set the type of database technology and the path/filename of the databases that store realm and user information created in the Authentication area of RealServer Administrator. This information is also used for higher-end authentication areas that limit access to clips and other content areas. For the most part, you can leave this section entirely alone. If you need to change the information, it's because you want to integrate a specific authentication database with other databases or front ends to manage this data you might be using. Most people will never go to these lengths. If you're interested in doing more with this section, consult the RealServer Administrator's guide. RealNetworks provides templates for all the major database servers as part of the installation process.

Step 7: Advertising

RealServer 7.0 offers increased support for advertising; however, the Basic Server doesn't include support for it, even though most of the configuration screens are here and work accordingly. Basic Server is therefore a nice learning system for administration, but it doesn't give you the power you might need. Also, you must install additional software on the higher-end server for more robust audio-based advertising.

General

The General page of the advertising administration options gives you two settings to tweak. The Connection Timeout setting determines in seconds how much time RealServer will wait when you're connecting to a Web server for advertising data before going on to the next clip. Server Timeout sets the time, in seconds, that RealServer waits for a reply when connecting to a Web server it is hitting to grab an ad. If the ad isn't available in the time frame set, RealServer will skip it and move on to prevent faulty or slow ad servers from holding up a pending broadcast.

NOTE
If a RealPlayer connected to a server has set its own connection and server timeouts below that of your settings here, those settings will supercede yours.

Ad Serving

On the Ad Serving configuration screen, you can make the bulk of your advertising tweaks.

> **NOTE**
>
> Although you can set ad serving options in the Administrator, the Basic Server does not feature advertising functionality and therefore will ignore these configurations. These options are enabled by Basic Server Plus and Professional Server.

Ad SMIL Generation

SMIL (which stands for Synchronized Multimedia Instruction Language and is pronounced smile) is a simple, tag-based markup language like HTML that is supported by RealPlayer. It enables many cool interactive features and deeper multimedia development than, say, the standard animated GIF. If you've created SMIL-based advertising, you can use this screen to point to where such ads are based and identify their characteristics. For more specifics on this language, check out the RealServer 7.0 Administrator's guide.

> **TIP**
>
> For more details on SMIL, check out the following:
>   **www.justsmil.com**
>   **http://www.inrialpes.fr/opera/people/Nabil.Layaida/smil/smil.html**

Part II Radio Station Software

Step 8: View Source

The View Source section deals with whether users are allowed to view the source code of underlying SMIL, RealText, or RealPix presentations. It's not exactly focused on audio-based broadcasting issues, so we'll skip them here. If you want to know more about them, check out the RealServer 7.0 Administrator's guide.

Step 9: Reports

You can extend RealSystem Administrator to include graphical and statistical reporting that goes beyond your own simple analysis of RealServer logs. The best RealServer reporting software is written by Lariat Software, and clicking on the Reports link of RealServer Administrator leads you to essentially an advertisement but also provides you a link to download a free copy of RealServer Basic Reports. After you've installed it (see the section "RealServer Basic Reports" later in this chapter), you can generate simple usage reports for your server such as those shown in Figure 6.23.

Figure 6.23
The free Basic Server Reports feature gives you simple but useful statistical reports from your RealServer logs.

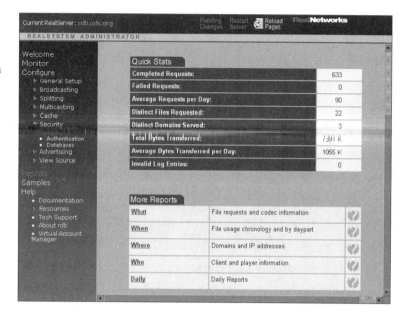

Other Links in RealServer 7.0 Administrator

Samples

The Samples section provides quick links to sample content that is available after installation. On your first use of the Remote Administrator, it's useful to click on a few of these links to ensure that the server is running and working properly.

Help

The Help section of RealServer Administrator contains five links, each of which pops up some information you can use to further your knowledge of RealServer or seek support help from RealNetworks. The Documentation link sends you to an HTML version of the RealServer Administrator's guide on Realnetworks.com. The Resources link opens a subset of links that point to other links for information on other RealServer-related products and user guides. The Tech Support link opens the tech support section of Realnetworks.com.

The About [Server Name] link (which says RDB in Figure 6.24 because that's the name of our RealServer) pops up a separate box containing all your licensing information, which may be useful when you're seeking phone or e-mail support from RealNetworks. The Virtual Account Manager link sends you to a section of Realnetworks.com in which you can enter a tech support area based on your purchase of RealServer (which, for Basic version users, is moot because you never purchased a version of the software).

Figure 6.24
You can click on the About [Server Name] link under Help to pull up basic information about your RealServer installation.

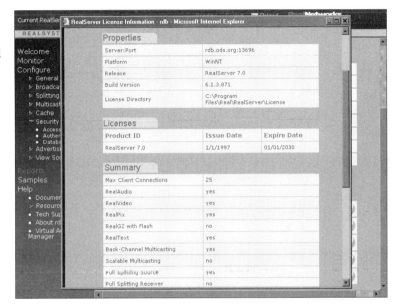

Monitoring Your Server

At the top of the menu on the left side of the RealServer Administrator is the Monitor link. This link activates the monitoring function of the RealServer 7.0 Administrator, which consists of a Java applet that shows short-term or current status of your server, including the Number of Players Connection, Memory Usage, File Usage, CPU Usage, and Bandwidth Usage. Clicking on the Options drop-down list in the upper-left corner reveals options that are more or less self-explanatory. The Configure option is the most important because you can use it to set how often the monitor checks to update information and the length of the period it appears on the monitor at any one time.

TIP

RealServer is also designed to work with the Windows NT Performance Monitor to show activity on one or more RealServers. This option is available if you are running RealServer on Windows NT and are viewing it from that same computer. A Performance Monitor file containing RealServer statistics, rmserver.pmc, is supplied during installation.

Broadcasting via Playlists with RealServer

If only creating playlists were as easy as using other radio solutions. If there is one easy target to gripe about RealServer, it is that, although RealServer has a playlist capability, setting it up is harder in comparison to setting up other server systems such as SHOUTcast, MyCaster, or icecast.

To create a playlist, you need to create a text file that contains all the relevant playlist information and then provide it to the server in a form that lets the server treat the playlist like a live broadcast. You can start by first corralling all your content and placing it in a valid content directory for RealServer on your system. (You can use remote content, but let's keep things simple to start!) Make a note of each file's name in your text editor—for example:

> Solartwins1.rm
>
> Solartwins2.rm
>
> Solartwins3.rm

This list of filenames will form the basis for your playlist, but it's a bit more complicated than just a simple list.

Playlists in RealServer work by a process known as G2SLTA (which stands for G2 Simulated Live Transfer Agent). G2SLTA takes a text file that is a playlist or script and makes it so that anybody linking to it hears what appears to be a live broadcast but in actuality is just a playlist most likely being looped. You make the playlist by using a text editor, and then you start a process on your RealServer that listens to the playlist much like it would a real live feed.

Step 1: Create Your Playlist

Creating a playlist is nothing more than creating a text file containing line after line of RealMedia filenames you want played during your broadcast (either in order or randomly).

NOTE

All content listed in a single playlist must be encoded at the same bit rate as every file in the list; RealServer does not re-encode the bit rates to match (like some other servers such as SHOUTcast do), and thus it won't work. Also, you should not combine SureStream files and non-SureStream files in your playlist, because the playlist system for RealServer doesn't handle them as well.

After you have listed all the files you want in your playlist, you're done. Save the file in a content directory with the name [*Playlist Name*].txt.

If you want to have your playlist also include Title, Author, and Copyright information, it can. RealServer playlists can offer three types of TAC content that will show up in the RealPlayer.

The first is the default setting. If you have encoded the TAC information with the file by using the RealProducer product, that information is passed through to the player, provided you have not embedded special TAC information in your playlist.

The second is the universal TAC setting. At the top of your playlist file, you can add three lines of text as follows:

Title: [title of broadcast here]

Author: [author of broadcast here]

Copyright: [copyright information for broadcast here]

Then you need to follow that information with your playlist files. This information is shown throughout the broadcast for every file and overwrites any previously embedded TAC information within the files themselves.

The third option is to embed unique TAC information in the line following each playlist entry. This type of information would look as follows:

Solartwins1.rm

Solartwins.rm?title="Puppet on a string"&author="The Solar Twins"&copyright="1999 Maverick Records/Solar Twins"

For the most part, you will probably want to use the first option—no playlist-embedded TAC information. You just need to make sure the information is in each file you've encoded for your broadcast.

Step 2: Activate Your Playlist

After you've created a valid playlist and positioned the content on the server accordingly, it's time to begin broadcasting. Broadcasting your playlist requires executing a command line on the server itself that initiates the G2SLTA system.

In Windows, you need to start a command prompt and run a .BAT file, whereas in UNIX, you will find an .SH file that does the same thing. With NT, you will find the G2slta.bat file located in your /realserver/bin directory.

Part II Radio Station Software

The G2SLTA program uses a simple command-line format, which includes the following parameters:

▶ **host**—The name of the RealServer or a specific domain or IP address

▶ **port**—The port number specified in your G2 Encoder setting, which is port 4040 unless you've changed it from the default

▶ **username**—The name of a valid administrator or user

▶ **password**—That person's password

▶ **livefile**—The name you want to give for the broadcast file

▶ **playlist**—The name of the text file containing the actual playlist

These items are followed by several optional switches that determine how your playlist is handled:

▶ **- r**—This switch determines whether files should be played in a random order. You use -r to force random play or leave it out to play files in the order they appear in the text file.

▶ **- nN**—This switch determines the number of files in the list the G2SLTA will play before ending. You can leave out this switch to force indefinite play. If you would like a list to play twice through and then stop, use -n(2*number of files in list) and increase the multiple for every continuous loop you want if you need it more than twice.

▶ **- bN**—This optional switch lets you force SureStream content to play at a specified bit rate. If you have SureStream files in your G2SLTA playlist, make sure you set this switch to a bit rate that is consistent with non-SureStream files in the list. N must be a number in thousands equal to the target bit rate; for example, -b20000 indicates a 20K bit rate.

In total, your command line follows this syntax:

Windows: g2slta.bat host port username password livefile playlist [-r] [-nN] [-bN]

UNIX: Same as Windows except that the name of the file is g2slta.sh

Step 3: Stop Your Playlist

To stop a playlist, you must kill the GSTLA file running in the background on your server. You do so by pressing Ctrl+C in the DOS Window for Windows NT or by using the Kill command with the process ID in UNIX.

Broadcasting Live with RealServer

To broadcast live with RealServer, all you need to do is run the RealProducer program and fill out the form for a live broadcast. This system then lets the local computer encode content on-the-fly as configured and send it up the line to the RealServer itself, which then makes it available to any currently connected listeners.

Step 1: Run the RealProducer or Producer Plus Program and Initiate the New Session Wizard

Usually, when you run RealProducer, it starts with the New Session Wizard (see Figure 6.25) unless you've turned off that option in the preferences (if so, choose New Session from the File menu). The New Session Wizard offers three choices: Record From File (convert to RealAudio), Record From Media Device (create a file on-the-fly but save it), and Live Broadcast (send immediately to a server). For now, choose Live Broadcast and click on Next to continue with the wizard.

Figure 6.25
To enable a live broadcast, you need to start the New Session Wizard.

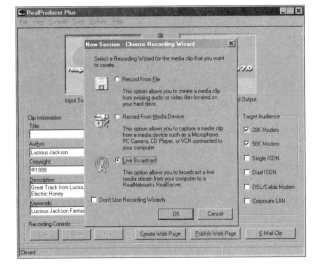

Part II   Radio Station Software

Step 2: Step Through the RealMedia Recording Wizard

To configure your live broadcast, you must step through a series of questions from the RealMedia Recording Wizard (see Figure 6.26). First, you start by choosing whether you're capturing audio, video, or both. Because you're setting up a radio show, you should check only the Capture Audio check box and then click on Next to continue.

Figure 6.26
You can start the live broadcast by choosing audio-only capturing

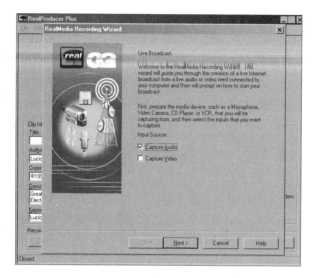

The next wizard screen is a simple information screen (see Figure 6.27) where you fill out basic descriptive information about the broadcast. Note that a good deal of this information will show up in the RealPlayer program, so make sure it's accurate and spelled correctly, because your listening public will see it. When you're done, click on Next to continue stepping through the wizard.

Figure 6.27
Here, you can define the details of your broadcast title, copyright, and other descriptive elements.

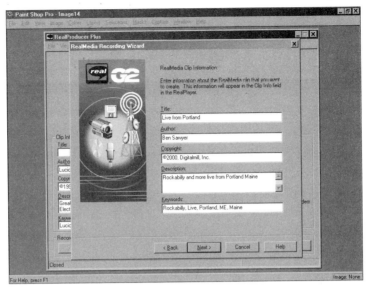

The third screen (see Figure 6.28) in the RealMedia Recording Wizard is an important one. You need to decide the file type that you want to create. It can be either SureStream or single rate. The SureStream format varies the bit rate as it broadcasts to different users. By analyzing the speed of connections to users, the RealServer system can automatically send through better quality streams to people who can accept it based on their bandwidth. However, SureStream works only for people connecting to a server that is using the RealServer program and clients connecting with RealPlayer. If you plan to just use standard HTTP streaming, then you must choose the single-rate setting. Because you are running RealServer, you should be okay with the SureStream setting.

Figure 6.28
You must decide whether you will be using single rate or the multi-rate SureStream method.

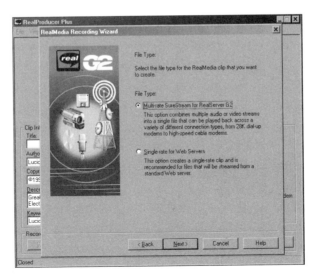

Part II Radio Station Software

After you choose SureStream and click on Next, you are greeted with a list of target audiences (see Figure 6.29) by bandwidth type for which you can include support. Check as many as you like. If you are going to broadcast over the Internet, we suggest that you choose everything but Corporate LAN. Click on Next to continue.

Figure 6.29
After choosing the SureStream setting, you must tell the RealMedia Recording Wizard which target audiences you want to reach.

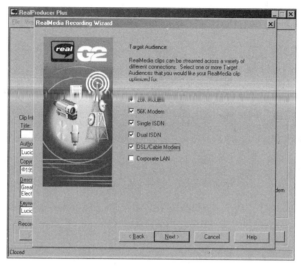

NOTE
You must have RealProducer Plus to target more than two audiences in this section of the RealProducer program.

After setting your broadcast rates, you must select the style of audio you intend to broadcast (see Figure 6.30). Choosing the audio format lets the encoder in the RealProducer program format the file for optimum quality and compactness given the type of content you intend to broadcast. When you're ready, click on Next to continue.

Figure 6.30
You must choose the style of audio you plan to broadcast so that the encoder part of the RealProducer program can optimize the audio quality.

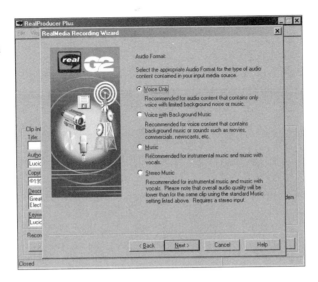

On the final configuration screen of the RealMedia Recording Wizard (see Figure 6.31), you type in the address, server port (usually 4040), filename, username, and password for the RealServer you intend to broadcast to. You optionally can choose to archive the broadcast at the encoder level (as opposed to or in addition to RealServer's own archiving features for live broadcasts discussed earlier).

Figure 6.31
Here, you can set your server address, port number, and login information so that you can broadcast correctly to the RealServer itself.

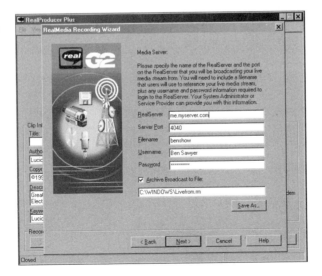

Step 3: Begin Your Broadcast

After you click on Next from the server configuration screen, you are provided with a summary of your settings. When you click on Finish, you are sent back to RealProducer's main screen. Here, you can tweak any of the settings for the broadcast (except the server login information, for which you must rerun the wizard). When you're set, you can click on Start from the Recording Controls in the lower-left corner of the RealProducer screen. The broadcast should start unless the server is not available or you configured the information wrong.

When you are in broadcast mode, your microphone and any other outgoing recording controls should be active. After you've completed your broadcast, click on Stop to finish. The RealProducer program then provides you with a Broadcast Complete information screen (see Figure 6.32) and some basic statistics for your broadcast.

Figure 6.32
After you've finished with your live broadcast, you can check statistics.

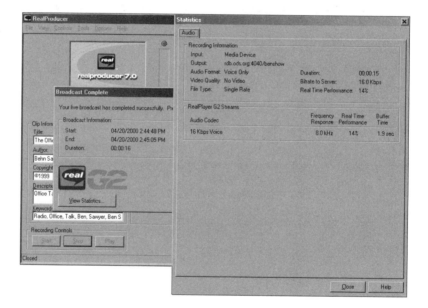

RealServer Basic Reports

If you want to add a reporting system to RealServer Basic, you can download and install a free version of Lariat Software's Basic Reports software that RealNetworks makes available off the RealNetworks Web site. The link is provided on a screen in the RealServer Administrator. After you've installed the software, you can look at a variety of simple reports that summarize your server's activity over a given period of time.

The installation itself is straightforward, but there are some worthwhile aspects to cover about the installation and operation of this software.

Step 1: Install the Software

You must first download the Basic Reports software from the RealNetworks site. The link is located in the Reports section of the Administrator. When you first install RealServer and click on the Reports item in the RealServer Administrator, you are taken to a section of Realnetworks.com where you can download the software. This link isn't made publicly available from RealNetworks, so you wouldn't find it otherwise.

After you've downloaded the software to your server, you must run the installation program, which includes a series of screens that include configuration options. You can redefine many of these options after installation.

The first few screens of the installation wizard cover copying the files to your system and accepting the license agreement for the software. Your first real configuration tasks are to choose a username and a password, which are used to gain access to the Basic Reports Configuration Manager (see Figure 6.33).

Figure 6.33
You must choose a username and a password for the Basic Reports system.

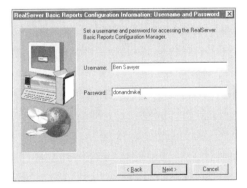

In the next wizard screen, you must show the Basic Reports system exactly where the RealServer logs are; by default, the system should point to the precise directory, provided you didn't make any special changes to the place where logs are stored during installation or configuration of the RealServer system itself. If you have made changes, or the system doesn't list the directory, click on Browse to find the logs yourself. Most likely, you'll find them in the program files/realserver/logs/directory.

Clicking through the installation wizard, you will come to the screen on which you set the interval used for report updating (see Figure 6.34). Set this interval to the number of seconds you want to have in between updates of your reports.

Figure 6.34
You must set the interval the reporting system will use to set the frequency (in seconds) of report updates.

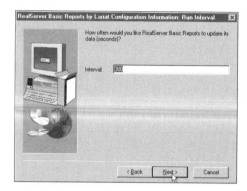

Installation continues with two more screens of configuration questions. The next screen in the wizard is very important. On the screen shown in Figure 6.35, you type the hostname of the RealServer you're installing the reports into. Set it to the Web domain or IP number of the server, not any internal domain names that might be suggested. Otherwise, when administrating remotely, the reporting system won't properly link through to the configuration screen. We know because we made this mistake ourselves. Luckily, there is a way around not having access to the Web-based configuration section of Basic Reports (see "Step 2: Configure the Reporting System" for more details).

Figure 6.35
You must make sure the hostname you type in during installation is the Web domain name and not the local server domain name if you expect to administer it over the Web.

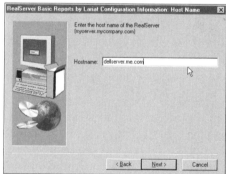

After setting the report interval and server domain name, you must provide a port number for the Basic Reports system to use to monitor the server. By default, it is port 8081.

After configuring the monitor report, the installation wizard greets you
with a yes or no question (see Figure 6.36). Click on Yes to install the
Basic Reports system as an NT service or No to install it as a standalone
application. When that task is taken care of, you need only confirm your
installation by clicking on Finish so that the system can complete the
installation.

Figure 6.36
Like the RealServer
itself, Basic Reports can
work either as an NT
Service or
a standalone
application.

Step 2: Configure the Reporting System

After the Basic Reports system is installed, the menu screen shown when
you click on Reports in the RealServer Administrator changes (see Figure
6.37). The Reports menu now shows several options, one of which is the
Configuration Manager. Clicking on this option takes you to a Web-based
form where you can make changes to all the items covered during
installation.

Figure 6.37
The new Reports screen
on the RealServer
administrator changes
to offer three menu
choices after Basic
Reports is installed.

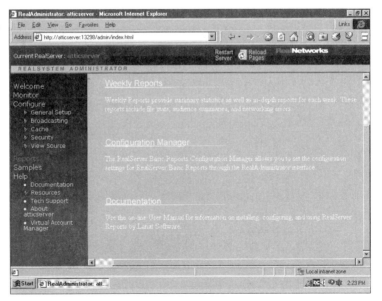

You can easily configure the report system in another way as well. Configuration settings are stored in a simple text file that is stored on the server system (see Figure 6.38). You can edit this file by using any basic text editor. This approach is useful if you forgot your password to the Configuration Manager (like we did) or have problems getting into the manager for any other reason.

Figure 6.38
An alternative way to configure Basic Reports is to edit the Basic Reports configuration file on the server itself by using a simple text editor.

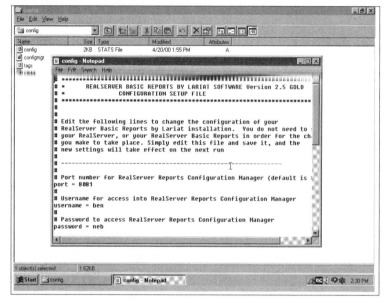

Step 3: Use the Reporting System

Using the reporting system couldn't be much easier. You simply click on the Weekly Reports screen for a list of available weekly reports. Then you can scroll down until you see a list of five additional reports (see Figure 6.39), which include the following:

▶ **What**—Shows you the top 10 media files requested and specific specifications for those files, including codec type, length, file size, and more.

▶ **When**—Shows you when files were requested in a matrix sorted by day and time of day. This simple report is useful for seeing when people are most likely to be listening.

▶ **Where**—Shows you who logged in from where using IP tracking.

▶ **Who**—Shows you details about specific clients who listened, including the underlying operating system and other player information.

▶ **Daily**—Provides a simple snapshot of the files transferred, server load, and most popular file for each day of the week.

Figure 6.39
At the bottom of each weekly report screen is a list of five other reports you can browse.

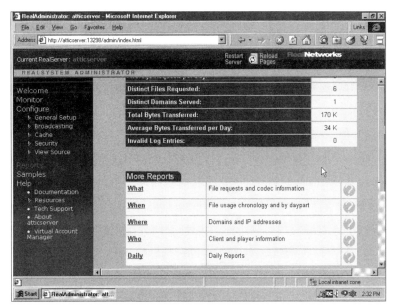

Really Robust

RealServer clearly benefits from the number of revisions it has gone through since its original debut. The one aspect you'll notice about RealServer 7.0—even the Basic version—is that it's a very well-designed and easy-to-use system but also one that is quite powerful. Although other server systems are much more conducive to personal broadcasting, RealServer is a strong choice to use either in conjunction with other server types or services or on its own.

The Basic Server is a great product, especially because it is free (even though it's limited to 25 streams), and it has much of the functionality of the higher-end versions.

Make no mistake—RealServer isn't for everyone. You need an NT or UNIX server to use it. And if you want more than 25 streams, it's a $2,000 cost. Its robustness and ease of use, though, clearly make it a strong choice for even small-sized broadcasters.

7

MyCaster and Windows Media Audio

This chapter could easily be titled "The Easy and the Not So Easy," because in it we cover two remaining major radio server programs: MyCaster and Windows Media Services. MyCaster is probably the easiest-to-use standalone radio server around. Destiny Broadcaster (see Chapter 8) may actually be easier, but MyCaster is more robust. On the other end of the spectrum is Microsoft's Windows Media Services. It packs a lot of power, but the administration and mixing of protocols are a bit tough to grasp at first. We're still learning the ropes ourselves. We can say, however, that both programs are important additions to the world of online broadcasting—MyCaster for its relative ease of use; and Windows Media Services because it offers a lot of power and, unlike its rival, RealServer 7, it is much less expensive (in fact, it's free with Windows NT or 2000).

MyCaster

When it comes to simplicity of broadcasting, MyCaster from Scour (**www.scour.net**) is the place to go. It's a powerful broadcasting solution specifically tailored for radio broadcasting; it combines a super-slick, Winamp-style client-side application with simple radio broadcasting-specific configuration screens. The installation, configuration, and use of the applet are easy enough for even the most novice broadcaster. MyCaster isn't a slouch, either. The latest 2.0 version (in beta when we wrote this chapter) combines chat, playlist editing, immediate messaging, and live voice/DJ mixing in one integrated application.

MyCaster uses MP3 as the broadcasting technology and is compatible with common MP3 playlist files (.M3U or .PLS files) that you might create in Winamp or one of the common MP3 management tools.

To use it, you simply load your playlist into the MyCaster applet and into your Winamp applet. Then you click on the Mute button on the MyCaster app (no sense in listening to two different streams) and let the applets both broadcast your content. Although people have to connect directly to your SHOUTcast station, you need only one outgoing station for your MyCaster application, allowing you to reach even more listeners.

Installing MyCaster

Installing MyCaster is straightforward. As you do with other server solutions, you download the system from the Web, which for MyCaster ███████ ███████ ██ ████████████████, ██████████ on the Free Download icon, and then clicking on the Download Now link.

After you download the program, you can run the mcSetup.exe program and step through the installation wizard. You are asked to accept a license agreement, choose an installation directory, fill out a user profile form (see Figure 7.1), and provide a password for the server system. That's it! After you've entered all this information, the application is installed, and you can begin to use and configure the program.

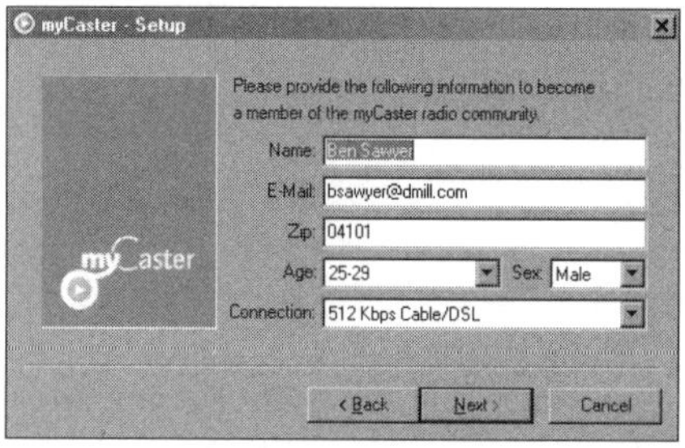

Figure 7.1
The first part of installing MyCaster involves filling out a user profile form.

Configuring MyCaster

In keeping with its ease-of-use mission, MyCaster doesn't have a ton of dialogs or text files associated with it. The program is broken down into one dialog with four major tabs for configuration, some of which are filled out from information you supplied during installation. One of these four is the About Tab, which doesn't offer any configuration settings, so in the end there are only three to worry about.

User Profile

The first tab of the Properties dialog is User Profile (see Figure 7.2). On this tab, you can define all your basic user information, which also includes the password you use to log in to your system. Any configuration here should be fairly self-explanatory.

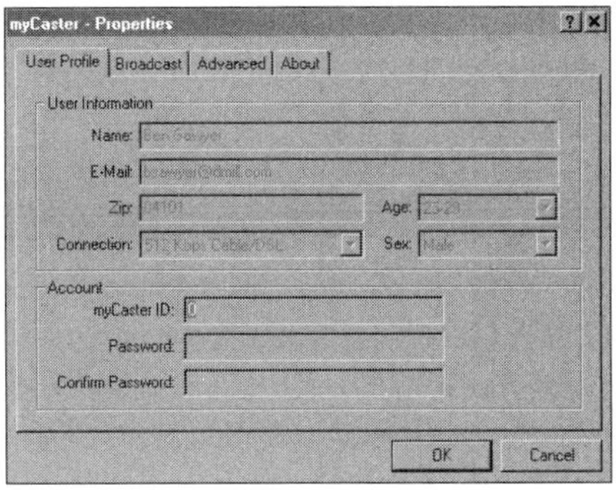

Figure 7.2
The User Profile tab is pretty much filled out from information you provided during installation, but you can update it here.

Broadcast

On the Broadcast tab (see Figure 7.3), you can input information that pertains to the stream you will be putting out from MyCaster. The Station Information section contains information on the name of your station, its home page, and basic genre(s) of music you will play.

In the Stream Settings section of the Broadcast tab, you can choose a broadcast stream format (that is, set the audio quality), the port number to use, and the maximum number of users who can connect to your broadcast. The IP address and stream password are unavailable to you unless you're on a machine that has multiple IP addresses assigned to it.

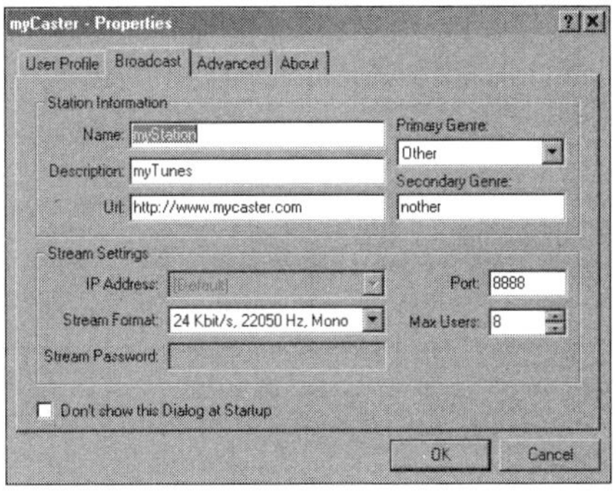

Figure 7.3
On the Broadcast tab, you can control bandwidth settings for your station.

Advanced

The Advanced tab (see Figure 7.4) contains a bunch of odds and ends. In the Version section, you can note what version of the software you have and choose a button to immediately download the latest version. In the Playlists section, you can determine whether MyCaster loads the last playlist upon startup and then starts immediately playing selections from that list. In the Show MyCaster In section, you can choose where a minimized MyCaster program is displayed: the taskbar, system tray, or both. If you want your broadcast to be private, select the Don't Show My Station on Directory check box on this dialog.

Part II Radio Station Software

Figure 7.4
The Advanced tab basically contains a bunch of odds and ends you can use to further tweak your use of MyCaster.

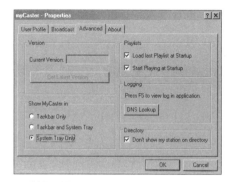

Broadcasting with MyCaster

To broadcast with MyCaster, you must configure the application correctly and then provide it with a playlist of some sort. You can build a playlist directly in the Playlist Editor or choose Load to load a compatible .M3U or .PLS list. After you've loaded your list, click on the Play button on the main MyCaster window to begin broadcasting. Note also that MyCaster 2.0 now features support for streaming content stored as either .MP3 files or .WMA (Windows Media Audio) files. However, remember that it broadcasts using only the .MP3 format.

MyCaster can also relay other streams, including icecast or SHOUTcast streams. To relay these streams, you must pull up the Open dialog (see Figure 7.5) of the program by pressing Ctrl+O or by choosing Open from MyCaster's main menu (which is available when you right-click on the application). At the bottom of the dialog is a Location field, where you can provide the URL and port number of a stream to relay. Entering this information adds that URL to your playlist, and you must then select it to buffer and repeat it out over your server.

Figure 7.5
On the Open dialog, you can enter a URL and port number if you just want to relay a stream from another radio station.

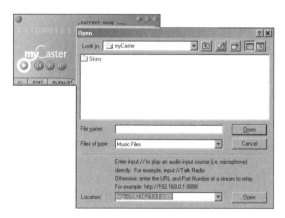

When your stream is heading out, you can basically sit back and enjoy pumping out your station or show. Using the DJ portion of MyCaster (see Figure 7.6), you can see how many current listeners you have and can adjust the outgoing mix, which includes the input level, the ratio of input to outgoing music, and the overall equalization of the outgoing stream. Using the input feature of MyCaster, you can combine the input from another source (which, for most of you, will be your microphone but can include the CD or any other input your sound card features).

Figure 7.6
Using the DJ portion of MyCaster, you can monitor and control the characteristics of your outgoing audio mix as well as drop in a little chat from your microphone.

To set the type of input MyCaster mixes in, follow these steps:

1. Right-click on the drop-down list on the DJ screen. Or you can choose Input from the main menu and then choose the input source from the submenu (see Figure 7.7).

2. After you set the level of your input, click on the Microphone button once to let the input into the outgoing mix. The Microphone button turns red to denote that the additional input is going out on the air. Click on it again to turn off the input.

3. Adjust the ratio of the input to music if people complain they can't hear you over the music.

Figure 7.7
Right-clicking on any section of MyCaster pulls up the main menu, which includes a section to check the input source.

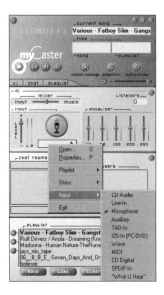

Part II Radio Station Software

TIP

If you want to broadcast but not have to listen to your own broadcast, just slide the volume on the main MyCaster screen all the way to the left or click on the Volume button once to mute it. Your broadcast will still go out on the air.

Communicating with Listeners While Broadcasting

One of the great strengths of MyCaster is that it features a built-in chat room and instant messaging feature. This nice, all-in-one solution contributes to the program's ease of use. Visitors to the MyCaster.com Web site can send you instant messages or join you in a chat room during your broadcast. To reply to or send an immediate message, you can click on the Instant Message button on the main MyCaster screen. To use the chat room, click on the Chat button. Both communication methods are fairly simple to use and should be self-explanatory. Note, however, that the immediate messaging shouldn't be considered a replacement for ICQ or other popular instant messaging programs. So, if you're building your own station page and want people to use those applications to communicate with you during your broadcast, you need to supplement MyCaster by using those programs as well.

In the preceding few pages, you've learned how to install, configure, and broadcast using MyCaster. Although MyCaster lacks some features of SHOUTcast, it makes up for that in ease of use. That will always be its role in the server space—power with simplicity. Future versions of MyCaster are in the works; they'll include logfile support, improved broadcasting capabilities, and more integration with listener features found on MyCaster.com.

Windows Media Audio/Services

Windows Media Audio is a new file format and streaming server system that debuted from Microsoft in mid-1999. As we stated earlier in this book, Microsoft has had a number of previous starts in the streaming media space, the latest being Windows Media Audio and Windows Media Services.

Although Windows Media Audio has won some excellent praise for its quality and compression capability as a codec , the associated server system isn't necessarily as well behaved as the format. In fact, when it comes to remote operation of the media server, Window Media Services can be a tough program to use. We suspect that at some point in the future the server will get more user-friendly. In the meantime, we've tried to help you work through most of the basics of installing and unicasting with the server (note that we don't cover multitasking at all in this chapter), which should help the majority of radio-oriented users.

NOTE

In this book and in the bulletin boards, articles and discussion about Windows Media Audio, you will see people mix and match up several names for what is essentially Windows Media Services. We use Windows Media Server, Microsoft Media Services or Windows Media Audio interchangeably at times to describe the actual server component. While most of the time here we've stuck to Windows Media Services, you will see these alternative terms used by people, so beware. For the most part, Windows Media Audio is the codec, and Windows Media Services is the set of services you install on Windows NT. When you see Windows Media Audio used in reference to the server, it's usually just shorthand for "I'm using Windows Media Services to broadcast audio only."

Installing Windows Media Services

Installing Windows Media Audio isn't too difficult. For NT4, it's a matter of making sure you've installed the latest upgrades and service packs and then downloading Windows Media Services from Microsoft's Web site. For Windows 2000, it's actually part of the initial installation, which you may or may not choose to install. Windows 95/98 users can't install Windows Media Services. However, remember that Winamp and other streaming media servers are able to read Windows Media Audio (.WMA files) and stream them out (although many do so in a different format). and those do work on Windows 95/98.

TIP

Windows 2000 owners can view a simple Windows Media overview of the installation procedure on Microsoft's Web site at **http://www.microsoft.com/windows/windowsmedia/en/Win2000/Intro.asp**.

You can find additional Windows 2000 issues in the Win2000 Issues FAQ at **http://www.microsoft.com/windows/windowsmedia/en/win2000/FAQ.asp**.

As you'll see, Windows Media Services is not too difficult to install, but pay particular attention to a few of the troublespots we talk about and the additional documentation and links provided in this chapter; they will prove to be quite useful in some key situations.

Step 1: Download the Windows Media Services and Tools

If you are not running Windows 2000 or you want the latest version (4.1 as of this writing), you can choose from two basic packages of tools and programs to download from the Windows Media site. They are the Windows Media Tools and Windows Media Services (which is the actual server component).

You can find links to download both components at the default download pages for Windows Media components:

▶ **http://www.microsoft.com/windows/windowsmedia/en/ download/default.asp**

▶ **http://www.microsoft.com/windows/windowsmedia/en/technologies/ services.asp**

Step 2: Begin Installation Procedure

After you have downloaded Windows Media Services to your NT/2000 machine, you need to run the wmserver.exe file to execute the setup program. When it is running, the setup program starts with some warnings and messages, including a license agreement. It then copies the files to your system and opens the installation wizard (see Figure 7.8).

Figure 7.8
After some basic files are copied, the installation wizard begins.

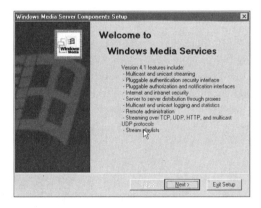

The installation wizard starts with the Welcome message shown in Figure 7.8 and then goes to a screen warning about system requirements. You can click on Next to quickly skip through these messages and get to the first choice presented by the installation wizard (see Figure 7.9). On this screen, you can choose whether you want to do the complete installation or install just the administration components. Going through these steps is an important aspect of Windows Media Services installation— especially if you want to remotely administer a server.

Figure 7.9
On this screen, you can choose complete or administration components.

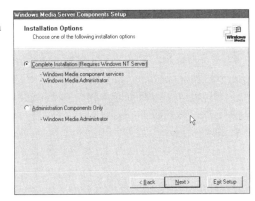

The Windows Media Services component (the actual server program) runs only on the Windows NT server. It must be installed on a Windows NT box. However, the administration components can be installed on a Windows 98/NT workstation/2000 professional system to be used as a remote administration program for the server. This capability is useful if you host from only one NT machine (perhaps as a dedicated server connected to the Internet at a hosting facility) but want to administer and manage it from your Windows 98 machine at home, at work, or on the road. If that's the case, you can download the wmserver.exe program to your NT/2000 system to do the complete installation. Then, for each machine that might need to administer the server, you can install just the administration components.

Right now, you should choose the complete installation; we'll return to the administration components issue later in this chapter. On the wizard screen, choose Complete Installation and then click on Next. The installation wizard prompts you to enter a directory into which it can install the Windows Media Server Components. The default is usually more than acceptable. On the next screen in the installation wizard (see Figure 7.10), you give the name of the root directory for content. The default directory of c:\asfroot is offered. This directory, also known as a *publishing point*, is the place where you will store all your content for on-demand streaming. Click on Next to continue.

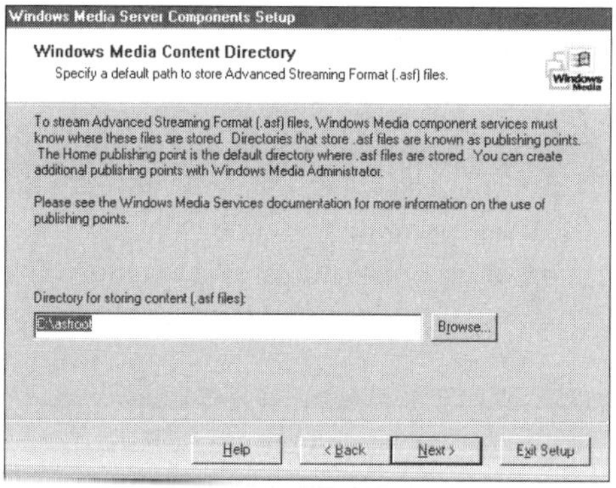

Figure 7.10
Here, you can choose the path for your overall default content directory.

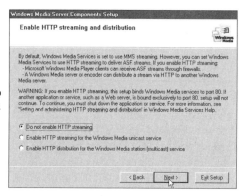

The next screen in the installation wizard is the Enable HTTP Streaming and Distribution screen (see Figure 7.11). This screen is very important as it relates to Windows Media Server and your overall server system. HTTP streaming is the process of using the HTTP protocol to send out streaming media files. It's useful for enabling people to listen to your files if they can't access your content through the normal mms:// (Microsoft Media Services) means. Many people behind firewalls and other corporate settings might have difficulty with such streams.

Figure 7.11
Although HTTP streaming is offered, it's recommended that you don't enable it if you use your media server on a machine you use to run Internet Information Server (IIS) on as well.

The problem with using HTTP streaming, as you'll read on the setup screen, is that by enabling it, you bind Windows Media Services to port 80, which is typically used by Web servers. This causes the setup to stop. You then have to shut down the service using port 80 (that is, your Web server) and install HTTP streaming. In addition, problems occur when you run both your Web server and your media server in a shared environment (that is, on the same machine). For more details on this problem, see the documents and help files on this topic. You can find them by using the search phrase "To enable HTTP streaming for Windows Media Server components that share a server with IIS" on Microsoft's search site or in the built-in help files that accompany Windows Media Services (choose the Search option). Click on Next when you're ready to move on.

CAUTION

For the most part, we suggest that you do not enable HTTP streaming and just move on to the final installation screen.

The final major installation screen for Windows Media Server concerns the account that will be used to run and administer it. You can create a new account known as NetShowServices or use an existing account on the system. The existing account must have Administrator status on the server as a whole in order to work.

After you have decided on Admin issues, click on Finish to complete the installation. The server needs to stop any IIS (Internet Information Services) that are running to install some components for logging and tracking usage of the Windows Media Server. Then you also need to reboot your server for the services to complete installation and start up properly.

As a final step, if you haven't done so already, you can download and install Windows Media Tools from Microsoft's site as well. This package contains the encoder and other tools discussed in this chapter and in Chapter 12. The Windows Media Tools package contains codecs and programs that enable you to create and publish Windows Media-compatible content. If you've installed the latest version of SHOUTcast properly (see Chapter 5), you should already have downloaded these tools.

Configuring Windows Media Services

Upon initial installation, Windows Media Services allows you to easily publish on-demand streams and send live-encoded streams for people to listen to. Unicasting is a fairly simple process, and no further configuration is needed, other than pointing streams to the right place or placing encoded content in the on-demand directory (that is, the main publishing point). However, like all servers, your server has tweaks and configuration issues you might want to address to make it run the way you will use it. These issues include multicasting capabilities as well.

Broadcasting with Windows Media Services

When the system is configured the way you want it, you can begin broadcasting with Windows Media Server. Broadcasting can be live or on demand, and you can have live or on-demand playlists as well. Before you begin, though, it is important to have some precise background on some of the file formats and protocols specific to Windows Media Services as it relates to audio broadcasting.

Formats and Protocols

When it comes to Windows media, the formats and options for broadcasting can be a tiny bit confusing. This difficulty mainly has to do with confusion over file formats for broadcasting audio and the use of stations and broadcasting points. Before we go any further, it pays to sort out these items because it will make deciphering the server's documentation easier, not to mention some of the basic uses we're covering in this chapter.

.ASF? What Happened to Windows Media Audio (.WMA)?

The first thing to know about Windows Media Server is that the main format of content for broadcast is what is known as an .ASF file. ASF (short for Active Streaming Format) is a format that itself contains data that is compressed using different codecs (depending on what the streaming data is—stills, video, or audio) and then encapsulated into a form that works for Windows Media Server.

For audio broadcasting, that codec is the Windows Media Audio format (WMA). When you create a proper .ASF file for broadcasting audio, you use the new Windows Media Audio codec. Where things can be confusing is that the .WMA format also is a standalone format (which was used early on mainly for digital downloads of music like .MP3s and are noted by the .WMA extension).

Because you can create pure Windows Media Audio files with the .WMA extension for downloading, you might think that .WMA files should be the files you will stream via Windows Media Server, but they aren't exactly.

Windows Media Server can stream .WMA files, .MP3 files, and .ASF files, but until version 4.0 of the services, all files streamed by the server had to be in the .ASF style format. So even today, most people still just use .ASF files, even if all that amounts to is .WMA files encapsulated in the .ASF format. If you've created a ton of media in the .WMA format, you can just stream those files by dropping them into a valid publishing point directory on your server and calling for it via the appropriate link on your system.

To create .ASF or .WMA files, you can use any number of encoding tools that support the .ASF format, some of which are discussed in detail in Chapter 12.

.ASX Files, Links, and Playlists

.ASF files are the actual files you want to stream. However, in many instances, you might not want to link users directly to an .ASF file. Instead, you might want to link them to a file that contains specific instructions on exactly what .ASF file to play, where to play it from, or—even fancier—link to a script containing a series of files and servers to get them from. A specific example would be to place a local file on your Web server that contains in it the URL for a stream that is sent from an entirely different server.

To do so, you need to create an .ASX file. .ASX files (also called Advanced Stream Redirector or ASX Metafiles) are nothing more than simple text commands and URLs in a format similar to HTML (they are actually based on the XML format) that tell the media player where to find a stream or streams to play. For example, the .ASX file in Listing 7.1 tells a browser that opens it to launch the media player and play one stream called intro.asf (perhaps containing an ad or station ID) and then play a stream known as currentshow.asf, which might be the main radio show the listener queues into.

Listing 7.1
A Sample .ASX File and Some .ASX Pointers

```
<ASX version = "3.0>
<Entry><Ref href="mms://24.95.36.2/shows/intro.asf" /> </Entry>
<Entry><Ref href="mms://24.95.36.2/shows/segment1.asf" /> </Entry>
<Entry><Ref href="mms://24.95.36.2/shows/bumper1.mp3?ext=.asf" />
    </Entry>
<Entry><Ref href="mms://24.95.36.2/shows/segment2.asf" /> </Entry>
<Entry><Ref href="mms://24.95.36.2/shows/signoff.asf" /> </Entry>
<Entry><Ref href="mms://24.95.36.2/shows/signoffsong.wma" />
    </Entry>
</ASX>
```

CAUTION
If you want to stream MP3 files using Windows Media Server, go ahead. However, if you want to mix and match them with .ASF streams, you should be careful how you structure your .ASX files.

Part II Radio Station Software

NOTE

In the line in Listing 7.1 that has an .MP3 extension, notice the use of an extra piece of code, ?ext=.asf. This code tricks the client computer into thinking that a typical .MP3 file is really an .ASF file and prevents that .MP3 request from spawning a player application that may be the default .MP3 file player (for example, Winamp); it continues to stream the audio through the standard Microsoft Windows Media Player, which is normally the default for .ASF files. This is an important aspect for playlists that might mix and match .MP3 content with traditional .ASF files.

For more details on the entire .ASX file language, see the documentation on the Microsoft Developer's Network (MSDN) site specifically at the following address:

http://msdn.microsoft.com/library/psdk/wm_media/wmpsdk/mmp_sdk/ overview/ASX_intro.htm

A complete reference to all the tags and attributes available in .ASX files is located at this address:

http://msdn.microsoft.com/library/psdk/wm_media/wmpsdk/mmp_sdk/ reference/asx/ASX_ElementsIntro.htm

At first glance, you might ask why you need .ASX files. Why not just link users directly to the .ASF file on the server they need to hear your broadcast? The biggest reason is your Web site. By placing in one .ASX file all the information about where players go to listen to your broadcast, you can reference the .ASX file from your site. To point people to an entirely different broadcast, you need only update the one URL contained in the .ASX file and note your site. For example, if you have a new morning broadcast every day, you could on your site (and any other sites linking to it) simply link to http://www.mysite.com/morning.asx. Then, every day, you could just change the URL in the morning.asx file to the .ASF file of your choice. There's no need for anyone to have to update every link on every page or every site every morning. Just one change, and it's all still current.

.ASX files also are useful when you want to have a playlist, as shown in Listing 7.1. By building an .ASX file filled with consecutive .ASF files, you can divide your content into multiple files that can be arranged as you need to suit your broadcast. You can play an intro file before a live broadcast. and you can play two shows back to back. When .ASX files are used in this form, they are known as *client-side playlists* and constitute the simplest form of Windows Media Server playlists.

TIP

Among the tools and server programs you install with Windows Media Services, you'll find ASX3TEST.exe, which is a command-line utility that does a syntax check on any .ASX file you give it. To use it, go to the directory you installed it into, run the program, and include the name and path of the .ASX file you want it to check (for example, enter asx3test c:\website\asxfiles\morningshow.asx)

Another form of playlist is the *server-side playlist*. Unlike .ASX files that can be put together by a simple text editor, server-side playlists must be put together by the Windows Media Administrator when setting up a Windows Media Station, which is part of the multicast section of Windows Media Services.

Protocols Used by Windows Media Server

You will find it useful to know these major protocols used by Windows Media Server:

▶ **Windows Media Server (WMS) protocol**—This protocol is the main streaming media protocol used by the Microsoft Windows Media Server, especially for server-to-client unicast streams. When you're linking to MMS streams, you use the prefix mms://.

▶ **Media Stream Broadcast Distribution (MBSD) protocol**—This protocol is used for machine-to-machine streaming, such as from the encoder to a server or between two different servers for relaying or server-to-server distribution.

▶ **Hypertext Transfer Protocol (HTTP)**—As described previously, the server does support HTTP streaming under certain conditions and configurations. You mostly need to use this if you want to reach behind firewalls that block other protocols like UDP or MMS but allow HTTP streaming.

Stations vs. Broadcasting/Publishing Points; Multicasting vs. Unicasting

With Windows Media Server, you will hear talk of *stations* and *broadcasting* or *publishing points*. The term *stations* refers to multicast configurations for Windows Media Services, and the term *broadcasting/ publishing points* refers to unicast configurations and use of Windows Media Server.

Multicasting is the process of sending out a constant single stream over a network; any client can then listen in on that stream. In multicasting, unlike in unicasting, there is not one stream for each specific client who wants to listen to your broadcast. Instead, a single stream is fed and split as close to the source client as possible to maximize outgoing bandwidth. If your network is multicast-compatible, you can configure Windows Media Server via the stations' configuration screens for multicasting. Because we are not covering multicasting in depth in this book, you can refer to the user documentation for more details.

Configuring and Administering Windows Media Services

If there is a part about Windows Media Services we don't like as much as other services, it's the configuration and administration part. To be fair, if the service is installed correctly, broadcasting on-demand content is very easy. You can just drop encoded .ASF files into your publishing root (if you changed the default during installation, it's c:\asfroot) and then point people toward the content using an .ASX file or a direct link to the file.

However, if you want to do fancier stuff such as a live show or address other configuration issues, then you need to use the Windows Media Administrator program. Unlike RealServer 7, which uses an entirely HTML-based system for administration and configuration (making it easy to remotely administer from any Web browser), Windows Media Server uses a proprietary program that must be installed directly on any Windows 98/NT/2000 machine that you want to use to administer a server. By default, the Windows Media Administrator program is installed on the same machine as the server itself is installed on. You can also optionally install the Administrator program on a remote server and then connect to it remotely and configure a server as well. This means you must have a Windows machine for configuring the server. We also had trouble configuring remotely, because we couldn't get the passwords and machine names to synchronize as they must to grant us administrative access remotely from a Windows 98 machine (more on this subject later).

Using the Administrator Program

The Administrator program (see Figure 7.12) consists of nine major configuration sections and a host of other pages that include documentation (which itself is pretty good). They include four screens that handle server configuration and five screens that cover monitoring.

Figure 7.12
The Windows Media Server includes its own custom administration tool.

With the configuration screens, unless you want to multicast, you need concern yourself only with the Unicast Publishing Points and the Server Properties screens. If you want to deal with multicast options, you must have only a multicast-capable network; in that case, you can read up on the included documentation pertaining to multicasting, which we won't cover here due to its complexity and because most people won't be able to enable a multicast session outside of their personal LAN.

Unicast Publishing Points

On the Unicast Publishing Points screen, you can add to the publishing points already configured with your installation of Windows Media Server. On initial installation, only one point is set up. The basic root home publishing point is shown in Figure 7.13. No other on-demand publishing points are created, nor are any broadcast publishing points created. To create new publishing points, you must click on the On-Demand button and choose New from the drop-down list that appears. Before choosing this option, make sure that the Use Wizard to Create New On-Demand Publishing Point option is checked.

Part II Radio Station Software

Figure 7.13
You can use the Unicast Publishing Points screen to configure other directories or live broadcast paths from which content can be accessed.

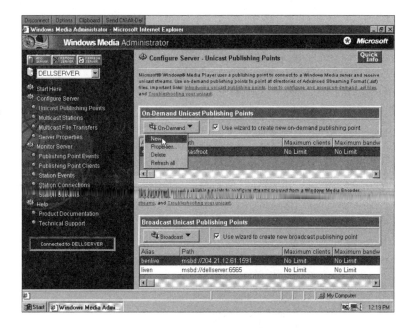

You'll learn how to create a new broadcast publishing point for live content in the "Doing a Live Show Step-by-Step" section later in this chapter.

Server Properties

On the Server Properties screen (which, due to problems we had with the server even after installing it three times, was unreadable), you can tweak server properties. They include whether you allow for HTTP streaming (an installation option as well) and what authentication methods you can use should you want to privatize access to certain streams and log connection information. For most public servers that aren't concerned with HTTP streaming, this screen can be left more or less alone.

Monitoring the Server

You can monitor the server by selecting any one of the five monitoring options on the left of the Administrator program page. The first two—Publishing Point Events and Publishing Point Clients—are the most important because the others—Station Events, Station Connections, and Station Streams—deal with multicasting setups.

The Publishing Point Events screen is pretty much the basic unicasting log screen for Windows Media Server. Here, you can see in detail all the related events that any publishing point has gone through during current operation of the server. The Publishing Point Clients screen shows you basic information about any client that is connected to any broadcast coming out of a publishing point on your server.

Remote Administration

To administer a server remotely, you must install the Windows Media Administrator program on the machine you will use to connect to the machine with the server on it. Alternatively, you can use a product such as Symantec's PCAnywhere (**www.symantec.com**) to remotely control the server.

If you use the Windows Media Administrator program, you can use it on either an NT or 98 machine. Install the Administrator program (which is available as a standalone option when running the original Windows Media Server installation program as noted earlier). Then, to remotely tie in to another server, click on the Add Server button in the top-left corner of the Administrator screen. Next, supply either a Windows network path or an IP address to the server you want to configure. When you're connected, you should be able to remotely configure the server as you like.

NOTE

Although it should be possible to use a Windows 98 machine to connect to an NT server running Windows Media Server and configure it, we had problems. The computer name and password must match that of an administrator on the Windows NT/2000 machine running the server. Thus, you might need to create a new login on your Windows 98 machine to properly connect remotely using the administrator on your system. In the end, we decided to can this approach to remote administration from a Windows NT machine over the Internet and instead just used PCAnywhere. It was easier.

A Final Note About Monitoring and Administration

As we wrote this chapter and Windows 2000 began shipping, Microsoft released an excellent document on running its Windows Media Services on Windows 2000 and released some specific tools for monitoring and stress testing as part of the Windows 2000 Resource Kit. To find out more details about these tools and practices, read the following document on Microsoft's TechNet site:

Best Practices for Windows Media Technologies
http://www.microsoft.com/TechNet/win2000/wmtbest.asp

Doing a Live Show Step-by-Step

With the Windows Media Server, as with most other media servers, a particular step-by-step process is required to get a microphone or other live input device to work. The process involves using the Windows Media Encoder tool, which is a free tool that installs as part of the overall Windows Media Tools download. It is featured and documented further in Chapter 12, but will be covered here as it pertains to live encoding for purposes of using a microphone with the Windows Media Server.

Step 1: Run the Windows Media Encoder Tool

You can run the Windows Media Encoder tool on the same system as the Media Server or run it remotely on another machine on the network or over the Internet. After you run the program, it should autorun the Welcome Wizard. Choose QuickStart from the Welcome Wizard. If the wizard doesn't run, choose New from the encoder's File menu.

Step 2: Select a Template Stream Format

We recommend that you choose 28.8 FM Radio Stereo for the template stream format, because you'll reach the largest audience. However, if you want to get a bit better quality, bump it up to the 56 Dial-up High Quality Stereo setting.

Step 3: Choose an Input

On the Input tab of the Encoder dialog, you can decide what to encode. Because you want a live broadcast, choose Live Source at the top of the tab. Then you must choose an Audio Capture setting. For the default setting, the system chooses what you've already designated in your Windows settings as your default capture card. You can choose the Custom setting and then make a selection from the drop-down list if you have a different card or input source you want to designate (this capability is useful if you have more than one card and want to encode two simultaneous live inputs).

Step 4: Choose an Output

On the Output tab of the Encoder dialog, you can designate where the resulting .ASF stream is sent. You have three major choices. You can designate ports (for both MSBD or HTTP protocols), initiate a connection to a Windows Media Station Manager, or send the stream to a local .ASF file. Because this is a live broadcast, you should use one of the first two options, and to keep things simple, you should avoid using the Windows Media Station Manager method. Therefore, you can choose the To Windows Media Server(s) over a Network option and then choose the

Allow Remote Server(s) to Connect via a Fixed Port option. Unless you know otherwise, you should note and keep the port numbers the encoder assigns to each protocol.

The Output tab of the Encoder dialog should look like the one shown in Figure 7.14.

Figure 7.14
If your Output tab is configured correctly for live broadcasting, it should look like this.

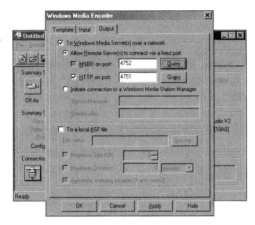

Click on OK or Apply to accept and check these settings. If another program is using the ports you selected, the encoder will notify you of a conflict. Simply click on Query to have it find another free port, note the number for your server, and click on OK.

Step 5: Build a Connection and Publishing Point for the Broadcast

After you set up the encoder, your next step is to go back to the Windows Media Administrator program and give it the information to connect to your live encoder and pull the information back to it for broadcast. You do so by creating a new unicast publishing point on the server and then giving it the information that lets it locate the live broadcast (which can be local on the same machine or remote via the Internet or your local area network).

On the Windows Media Server, run the Windows Media Administrator program and choose Unicast Publishing Points under the Configure Server section. To create a new broadcast publishing point (as opposed to On-Demand publishing points), click on the Broadcast button and choose New from the drop-down list (make sure you have the Use Wizard to Create New Broadcast Publishing Point option checked).

The QuickStart Wizard then runs (see Figure 7.15). The wizard has five screens and is fairly simple to set up, provided you've got the encoder running properly.

Figure 7.15
The QuickStart Wizard
makes it easy to set
up a new live
broadcasting point.

On the next wizard screen (see Figure 7.16), you can choose from an
existing publishing point or create a new one. Choose Create a Broadcast
Publishing Point to start a new publishing point for your live source.

Figure 7.16
Choose whether you
want to create a new
publishing point or
edit an existing one.

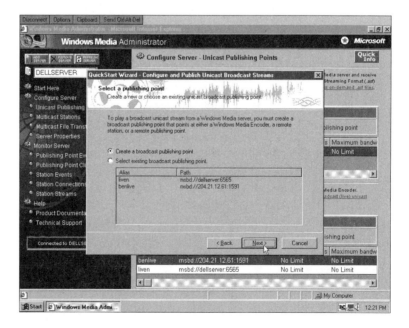

Because you're creating a new publishing point for this example, you need to define what style of source you're using to pull content from. You have three choices: Windows Media Encoder, Remote Station, or Remote Publishing Point. For this example, choose Windows Media Encoder, because this is a live broadcast. Click on Next when you're ready to continue.

On the next wizard screen (see Figure 7.17), you set information that tells the server where to find the encoder and what to use as a name for the broadcast (which is part of the file URL people will use later). The screen begins with a field titled Alias that will be the name for the broadcast. You should use a simple, intuitive name such as mytalkshow or livefromoffice to help denote the broadcast from any other content coming out of the server. The Path field indicates the direct network or IP address (with port) to the encoder you are running to generate the live feed. Having the port information from the previous setup of the encoder is important, because you plug it in here. Note that, by default, the server sets the port to 7007, so if you've changed it by choice or necessity on the encoder, you need to change it here as well to match.

Figure 7.17
You must tell the server the location of the path to the incoming stream.

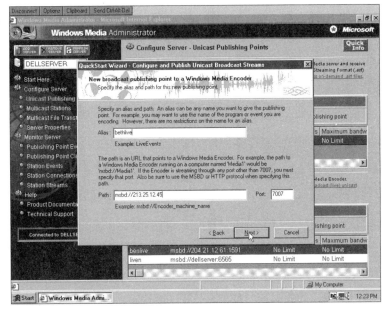

After setting path and alias names, you click on Next to go to the next wizard screen to select the publishing method (see Figure 7.18) Here, you are shown the exact URL that people use in the Media Player program to access the stream. You can choose the protocol prefix you want to use (by default, it's mms:), and if necessary, you can change the URL name (for example, to a direct IP address). The list of checkboxes below the URL name provides several ways you can have the wizard automatically generate files or code snippets that you can e-mail or embed in a Web page to generate links to the new stream. We find the easiest choices to work with are to have the wizard create and save an .ASX file to a folder on our Web page directory.

Figure 7.18

Here, you can choose the publishing method to develop the URL and optionally create the needed tags and .ASX files to publish links to your stream.

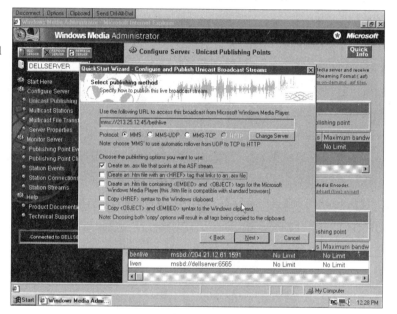

When you finish making selections on this screen, click on Next to move to the next wizard screen, which contains a summary of the information you queued in (see Figure 7.19). On this screen, click on Finish to generate the publishing point and any associated files you asked for on the previous screen. After clicking on Finish, you get confirmation if the publishing point was successfully completed. Choose Close to return to the Windows Media Administrator, or choose Restart to create more publishing points.

Figure 7.19
Before you finalize the publishing point, review the configuration. You can back up in the wizard to change anything that's not correct.

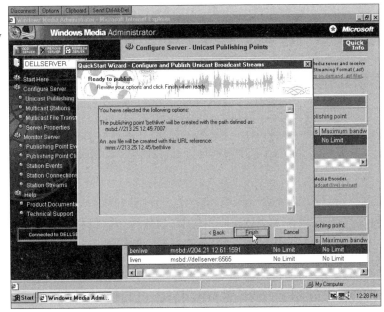

TIP

To edit an existing publishing point, right-click on its entry in the list and choose Properties from the menu that appears. Using this menu, you also can delete a publishing point. On the Properties screen, you can set bandwidth limitations (by number of users or maximum allowed bandwidth) for this publishing point.

Step 6: Test

After you've completed all these steps, you need to test the stream. Go to another PC or have a friend try to call up the stream on your server. If you've set up the encoder and your microphone on your sound card, you should be able to speak and have the audio pumping out on the other side of the server.

If you don't hear any sound, make sure you've set up the publishing point correctly, that the ports on the encoder and publishing point match, and that the microphone or line-in audio is working properly. Other than that, restep through the entire process and double check everything to ensure it's set correctly. You might also check the microphone in another program that uses it to make sure it's not muted or improperly configured.

Part II Radio Station Software

Proprietary Power, But It's Free

We've beat up on Windows Media Server a bit here. In reality, it's not a bad server. It's fairly quick to install, it's got some robust features, and it supports a very promising up-and-coming codec in the Windows Media Audio format. The problem is that, if you decide to use it, you will be a bit locked in to the Microsoft way of doing things. That means using the .ASF and .WMA formats, which not all the popular media players support (as opposed to MP3, which most, if not all, do). It also means using Microsoft's method of administration, which, to be honest, is not nearly as open as other systems. Finally, it is a Windows NT/2000-only product. Windows 98 users and Mac/UNIX/Linux users must look elsewhere for a server.

On the other hand, for Windows 2000/NT users, Windows Media Server is a strong contender that can serve many streams (given bandwidth capabilities) and doesn't cost any more than NT or Windows 2000 to begin with. That's a big plus for many companies and individuals. So, although this server has a few potholes, it is a powerful addition to the broadcasting realm and worth knowing more about and using.

8

Alternative Server and Radio Station Solutions

The Internet radio station and show industry is growing rapidly, and many people have launched new products or services for those interested in broadcasting to friends or the greater Web population. In the preceding three chapters, we've covered close to a half-dozen of the best tools and services. However, let there be no stone unturned. In this chapter, we're going to survey and explain all the remaining products and services that are available to help you place a station or create a show on the Web.

In Chapter 9, you'll also learn about some companies such as Live365.com that help you outsource your broadcast so that you don't have to provide all the outgoing bandwidth yourself. For now, though, we want to explain a few other useful products that have a place at the table and are thus worth knowing about and knowing how to use.

icecast

With the arrival of SHOUTcast came the birth of icecast, an open source audio streaming server system. *Open source software* is software that actually lets you get into the source code and modify it. For example, icecast was developed as an open source project under the GNU Public License, which dictates how it can be used. According to the license, you generally can use the open source code for free, but all modifications to the source code should be contributed back to the general public for further use and modification.

Each open source project tends to have a community of users and programmers who support it, but it also usually has one or several core programmers who are the force(s) behind it. In the case of icecast, the project and program were created in January 1999 by Jack Moffitt and Barath Raghavan. Many other people and groups have contributed to the project since its inception. Particularly helpful was Green Witch, a startup devoted to online broadcasting which helped fund the work of Moffitt and others. In January 1999, iCAST.com purchased Green Witch, and with that purchase came further support of icecast. At the time of this writing, it isn't clear what iCAST will be doing with icecast, although

Part II Radio Station Software

we suspect it will be something similar to an outsourcing service like
Live365.com, which is discussed in the following chapter.

Using icecast

While icecast is more complex to use than SHOUTcast, structurally it
works in a similar manner. However, due to its more complex nature and
our space limitations, we can't go into every nuance. Still, the following
sections provide a good overview as well as some additional pointers if
you want to explore broadcasting with icecast.

Step 1: Acquire and Install the Server

You can download icecast from **www. icecast.org**. As an open source
product, it is available in both compiled and uncompiled forms and for a
number of platforms. For example, it has been ported to Windows
95/98/NT, Solaris, and Linux.

Unless you're familiar with creating compiled binaries from source code,
you should not download the source code versions. On the download
page of icecast.org, you can download precompiled binaries to install and
run. Download the binary for the platform you want to use and extract
the compressed archive to your hard drive. Each archive contains the
following:

▶ The icecast server program

▶ Shout, a program that helps you send content via the icecast server

▶ Documentation stored in the docs directory

▶ A boilerplate configuration file stored in the etc directory

▶ A folder and some files that hold server log information

▶ Some template HTML files used for Web-based administration
   updates

Step 2: Configure the icecast Server

Configuring the icecast server involves editing the icecast.conf file and
saving it in the appropriate directory, much like the SHOUTcast server.ini
file works. Comments in the boilerplate icecast.conf file explain what
each option does, but only a few are most important, including hostname,
port number, and security passwords.

NOTE

The documentation for version 1.30 of the Windows binary of icecast says the
icecast.conf file is located in the docs/ folder. It's not. It's located in the etc/
folder and should be placed there instead of the docs folder.

For further explanation of the options that you can configure in the icecast.conf file, refer to the manual.html file included in the docs/ folder with icecast.

Step 3: Run the icecast Server

The icecast server, even on Windows, is a command-line program. That is, it runs from the DOS prompt on Windows and traditional command-line consoles on Linux and Solaris machines. To run the icecast server, you must make sure your icecast.conf file is set properly and then run the icecast binary (icecast.exe for Windows users). A command line pops up (or not, if you run it initially from an already-open command line), and after you run through some initial setup items, it displays a prompt that looks like this:

    ->

At this point, the server is running and is in Admin mode (see Figure 8.1). It can receive content from a source that you need to supply or configure.

Figure 8.1
Icecast is a command-line system that runs on Windows, Linux, and Solaris systems.

Part of running the server is passing commands to the server itself when it is in Admin mode. A complete list of commands and parameters you pass through with them is available in the included manual file. Typing HELP when you're in Admin mode brings up a list of the commands as well.

TIP

Before you run icecast, it is strongly recommended that you read the manual and familiarize yourself with the command prompts. Otherwise, you'll end up initially frustrated when you run the server. If you're an old pro with command-line interfaces, using it should be straightforward. If you're new to this type of interface, you'll want to put in some up-front study time.

Step 4: Supply Content to the icecast Server

The hardest part about using icecast is getting content streaming out of it. When the server originally runs, it doesn't do anything to begin streaming content. Instead, you need to send it a source feed (using Winamp, LiveIce, or shout).

Winamp can send source to an icecast server. To use it, type the location of the server and its password into your SHOUTcast DSP source dialog (see Chapter 5) and then connect.

LiveIce is a command-line program you can use to send encoded source to the icecast system. See the LiveIce documentation for more details on how to use it.

NOTE

No precompiled version of LiveIce is available on the icecast.org site. You need to compile it from the source located at **http://cvs.icecast.org/cvsweb.cgi/liveice/**.

Shout is a command-line program that is included with the icecast server distribution. You can use it to send content to your server by referencing files stored on the server; those files are then fed directly back out via icecast. This process is similar to the G2SLTA (G2 Simulated Live Broadcast) system described in Chapter 6. Like that system, your files *must* be pre-encoded at the same bit rate as all the files in the broadcast and the rate the server is configured for. Otherwise, it won't work.

CAUTION

Shout is not SHOUTcast; it's a separate application tied to icecast. Don't confuse the two, even though it's easy to do so.

See the shout documentation for more information about commands it offers and how to construct shout-compliant playlists.

TIP

In some of the distributions of icecast (Windows especially), the Readme file for shout is not included at all. To find it, go to the repository of all icecast-related files located at cvs.icecast.com (see Figure 8.2), and click on the shout folder (the direct URL is **http://cvs.icecast.org/cvsweb.cgi/shout/**). There, you'll find links to all the related shout files, including the readme.shout file, which you can download.

Figure 8.2
The icecast repository holds all files related to icecast, including some missing documentation.

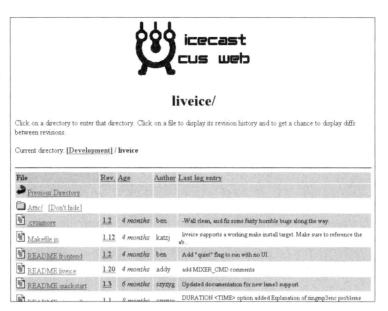

liveice/

Click on a directory to enter that directory. Click on a file to display its revision history and to get a chance to display diffs between revisions.

Current directory: [Development] / liveice

File	Rev.	Age	Author	Last log entry
Previous Directory				
Attic/ [Don't hide]				
.cvsignore	1.2	4 months	ben	-Wall clean, and fix some fairly horrible bugs along the way.
Makefile.in	1.12	4 months	katzj	liveice supports a working make install target. Make sure to reference the ab...
README.frontend	1.2	4 months	ben	Add "quiet" flag to run with no UI.
README.liveice	1.20	4 months	addy	add MIXER_CMD comments
README.quickstart	1.3	6 months	szyzyg	Updated documentation for new lame3 support
README	1.1	8 months	szyzyg	DURATION <TIME> option added Explanation of xingmp3enc problems

Step 5: Administering the Server

You administer the server completely through the command-line system. You can telnet to your server using any standard client, and you can use a Web-based interface that, for the moment, just provides Web-based status reports (although we suspect in the future it will provided integrated administration functions).

You can access the Web-based console by typing http://server.name:8000/list.cgi into your Web browser. The files contained in templates in your icecast folder can be modified to customize the look and feel of your Web reports as needed.

Advanced Options Available with icecast

The most advanced option with icecast, of course, is the access to the source code. If you're familiar with C programming, you can dive into the source code and begin hacking away to fix bugs you find and modify it to add your own new features. Of course, icecast asks that you supply these fixes back to the people there so that, as they release new versions of it, they can include the latest round of contributions.

Icecast also lets you mix multiple streams through it into one broadcast. You do so by using the LiveIce application; see that documentation for more information.

Part II Radio Station Software

A final useful item for icecast users is the icedir system. Unlike other server systems such as SHOUTcast, the directory server system that lets sites display a listing of all the servers that are broadcasting using their system isn't accessible to you. That is, you can't, as an interested site operator, display a directory of servers for users to click on. With the icecast system comes icedir, which is a series of programmed scripts that you can install on your Web server and, with it, begin running a directory server of your own. In fact, several sites, such as **www.linuxpower.com**, run their own directory servers. Icecast broadcasters can optionally list any number of compliant directory servers in their icecast.conf files.

A final use of the icecast system —especially with its directory server system, icedir—is that, with it, you can set up a number of icecast servers all running different shows and streams. Then, using the icedir system, you can create an easy-to-navigate directory of all your shows. With that directory in place, you can run your own version of big Internet radio aggregators such as spinner.com or netradio.com. Doing so would take a bunch of work, and it is recommended only for more advanced users familiar with icecast and server-side development and administration. But the fact that it is possible is a great reason to explore icecast.

Exploring the icecast Documentation and Getting Further Support

The documentation included with icecast isn't too bad; you just need to spend the time reading it all. We've pointed out some holes in it. If you find problems, you might try the code/documentation repository located at **http://cvs.icecast.org**. You also can find a full support system on icecast.org that is delivered via message boards, where you can directly contact many members of the extremely helpful icecast development team.

With its commitment to open source and its strong set of tools, icecast is a great radio solution for the Internet. It's not for everyone, but it does occupy an important role in the development of all Internet radio.

RadioDestiny Network

RadioDestiny Network (see Figure 8.3) offers an MP3 and Internet radio player, chat, news, and, of course, the capability to broadcast to the world, which is what we'll focus on here. An especially cool feature of RadioDestiny is that it offers a Java-based playback applet that you can embed in your page. Using it, you can automatically tune listeners into your station the second they hit a Web page featuring the RadioDestiny clipstream applet technology.

NOTE

Mac users, rejoice! RadioDestiny has a Macintosh version that was in beta during this writing. It's available on the RadioDestiny Network site.

CAUTION

Radio Destiny Broadcaster does not offer MP3 streaming on your PC. You must first convert MP3 files to .WAV files (there is another workaround, but it's not worth the effort). The Mac version does directly support MP3 streaming directly, however.

Figure 8.3
RadioDestiny Network offers an MP3 and Internet radio player, chat, news, and, of course, the capability to broadcast to the world.

Locating Services for Commercial Broadcasters

RadioDestiny offers different services for different levels of broadcasters. Commercial broadcasters can use Radio Destiny Broadcaster. For more information for commercial broadcasters, go to **www.radiodestiny.com/broadcast/commercial.shtml.**

RadioDestiny also has repeater technology (in trial stages as of this writing) that enables you to choose the number of listeners you want to support. At the time of this writing, each block of 10 streams costs $500 a year. For example, if you need to support only fifty simultaneous listeners, the annual cost would be $2,500. For more information, visit **www.radiodestiny.com/broadcast/repeat.shtml.**

Building a RadioDestiny Internet Radio Station

There aren't a ton of steps involved with Radio Destiny. However, there are a few catches worth noting as you read through the following step-by-step instructions on how to build a station using the RadioDestiny software.

Step 1: Download and Install Radio Destiny Broadcaster

For noncommercial broadcasters to start broadcasting free of charge, go to **www.radiodestiny.com/broadcast/quick.shtml** and follow the directions. Start by downloading and installing Radio Destiny Broadcaster by clicking on the Download Now button.

After you've downloaded the files, run the setup software. You then are asked to fill out a number of forms and accept user license terms. For example, you need to set the directory you want the broadcaster installed to, fill out user registration forms, and fill out a station information screen.

The Station Information dialog (see Figure 8.4) is straightforward, except for the Category description. Type your category by using a *category**style* format—for example, \music\country. Table 8.1 shows the suggested formats Destiny Broadcaster wants you to use.

Figure 8.4
On the Station Information dialog of Destiny Broadcaster, the only difficulty is figuring out how to fill out the category description.

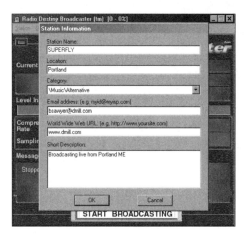

Table 8.1
Destiny
Broadcaster Formats

Category	Style
Music	Country Dance/Tech Religious Contemporary Rock Classical
Jazz	R&B Blues
Folk	World Miscellaneous
Talk	Radio Information
Scanners	Weather
News	Stocks/Financial Sports
Soap Box	Political Religion Rants General What?
Special Interest	College Adults only Computers Gaming Comedy Regional
Mixed Format	
Children's	

After you answer these configuration questions, Radio Destiny
Broadcaster will run, and you will see its main screen (see Figure 8.5).

Figure 8.5
Radio Destiny
Broadcaster is ready
for action.

Step 2: Launch and Further Configure the Software

You can launch the Broadcaster by opening the Start menu and choosing Programs > Destiny > Radio Destiny Broadcaster, although it will run right after initial installation and configuration. The player includes a level indicator, start time, elapsed time, and information on compression rate, sampling rate, number of listeners, rejected listeners, and messages.

Just because the Broadcaster is running, however, does not mean you are finished with the configuration. Under the Options menu are two menu items that offer further configuration—Settings and Expert Settings.

Choosing Settings pulls up the Options dialog (see Figure 8.6). Here, you can choose the Broadcast mode: Script or Live. Audio Type is a drop down list from which you can choose Voice or Music. If you choose the audio type, Radio Destiny Broadcaster can optimize output for the style of the broadcast. If you've selected the Script option for the Broadcast mode, you can type the name of a script or click on Browse to find a script on your system to use. Finally, you need to set the connection rate you have on your broadcast system.

Figure 8.6

In the Settings dialog (labeled Options), you can decide the type of broadcast mode and the style of the broadcast audio.

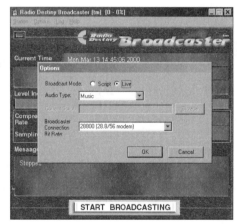

The Expert Settings dialog lets you specify higher-end settings for your broadcast. These include the following:

▶ **Specify IP**—Using this check box and drop-down list, you can set the IP address you are broadcasting with. This option is useful for machines sporting more than one IP address.

▶ **Auto Bit Rate**—If a listener is using the Destiny Media Player, the broadcaster will send a stream best suited to his connection, resulting in better audio quality. This should be checked, however, only if you yourself are sending out your broadcast on a high-speed line. If you are using a modem line, then you should uncheck this option.

▶ **Autostart Broadcasting**—When this option is checked, Radio Destiny Broadcaster will automatically begin broadcasting the second it is activated.

▶ **Stream Bit Rate**—By using this sliding bar, you can set a more precise bit rate for your broadcast. As you set it, the number in parentheses above the bar after the bit rate indicates which modem type is the minimum needed to listen to your broadcast at that bit rate.

▶ **HTTP Proxy**—If you are behind a firewall, clicking on this button opens a dialog in which you can adjust proxy settings to enable broadcasting through a firewall.

Step 3: Provide an Audio Stream

You can provide audio streams in one of three ways:

1. Hook up a microphone, CD player, or other audio source through your recording input on your sound card.

2. Build and provide a script of .WAV files stored on your hard drive. For more details on this approach, see "Building a Script with Destiny Broadcaster."

3. Play a CD from your computer's CD-ROM drive.

Step 4: Begin Broadcasting

Click on Start Broadcasting at the bottom of the Broadcaster screen to do just that. It's that easy. The bar then changes to Stop Broadcasting, which you can click to shut down a broadcast.

Building a Script with Destiny Broadcaster

If you decide to run Destiny Broadcaster in Script mode, you first need to build a script of files to play in the Script Builder (see Figure 8.7). To add a file, click on Add Sample. You can use Edit Sample to refine a sample already in the list. The rest of the buttons—which include Remove, Duplicate, Load, and Save—are fairly self-explanatory. Click on Done when you're finished, and then click on the Start Broadcasting button at the bottom of the Broadcaster to begin playing your script.

Part II Radio Station Software

Figure 8.7
You can use Destiny Broadcaster's Script Builder to create your script of files.

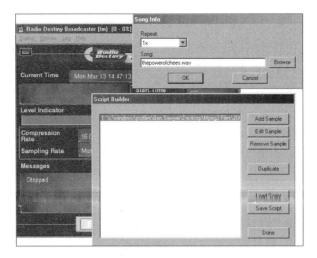

Using the Log Files

Broadcaster automatically creates log files. By using the Log menu on the main Broadcaster screen, you can look at logs of each of the past seven days. Click on the day you want, which causes the log file to appear in your Notepad. You can take the contents of any log file and use the Log File Analyzer located on the RadioDestiny Web site (see Figure 8.8). After you've submitted the file, the form provides a simple response telling you, for example, the total number of listeners, unique listeners, high-speed listeners, and most active time of day.

Figure 8.8
On destinyradio.com, you can submit a log file for automatic analysis.

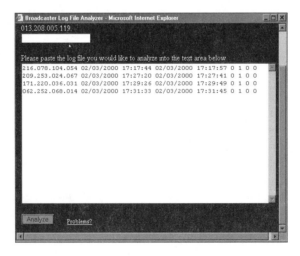

clipstream

Clipstream (**www.clipstream.com**) is a product that enables you to add streaming audio to your Web pages, but more importantly, it plays Destiny media files. Users don't need any plug-ins, and you don't need any special servers. If you have a Web page, you have what you need. The basic package costs $99 and includes a license for a single Web site, up to ten pages with clips and up to thirty clips total. You can run a show with it, and it supports some playlists embedded into a page. It's not the optimum solution, but it is a nice twist. Because it is a Java applet, users don't need to have a specific player, and it's completely cross-platform. Everything must be prerecorded, though, which makes it more conducive to on-demand shows than live, looped playlists. It's also more conducive to talk shows than musical ones.

If you want to hear some samples, check out **http://www.clipstream.com/samples/index.html.**

1.   To try the free trial unit, go to **www.clipstream.com/ download/index.html** and download clipstream for either PC or MacOS, install the clipstream compressor (see Figure 8.9), and visit the Quick Start page to begin using clipstream.

Figure 8.9
The clipstream compressor is ready to go.

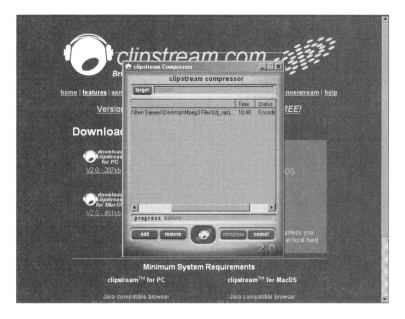

2. After you have installed the software, choose or create an audio file you want to stream. For clipstream's tips on this process, go to **www.clipstream.com/help/audio.htm**.

3. Compress your files with the clipstream compressor by first clicking on the Add button to choose your selections. Choose the target drive and folder by clicking on the Target button. Each track is added to the compressor display screen, and the target folder indicates where you want the compressed versions of your file(s) saved. The two compressed audio files and the player applet (clipstream.zip) must be saved in the same folder as the Web page on which you will present the stream. Do not unzip clipstream.zip.

4. Click on Compress.

5. Purchase a code key at **www.clipstream.com/purchase/index.html**. You can test the clipstream on your local hard drive, but clipstream will not work on your Web server until you purchase a code key and register the URL.

6. Generate the necessary Java code for your Web page. For help, visit the clipstream Applet Code Generator at **http://www.clipstream.com/codegen/codegen.shtml**.

LAUNCHcast

LAUNCH.com combines LAUNCH's original editorial content with personalization capabilities to create an interactive online music community. LAUNCH.com offers artist biographies, album reviews, concert reviews, and exclusive features, chats, and interviews. Personalization capabilities enable members to create customized music home pages and to receive content that is tailored to their own tastes.

Using LAUNCHcast (**www.launch.com/music/launchcast/**), you can create your own radio station based on more than 50,000 songs and more than 70 genres. You can rate songs, albums, and artists to influence the frequency with which your station plays them. You can also subscribe to other LAUNCHcast stations to allow their ratings to influence your station.

LAUNCHcast does not allow you to create a playlist with specific songs, but the more songs, albums, and artists you rate, the more personalized your station's playlist will become. Ratings allow you to virtually eliminate songs from your station and increase the frequency with which your favorites are played. Your station will play only songs from the genres you choose.

Building a LAUNCHcast Station

To build a station, click on the Create Station Here button on the LAUNCHcast main page (**www.launch.com/music/launchcast/**). To become a member (there is no charge), fill out the application form, which includes a username and e-mail address.

You can also join LAUNCH by selecting the Join Now button near the top of the LAUNCH home page (**www.launch.com**). After you fill out the form, the Web page will bring to you a page that congratulates you. Here you can select a link to start your radio station.

After signing up, you can use a number of optional features to automatically personalize your station. The more you use, the more you can define your automatically generated playlist. First, you can use LAUNCHcast to select from several traditional radio stations in your area (see Figure 8.10). But don't be alarmed if there are no radio stations from your area.

Figure 8.10
You can select from a list of local radio stations to influence your playllst.

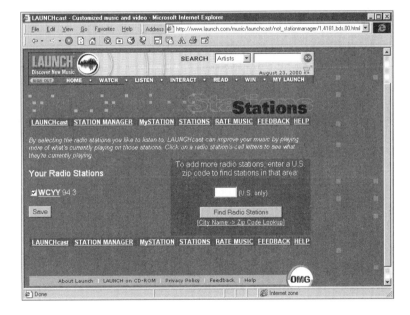

Then you can select other LAUNCHcast stations that match your personal tastes, and their playlists will influence yours (see Figure 8.11).

Figure 8.11
You also can select other LAUNCHcast stations to influence your playlist.

After you click on Play on the main screen, you might need to have Flash 4.0 automatically installed on your computer. If you don't already have Flash 4.0, you will not see a spinning LAUNCH logo and therefore you should click on the appropriate button. When you see the spinning logo, click on the appropriate button.

Next, you need to configure your computer with Windows Media Player. If it is not configured already, simply follow the instructions and continue after you hear the prompt.

Then you can choose your connection speed (28.8, 56K, and high-speed) to listen. If you aren't sure, choose 28.8, which is guaranteed to work. You can always change the speed later in your Station Manager to get better quality.

Using the Station Manager

To get your station ready to go and to make changes, go to your Station Manager (see Figure 8.12). Here, you can rate and review music, select DJs or radio stations to influence your playlist, set your options for new music and connection speed, change your mood profiles, select the genres of music you prefer, and promote your station.

Figure 8.12
You can use the Station Manager to customize your station.

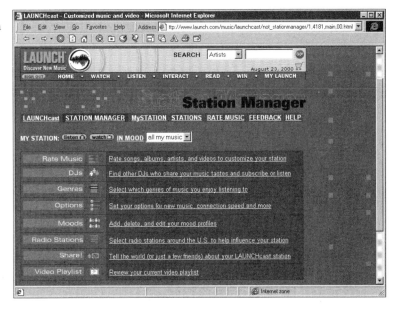

Rate Music

You can use the Rate Music option to rate some of the most popular artists on LAUNCH, as well as search for specific albums or artists. If you have a lot of time on your hands, you can cruise through the list of more than 2,600 albums in the rock genre alone.

DJs

LAUNCHcast offers featured DJs and popular DJs (most subscribers) whose playlists can influence yours if you so choose.

Radio Stations

Initially, you are given the option to add radio stations from your geographical area. In the Radio Stations area of the Station Manager, you can add stations from other areas by entering the zip code of your choice. If you don't know the zip code of a certain city, you can use the zip code finder by entering the name of the city.

Options

In the Options area (see Figure 8.13), you can change the connection speed, decide whether to play music with explicit lyrics, and choose a mix of new music and music you have rated. To ensure a variety of music, your station will play mostly new music until you have at least one hundred ratings.

Part II Radio Station Software

Figure 8.13
In the Options area, you can further personalize your station.

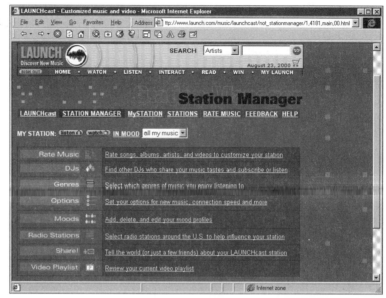

Moods

In the Moods area of the Station Manager, you can create "sub-stations." These moods can include some or all of the radio stations, genres, and DJs you have selected. Click on Create a Mood, choose a Mood Name, and select the genres, stations, and DJs you want as part of this mood. You can use moods to play certain types of music at certain times. When you play your station, you can either play all your music or just music from a specified mood.

Genres

In the Genres area, you can check the boxes for the genres you want your station to play. Your station will not play any unchecked genres.

Share

You can use the Share options to e-mail your friends about your station and provide the HTML code to link to your station.

Launching Your LAUNCHcast

After you have set up everything with the Station Manager, click on Play and off you go. The whole process takes just a few minutes. The LAUNCHcast player (see Figure 8.14) enables you to rate songs as they play and view other stations that play similar music. The more songs you rate, the more personalized your station can become, playing what you like and eliminating what you don't.

Figure 8.14
Here, you can see the
LAUNCHcast player
in action.

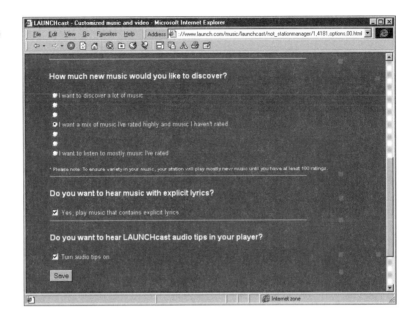

iCAST

iCAST (**www.icast.com**) offers the iCASTER player for those who want to listen and also enables you to create and broadcast a media library. iCAST wants people to broadcast content that they have created—primarily their own music. To begin using iCAST, click on the Media Upload link on the home page (see Figure 8.15).

Figure 8.15
iCAST provides
the means to get your
music heard.

iCAST provides exposure, feedback, and, potentially, income to artists. Artists can upload MP3, .AVI, .ASF, .WAV, .MPG, .MID, .MOV, and .AU files. The content you upload to iCAST must be free and clear of all rights. In other words, it should be your work. To quote the iCAST terms of agreement: "You retain full ownership of and all right, title, and interest in and to the Content, including any related copyrights, subject to the non-exclusive rights granted to (iCAST) under this agreement." Although we know people often skip the terms of agreement on many sites, we suggest you read iCAST's, because it is your content that you are uploading.

After you have agreed to the terms of service and checked the appropriate box, click on the Upload Your Media button. If you are not already an iCAST member, you need to register at this point.

What about QuickTime?

Apple fans might now be wondering about QuickTime and the QuickTime Streaming Server (located on the Web at **www.apple.com/quicktime/servers/**). Once it seemed that QuickTime would be a major component of Internet audio broadcasting. So far it hasn't been, but that could change. Mac fans and open source software proponents may want to take a peek at the latest server software Apple is developing.

For Mac users, QuickTime Streaming Server is available from the QuickTime Web site (as noted in the preceding paragraph). To run it, you will need the latest version of Mac OS X Server. Then you should download QuickTime Streaming Server 2. The requirements for this server are a Power Macintosh G3 computer or Macintosh Server G3 with 64MB or more of RAM (512MB is recommended), and at least a gigabyte of hard disk space.

From there you can set up and configure the server following the included documentation. There is also support for a broadcasted playlist. Check out the QuickTime Streaming PlaylistBroadcaster feature by visiting the documentation for it at **http://til.info.apple.com/techinfo.nsf/artnum/n60463**.

From QuickTime to Darwin

If there was a knock on QuickTime Server, it was that it was a Mac-only product. All that changed with the release of Darwin. Darwin is the codename for an open source adaptation of Apple's QuickTime Streaming Server. The Server, which can be found at **http://www.publicsource.apple.com/projects/streaming/** is available for FreeBSD, Linux, and Solaris systems. There are executable versions on the site as well as source code. Documentation is included in the download.

With Darwin, Apple is moving toward an innovative approach to its streaming server system. While it will continue to build and maintain QuickTime Server only on the Mac, it is working with open source to see its streaming software proliferate to other platforms. While other products detailed in this book are easier to use and are more focused on radio than QuickTime, it is good to see one of the innovators of multimedia and streaming media becoming more aggressive. If you are a tinkerer, Darwin may be a fun broadcasting system to play with. However, if you are trying to keep it simple or work with a Windows-based platform, neither QuickTime Server nor Darwin are your best—or even next-best—options.

Which Product Should You Use?

By now, you have been introduced to more than a half-dozen major and minor technologies that enable you to broadcast a radio station or show on the Internet. That begs the question, "Which one should you be using for your station or show?" This issue was covered back in Chapter 4, where we did an overview of all the major technologies. Now that you've read more details about how to use them, you should have an even better understanding of which are best for you.

The way we look at this issue, the serious commercial broadcaster will want to settle on one specific technology and get to know it very intimately; it is, after all, the most critical component. For the hobbyist, however, we recommend playing with all the available technologies and using as many as possible. Use SHOUTcast or icecast to reach an MP3-minded audience, use RealServer to reach users of RealPlayer, and use products such as Windows Media Server or MyCaster to reach still further other audiences. Radio Destiny Broadcaster and QuickTime Streaming Server are solutions for Mac radioheads, and it also offers some additional repeater options to cast a wider net. Finally, if you want to tinker with the real innards of a server and have a programming background, the Darwin or icecast open source systems should be worth a download.

In the end, you should appreciate that you have so many products to choose from and use. So why choose one? Look for a mix of technologies that lets you gain more audience and build listenership.

9

Outsourcing and Station Hosting

Up until now, most of what we've talked about is how to set up your own server and manage it. However, setting up a server isn't the only way to get your broadcast online, and it might not be the best way. If you don't have the bandwidth or the server capacity to meet the demands of your audience, then outsourcing your Internet broadcasting is a good idea. In this chapter, we'll cover all the ins and outs of outsourcing your broadcast.

Types of Outsourcing

You can find essentially three types of outsourcing in the Internet radio industry. The first is what we call *full-service outsourcing*. The companies involved with this type of outsourcing offer everything: They take your content, set up the server, and provide all the infrastructure and expertise to broadcast your station or show to the masses. Companies such as Yahoo! Broadcast Services, Evoke.com, and Real Broadcast Network are great examples of such services.

The second group is made up *audio hosting providers*. These providers are pretty much traditional Web hosting companies that also offer some level of audio server capability (most use RealServer) and will, for an extra fee, provide access to that server for you to broadcast.

The third group is known either as *repeater services* or *audio homesteading services*. This group is made up of companies such as Live365.com and AudioRealm.com. You send them a single stream or upload files to a server, and they will give you the outgoing bandwidth to reach users. In exchange for this free service, they sell advertising on your stream (periodically interrupting it for a small commercial or offering banners on their site, and so on) and other services.

Why Outsource?

For most 24/7 broadcasters, outsourcing is not necessarily the best option, but for anyone doing spot broadcasting or a remote show, using an outsourcer can be a smart, user-friendly option for broadcasting. If you're a 24/7 broadcaster, you might want to use a homesteading service such as Live365.com either in place of your own bandwidth or in addition to it.

The key reasons to outsource are as follows:

▶ **Scalability and bandwidth**—Large outsourcing companies specialize in being able to support large audiences up to tens of thousands of listeners. Although 95 percent of most online broadcasts attract audiences of 3,000 or fewer, for those special events when you might attract a large simultaneous audience, an outsource broadcast is just the ticket.

▶ **Speed**—The speed at which you can produce a broadcast via an outsourcer is much faster than if you do it yourself (assuming you don't already have the necessary equipment).

▶ **Remotes and expertise**—Expertise for your broadcast is something an outsourcer has that you might not have. Especially for remote broadcasting in which you might need local knowledge and expertise, an outsourcer can be a key partner.

▶ **Ease**—Using a quality outsourcer takes all the headache out of running a broadcast server. You can simply supply via telephone, upload, or satellite some audible audio stream, and the outsourcer will take care of the rest.

▶ **Cost**—Although more expensive in some ways, outsourcing can be cheaper for remote broadcasts when you factor in costs for equipment and setup.

Evaluating Top-Tier Outsourcing Systems

You can go to a number of places to outsource your broadcast, but only a few select companies are focusing directly on high-end hosting of streaming media. We've selected three of the best top-tier providers to consider and provided background on their services.

Evoke.com

Formerly known as vStream, the outsourcing company now known as Evoke.com is based in Boulder, Colorado. It offers support for both RealAudio and Windows Media Audio. The company offers three services: voice-based e-mail, Web conferencing, and Webcasting. Its Webcasting division has handled broadcasts for a number of major companies, record labels, and broadcasters.

Unlike RBN, Evoke.com doesn't require a set number of months for a contract. Instead, all of its pricing is based on audience size, number of megabytes streamed, and size of storage needed for your broadcast. It can handle live feeds, on-demand shows, and satellite feeds as well. You need to call for a quote, but pricing is in line with RBN and other top-tier outsourcers.

Real Broadcast Network

Real Broadcast Network (RBN) is the Internet broadcast outsourcing arm of RealNetworks. It arguably has the most advanced streaming infrastructure around and can scale to handle the largest broadcasts. RBN's broadcast facilities can take live, satellite, and uploaded feeds, and the price is fairly reasonable. The key downside to RBN is that it serves out content only in Real-related formats (that is, RealAudio). Thus, if you want to serve out content either in the MP3 format or in Windows Media Audio, you need to work with a different broadcast outsourcer. Whereas the RealServer can serve MP3 audio via plug-ins and the RealPlayer can listen to MP3 audio, RBN doesn't support it.

Pricing for RBN is based on the size of the contract you sign. At the time of this writing, pricing was offered in the form of three-month and twelve-month contracts. A twelve-month contract, which includes plenty of room for storage of media and good bandwidth, is approximately $1,000 per month. For three-month contracts, the per month cost is much higher. With RBN, as with other outsourcers, when you have streamed a certain amount of content within a given month, you are charged a rate per megabyte, which can send the cost higher. Overall, RBN's pricing is pretty decent, but given the requirement for a three-month or twelve-month contract, it's not the best outsourcer for event-based or short-term broadcasts.

Akamai

Another major streaming services company is Akamai (**www.akamai.com**) which offers streaming services of many kinds. Focused mostly on business-based streaming and broadcasting, this is a top-tier company that supports a variety of formats.

Yahoo! Broadcast Services

Formerly Broadcast.com, the division of Yahoo! Broadcast known as
Yahoo! Broadcast Services works as an outsourcer. It lets you take
advantage of its well-developed Dallas-based Internet broadcast facility.
Yahoo! Broadcast supports broadcasting in Windows Media and
RealMedia.

Second-Tier Audio Hosting Providers

Any Web hosting provider that lets you set up and run streaming audio
can be categorized as an audio hosting provider. In fact, many Web hosting
companies are branching out to offer audio streaming services as part of
their overall Web hosting services. Although these types of audio hosting
providers claim to offer the same product as Evoke.com or Yahoo!
Broadcast, more often than not, they don't offer the same level of service.
Typically, they offer you some level of server access and Web connectivity,
but even medium-sized Web hosts may not have the distribution and
backbone access networks of top-tier outsourcers. For smaller-sized
broadcasters, these limitations might not be an issue whatsoever, but for
large broadcasters and event-style broadcasts, these second-tier providers
may not provide the level of scalability, expertise, and round-the-clock
monitoring that may be necessary.

Questions to Ask
Your Outsourcing Company

You should ask any potential outsourcing company a number of questions
before making a decision.

Can the company handle your type of audio stream?

Not every outsourcer or audio hosting provider enables you to broadcast
in every given audio format. Most support RealAudio, and some support
Windows Media Audio. Very few support MP3 audio.

What encoding services does the company offer?

If you're going to need onsite encoding, you had better ask what type of
encoding services the company can offer; otherwise, you need to do the
encoding yourself.

What promotional help can the company give you?

A key part to any good outsourcing company is promotional capability. The best companies can offer some level of promotional support to help you build an audience. Some companies charge extra fees for promotional opportunities, whereas other companies do a number of things beyond just pumping out the stream as part of their overall service. Before you choose an outsourcer, ask the company what promotional capabilities and services it brings to the table and what, if any, extra fees are required to take advantage of those services.

TIP

Yahoo! Broadcast Services does not automatically promote any broadcast it hosts. Its policy is to pick broadcasts for promotion that its editors feel will be of interest to the general audience. Although advertising opportunities are available, in addition to general promotion, no distinct promotional quid pro quo is offered with a Yahoo! Broadcast Services-hosted station or show.

What's the largest broadcast the company has handled?

Although it's unlikely your broadcast—be it an event or just a traditional show or station—will top out the best broadcast networks, you can get a good idea of a company's capacity and scalability by finding out about the larger-sized broadcasts it has handled. Most of the top-tier providers have handled broadcasts with thousands of simultaneous listeners, so with them, you probably have little to worry about. For smaller-sized audio hosting providers, however, you should ask about their bandwidth availability, largest-sized audience, and latency issues.

How does the company's network fare to your key geographic audience?

Most top-tier services have excellent access to the fastest types of lines and the major Internet backbones. However, this access doesn't guarantee that their streams will have good reach to your desired location. Chances are, if it's within North America, any of the top-tier services can broadcast very well to your desired audience. If, however, you're trying to reach audiences in Europe or Asia, you might want to consider working with local companies or divisions in those markets.

Part II Radio Station Software

Audio Homesteading Services

An *audio homesteading service* is the Internet radio equivalent of GeoCities or Tripod. This service supplies you a method with which to send out an audio stream for free, and in return, it offers you additional services for a fee or piggyback advertising on your stream and station home page. It's the typical symbiotic relationship of many free-oriented Web services, and for the hobbyist broadcaster, an audio homesteading service is a great tool.

Most hobbyists and personal radio station operators don't have the available bandwidth to broadcast a station to the masses, let alone 50 or 100 listeners. Even those users who have access to a DSL or cable modem connection might not want to or be allowed to use all their available upstream bandwidth to broadcast their stations. Additionally, homesteading services can help you promote your station, help give you content, and in some cases, provide you with umbrella rights protection from ASCAP, BMI, and other rights organizations (they don't all do that, so be sure to look at the details!).

Right now, a couple of homesteading services are out there, with the best known being Live365.com.

Introducing Live365.com

Live365.com got started in early 1999 when SHOUTcast first appeared. Realizing that people would need bandwidth and other radio station services, this startup offered SHOUTcasters the ability to send them streams, which they would then rebroadcast and aggregate via their servers and site. The result was Live365.com.

Live365.com offers two types of services. LiveCast lets you supply a live stream to Live365, which it then sends back out via its large supply of bandwidth. EasyCast lets you store up to 365MB of data, which can then be broadcast to your audience.

Using LiveCast

LiveCast, as a service, has two options: You can provide a source stream via Winamp and its SHOUTcast source DSP plug-in, or you can use the built-in LiveCast Java applet to broadcast your MP3 files.

Step 1: Register for Live365.com

To begin using any of Live365.com's services, you must first sign up as a registered member of the site. To do so, go to the site, and click on the sign-up link, located in the upper left hand corner of the screen below the Live365.com logo, which takes you to the sign-up form page.

Using the form to register is about as easy as it can get to register for a site. You just enter the information and click on I Accept (which means you accept the terms of service), and your registration will go through (provided you picked a unique username). At that point, Live365 sends you a confirmation e-mail that means your initial registration and login are accepted. You can just click on the link supplied in the e-mail and type your password to go to a general Welcome screen. However, while generally registered, you are not registered to broadcast. To do so, you must click on the link that reads Register to Broadcast.

Step 2: Register to Broadcast/Choose Your Broadcasting Method

After registering for Live365.com, you need to instruct the service how you plan to broadcast with it, because you will be told that you aren't currently signed up to broadcast. You have these three major choices for broadcasting via Live365.com (see Figure 9.1):

▶ **EasyCast**—You can use this service to upload MP3 files to Live365.com, arrange a playlist, and then broadcast it.

▶ **Broadcast Live**—Using the LiveCast applet or Winamp, you can broadcast your MP3s directly to Live365.com, and this service will repeat it out to a larger group of listeners.

▶ **Relay Broadcast**—You can use this option to have Live365 connect to an existing broadcast and repeat from that server out to even more listeners.

Figure 9.1
On this screen, you can choose which broadcasting service you want to use.

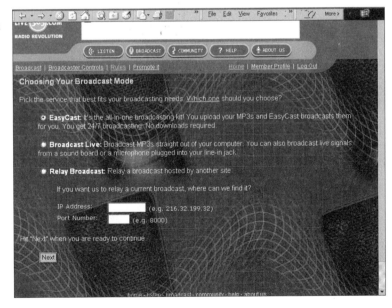

Choose the type of broadcasting service you want to use, and then click on Next. If you choose the Relay Broadcast option, you need to provide Live365 the exact IP address and port number of your SHOUTcast/icecast or other MP3 server broadcast.

Step 3: Using Winamp with LiveCast

To use Winamp for your LiveCast source, simply choose Broadcast Live from the screen described in the preceding section. When you click through, you are given confirmation of your choice. Click on the Broadcast Controls link to move through to the Broadcast Live screen.

The Broadcast Controls screen (see Figure 9.2) gives you three options. You can broadcast live using Live365.com's own LiveCast applet, or you can use "other tools" such as Winamp by clicking on the Other Tools button. Alternatively, you can choose Switch Broadcast Mode if you want to switch to a different broadcasting mode instead of using LiveCast.

Figure 9.2
The Broadcast Controls screen gives you three choices

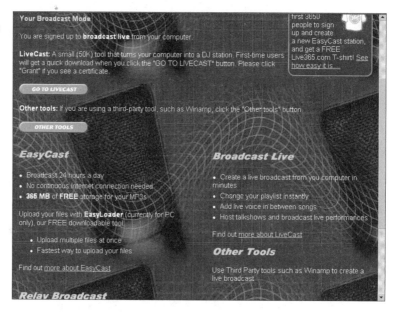

To use Winamp as the source for your LiveCast, choose Other Tools from the Broadcast Control screen. Live365.com then gives you a server IP address and port number (see Figure 9.3).

Figure 9.3
When you choose the Other Tools/Winamp method for LiveCast, you are assigned a unique IP address and port number to use.

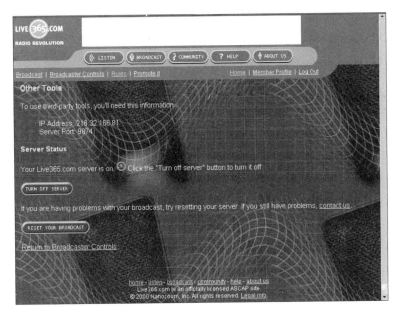

Plug this information into the server information dialog (see Figure 9.4) of the SHOUTcast Source DSP and then click on Connect to send it to the server.

Figure 9.4
Using Winamp's SHOUTcast Source DSP plug-in, enter the address and port number Live365.com assigned to you.

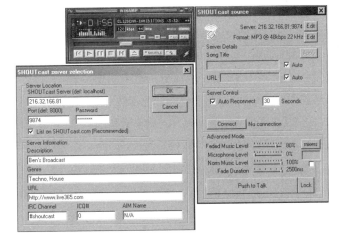

That should do it. With very little effort, you're now up and broadcasting via Winamp to the Live365.com servers, and from there, many more listeners can connect to your stream and listen away.

Part II Radio Station Software

Step 4: Using the LiveCast Applet

An alternative to using Winamp to send your stream to Live365.com is to use the services built in the LiveCast applet. Using this Java-based system, you can select files from your local machine, arrange them in a playlist, and then stream them to Live365.com right from your browser.

The big hang-up with LiveCast (and with EasyCast, which is described later) versus using Winamp is that you must encode your MP3 files at the exact same bit rate that you'll be broadcasting in. Also, due to bandwidth considerations, you can't broadcast MP3s encoded at a bit rate higher than 56kbps. Thus, you will probably be required to re-encode all your current MP3 files to a lower bit rate of 56, 32, or 24kbps because most MP3 files for local listening are encoded at 128kbps or higher. See Chapter 12 for more details on encoding your MP3 files.

After you have encoded or re-encoded the files you intend to broadcast, you can go to the LiveCast screen (see Figure 9.5) and set up your broadcast. On this screen, you have to fill out four items that describe your broadcast:

▶ Broadcast Title

▶ Broadcaster Web Site

▶ Minimum Connection Speed

▶ Genre(s)

Figure 9.5
On the LiveCast applet screen, you can configure and broadcast directly from any Web browser.

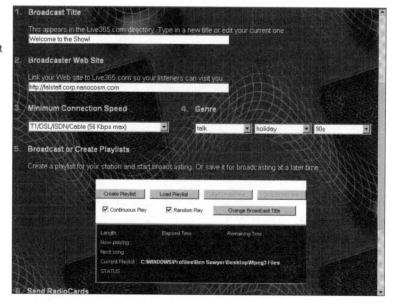

After filling out these four items, you must load files or a playlist into the LiveCast applet. Click on Create Playlist to bring up the Playlist Editor (see Figure 9.6), which enables you to locate files on your local machine and add them to a playlist. The dialog box is split into two list windows, with the left side showing MP3 files on your local machine (provided you have tuned it into a folder on the machine that has MP3 files) and the right side showing files you've selected for broadcast. Note that only MP3 files that are encoded at 56kbps or lower show up on the left side. If you check Only Show Best Files for Your Connection, the applet lists only files that have been encoded at the bit rate level you selected for your broadcast.

TIP

When you're tuning the LiveCast applet to a folder on your machine containing many MP3 files, loading all the files into the applet's list can take a decent amount of time (three to five minutes or more). Be patient because the applet is reading all the ID3 tag information to denote the length of the file and the bit rate at which it is encoded. The applet might seem to be stalled, but it really isn't.

Figure 9.6
LiveCast includes a
Java-based Playlist
Editor.

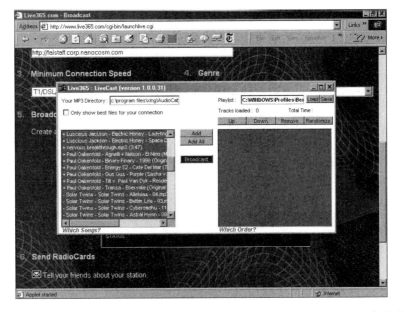

When you see a file that you want for your broadcast, select it and click on the Add button in the middle of the dialog box to send it to your playlist. When you're on the playlist side of dialog box, you can move files up or down in the playlist or randomize the list by using the buttons labeled as such in the upper-right corner of the dialog.

After you have created your ideal playlist, click the Save button on the editor to save the playlist for future use.

When you are satisfied with your playlist, click on the Broadcast button to begin broadcasting your station.

Using EasyCast

EasyCast doesn't have a live feed to Live365.com. Instead, you can store all your MP3 files on its servers directly, and then you can develop a playlist, set some additional parameters, and begin streaming to your listeners.

Using the EasyCast screen (see Figure 9.7), you can set your basic broadcast parameters and then upload songs to your 365MB of server space. When you're done uploading, songs can be arranged into playlists and broadcast. With EasyCast, as with the LiveCast applet, you must supply MP3 files that are encoded at 56, 32, or 24kbps bit rates, or they will be skipped and will not be played.

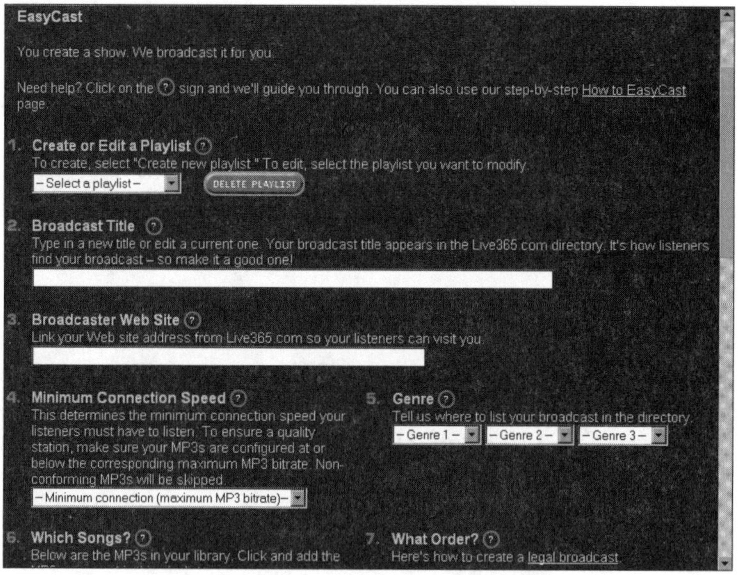

Figure 9.7
Using EasyCast, you can store MP3 files directly on Live365's servers and broadcast them from your online vault.

To upload MP3 files to your site, you need to go to the upload page of EasyCast. Then click on the Browse button to bring up a file open dialog box (see Figure 9.8) and find the file you want to upload. After you've selected it, click on the Upload button, and the file is uploaded to Live365.com. When the file is finished uploading, the page refreshes and the uploaded file will appear in the Your MP3 Library list. At that point, you can select any file from the list and choose Delete to remove files from the archive. When your list is complete, click on the Go to EasyCast button.

Figure 9.8
The Upload Page of EasyCast is a browser-based uploading service.

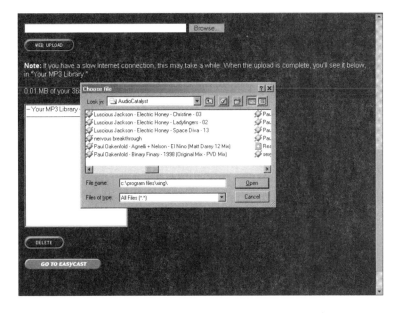

After you've uploaded a bunch of files to your MP3 archive, it's time to create a playlist. On the EasyCast main screen, you'll see two lists (see Figure 9.9). The list on the left is your archive, and the one on the right is the current playlist. Choose the files you want, and click on the Add button to move them over to the playlist. You can use buttons to move items up and down the playlist as well as delete, alphabetize, and randomize the playlist. When you're done, you can save the playlist to Live365.com, and you can have multiple playlists as well.

Figure 9.9
Playlist editing with EasyCast consists of moving files from your archive onto a list and then arranging that list as desired, all via a simple Web-based interface.

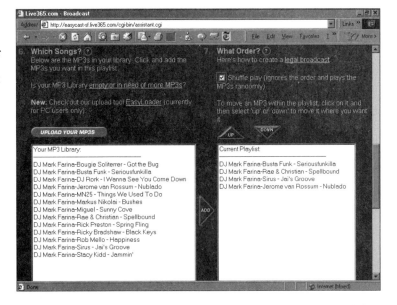

Part II Radio Station Software

When you have a playlist set the way you want, click on Broadcast Now! to begin broadcasting your station or show.

Live365.com's EasyLoader

To make it easier to upload content to the EasyCast service, in the spring of 2000, Live365 introduced EasyLoader, a Windows application that you download to your computer which makes it easy to batch upload your MP3 files to the EasyCast service. Not only will it batch upload, but it will convert the bitrates to match your outgoing bitrate. This is a great feature that means you can avoid having to separately encode for purposes of using their service.

The EasyLoader applet (Figure 9.10) is fairly simple to use. It is essentially a modified common Windows Open/Save dialog box. In the file listing window, find and select (use CTRL when selecting multiple files) as many MP3 files as you wish to upload. Enter your account information and password, and when you are satisfied, hit the upload button to begin the conversion and upload process.

Figure 9.10
By using the EasyLoader applet, you'll save yourself a lot of time with this batch uploader/converter for the Live365.com EasyCast Service.

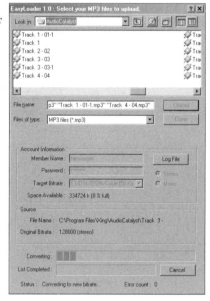

EasyLoader will check all the files and, if they are not of the target bitrate you've set for your broadcast, will convert them to the proper bitrate while uploading. When the EasyLoader application is done, you can get a log of its work by clicking the Log button to ensure all the files were able to upload properly.

The EasyCast solution provided by Live365.com is easy to use except for the fact that, with its default Web-based interface, you must upload one file at a time and it must be in the bitrate of your target broadcast. By using EasyLoader, you avoid this one tough aspect of the EasyCast service.

Alternatives to Live365

Live365.com was the first audio homesteading service out of the gate, but it isn't the last. A few other companies are getting into the mix as well. Not every one of these services is as flexible as Live365, and some aren't open to all comers automatically like Live365.com, but you might want to consider them. Not only can they be viable alternatives, but if you're really trying to enjoy the idea of broadcasting, you might use all these available services to reach out to an ever wider audience or to launch different genres of stations for yourself, your friends, or the greater Internet masses.

AudioRealm.com

AudioRealm.com (shown in Figure 9.11), a Texas-based company, is offering access to its streaming servers for select stations that are attracting audiences, providing good content, and using their SAM broadcasting tool (see Appendix D).

Figure 9.11
AudioRealm.com is another company offering bandwidth homesteading.

MyPlay.com

MyPlay.com (shown in Figure 9.12) is an online MP3 vault that also allows you to set up an on-demand radio station. It works in a fashion similar to Live365's EasyCast system. First, you upload your files to your private online vault, which can hold up to 250MB of MP3 data. Then you create a playlist and post it on the site for people to listen to. When your playlist is up, anyone on the Web can connect to the MyPlay.com service and listen to your tracks.

Figure 9.12

MyPlay.com offers an on demand radio station system that works in a fashion similar to Live365's EasyCast system.

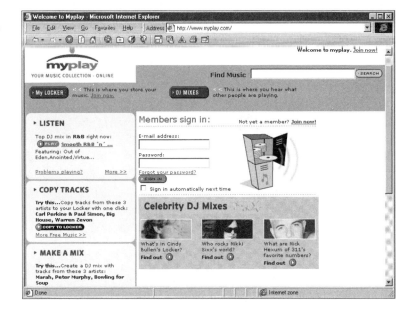

Note that to reach the widest possible audience with your station, you should encode your MP3s at a bit rate much lower than 128kbps. Like Live365.com, MyPlay.com doesn't recast your MP3 files to lower bit rates when they are streamed. To reach users with 28.8 modems, you need to encode your music at 24kbps. Higher rates such as 32kbps or 56kbps are also possible, but you will be shutting out lower-bandwidth modem users as you raise the bit rate.

Using MyPlay.com to Create an Online Radio Station

MyPlay.com is fairly easy to use. In four easy steps, you can post a playlist and have it available to the public.

Step 1: Register for MyPlay.com

To use MyPlay.com, you first must register with the service. To do so, enter your e-mail, password, and username preferences. Then click on login, and if your username is accepted, you are sent to a music test screen (see Figure 9.13)

Figure 9.13
The music test screen of MyPlay.com ensures you have your system properly configured.

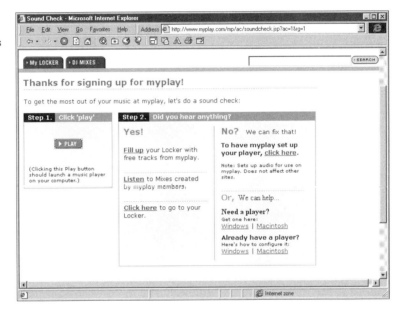

Part II Radio Station Software

Click on the Play button on the music test screen, and if you hear music, then you have a system correctly configured for MyPlay.com (you should be fine if you're already stocked to the max with audio players that are properly configured). Click on the Click here to go to your locker link to move straight into your private MP3 vault.

Step 2: Stock Your Online Locker

When you first get to your locker, you will find only one file in it: a welcome message from MyPlay.com's founders, Doug and David (see Figure 9.14). To add files to your locker, you must choose from one of three links under the heading Add Music, on the left side of the screen.

Figure 9.14

Your locker is pretty empty when you first set up MyPlay.com.

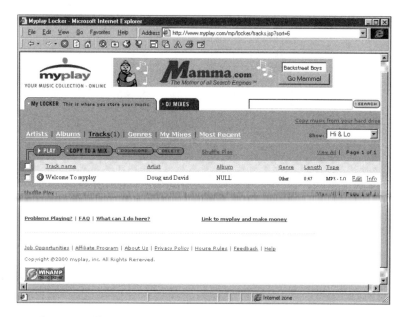

MyPlay.com offers four ways for you to get music into your locker. First, you can add tracks from music that MyPlay.com makes available to its users. Second, you can add tracks from partner sites on the Web that allow you to add free tracks to your MyPlay.com locker. These sites include eMusic, Tunes.com, and Knitting Factory Records, to name a few. A third option is to upload tracks directly from your computer via a Web-based form. Finally, Windows users can select to alternatively use the MyPlay.com DropBox, a special applet that you download to your computer. Using this applet, you can just drag MP3 files from any folder on your system and automatically upload them to your locker.

To add a free track from MyPlay.com, choose Free Tracks from the Add Music menu. Then, on the Free Tracks screen (see Figure 9.15), click on the either +128k link or the +28.8k link to add the music to your locker. The 28.8k links are better if you intend to make your playlists available to the widest possible listening audience.

Figure 9.15
MyPlay.com offers free tracks you can include in your broadcast.

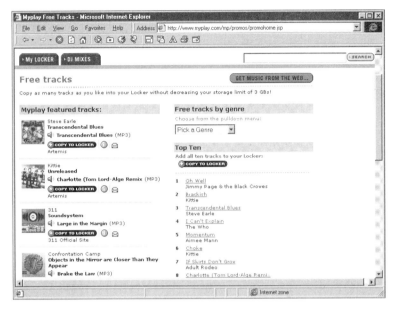

To add a track from other sites on the Web, choose From the Web from the Add Music menu. You then go to a screen highlighting other partner sites and music you can remotely send to your MyPlay.com locker. From there, you can select any song you think would be interesting. A separate window launches for that service and song; there, you will find green + (plus) links to add the song to your MyPlay.com locker (see Figure 9.16). Click on the link to begin the transfer.

Figure 9.16
In addition to free tracks on MyPlay.com, partner sites offer you tracks as well.

If you want to add a track from your own computer, the most direct way is to choose From My Computer from the Add Music menu. Doing so launches a simple form that includes a Browse button. You can use this button to select a single track from your computer to upload to your locker (see Figure 9.17). If you want to do a batch upload, you need to use the MyPlay.com DropBox applet.

Figure 9.17
You can use this form to upload from your computer to your MyPlay.com locker.

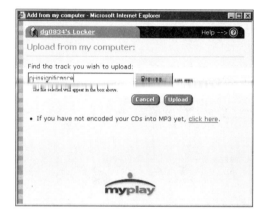

To do easier batch-style uploads, you need to use the MyPlay.com DropBox, which is a Windows 95/98-based application (with other platforms forthcoming). A link to the DropBox download page is included on the menu on the left side of MyPlay.com, or you can find it directly at **www.myplay.com/mp/locker/client.jsp**. When you're on the page, click on the Download Now! button, and the applet will begin to download. You must confirm to accept the download and then run through a simple setup program. You need to restart your computer, but at that point, it will be set up.

You can initialize the DropBox applet by choosing the Launch DropBox program from your Windows Start menu. The DropBox Applet, when first run, prompts you to indicate how it should be displayed (we choose to make it appear in the system tray only). When it is running, it displays a small box in the lower-right corner of your machine (see Figure 9.18). If that box is not there, you can right-click on the system tray icon and choose Display DropBox from the menu. When the applet is running, simply drag any MP3 file(s) from any folder to your DropBox (or right-click on them and choose Send to My MyPlay Locker from the menu), and it is uploaded.

Figure 9.18
The MyPlay DropBox applet makes batch uploading to your locker a snap.

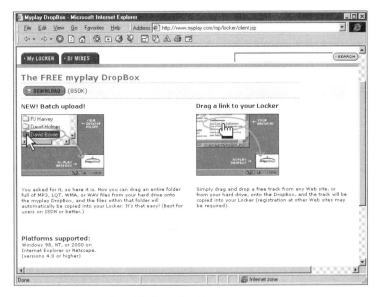

Step 3: Create and Publish a Playlist

To begin creating a playlist, choose Create a Playlist from the Organize Music menu on the left side to bring up the Edit Playlist page (see Figure 9.19). On this page, the first thing to do is to select a genre from the genre drop-down list. The page does not let you move on to select tracks from your vault until you select a genre. You might also want to type a name for your playlist in the field provided at the top of the page. In the description box, you can type a brief description of the playlist, such as the types of music and names of artists in the playlist.

Figure 9.19
The Playlist Editor includes some basic configuration fields and a simple playlist ordering interface.

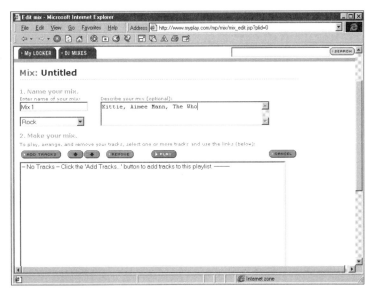

If tracks are already in the playlist (for example, you're re-editing a previously created playlist), they are listed below. You can use the up and down arrows to move tracks up and down in the playlist and choose the Remove button to delete a song from the playlist. Buttons and links are also provided to play any individual file on the playlist in case you need to hear it first; you also can select all, none, or invert the selections on the list.

TIP

You can use the Shift and Ctrl keys along with mouse clicks to highlight multiple files within the playlist.

To add tracks to your playlist, you click on the Add Tracks button, which takes you to the Add Tracks page (see Figure 9.20). To add tracks to your playlist, check off the tracks you want in the playlist, and click on the Add Tracks To button. Doing so returns you to the previous playlist editing page, where you can set your arrangement.

Figure 9.20
To create a playlist, you first have to select files from your vault to load into the initial playlist.

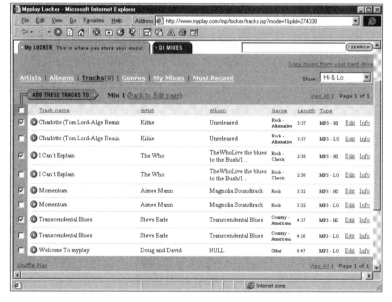

When you are done editing your playlist, click on the Save button. To publish your playlist, choose Post a Playlist from the Share Music menu on the left side of MyPlay.com. This way, you can first select the playlist you want to post. When you click on Post, MyPlay.com analyzes the playlist to see whether it is compliant with the DMCA guidelines. If it is not, you are given a warning screen. If it is compliant, the playlist is posted and can be accessed by people coming to MyPlay.com.

MyPlay.com tries to strictly enforce the statutory license broadcasting rules outlined in the Digital Millennium Copyright Act (DMCA), which means building a playlist that conforms to the rules outlined in Chapter 16.

It also means that your published playlists may stay active for only two weeks, at which point playlists that have been unchanged and unattended for two weeks are removed from the service. So, if you plan to use MyPlay.com for broadcasting, you should make sure you absolutely keep juggling that playlist and conform to the basic rules of the DMCA statutory license.

Step 4: Finding and Promoting Your Playlist

When your playlist is active, you can find it by browsing through published playlists. You can also use the E-mail a Playlist option on MyPlay.com to e-mail a direct link to the playlist. Each unique playlist has a playlist ID number associated with it that is embedded in a link that starts automatically streaming a playlist to a user. To embed a playlist link on your personal Web page, find it on the playlist, copy the shortcut (right-click on the green play link and choose Copy Shortcut), and then paste that link into your Web page. A typical playlist link looks as follows:

http://www.myplay.com/mp/playlist/now_playing.jsp?plid=30814&start=1

Playlists that are popular make it into top-ten lists published on MyPlay.com. It has an overall top ten and a top ten for each genre category.

Part II Radio Station Software

Soak Up That Bandwidth

Bandwidth isn't cheap. A T1 line costs at least $1,000 per month and can cost as much as $1,500 per month, depending on the area of the country you're in (and the service level you purchase) plus the quality of the ISP. So, if you want to make the most of broadcasting—especially as a hobbyist—you need to piggyback on someone else's bandwidth. That is precisely why companies such as Live365, MyPlay.com, and AudioRealm have come into vogue. They can derive revenue to pay for bandwidth by earning advertising dollars from your streaming content. In some cases, they may even cut you in for some money they generate due to the audience you create, if you're an exceptionally great broadcaster. (If not, a number of services have plans for this sort of payment scheme in the future).

Professional broadcasters also can take advantage of bandwidth available. Depending on your reach, broadcast frequency, and needs, having a commercial outsourcer such as Evoke.com or RBN transmit your streaming audio for you could be cheaper than having your own T1 line(s). First, you don't have any of the management or equipment headaches, and second, you pay only for the bandwidth you use. With a T1 line, you pay a monthly fee whether or not you use all the available power it offers you.

So, whether you're a commercial broadcaster, professional, or hobbyist, there are many reasons to take advantage of outsourced bandwidth and services. If you're a hobbyist, one great idea is to use the services of MyPlay.com, Live365.com, MyCaster, and others as they appear to proliferate your broadcasts and find as many listeners as you can. If the bandwidth's there, why not soak it up and make the most of it?

10

Building a Web Site for Your Station

Every good radio station should have an accompanying Web site or some sort of Web components. Although many people run a station, the true pros or hobbyists want to have some sort of Web presence. And having a Web presence is actually one of the best aspects of having an Internet radio station.

It's important to understand that a Web presence need not necessarily be a conventional Web site. For example, you might have a single-page site and use communications functionality such as a chat room or ICQ messaging to maintain a presence on the Web. Or you might just use the automated screens generated by the SHOUTcast (see Chapter 5) server system.

Deciding What Makes a Good Complementary Site

In general, a good radio site is not unlike most corporate or personal Web pages: it explains all the information and background about the station and provides a way for visitors to interact with the people behind it.

Overall, a good radio show or station Web site should do the following:

▶ Provide information about the station or show and the people who run and host it

▶ Provide a means for visitors to interact with the station, whether by sending in music requests or asking on-air or off-air questions

▶ Provide extended features and content based on the programming of the station

Part II Radio Station Software

Although every radio site is different, we can map out some general areas to provide a solid outline of the types of pages and features a complementary Web site for an Internet radio station or show should have. You need not create a site with every page or feature we've listed, but for the rest of the chapter, we'll cover in detail how to implement each one of these ideas:

Informational Pages

About station—Tells users basic information about the station

DJ biographies—Provides background information on show hosts or station DJs

News page—Gives the latest station and related news

Guest biographies—Provides biographical information about past and present guests

Broadcast schedule—Gives a weekly view of upcoming broadcasts

Music library—Lists songs and material in regular rotation

Downloads page—Provides links to products and tools that listeners should have

Interactive Pages and Features

Message boards—Provide the means for people to post messages

Chat room and IRC chat—Give users the chance to chat live with DJs and fans

E-mail mailing list—Lets listeners sign up to be notified about cool events

Question/request form—Provides an onsite form to request a song or ask a question

Immediate messaging—Gives listeners a quick way to interact with the on-air DJ

Current and past playlists—Give the title of the current song being played and the last ten

Voice chat—Provides a means for people to chat live with DJs

E-Commerce Pages

Links to record stores—Provide links to CD stores as a key source of revenue

Links to other stores—Provide links to other relevant e-commerce sites

Miscellaneous Features

Webcam—Lets users see into your studios

Building Your Informational Pages

Building a good site—whether it be for your station, show, or any Web topic—requires that you have some basic understanding of Web design, Hypertext Markup Language (HTML), and some graphics. If you don't possess these skills and have never built a page before, this book can't help you. Table 10.1 lists some very good books you can use to acquire skills and knowledge about designing Web pages and graphics.

Table 10.1
Books for Web Design and Graphics Help

The Best Web Design Books Worth Having

HTML 4 for the World Wide Web: Visual QuickStart Guide, 4th Edition by Elizabeth Castro (Peachpit Press, 1999, ISBN: 0201354934)

Web Design in a Nutshell by Jennifer Neiderst (O'Reilly and Associates, 1998, ISBN: 1565925157)

JavaScript for the World Wide Web: Visual QuickStart Guide, 2nd Edition by Tom Negrino and Dori Smith (Peachpit Press, 1999, ISBN: 0201354632)

The Web Style Guide by Patrick J. Lynch and Sarah Horton (Yale University Press, 1999, ISBN: 0300076754)

Web Design Wow by Jack Davis and Susan Merritt (Peachpit Press, 1998, ISBN: 0201886782)

Designing Web Usability: The Practice of Simplicity by Jakob Neilsen (New Riders, 1999, ISBN: 156205810X)

The Best Web Graphics Program Books Worth Having

Photoshop 5.5 for Windows and Macintosh: Visual QuickStart Guide, by Elaine Weinmann and Peter Lourekas (Peachpit Press, 1999, ISBN: 0201699575)

Paint Shop Pro 6 Power! by Lori J. Davis (Muska & Lipman, 1999, ISBN: 066288920)

Designing Web Graphics by Linda Weinman (New Riders, 1999, ISBN: 1562059491)

PhotoImpact Solutions by Jason Dunn with Kate Binder (Muska & Lipman, 2000, ISBN: 1929685122)

HTML Resources Web Sites

Microsoft HTML For Beginners
http://msdn.microsoft.com/workshop/author/html/beghtml.asp
Straightforward HTML instruction

Netscape's Documentation Site
http://developer.netscape.com/docs/manuals/index.html
Netscape offers documentation on a number of Web technologies, including HTML

W3C's HTML Home Page
http://www.w3.org/MarkUp/
Includes HTML specifications and guidelines on using HTML.

Part II Radio Station Software

Main Page

Your main page can be anything you want, but however it looks, you should make sure it provides all the vital information about your station, especially how to access your broadcast. Many stations place a clear button or link to the audio stream prominently on the home page. That link is server specific, so refer to the specific chapter for each server for information on setting it up. In some cases, you need to configure or have your Web host configure your Web server's MIME type to match some of the special Internet radio data types, such as SHOUTcast's .PLS file format.

About Station or Show Page

The first place many people turn to on any Web site is the About page. Without it, you or your company is a mystery to your site's visitors. By providing an About Station or Show page, you can explain when your station or show was started, what the main format is, why the station or show exists, when it broadcasts, and so on.

DJ Biographies

The people behind your music, news, or call-in show should never be mysterious voices to your listeners. A great way to make sure of this is to post biographies of the people behind the station.

TIP

Biographies can be more or less boring if they're done in a formal style. Instead of doing plain old bios, you can have your DJs explain what in their life makes them fans of the music they play or what their expertise is. You should always relate the bio to the content that DJ produces.

News Page

Adding a news page to your Web site is simple enough, but you can make use of a few tricks to provide for a much more enhanced onsite news section.

First, you can include basic station-related news, such as upcoming specials, news about new DJs, or details on contests. This you'll just have to do on your own, writing it up and placing it on a page. If you've never written news items for the Web, remember this one point: Keep it short and simple.

You should also place links to relevant news sources on your site; however, just placing links is a little on the lazy side. If you really want to jazz up your page, you can provide links and forms that let people do more than just click through to another news site. Next, we'll provide some ideas and HTML code snippets you can use.

One of the best places to go for free news content is iSyndicate (**www.isyndicate.com**). This site specializes in distributing free and paid-for syndicated content to Web sites. The free content includes major headlines and photos you can embed directly onto your own site. You can start by going to the iSyndicate home page and registering for the service. iSyndicate then sends you a password to log in to the site and configure content.

When you log in for the first time, you are greeted with an iSyndicate screen that shows five headline blocks (see Figure 10.1). You can also create your own headline block by entering the name of a new block in the Create field and then clicking on the Create button.

Figure 10.1
iSyndicate offers several content categories you can choose from.

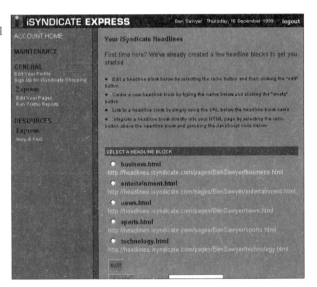

Creating a "music news" block is simple enough. First, you can enter **music news** in the Create field and then click through. iSyndicate then shows you various content categories it offers.

Choosing Entertainment brings up subcategories, including Music. Clicking on Music yields (at the time of this writing) eighteen distinct sources of content iSyndicate offers; they include LAUNCH: Music News, RollingStone.com: News, and Billboard Music News, among others. To add a source to your custom headline block, click on the appropriate link. iSyndicate then replies with a sample of the headline content and displays an Add button you can choose to confirm adding that particular piece of content to your headline block (see Figure 10.2).

Figure 10.2
You can preview the content and then click on Add to add it to your headline block.

After an item is added to your headline block, you must set its preferences, as shown in Figure 10.3. For example, you need to set the position in the headline block among other content items and the number of headlines to display. After you set these preferences, choose Save Changes to register them or choose Add More Content to go back to the previous menu and add other headline content.

Figure 10.3
Here, you can set your headline preferences.

After you choose Save Changes, the site shows you a preview of your headline content (see Figure 10.4). At the top of this page are five buttons. Content sends you back to the previous page, where you can set preferences for headlines or choose more content; Preview shows you the preview page; Publish takes you to a new page where you can get the code to enable the content on your site; and Cancel, of course, kills the entire process. Style takes you to a page where you can customize the look and feel of the content (see Figure 10.5). Formatting the style here is as simple as making choices from a Web form, configuring your style as you like, and choosing Save to preview the content as styled.

Figure 10.4
You can view the headline content before you get started.

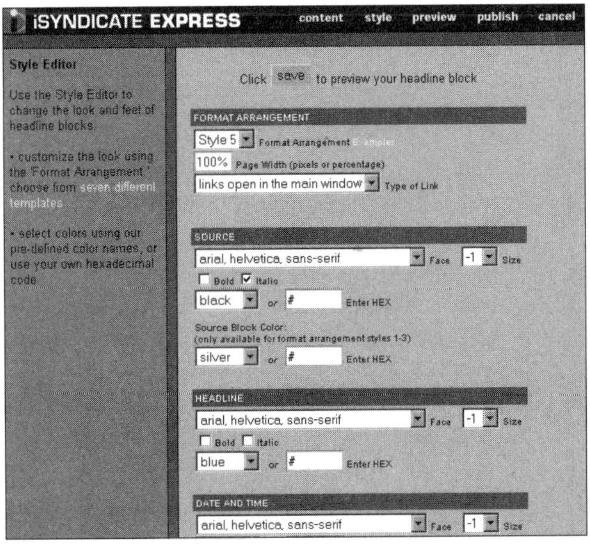

Figure 10.5
Customize the look and feel of your content with the Style Editor.

After you get all the headlines you want and have configured the look and feel, it's time to publish your content on your site. Choose Publish at the top of the page to confirm the changes, and you are taken to the Publish menu, from which you can select the headline block you want. When you do, in the JavaScript box below the code to embed in your news page, you will see the following:

```
<SCRIPT LANGUAGE="JavaScript"
SRC="http://headlines.isyndicate.com/pages/BenSawyer/musicnews.
js"></SCRIPT>
```

You can place this code on your instant music news page for your station.

Another idea to spice up your news page is to add other content from iSyndicate—for example, major news headlines, photos, and other content. You should take the time to explore the site because it has a lot of cool content you can add for free.

A popular news ticker application is 7am.com. You can place this small Java applet on your page to deliver major world headlines. To place it on your page, go to the installation page and follow the simple instructions at **http://www.7am.com/ticker/code.htm**.

Guest Biographies

Although guests on your station or show will surely be introduced with short bios, if your listeners want to know more details, they might hit your Web site to see whether you've posted further information about the guests. Guest biographies are great content for your site. Here are some suggestions of what to include:

▶ URLs to guests' personal or company home pages

▶ Photos of the guests and anything else relevant to their appearance, such as book covers, album covers, or software downloads

▶ Enhanced biographies versus what is read on-air

▶ Links to books they've written or other associated products

Broadcast Schedule

If you run a station that broadcasts distinct shows at specific times, or you have a show or station that broadcasts only at distinct times, publishing a schedule on the site for users is a good thing to do. Otherwise, you'll never maximize your listenership for specific content you broadcast.

Figure 10.6 shows a simple Web-based schedule for a fictitious station. It is simply a well-designed table using HTML; in it, you can insert the necessary information to alert listeners to what is playing on the station or when your station is broadcasting.

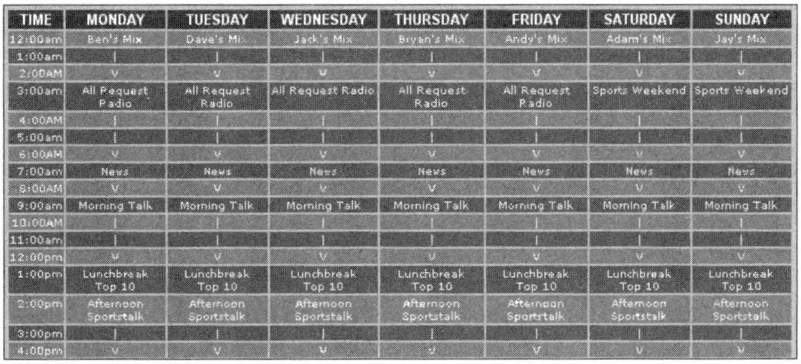

Figure 10.6
If you run different shows and themes throughout a week, use the Web to publish a schedule of your station's content.

TIME	MONDAY	TUESDAY	WEDNESDAY	THURSDAY	FRIDAY	SATURDAY	SUNDAY
12:00am	Ben's Mix	Dave's Mix	Jack's Mix	Bryan's Mix	Andy's Mix	Adam's Mix	Jay's Mix
1:00am							
2:00AM							
3:00am	All Request Radio	All Request Radio	All Request Radio	All Request Radio	All Request Radio	Sports Weekend	Sports Weekend
4:00AM							
5:00am							
6:00AM							
7:00am	News	News	News	News	News	News	News
8:00AM							
9:00am	Morning Talk	Morning Talk	Morning Talk	Morning Talk	Morning Talk	Morning Talk	Morning Talk
10:00AM							
11:00am							
12:00pm							
1:00pm	Lunchbreak Top 10	Lunchbreak Top 10	Lunchbreak Top 10	Lunchbreak Top 10	Lunchbreak Top 10	Lunchbreak Top 10	Lunchbreak Top 10
2:00pm	Afternoon Sportstalk	Afternoon Sportstalk	Afternoon Sportstalk	Afternoon Sportstalk	Afternoon Sportstalk	Afternoon Sportstalk	Afternoon Sportstalk
3:00pm							
4:00pm							

Music Library

If you have a music-oriented station, you must remember that it's a violation of the statutory license to specifically detail a schedule of music you will play ahead of time. Although you can list current songs played, past songs played, and the song or songs you expect to play sometime in the next hour, you can't say that you will play Song X at 4:15 p.m. tomorrow.

This restriction doesn't mean, however, that you can't publish on your site all the music that is in your library that you will be putting in regular rotation from time to time. This full library list can be fun for listeners to look at to get an idea of the kind of station you have. It also enables listeners to make requests or even offer to trade music you have in your collection (provided it is freely tradable to begin with; don't start swapping the Metallica and Korn now).

Publishing a music library on your site is easy enough if you use MP3 files as your content. Using the Winamp Player, you can take any playlist currently loaded into memory and output it as an HTML file. In the Playlist view, you can simply select the MISC button and then choose Generate HTML Playlist from the menu (or press Ctrl+Alt+G), and Winamp will generate a playlist instantly, as shown in Figure 10.7. You can post that file as is or edit it to conform to the style of your site.

Part II Radio Station Software

Figure 10.7
Winamp can automatically generate an HTML playlist for you to post on your site.

WINAMP
playlist

75 tracks in playlist, average track length: 4:26
Playlist length: 5 hours 32 minutes 45 seconds
Right-click here to save this HTML file.

Playlist files:

summer daze
Solar Twins - Puppet
Track 15 - 15
DJ Rap - Learning Curve - Live it for today - 06
Paul Oakenfold - Binary Finary - 1998 (Original Mix - PVD Mix)
Track 2 - 02
Def Leppard - Let It Go
Solar Twins - Swayambhu
Track 1
Track 1 - 01
DJ Rap - Learning Curve - Bad Girl - 01
Solar Twins - Love Your Love
Track 13 - 13
Solar Twins - Astral Hymn
friends
Track 4 - 04-1
Solar Twins - Rock The Casbah
Solar Twins - Out There
Solar Twins - Living Your Dream
Solar Twins - Cybersadhu
DJ Rap - Learning Curve - Stories From Around The World - 10
Track 5 - 05
Track 3 - 03
Solar Twins - Puppet
Solar Twins - Alleluias

Downloads Page

Some broadcasters might want to put downloads in a section on the station's home page, whereas others may decide to give them their own page. Wherever you decide to place downloads, by all means, you should include links to all the relevant products listeners of your station will want to have. For example, you can recommend the following:

▶ Players to listen with (for example, Winamp, Real Player 7, and so on)

▶ Programs that enhance incoming streams (for example, WowThing! or Qsound)

▶ Programs that you use to interact with your listeners (for example, ICQ or IRC Chat)

The links to these items are shown in Chapter 4.

TIP
Other items to include are links to programs that let people create their own stations. Remember that the next group of broadcasters will most likely emanate from people who are first listeners themselves. Help the industry grow!

Building Your Interactive Pages and Features

One of the key powers of the Internet lies in its capability to foster interactivity between you and your listeners as well as among listeners themselves. To promote such interactivity, though, you need to install features on your Web site to enable communications to take place.

Message Boards

Adding a message board to your site can be somewhat of a cumbersome process. This difficulty is compounded by the fact that, of the more than three dozen forum and message board hosting services, most of them are truly awful to use.

That being said, there are some easy ways to add a message board to your site for free, and if you want to purchase a product, there are some good packages to consider. Some hosted services are also available—although to date no clear leader is doing a great job in this area.

For free message boards, two leading services you can use are ezboard (**www.ezboard.com**), which is quite powerful and has many customizable options; and boardhost (**www.boardhost.com**), which is a much simpler service. If you think you'll have heavy usage of message boards, go with ezboard, which uses definable topic areas, folders, and other subcategories. If you want a casual, free-floating style that is more spur of the moment, your users will find boardhost much easier to manage and use. Figure 10.8 shows a boardhost site with a discussion underway.

Figure 10.8
Boardhost is a simple system that makes it easy for people to post messages to a bulletin board related to your station.

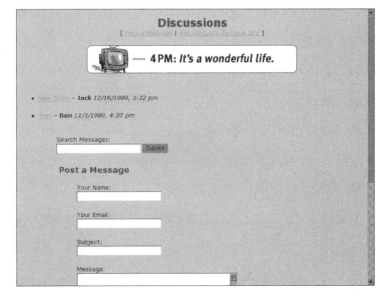

You set up both boardhost and ezboard by registering with the particular service and then using a series of Web-based forms to configure the rules and look of the board. After you have it set up, you can link to it from your station site, giving your visitors a forum for public posts. Both sites make it easy to add forum messages, delete unsavory postings, and place some limits on the content that is posted.

Even with the customizability of an ezboard, you might decide to do something a little more specific and professional and devoid of the banner ads associated with free board services. WebBoard from O'Reilly Software (**www.webboard.com**) is a good system to install on your own server, as is Allaire Forums (**www.allaire.com**).

For commercially hosted boards, Well Engaged (**www.wellengaged.com**) is a well-known and reviewed premium discussion board. Well Engaged's boards are used by E*Trade, Adobe, and Sportsline.com, among others.

Chat Room and IRC Chat

Adding a chat room to your site is easy enough. You have two choices: You can pay a service to host a room for you, or you can register and embed a free room on your site. You can also buy your own chat servers, but doing so is truly a waste of money for all but the highest end sites. The difference between a commercially hosted room and a free one is that the free room shows advertising banners while people are logged in to your chat room.

A good choice for both hosted or free chat rooms is ParaChat from Paralogic software (**www.parachat.com**). The company, which was acquired by XOOM.com (now part of NBCi), distributes the free chat room through the XOOM.com service, and the hosted version, which is ad free, through its Parachat.com site.

To get a free chat room, you first need to register with XOOM.com as a member. Then go to the Member Services page. Under the heading For Your Page, choose the Chat link, which will take you to a page where you can register for a chat room (see Figure 10.9). When registering for a chat room, you must supply the exact URL for the page on the Web that will feature the room. You can add an optional topic but leave *unchecked* the box that requires people to be XOOM.com members to join the chat room. Choose Create My Chat Room, and XOOM.com then displays a page of HTML code that you can cut and paste into the page that will feature the chat room.

Figure 10.9
Here, you can register for a free XOOM.com chat room.

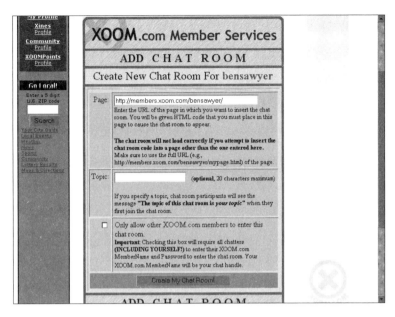

We recommend that you put the chat room on a separate page on your site that you can link people to. People visiting this page will be greeted by a Java applet (they must be able to run Java applets). On this page, they must provide a chat room name and, once accepted, are logged in for chatting, as shown in Figure 10.10. Your chat room can have up to 25 users maximum at any one time.

Figure 10.10
Your site's visitors can chat in a free XOOM.com-supplied chat room.

To obtain a commercially hosted chat room from Paralogic, go to the ParaChat site (**www.parachat.com**) and sign up for the hosted solution, which runs $50 or more a month, depending on the maximum number of users allowed and whether you pay annually. The basic service gives you a maximum of 25 users in your room, and if you pay up front for an entire year, the cost is $50 a month.

To obtain the room, fill out an order form and supply a credit card number on the Parachat.com Web site.

E-mail Mailing List

If you want people to keep tuning in and returning to your site, you need to remind them to do so. The best way to do that is to use e-mail reminders. A good type of reminder might be a newsletter or a few small paragraphs detailing the latest show or station happenings, upcoming guests, new music in rotation, and so on.

To capture e-mails, you need to provide a form on your site. Using that form, people can add their names to a database that keeps track of the names and automatically sends out e-mails to them.

To achieve this goal, you can use commercial services such as SKYLIST (www.skylist.net), or you can make use of two ad-supported free services: ListBot (**www.listbot.com**) or ONElist (**www.onelist.com**).

Both ListBot and ONElist are great services suitable for most small-sized stations or shows. With either service, you go to the site, fill out some forms to register for the service, and then you are supplied with code to place on a page on your site. This way, people can enter their e-mail right on your site to subscribe. Both lists let you set up as public or private and allow you to moderate members, add members, or remove them. ONElist is a little more flexible and robust in terms of list management, whereas ListBot offers the capability to compile (with permission) various demographic information. Both have no limits on the number of members. ListBot offers ListBot Gold, a $99/year service that lets you send out larger-sized messages that don't feature ads to up to 5,000 users per month.

Both services are managed entirely through a Web-based interface, although you can optionally moderate some features via e-mail interaction with the service. Both services also let you define a list as an announcement style (in which only you can post to the list) or as a discussion style (in which you and any other member can post to the list). If you do decide to go with a discussion-oriented list, be sure to set it to Moderate; otherwise, you risk allowing people to post anything and everything to your list whether you like it or not. With moderation set on, you can approve or disapprove of any message.

Question/Request Form

If you're featuring a talk-based format or show, you might want to provide an onsite form for people to send in on-air questions or comments. If you feature a music-based format or show, you might want to add an online request form. In either case, you need to design a Web form and set up a system to send the submitted information to the station's DJ, producer, or show host.

When it comes to designing forms, you need to be familiar with the basics of developing Web-based forms using your favorite Web editor or HTML code. All the books described in Table 10.1 have sections on this topic. You also need to configure the forms and your server system to send the information to the correct recipients. Every Web hosting provider and server system handles form remailing differently; there is no standard way to instruct you to do this. You should check with your Web hosting provider for specific instructions. Most systems require you to embed in the Web page hidden codes that name the recipient e-mail addresses and other traits for the system to execute mailing the forms when they are submitted.

Another way to execute such forms is to create simple ICQ-based forms.

Adding a Caller, Request, or DJ Message Form with ICQ

A cool way to add a request or DJ message form for your station is to use ICQ instant messaging and a Web-based form that lets people go to your site and ICQ you directly from your site. Your visitors' messages come through right away, so using this type of form is a great way to extend immediate messaging capability without requiring your listeners to have ICQ.

To add an ICQ form to your page, you can modify the following code as you see fit (be sure to place your ICQ number where the code mentions it):

```
<html>
<head>
<title>Untitled</title>
</head>
<body bgcolor="silver" link="#0000A0" vlink="#000068">
<table border="0" cellpadding="0" cellspacing="0">
<tr><td colspan=2>
<form action="http://wwp.icq.com/scripts/WWPMsg.dll"
   method="post">
<font face="arial" size="3"><b>Send in your request via
   ICQ!</b><hr></font>
</TD></tr>
<tr><td><font size="-1" face="Arial">Name:</font></td><td><font
   size-"-1" face="Arial">Email:</font></td></tr>
<tr>
<td><input type="TEXT" name="from" value="" size=30
   maxlength=40 onfocus="this.select()"></td>
<td><input type="TEXT" name="fromemail" value="" size=30
   maxlength=40 onfocus="this.select()"></td>
</tr>
<tr><td colspan="2">
<div align="center"><font size="1" face="Arial">It is
   recommended to enter your e-mail so a reply can be sent to
   you.<br><br></font></div>
```

```
<font face="arial" size="-1"><b>Your Message:</b></font>
</td></tr>
<tr><td colspan=2>
<font size="-1" face="Arial">Subject:</font><br>
<input type="TEXT" name="subject" value="" size=64
   maxlength=20 onfocus="this.select()">
</td></tr>
<tr><td colspan=2>
<font size="-1" face="Arial">Message:</font><br><textarea
   name="body" rows="6" cols="55"
   wrap="Virtual"></textarea><br>
<font face="ms sans serif" size="-2"><b>Note</b>: only the
   first 450 characters of the message will be
   transmitted<br></b></font>
</td></tr>
<tr><td colspan="2" align="center">
<input type="HIDDEN" name="to" value="PUT YOUR ICQ NUMBER
   HERE!">
<input type="SUBMIT" name="Send" value="Send
   Message">  
<input type="reset" value="Clear">
</td></tr>
<tr><td colspan=2 align="center">
<font size="1" face="Arial"><br>
Your message will be delivered to the user immediately,
   appearing on the DJ's screen<br>
if they are not logged on, they will receive this message as
   soon as they connect to the net.<br><br>
<b>Please note</b>: Your message is stamped with your IP
   address and the time of sending.<br><br>
</font>
</form>
</td></tr>
</table>
```

The great thing about this form process is that messages are sent as soon as possible to the DJ's ICQ—and therefore can make it on the air right away.

Current and Past Song Playlists

When you get to Chapter 16, which discusses the legal ins and outs of running your station, you'll see that one requirement of the statutory license for Internet radio stations is that you must do your best to publish, at the time of playing, every song name and artist you feature on your stations if you're playing commercially published music. For many systems, publishing playlists isn't a difficult process. In fact, SHOUTcast actually streams the title of a song down to the player itself, and the MusicTicker plug-in for SHOUTcast can display current songs and the last ten or more songs you played right on your Web site.

Adding Dynamic Playlists with MusicTicker

The MusicTicker Plug-in by Atul Varma enables you to output information about your current playlist to an HTML page that you might display on your server (see Figure 10.11). The idea is to make it easy for people to see the current file playing on your station and some of the files that have been played recently. This list makes it easy for users to find the names of a song you may have played 10 or 20 minutes ago.

Figure 10.11
MusicTicker lists the songs most recently played on the Amish Web Posse's Station site.

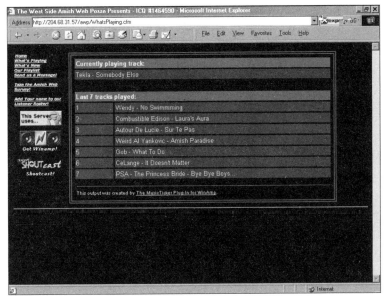

Part II Radio Station Software

MusicTicker can also monitor Winamp's playlist for better compliance with the statutory license rules for operating an Internet radio station. Although it isn't perfectly compliant with all the rules, it does check tracks so that different songs by the same artist are not played consecutively and the same song isn't played twice in the same hour.

To use the MusicTicker plug-in, you must install the gen_mticker.dll file and the mt_subs.inf file in the Plug-ins folder of your Winamp folder (you have to restart Winamp to be able to use it). You should also copy the mticker_pow.gif file to the folder you will output the mticker HTML file to.

You can find the most current version of MusicTicker on Varma's site at **http://www2.kenyon.edu/People/varmaa/mticker** or in the General Plug-ins section of the Winamp Web site.

Using the MusicTicker Plug-In dialog (see Figure 10.12), which you get by selecting it from the plug-in preferences section of Winamp, you can set the various features of the program. You just click the Enable MusicTicker check box to make MusicTicker active.

Figure 10.12
You can set preferences in the MusicTicker Plug-in dialog.

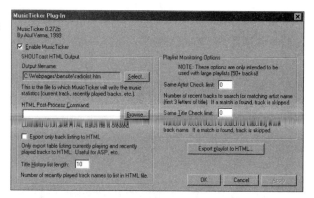

In the Output Filename field in this dialog, place the filename and path to the place where MusicTicker should output the HTML file. You can click on the Select button to open a File dialog to accomplish this task.

Sometimes you might want to have another program or process run after the new HTML file is created so that you can do something to it or with it. For example, you might launch an FTP process that uploads the new file to your remote Web site for your station. To do so, you type the name of the file to execute and any parameters to pass along with it in the HTML Post-Process Command field. Selecting Browse opens a standard File Open dialog from which you can pick the executable or batch file.

In the parameters section (i.e. the actual text that follows the name of the file to run which you put in the HTML Post-Process Command field), you can also use some special symbols, like those shown in Table 10.2, to pass parameters to a program about the currently playing song and recently played songs.

Table 10.2
Special Parameters to Pass via MusicTicker's Post-Process Command

Parameter	Description
%f	Inserts the name of the HTML output filename you created as a parameter
%0	Uses the name of the currently playing song as a parameter
%1, %2, ... %n	Passes the name of the song played *n* times ago (for example, %2 equals two songs prior) as a parameter
%%	Inserts a single % (percent sign) if needed as a parameter

TIP

If a path or program name has a space as part of its filename (for example, c:\Program Files), you must put quotation marks around the pathname or filename before the <u>parameters</u> section.

The Export Only Track Listing to HTML option is for advanced users who might want to export just a stripped-down version of the track listing so that it can be used with ASP or other HTML application systems like Allaire's ColdFusion. Essentially, it gives you raw output you can use to meld with another HTML file using a program you've created. See the Readme file that comes with the MusicTicker distribution for more information.

The Title History List Length setting lets you limit the number of recently played files that MusicTicker will output. Most people tend to pick a number between 5 and 10. Note that this number doesn't include the song currently playing.

Setting Playlist Monitoring Options

As we stated earlier, MusicTicker can also monitor your song lists to prevent certain songs from playing if they fall outside the criteria of being from an artist whose work was recently played or a song played within the same hour. In the Playlist Monitoring Options section of the MusicTicker Plug-ins dialog, you can disable these options if you don't want MusicTicker changing your playlist. One aspect of this feature that is annoying (however, interesting) is that the song must be played for a few seconds before MusicTicker can analyze the playlist and the song's information and skip to the next song. The author claims to be working on fixing this problem.

You can use the Same Artist Check Limit field to set the number of songs that MusicTicker goes back when checking to see whether the current song is from an artist just recently played.

TIP

MusicTicker checks the title of the MP3 as output by Winamp. This usually is the default setting of "Artist name—Title name." If songs aren't output this way (because they are devoid of the information or you changed the settings in the Nitrane Preferences), then this feature doesn't work.

In the Same Title Check Limit field, you can place the number of songs MusicTicker goes back to see whether a currently playing song title matches one of the previously played titles. Make sure to keep this number lower than the total number of songs in your playlist.

Part II Radio Station Software

Plugin.ini Variables

MusicTicker includes settings found in Winamp's master plugin.ini file (found in the winamp\plugins folder). In it, you can set options that are in the dialog box and a few additional options not found in the current dialog. Table 10.3 covers the major settings for the [MusicTicker] section of plugin.ini file.

Table 10.3

Variables Found in the [MusicTicker] Section of Winamp's plugin.ini File

Variable	Description
EnableHTMLOutput	When this variable is set to 0, MusicTicker cannot output an HTML file. If it is not to 0, HTMLPostProcessCmd does not execute either.
HTMLTitle	This variable identifies the text placed between the <TITLE>...</TITLE> HTML tags in the file that MusicTicker outputs.
HTMLBodyProperties	This variable identifies the text that goes inside the <BODY> tag of MusicTicker's HTML output file—not between the tag, just inside it. You can use this variable to introduce attributes such as background images, link colors, text colors, and so on. See an HTML guide for more information.
HTMLFont	This variable specifies the base font for the entire HTML document created by MusicTicker.
HTMLHeader	This variable specifies what is at the beginning of the HTML output page, before MusicTicker writes the table about the currently playing or recently played songs.
HTMLListColor1	This variable sets the background color of the table cell for the track listing of the current song. You can use '#000000 BACKGROUND=" picture.gif"' if you want to use an image instead of a color for the background. Note that not all browsers support this feature.
HTMLListColor2	This variable is the same as the preceding, except that it's used for all past tracks played.
HTMLServerOfflineMsg	This variable specifies the text to display instead of the current track if the server source (that is, Winamp) is not running.
HTMLFooterImage	This variable indicates the filename and pathname of the "Powered by MusicTicker" image. You can use a different image for the footer, but this image is always linked to the MusicTicker home page.
HTMLRefreshTimeout	This variable indicates the value used for the META REFRESH tag in MusicTicker's output HTML file. The number is set in seconds and is used to generate the amount of time before the page displaying MusicTicker information checks for a new version of the HTML page.
EnablePlaylistMonitoring	You can set this variable to 0 to disable MusicTicker's playlist monitoring.
TitleCheckCount	You should increase the variable amount here only if your HTML output is giving you garbage track names.

Part II Radio Station Software

TIP

Advanced MusicTicker users can also use a substitution system that substitutes words found in artists' names and track listings with othertext (for example, you can change Lincolnvile to <A HREF="http://www.lincolnville.com"> Lincolnville</A>) so that you can create even more robust ticker outputs. See the file titled mt_subs.txt that comes with MusicTicker for more information about this powerful and advanced feature.

Posting MusicTicker's Output to Your Site

You can post the outputted ticker HTML file to your Web site in two ways: easy and harder. The easy way is if the machine playing Winamp is the same or on the same network as your Web server. At that point, all you need to do is set the pathname to the place where the program should output the HTML file, and you're done.

If, however, the Web server that people connect to is remotely hosted (for example, via Tripod or Geocities or your own hosting provider), you need to use the HTML Post-Process command to initiate an FTP program and pass to it the server connection information and the file to upload. Novices might not find this task easy. If you need to do so, the plug-in's author recommends using WS_FTP; he has included instructions in the readme.txt file with the program for executing it using the HTML Post-Process command.

Voice Chat

Adding voice chat can be a fun way to spice up your site. Hearme.com is the leading company in the voice chat world. To add voice chat to a site, you should first register with Hearme.com. You don't *have* to register, but doing so opens up other options for your site. To add the most basic voice chat room to your site, you can simply cut and paste the following HTML code into your page:

```
<!-(c) HearMe, 1999. Freely reproducible subject to
   VoicePresence(tm) agreement at www.hearme.com ->
<SCRIPT
   SRC="http://vp.hearme.com/products/vp/embedded/scripts/vc.js">
//- IE 3.0 Message --
document.writeln("<TABLE BORDER=1 CELLPADDING=5 WIDTH=130
   HEIGHT=260>",
"<TR><TD align=center>To voice chat with others using Hearme's
   VoicePresence, ",
"you will need Internet Explorer 4.0 or
   above</TD></TR></TABLE>");
</SCRIPT>
```

If you want to add other features to this room, you can visit the customizing page for the VoicePresence application, which is located at **http://www.hearme.com/products/vp/embedded/doc_reference.html.**

The big problem with voice chat on your site is that, if you don't have an audio card that supports multiple streams, you cannot interact with listeners if you're already running a sound application. If you get a higher-end sound card such as SoundBlaster Live!, though, you can run multiple audio streams.

If you run a SHOUTcast server, you can set up the chat room and then, using the Linerec plug-in, you can from time to time stream out the banter from the voice enabled chat room. See the chapter on SHOUTcast server (Chapter 5) for more details on how to send incoming audio back out to your listeners.

Providing Product Links

Although Chapter 17 goes into more detail about commercializing your station, one key component of a good complementary Web site is providing the means for people to click through to products they can buy that are mentioned or featured during your broadcast. Whether or not you decide to make these links revenue generating, product links are good features to add to your station via its complementary Web site.

Links to Record Stores

When it comes to commercializing your station, you can take several steps, all of which are covered more extensively in Chapter 17. However, as part of building a site, you might want to add some links to various online CD stores where people can click through to purchase a CD from an artist or album you've played on your station.

Adding these links is fairly straightforward. If you want to make money by recommending albums, you need to sign up for one of the major affiliate programs on the Web. If you are going to do so, though, you'll be commercializing your station, which means you'll probably have to pay fees to the ASCAPs and BMIs of the world.

We will assume you want to link for profit, and doing so requires you to set up the affiliate campaign with the store of your choice. You can choose from many CD stores on the Web. However, you should link to a store that your customers may already be registered with because that increases the likelihood they'll purchase a product. You also want a store that carries a lot of inventory and has good customer service because, again, that will increase the likelihood of sales. Table 10.4 lists the major CD stores worth checking out on the Web and the URLs of their affiliate information pages. Note that some popular music stores such as cdpoint.com and checkout.com don't offer affiliate campaigns.

Table 10.4
Major Online CD Stores

Store	Affiliate Information/Registration Page
CDNow **www.cdnow.com**	Click on the Sell Music link on the right side of the home page.
Amazon.com **www.amazon.com**	Choose Sell Items from the bottom of the home page and then choose Amazon Associates from the resulting page.
Barnes and Noble **www.bn.com**	At the bottom of the right column on the home page, click on the Affiliate Network link.
Tower Records **www.towerrecords.com**	Click on the Affiliate Program link at the bottom of the home page.

Most affiliate programs work the same way. You register with the store, giving it your home page URL and other contact information (so the store knows where to send the checks!). From there, you are given snippets of HTML code to use or a code to embed in any URL that you point to on that site; this code lets the store track the people you send to it from your site. Most affiliate programs give you 10 to 15 percent of the resulting sale, but many won't pay you until you've earned at least $20 to $25 in a given time period.

Links to Other Stores

Providing music recommendations is certainly one of the best ways to create revenue for your site, but you also can be set up as an affiliate to literally hundreds of other interesting stores. Books and videos are also great sources because many music artists also have complementary books and videos. Talk-oriented stations can link to relevant books and movies as well.

Also worth linking to are software and hardware stores so that you can link to portable MP3 players, sound cards, and various audio software. Table 10.5 lists some other popular stores to link to as part of your product-linking efforts.

Table 10.5
Popular Online Stores

Store	Product Type	Affiliate Information/Registration Page
Amazon.com	Nearly everything	Choose Sell Items from the bottom of the home page and then choose Amazon Associates from the resulting page.
Gigabuys.com	Hardware and some software	Click on Site Map at the bottom of screen and locate Affiliate Programs under the Gigabuys Services heading.
Beyond.com	Software	Click on Affiliates Programs under the About Beyond.com section on the left side.
Reel.com	DVDs and videos	Click on the Producer Program link on the left side of the home page.
EToys.com	Toys and gadgets	Click on Help from the top menu and then click Affiliate Programs under the Additional Topics heading.

Adding a Webcam Feature

After all that we've suggested, what else could you add to your Web site? For the most part, you can add whatever else you think would expand your audience and enhance your station. Both of us could think of only one other feature to add.

As we stated in the Chapter 4, a Webcam is a nice addition to a complementary Web site. Although radio broadcasting should focus on good audio content, it can't hurt every once in a while to give people a Webcam image so that they can see into the studio, view the DJ, or maybe get an image of a guest during an in-studio interview.

The procedure for installing a Webcam varies from device to device; many now use USB ports to interface with your computer, making the installation very simple. All cameras come with some level of software included, but some packages are better, as we mentioned in Chapter 4.

Most Webcam software works by taking pictures either on cue, constantly, or at various intervals (for example, every 30 seconds); then the software uploads the graphic to a Web server or transfers it to a directory on an existing Web server. You have to provide a page that then shows this graphic to users.

In most personal radio cases, you run the Webcam as part of the local machine and then have it upload the imagery to your server. With the packages we've recommended, you just provide it with the proper FTP information (address, password, directory to place the imagery in) and then let it go.

When you're designing the Webcam page, you can force the page to refresh in an interval that matches the camera's upload rate. That way, if people keep the page up, it constantly reloads new images. You set it up this way by placing a special META tag in the page that displays the picture. The following code should go in the <HEADER>...</HEADER> section of your Web page:

```
<META HTTP-EQUIV="Refresh" content="60" URL="thispage.html">
```

In the content section, you should replace 60 with the number of seconds you want in between refreshes. The URL of thispage.html should be the same filename as the page you place this tag on, so it will continually refresh.

Building a Great Site

The best Internet radio stations or shows are never just ethereal broadcasts. As this chapter proves, you can do a great deal to build not only an interesting site, but also one that integrates ways to interact with the station. That capability is one of the most powerful aspects of Internet radio, leveraging the power of a Web site to create something that is distinctly community oriented and different from regular radio.

Building a site also makes it much easier to promote your station. By promoting the pages themselves, you can gain listeners who come across your site and then log on to your stream. Chapter 15 will help you with the basics of Web site and Internet radio station promotion, so after you've finished building your site, be sure to read that chapter as well.

Part II Radio Station Software

Part III

Preparing Content
for Your Station

11

Digitizing and Formats

When it comes to digital audio, a lot more than just sound comes out of your speakers or headphones. In Chapter 2, we covered some basic details of the file formats used in Internet radio. Most Internet radio-related audio formats are usually the result of an encoded raw digital audio file or CD track that is compressed and stored in a format conducive to quality streaming over the Internet. In the cases in which you are encoding from the raw CD track, you don't need to understand much about the actual digital structure of that file. However, ripping CD tracks (i.e. converting to digital audio directly from a music CD) isn't always what streaming audio development is about.

In many cases, you might be creating a file from a recorded interview, from taped sound effects, or from a DAT tape, MiniDisc, or other form of audio acquisition. Because not every piece of encoded audio starts from a CD track or a live broadcast stream, this chapter is devoted to teaching you the basics of working with computer audio and recording, digitizing, and editing raw audio. As the saying goes, garbage in, garbage out. In other words, if you record garbage, your audio will sound like garbage. In this chapter, we'll explain many of the ins and outs of using digital audio so that you can create the highest quality raw audio that is eventually encoded into one of the top file formats used by streaming audio servers.

Digital Sound Basics:
How Computers Capture Sound

At the most basic level, computers capture sound by taking a stream of analog music and converting it into a digital form using special chips known as *Digital/Audio Converters (DACs)* but more commonly called *A/D, D/A converters*. These chips can read the analog signal and create the digital 1s and 0s that eventually let your computer play back.

Sampling

Although sound is a constant stream, a computer needs to take a small segment of that sound at constant intervals to record it. These intervals of captured sound are known as *samples* (think of this concept as sampling a continuous stream of sound). The more frequently you sample the sound stream, the higher quality playback you can achieve. In audio recording, samples are measured in the thousands per second (kHz) range. Of course, the more you sample the music, the more data you accrue, and the larger the file becomes. Most high-quality CD-style samples are collected at a 44.1kHz rate. When sampling at a lower rate for smaller files, most programs offer 22.05kHz (½) or 11.025kHz (¼) rates.

Resolution

Although sampling determines how often you capture a segment of sound, it doesn't determine the quality of the frequency sample. The quality is determined by the resolution of the sample, which is measured in bits per sample. The *bit rate* of a file determines the quality of the sample taken. Sixteen-bit samples allow frequencies with a larger range to be captured, whereas 8-bit samples cut off some of the higher and lower frequency range sounds, causing the sound to be inferior. In cases in which the fidelity of the sound isn't as important (say, for spoken word or narration), dropping the bit rate to eight isn't a bad idea. For full-range music, however, dropping the rate results in sound that is sub par as compared to the original recording.

Channels

The term *channels* refers simply to whether the sound file is stereo (two) or mono (one). Remember that, when you're recording for music files, you'll want a stereo file that is twice as big in size as a mono (single channel) recording. For voice recordings, mono can be perfectly suitable, especially if you're looking to build a show or station that broadcasts at extremely low bit rates.

File Size

How do sample rate, bit rate, and channels affect file size? Table 11.1 shows the approximate number of megabytes (before encoding to MP3) that each style of recording requires. MP3 size varies based on the quality of the recording. For high-quality 16-bit stereo recordings sampled at 44.1 kHz, for example, you can figure on a 10:1 to 12:1 compression ratio when converting to the MP3 format. Note that you can achieve even higher compression when you're converting to Windows Media Audio or any encoded format that offers greater compression than MP3.

Table 11.1
File Sizes for One Minute of Sound Recorded at Various Frequencies, Bit Rates, and Channels

	44.1kHz (stereo)	44.1kHz (mono)	22.05kHz (stereo)	22.05kHz (mono)	11.025kHz (stereo)	11.025kHz (mono)
8-bit	5.0MB	2.5MB	2.5MB	1.3MB	1.3MB	.6MB
16-bit	10.1MB	5.0MB	5.0MB	2.5MB	2.5MB	1.3MB

Acquiring Audio: Recording Principles and Practices

Depending on the type of station or show you are going to have, you might need to capture audio remotely or under other circumstances before it is digitized and encoded for broadcast. For example, you might do an interview with a local politician at city hall or record a concert broadcast at a local nightclub. You might do a phone interview that won't be played live and thus need to record it. Whatever the reason for your need to record audio, you need to understand the basics of recording for Internet radio. In the following sections, we'll give you the details.

Studio Versus Remote

Essentially, the two types of recording are in-studio and remote. The difference basically depends on whether your in-studio recording situation is different than when you're out and about. If you have better acoustical facilities, and perhaps access to a mixer and tape decks (or even the ability to record directly to the PC), then you will have potentially more control over the recording in the studio.

When you're in a remote setting, you have to use a portable recording device unless you've been given enough time to haul out nice equipment—like what you might have back in your studio.

We suspect that most of you, however, will be taping either interviews or local events with a portable recording system. An overview of portable recording hardware, therefore, seems like a good place to start.

Portable Recording

Most people use some or all of the following four types of portable recording devices these days:

▶ **Digital Audio Tape (DAT)**—A popular choice for portable recording for most audiophiles is the DAT tape deck. DAT records audio data in a digital form and stores it on a tape much like a VCR works. Several are suited for portable audio, and although MiniDisc is also popular and easier to edit with, many pros use DAT. DAT can record longer sessions in one sitting (MiniDiscs are limited to 64 to 75 minutes at best quality, more at lesser quality settings).

TIP

Popular models of portable DAT recorders include Sony's TCD-D7, TCD-D8, and the TCD-D100. You can find a wonderful FAQ and tons of additional resources on these products located at **www.rockpark.com/d7**.

▶ **MiniDisc (MD)**—Invented by Sony, the MiniDisc is a magneto-optical solution, similar to a CD but much smaller. Although a dud as a device for pre-recorded music (Sony thought it might replace cassettes), it has bounced back as a recordable format. The MiniDisc is very popular for portable recording. Not only is sound quality excellent, but the editing process with MiniDisc also is much easier and less expensive than with DAT.

TIP

The SONY MZ-R90 and MZ-R55 are good. However, you might want to check out some of the better MiniDisc resources on the Web for more information. You can find the MiniDisc FAQ at **www.hip.atr.co.jp/~eaw/minidisc/minidisc_faq.html** and the MiniDisc community site at **www.minidisc.org**.

▶ **Cassette/MiniTape**—This device is the old standby. Although cassette taping is the cheapest form (tapes and players are both inexpensive), and both in mini and regular form are very unobtrusive, the quality of recording isn't nearly as good as DAT or MiniDisc.

▶ **Digital Audio Recorders**—As the MP3 format has spawned a number of portable memory-only devices for playback, the same technology is now being used for portable recording. Although this type of recording is a more expensive option, editing and converting the audio to your computer are a snap. However, as of 1999, devices uniquely designed for recording professionally aren't on the market.

Which to Use?

When it comes to deciding once and for all which type of portable recorder to use, you will find proponents for both DAT and MiniDisc. DAT seems to have a slightly better quality, which is due to the fact that it doesn't compress the audio data it records; MiniDisc does. However, MiniDisc is much easier to use and somewhat less expensive. We therefore recommend MiniDisc, unless you are a true stickler for audio quality. The difference is slight enough for experts to tell, but not wide enough to show any difference when recorded to an encoded format for broadcast. Finally, you should consider getting a cheap analog tape recorder for backup in case your more expensive digital recorder fails to work when necessary.

Microphones for the Road

Assuming you have your desired choice of portable recording device, you now need a microphone of some sort for recording your portable audio. Some of the portable MiniDisc and DAT products available include a microphone with your purchase. If you didn't get one or are considering an upgrade, you should look for several types of microphones for onsite recording and might want to have one of each for various situations:

▶ **Omni-directional**—A microphone that is omni-directional picks up all sound around the microphone. This type of mic is useful for recording meetings, press conferences, and interviews for which you want to capture multiple voices or event-related sounds without positioning the microphone. The downside is that it can pick up extraneous background sounds you might not want.

▶ **Uni-directional**—A microphone that is uni-directional limits the amount of sound you can pick up to just that in front of the microphone head. This type of mic is good for focusing the recording on a specific subject. Remember, however, that for interviews, you have to tilt the microphone toward the voice you're trying to capture.

▶ **Clip-on**—This type of microphone is used for interviews mostly. This type of mic is great because it is completely unobtrusive. The problem is that a clip-on mic can pick up lots of extraneous noise if the subject moves around a lot.

Getting Your Audio Back

In Chapter 14, you will find a great deal of information about broadcasting from a remote location. Much of that information can apply to how you transfer your recorded audio back to your home base for broadcast—especially if the idea is to do as much of a remote feed as possible (for example, when you're at a trade show or conference). However, we need to cover some basics here as they pertain to sending back some recorded audio for broadcast.

You can get your audio back to the station in four ways. The first is to just return with the recorded audio in hand; this approach is fine unless you're screaming to get a hot interview on the air. To get something back quickly, you need to send it back over a phone line. The best way to do so is to have a portable computer that can digitize and either e-mail or FTP the files back. Presuming the files aren't too big, digitizing them can be an effective means of transfer. Otherwise, you need to feed the audio back down over the phone line, thus losing quality but gaining efficiency if the broadcast requires such. To get audio back to studio via phone lines, you need to set up two phone line recording devices, one on each end, and then transfer the audio back to the studio. The drawback of this quality of the recording. ISDN lines could improve the quality greatly, but in many remote locations unless pre-staged (i.e. you set up with enough lead time or the facility has installed ISDN access for previous or upcoming Webcasts), you are not going to have outgoing ISDN access.

In the end, for most voice interviews, phone-line quality is sufficient as long as the interviews don't drag out too long, and the listeners realize the phone feed is being used because they're getting breaking news. In fact, hearing someone over the phone usually heightens the urgency or importance of the broadcast. Every time you see a reporter on the phone on a TV broadcast, don't you usually get the feeling that the news being reported is too critical to have waited for a satellite up-link or for recorded audio to make it back to the studio?

From Tape to Hard Disk: Digitizing Sound Files

You can acquire the original source audio files in two major ways. The most direct way is to "rip" audio right from a recorded CD audio track file. In this case, there is no digital-to-analog and analog-to-digital process. The computer simply reads the CD information and makes the correct conversion to an audio file. Programs that do so are known as *rippers;* they're discussed in more detail in the following chapter. Note that the most popular ripper, Xing's AudioCatalyst 2.0, supports only encoding to the MP3 format. However, if you want to encode a file into another format, you can rip it to just a raw audio .WAV file and then encode it to formats such as RealAudio or Windows Media Audio.

The other common way to acquire audio for creating MP3s is to convert any analog audio source coming into your sound card into a raw digital form (such as .WAV). To do so, you need to understand the intricacies of sound cards, line noise, and digitization software.

The Issues That Control Good Sound Acquisition

Just getting the best sound card you can afford does not guarantee you good sound acquisition. Ensuring sound card quality is just one step among many that will help you ensure you're generating clear source sound files for encoding into the MP3 format. The following sections describe the other steps involved.

Using a Quality Card

In Chapter 4, we described the major sound cards you can get to power your station. Nothing separates a quality sound card more than its recording capability. Lower-end cards produce electrical noise and other artifacts that can affect the quality of your digitization process. For the most part, a SoundBlaster Live! or Diamond Monster sound card can do an adequate job of digitizing audio for broadcast. Neither of these well-done consumer-focused cards is a slouch. However, if you plan to record and digitize a lot of audio for your broadcast, you should consider getting a higher-end card with the best frequency range and noise reduction you can afford.

TIP

We recommended some good cards and brands back in Chapter 4. If you want to be even more discriminating, check out the sound card comparison information on the Web at **www.rockpark.com/soundcards/**.

Killing Background Noise

One of the most important things you can do is find ways to kill the background noise that can be associated with your recording setup. Background noise can be a very slight hum or other forms of noise that distort the sound coming through your sound card. You can see whether background noise occurs in your setup by recording 20 to 30 seconds of sound with no music (see Figure 11.1). From there, you can decide whether you have too much noise or an acceptable setting. For the most part, noise shouldn't be a problem.

Part III Preparing Content

Figure 11.1
You should record
moments of silence
with your digitization
software to see how bad
background noise is.

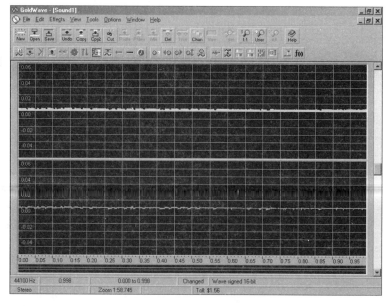

TIP

Your computer also makes noise. With all the electronics inside it, things can
get a bit noisy if the card isn't well shielded and grounded. Again, the degree
to which you can produce less noise improves the higher you go up the
product chain of sound cards.

Cleaning Tape Heads and Records

One of the most critical steps you can take when coming off a regular
cassette tape or a vinyl record is to clean everything as much as possible.
Using a quality tape-head cleaner found in many record stores for $10 to
$15 can help keep your tape deck in good shape. DAT decks require
special cleaning, and many times people periodically replace the DAT
heads over time (the aforementioned DAT page has tips on cleaning and
maintaining heads).

Wiping records clean of dirt and dust and buying a new needle will help
with LPs. And for MiniDiscs, although SONY claims you can re-record
one million times before degradation, most people go to new discs after a
few dozen rewrites.

Using a Mixer and Other Music Hardware

Mixers and hardware equalizers are not required by any means, but if
you have them, they can be useful—especially if you have experience
optimizing audio via these types of devices. Depending on your setup and
the nature of the recorded audio itself, passing a recording through a mixer

and perhaps a hardware equalizer can also be a useful optimization. Although you can equalize and mix audio using the digitization program itself, by passing audio through these types of devices, you can attempt to do that before getting into the software itself, where performing these types of processes isn't necessarily as easy. This way, you also can apply changes to the audio as it's being captured, tweaking the mix and equalizing it throughout the capturing process.

However, if you do decide to place such hardware between your recordings and the computer, you should test for noise, because each piece of equipment along the line can potentially add noise to the audio stream heading into your computer's sound card.

Deciding Which Cables to Use

Trying to talk about cabling with stereo fanatics, engineers, and audiophiles is bound to drive you crazy. You'll hear many opinions, lots of hype, and several ideas about which types of cabling you should use to connect various audio devices. In most cases, you will use a simple RCA-style cable to connect out-jacks to in-jacks on your sound card.

By far, the most commonly used "quality" audio cabling is Monster Cable (**www.monstercable.com**). The problem with this cable is that it is so often talked about and widely used, it has its share of supporters and detractors. Overall, the quality of this cable is very good and probably better than anything you'll find that comes from a no-name or low-end cabling company that sells to the mass market. The construction is sturdy, and the price is reasonable. If you want to go the extra mile to provide a quality signal to your card, using Monster Cable to patch your audio into your sound card isn't a bad step.

If you're interested in alternatives and higher-end options to Monster Cable, you can try two other well-known audio cable manufacturers. Nordost (**www.nordost.com**) and AudioQuest (**www.audioquest.com**) are two recommended cabling manufacturers used by audiophiles worldwide.

> **TIP**
>
> In some cases, you might try to pass the audio through a graphic equalizer to remove the frequencies causing noise in the background. This trick can be problematic, because equalizers can change the sound quality of music when it begins playing. Do so with caution.

Optimizing Your Hard Drives

When sounds are captured in digital form, they are stored either in memory or directly on the hard disk. This point is somewhat important because quality sound files take up a lot of space. A normal file size for a musical track on a CD can be 40 to 50MB. As your sound card and the program you use to capture audio digitize sound, the computer memory fills up, and if the memory is not sufficient, the sound spills onto your hard drive. The hard drive captures the sound as fast as it can, but poorly optimized hard drives might not offer optimal quality. Optimizing your hard drive (i.e. defragmenting it) provides for the best performance.

Most new PCs today have very fast drives, with good transfer rates—so there isn't a ton to worry about. However, if you're looking for that next way to optimize for quality sampling when you're shopping for a new system or a new hard drive specifically for digitizing capabilities, look for ultra-fast hard drives and hard drive controllers. Many digital music developers use SCSI hard drives for their speed versus cheaper and more prevalent IDE drives (which most of you will have). A new IDE controller, the ATA-66, is a faster breed of IDE technology. At the very least when looking for a drive, look for drives that have very high transfer rates and low seek times.

The Digitizing Process

At this point, your audio is recorded (or is going to be recorded directly to your computer), and you have the best sound card you can find and have done as many of the optimizations as possible. Assuming you've evaluated the various digitizing and editing packages mentioned in Chapter 4, you're now ready to digitize your audio.

When you aren't ripping a track directly off a CD, you have to record it from your sound card and store it in a format that is a perfect representation of the sound captured. For PCs, that means a .WAV file, and on Macintosh platforms, that might be an .AIFF file. Both of these formats can store raw captured sound with no encoding or loss of data in order for later compression via encoding by every major digitizing and editing package available.

Being Windows users, we use Sonic Foundry's Sound Forge for our digitizing. Sound Forge is a top-rated product and, aside from having a plethora of editing options, it can encode files into several common formats for broadcasting, including RealAudio, Windows Media Audio, and MP3. SoundEdit 16 for the Macintosh is a similarly styled package. If you can't afford Sound Forge, you can get Sound Forge XP for under $80. If you want to use a good shareware package, CoolEdit and Goldwave are both excellent options. However, remember that for some of the lower-end packages, you might need to optionally use a standalone encoding product to finally render your files for broadcast. We'll cover these products in the next chapter.

Capturing Your Audio

Capturing audio, in almost every program, is about as simple as pressing the Record button. After you've conditioned your setup and queued the music on your tape, record, MiniDisc, or DAT, you should press Record on the capture software and then initiate Play. Later, you can trim the file to capture just the sound.

> **TIP**
>
> For every minute of high-quality audio, approximately 10MB of space is needed on your hard drive to store the file. Be sure to calculate the length of your recording and prepare the necessary space accordingly.

In some cases, the software you use will save the file as it captures it, but you should be sure that after you have your captured file, you save it first—just in case something goes wrong during the editing and enhancing period. Also, beware that on slow machines, if you begin to capture a long file, the rest of the file will start writing out to disk when RAM is full; if your system isn't fast enough, it can bog down. If that's the case, you can break up the digitization into smaller sessions. Most well-powered machines (Pentium 266, the equivalent or better with 64MB of RAM) should be more than adequate for anything but the most difficult or higher-end of digitization processes.

Enhancing the File

With all the major packages listed in Chapter 4 available to you, you can perform a wealth of effects on your sound file. In many cases, you'll probably want to leave the file as is. If you've managed a good, clean capture, why fix something that isn't broke? Processes common to all the major sound editing packages are worth being familiar with, however. As you gain expertise with them, you will find yourself more able to improve various styles of recordings. Also, if you've passed audio through a mixer before, you may have used that device instead of the software's tools to fatten sounds and bring out the best in the digitized version.

> **TIP**
>
> Check your sound system setup on your control panel.

DC Offset

One of the top items you can look for to help improve the quality of your digitized audio is what is known as the *DC offset*. DC offsets happen when the equipment and lines feeding into your sound card aren't properly grounded. DC offsets are usually caused by electrical mismatches between your sound card and microphone. This problem can be common to lower-end sound cards. This is one of the types of noise that we talked about earlier in this chapter. By digitizing a few seconds of silence, you can see how bad the DC offset is on your setup.

A bad DC offset forces the baseline of your audio to be slightly off the 0 axis or centerline of your digitized audio. You might have to zoom in on your audio to see how bad it is. If the sound has a significant offset, you can easily correct it by using your editor. Every decent sound editor, like those mentioned in Chapter 4, has a DC adjustment function.

After you zoom in on the file, look to see what the offset is. Your editor should have numbers along the side or a graph overlay that helps. Then, after you've digitized the file, you can apply the opposite amount of offset (for example, if the offset is 85, you can apply a -85 DC offset filter) and improve the sound. Some programs can even calculate the offset automatically and adjust it accordingly.

Equalization

Just like a graphic equalizer on your stereo or the one included in Winamp, most sound editing packages let you adjust the various frequency bands and apply those changes to the file (see Figure 11.2). Equalizing is really an issue of what sounds best to you.

Figure 11.2
Most digitization packages, like Sound Forge XP, shown here, feature built-in equalizers that you can use to improve frequency ranges in your files prior to encoding them.

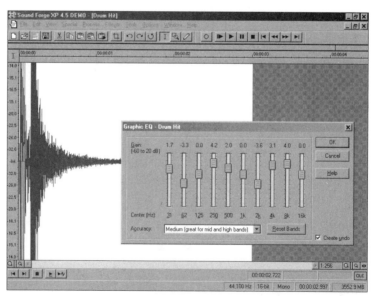

TIP

Because the MP3 format uses a perceptual encoding technique, it drops out very high-end and low-end frequencies in the file. Using your equalizer to fatten the middle frequencies just a hair (2 to 3kHz) can sometimes be a nice adjustment that specifically takes into account how the MP3 format changes the audio upon encoding. To some extent, you might have to experiment and encode a few files to be certain.

TIP

Real recommends on its site that for voice-only content, you can make the file better by cutting frequencies below 100Hz and carefully boosting frequencies in the 1 to 4kHz range.

Normalization

Normalization helps you maximize the volume of a file without distorting it. The function scans the audio data and then applies a gain to the levels in the file to a specified amount of increase. Every good package has a normalization (sometimes called *maximize*) function.

When you're running this process, you can set a normalize factor between 0 and 100 percent of the maximum value. It is possible for a normalization process to maximize the frequencies out of range. For the most part, though, you can avoid this situation by setting the process to hit the 90 to 95 percentile (some editors don't do a good job normalizing to 100 percent anyway). You then can play back the resulting file and listen for any clicking sounds that would indicate the process caused some frequencies to shoot out of range.

You should perform this step at the end of your enhancement process because, when the file is maximized, you can create distortion if you run filters after that process.

Dynamics Compression

Performing a normalization maximizes the audio by filling out the captured audio's loudest parts. This favoring of the peaks in your audio disfavors the valleys; thus, quieter sounds in a file can lose their part in the mix and not encode as well, according to Real's content development guide. To compensate for this problem, Real recommends using dynamics compression—a tool not found in every audio editing package (but found in Sound Forge). Dynamics compression evens out input levels by cutting off high inputs when they go above a set threshold; this evens out the sound and gives a better ratio to quieter parts of your file. You can control *attenuation* (the process of turning down high levels in a file) by specifying a compression ratio. After you've run this process, you can then use an equalizer to readjust various levels as needed.

Part III Preparing Content

Real specifically makes this recommendation: "For multipurpose dynamics compression, set the threshold to -10dB, the ratio to 4:1, and the attack and release times to 100ms. Adjust the input level to get around 3dB of compression and an output level around 0dB."

What About Output?
Drivers and Speaker Issues

Just because you captured your sound correctly, touched it up, and encoded it perfectly doesn't mean you have achieved sonic nirvana. Before you finish reading this chapter, you should take some time to understand the role of speakers and sound drivers on your setup.

Most computers today come standard with multimedia speakers. However, most speakers that come with computers aren't as good as those you would get with even a modest stereo system. In addition, positioning them too close to your monitor or other computer equipment might add interference. Some computer audiophiles solve this problem by running their computers' sound output through their stereo systems, whereas others purchase above-average computer speakers like those produced by Boston Acoustics or Bose.

▶ **Boston Acoustics (www.bostonacoustics.com)**—Boston Acoustics offers a complete line of add-on multimedia speakers ranging from its lower-end BA-635 system, which runs $99, to its higher-end MediaTheater line, which runs $299 and includes a subwoofer and optionally (for another $99) a surround-sound speaker.

▶ **Bose (www.bose.com)**—Bose produces two specific products, both of which are two-speaker setups. Its high-end Acoustimass multimedia speakers cost $499 and have been highly rated by a number of computer magazines. Bose also has a lower-end offering, the MediaMate line, which runs $199 for a pair.

In terms of sound card drivers, you should familiarize yourself with the options your drivers allow for, because some can affect the way sound is played back. First and foremost, you should check the manufacturer's Web site for your card and make sure you've updated your drivers to the latest versions.

TIP

For some reason, sound card companies often like to post beta drivers. Although these drivers are more advanced, they're not final release drivers. You should be careful about updating to what appear to be the latest drivers when, in fact, they may be beta releases. Always look for the last fully released update. Also, when you're checking for new driver updates, it's best to check your computer manufacturer's Web site first before checking the sound card manufacturer's site.

For Windows users, some sound cards can give special features on how the playback of your sound happens (see Figure 11.3). When you're capturing and tuning your audio, you can turn off these features so as not to be confused by the special effects of your particular sound card.

Figure 11.3
Some sound cards have special playback settings that you can reset to normal when you're trying to tweak your recorded sounds.

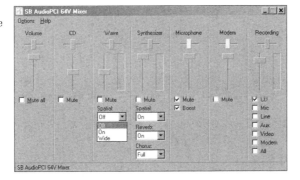

Also, you should be sure to check the recording properties of your card using the volume control found in your Windows system tray (see Figure 11.4). These properties control the amplitude and balance of incoming audio streams during recording.

Figure 11.4
The volume properties control found in your Windows System Tray (double-click to activate) lets you tweak amplitude and balance of incoming audio.

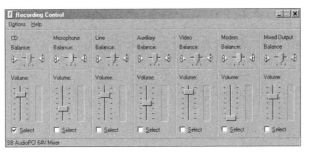

To get to the recording properties, you can bring up the volume properties control by double-clicking on the speaker icon in your Windows system tray. Then, under the Options menu, choose Properties to bring up the volume control Properties dialog (see Figure 11.5).

Figure 11.5
Using the Options menu commands, you can switch volume control properties mode between playback and recording.

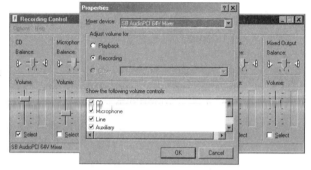

Choose the Recording option from the Adjust Volume For area and make sure that you have selected at least CD, Microphone, and Line Balance in the check boxes below. Click on the OK button, and your volume control panel will change to the recording volume controls, as shown in Figure 11.6.

Figure 11.6
The three recording volume levels that are most important are CD, Microphone, and Line.

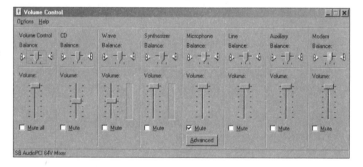

TIP

Most of the time, you'll be recording through the line input. If you have a microphone attached to your sound card at the time, you should mute the mic input to reduce possible noise interference during recording.

You also should check the multimedia control on the control panel to see whether you've set your sound card settings to the optimal settings. Many drivers, like the SoundBlaster PCI card driver, have a setting that lets you increase the quality of the card's sampling rate—a sure way to improve sound capture quality.

Depending on the features of your sound card, you might have additional playback and recording options. By thoroughly examining both your control panel settings and the volume and balance adjustments to your sound card, you can ensure you're creating the optimal conditions for recording and tweaking your digital audio prior to creating the final MP3 files.

What's Most Important for Good Audio?

Getting a good raw audio file captured on your computer is always a process of trial and error. In fact, many times you might not be satisfied until encoding the file, hearing the problems post-encoding, then tweaking the original file, and encoding again. However, as you repeat this process a few times, you'll begin to see that if you get a good original capture and then perform some of the basic tweaking functions covered in this chapter, you will have little left to do. Mastering your encoding process, which is covered in the next chapter, and getting continuously better with the sound editing and digitizing package of your choice will only enhance your ability to give listeners the best sound possible.

No amount of good capturing, editing, and encoding, however, will replace the most critical aspect of having good audio for your radio station or show: The actual audio needs to be interesting. No matter how pristine the audio, if the actual topics, hosts, or guests are boring, it won't help. If the music you broadcast is poorly played, you're not going to attract listeners just because you tweaked the audio file to the max. Before you go so far as to master recording, digitizing, and encoding audio, you should ask yourself the most important question, "Will anyone care to listen once I've done that?"

12

Encoding
Step-by-Step

What Is Encoding?

As you learned earlier in this book, to broadcast audio over the Internet, you must reformat it so that it can be easily streamed out over the Web. The process of converting audio from a raw form into a streamable format is known as *encoding*. Encoding is a two-part process. First, you compress audio to make the file size smaller. The smaller the file, the better it is able to stream. Second, you arrange the compressed data in a way that it is easy to send out in small chunks that can be expanded on the other end of the network and result in audio. For this reason, it's a misnomer to call encoding *compression,* because compression is only one part of the encoding process. Encoding can also include adding extra meta information that describes the file's data, adding digital watermarking to protect copyright, and so on.

When audio is encoded in a proper form, it can stream out over the Internet using any one of the server types already described in Chapters 4 through 8. It also is important to understand that encoding can take on one of these two forms:

▶ *Pre-encoding* involves rendering the information to be streamed into the needed format and then storing it on a computer for later broadcast. Every time you make an MP3 file or a RealAudio file, for example, you are pre-encoding your content.

▶ *Live encoding* involves a system that can quickly compress the incoming audio stream and then broadcast it; as it streams out, the system dumps the current data to move on to the next piece.

In many cases, you might decide to simply encode on the fly instead of constantly creating pre-encoded (or recorded) files for broadcast. You can even combine the two, encoding on the fly for a live broadcast, while simultaneously collecting the outgoing broadcast in a file for later repeat broadcasts.

In this chapter, we'll discuss the encoding formats a little further and specifically cover step-by-step the major tools you can use to render your station's or show's content for broadcast. We'll cover live encoding as well, wherever applicable. For more details on live encoding and remote broadcasts, see Chapter 14.

What Are the Issues to be Concerned About When Encoding?

When it comes to issues and major concerns, encoding is a little like audio recording: Quality is a factor of how much you care to push for the best. You can get basically well-encoded files without much effort by just running the major tools through their paces. Or you can go a little further and try to produce the highest quality content because you care enough to do so. The difference in encoding quality comes down to several factors:

1. What is the shape of the original source file? You shouldn't forget the adage, "Garbage-in, garbage out!"
2. What is the codec you are choosing to encode to?
3. What is the bit rate and sample rate of the resulting file?
4. What is the quality of the encoder software you are using?
5. What additional tweaks do you add to your process?

The major issue is quality, but you must consider other issues as well. They include the following:

1. What time should you encode your content?
2. What copyright protection can you include?
3. What meta information can you tag on, and how easy is it to do so?
4. Do you want to encode to multiple formats or quality levels?

What Are the Best Ways to Encode Content?

The best way to encode your content is to use top-of-the-line products and software to create the cleanest audio and encoded files you can make. However, with that as a mission, many specific situations come up concerning how you want to encode a certain file—or which products may work best (e.g. quality of file versus speed of encoding). That means having as thorough an understanding of the various encoding tools for each format as possible is helpful. It will let you make the best decision for whatever given encoding task you find yourself in.

NOTE

Live encoding is not a whole lot different from encoding from prerecorded files. You first need to set up the encoder by setting the characteristics of the outgoing stream (for example, bit rate, frequency, and so on). For a source file, you need to identify the device on your system (most likely a specific sound card and driver installed on your system), and you also have to specify where to send the outgoing files. Also, most third-party programs don't support live encoding, so instead you need to turn to the encoder programs supplied by Microsoft and RealNetworks for live encoding for those server types.

For MP3 live encoding, if your machine is fast enough and you have SHOUTcast, you can encode live using that system and then send out the program to a server for your station. You can also use a hardware-based encoder like those from Telos Systems that can provide better quality and alleviate your onsite computer needs. You can find more details on live encoding in Chapter 14.

The Basics of Encoding and Using Encoding Tools

When it comes to Internet radio, you basically need to deal with three major formats for streaming audio: MP3, RealAudio, and the newer Windows Media Audio (WMA) format from Microsoft. Yes, we've mentioned other formats, but your choice mostly (for now) comes down to these three formats.

By now, you've probably decided which one of these three formats you want to broadcast in, either because of your server choice or because of some technical choice. With that format choice in mind, you need to choose a tool that can get your raw audio into the format you will use to originate your broadcast.

In general, you should either use a tool specifically tailored to encoding in the format you plan to use or a general-purpose audio editing/encoding tool you may already be using. The trick in deciding which tool to use overall is understanding which of the tools you select does the best job at encoding your files. For example, all MP3 encoders are not created equal. Many professionals prefer Opticom's MP3 Tools or AudioActive's tools versus the more popular Xing Encoder. In addition, many people use the Blade Encoder, a freely available encoder that isn't considered to be of the highest quality.

When it comes to encoding tools, some are faster than others. Some companies use hardware encoding tools to help speed up what can sometimes be a laborious process for many computers.

When it comes to producing content, we choose to use or recommend the following major tools. For overall encoding, Sonic Foundry's Stream Anywhere product supports all the major formats including RealAudio, MP3, and WMA. For MP3 specifically, we recommend AudioActive's encoder and its hardware encoder if you choose to use a hardware solution. We also like Xing's AudioCatalyst for a low-cost and good CD Ripper/Encoder. AudioActive's products seem to win the audiophile vote, but AudioCatalyst from Xing is inexpensive and a breeze to use. RealProducer and RealProducer Plus from RealNetworks also are good tools that are easy to use and well tailored to sites broadcasting using RealServer.

We'll cover how to use all these major tools in this chapter.

Using Stream Anywhere

Stream Anywhere from Sonic Foundry is a combination product that offers simple audio editing with encoding for RealAudio and Windows Media. It does not support MP3 encoding, but you can find plenty of other programs for that task. As a tool that includes both WMA and RealAudio support under one roof, it's a great product.

Using Stream Anywhere is a straightforward process; just follow the steps outlined in the next few sections.

Step 1: Open a Source File

To begin using Stream Anywhere, start by opening an original source file in the program. To do so, choose the Open icon on the toolbar, or choose the Open/Add selection (Ctrl+O) from the File menu. Then find a source file (which can include .WAV, .AIFF, and MP3 files, among others) on your machine.

Step 2: Tweak Selection

After Stream Anywhere has loaded the file, its key characteristics are displayed. If you have the program in the Full View mode (to do so, choose Full from the View menu), you can see a graphical representation of the file and its timeline on the bottom of the screen, as shown in Figure 12.1.

Figure 12.1
The Stream Anywhere screen displays a graphical chart of the source file when loaded.

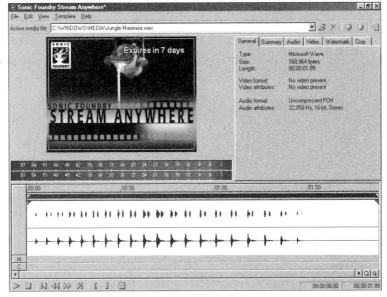

You can use this portion of the program to limit the selected area of a file to encode, as well as to set fade-in and fade-out spots for the file. By dragging the two yellow triangles just under the timeline, you can change the selected area of the source file. By dragging the two red triangles that are just below the yellow ones, you can set the fade-in and fade-out points. You can use the controls at the bottom-most part of the program to play and preview the source file and selected area, as well as reset the selection points.

Step 3: Set Summary and Audio Attributes

After you select the audio source file and set the selection and fade points, you can enter Summary information by clicking on the Summary tab (see Figure 12.2) and filling it out as needed.

Figure 12.2
You can fill out the information in Stream Anywhere's Summary information tab.

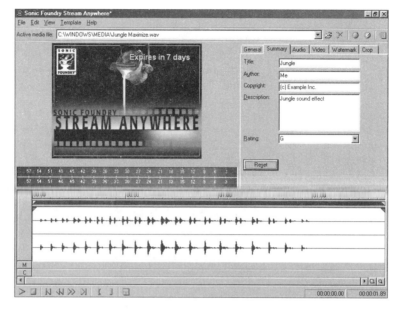

You also can set some basic audio processing attributes. To do so, click on the Audio tab (see Figure 12.3), and then check the Audio Processing box to set a volume increase for the file and some basic equalizing tweaks. By clicking Normalize Audio, you can set normalization characteristics to use.

Figure 12.3
You can choose from several options on Stream Anywhere's Audio settings tab.

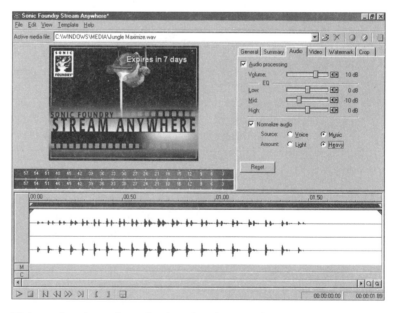

This product has other tabs, but they have to do with video encoding and thus aren't a concern for radio operators.

Step 4: Begin Encoding

With everything set, you can begin the encoding session. To get started, click on the Encode button on the toolbar, or choose Save as Streaming Media from the File menu. When the basic encoding dialog appears, as shown in Figure 12.4, you can choose from a number of encoding options.

Figure 12.4
When you're ready to encode your source file, you can set various file attributes.

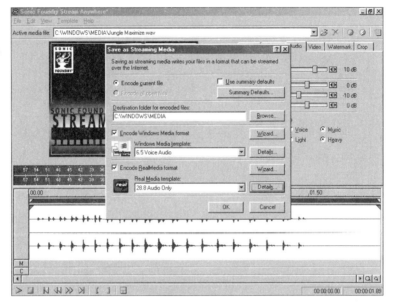

First, you must tell the program whether to encode the current file or all currently open source files (this capability is useful for using multiple files in one encoding session). Next, you can choose the Summary Defaults option, which lets you define summary information for all encoded files. If you've individually entered summary information for all your source files, leave this option unchecked.

Next, you must pick a destination folder for encoded files. Click Browse to set the folder, or type in a path directly.

Finally, you can tell the encoder which of the two supported formats you want to have encoded files rendered in. Stream Anywhere lets you encode files out to both formats simultaneously.

For each encoder choice, you can choose a template that lets you set the bit rate and frequency the final file will have. If you want to further tweak this setting, you can run a wizard or directly configure it by clicking on the Details button. For the most part, the templates included give you most of the basic choices you might want.

When you're done, click on OK to begin the encoding process.

Part III Preparing Content

Many More Options

This basic step-by-step process outlines how to use Stream Anywhere, but you can choose from many more options than we can cover here. They include a scripting feature for automating batch jobs and a template system to save common encoding sessions for repeated use.

Encoding for RealAudio

Aside from using an audio editing package for encoding RealAudio files, you can use two standalone programs to encode your content for broadcast in RealAudio. The first is the basic RealEncoder product, which is a no-frills freeware encoder tool that RealNetworks offers on its Web site. Next are RealProducer 7 and RealProducer 7 Plus. Producer 7 is free for download from RealNetwork's site, whereas the Plus version, which includes greater control over encoding parameters, cost $149.95 at the time of this writing.

Using RealProducer

RealProducer is a good product for encoding to the RealAudio format, and it's especially good for RealServer users because it makes sending out a live encoded stream to your server a snap if you require that capability as well.

With RealProducer, you can choose to set up your encoding process by using a wizard-based configuration scheme, or you can just go to the main screen and individually configure the system to encode a file as you need it. RealProducer not only lets you encode from an existing file, it also captures and encodes directly in real-time as well.

For purposes of explaining RealProducer, we're going to step through encoding from an existing file, which is easy if you use the wizard system included.

Step 1: Start the Recording Wizard

To start the Recording Wizard, simply choose Record From File from the menu when you start the program, or from the main menu of RealProducer, choose File > Recording Wizards > Record From File to begin. In either case, the first screen of the Recording Wizard then appears, as shown in Figure 12.5. In this wizard screen, you can enter the name of the file you want to encode (click browse to pull up the open dialog to select a file from your computer or network). Your source file can be many types of media, including .WAV files, MP3 files, .AU, and more. Click on Next to continue.

Figure 12.5
You can start the
encoding process by
telling the program
which source file you
want encoded.

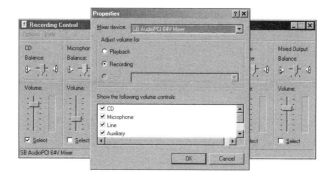

Step 2: Define Clip Information

In the next wizard screen, as shown in Figure 12.6, you can attach basic
meta information that is attached to the RealMedia clip, including
copyright information, keywords, title, and producer. After you enter this
information, click on Next to continue.

Figure 12.6
In this wizard screen,
you can enter
descriptive information
about the clip.

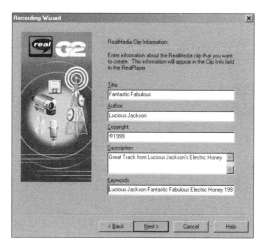

Part III Preparing Content

Step 3: Define File Type Information

RealAudio supports two types of streaming formats: SureStream and Single-Rate (see Figure 12.7). SureStream encodes the file in such a way that if it is served using a G2, Server 7, or higher RealMedia Server, the listeners get the best sounding stream their connections to the server can provide. The Single-Rate function forces the encoder to optimize the stream for one specific bit rate, which is good if you plan to stream the file out using a non-RealServer process, such as just embedding it on a Web page.

Choose SureStream if you're going to serve it out using a Real G2 or 7 level server. Then click on Next to continue to the next step.

Figure 12.7
Here, you can choose between SureStream or Single-Rate encoding.

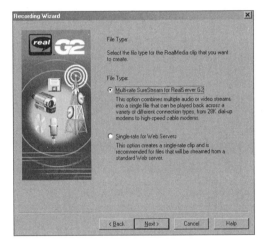

Step 4: Define the Optimized Connection Speed

When you encode the file, you can have RealProducer optimize it for as few or as many of the major Internet connection speeds people have on their systems. Choose from the available list on the screen, as shown in Figure 12.8, and then proceed to the next part of the wizard process by clicking on Next.

Figure 12.8
Choose the connection speeds you want your stream optimized for.

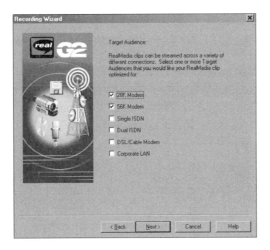

Step 5: Choose the Audio Format

After you set connection priorities, you can further instruct the encoder on how to optimize your stream by choosing the style of the recorded audio in the next wizard screen, shown in Figure 12.9. Choose from the four options, and note that, while Stereo Music as a setting gives quality as a result of its stereo attribute, the overall quality of the music isn't as good because some overhead is used in the file to affect the stereo process. After you make your choice, click on Next to continue.

Figure 12.9
Here, you can tell the encoder what style of audio you want to encode.

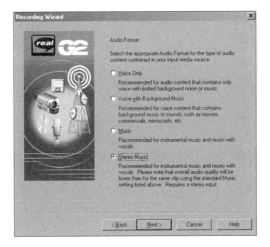

Part III Preparing Content

Step 6: Choose the Output File

The final step in the Recording Wizard is to choose the location and filename of the resulting encoded file. Enter this information into the text box shown in Figure 12.10. Then click on Next to continue the process.

Figure 12.10
On this screen, you can choose the outgoing filename and location.

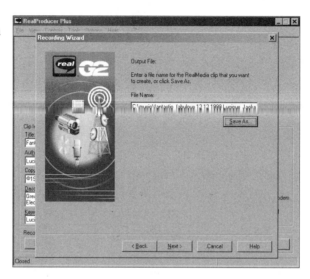

Step 7: Review and Finish

Although there is nothing left to configure, the final screen of the wizard lets you review the configurations you gave it, and if you want to change something, you can merely backtrack through the various screens to change specific items. Click on Finish to confirm the setup. From there, you are taken to the main screen of RealProducer, where you can initiate the encoding process or further refine or change the encoding setup.

Going the Extra Mile with RealProducer Encoding

On the main encoder screen, as shown in Figure 12.11, you can see all the major configuration choices and edit them. At the bottom of the screen are several buttons that you can use to begin the encoder process (Start, Stop, and Play) and to the right of them are Web Publishing options that enable you to create a simple Web page sporting the clip or set it up in an e-mail.

Figure 12.11
On the main screen for
RealProducer, you can
edit the configuration of
your clip.

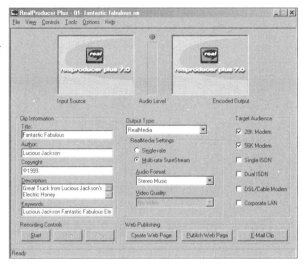

Most of the menu items are duplicates of options available on the main
screen; however, a few areas are worth pointing out further.

▶ **Statistics**—When you're doing live encoding or if you want to check
on the progress of an encoding session, you can view statistics for the
process. To do so, choose Statistics from the View menu to open the
Statistics dialog box (see Figure 12.12).

Figure 12.12
You can review
information on your
audio clips by using the
Statistics reporting
feature of RealProducer.

▶ **Preferences**—If you choose Preferences from the Options menu, you can set some additional features and preferences for your encoding process. Most of the items under the Preferences dialog concern video, but on the General tab, you can set characteristics for new session startups and indicate which directory should be used for temporary storage. On the SureStream tab, you can set the Player Compatibility level for SureStream files; you can choose only RealPlayer G2 or higher or RealPlayer 5.0 or higher. On the Live Broadcast tab, you can set the protocol to use for transmitting live encoded files back to a server. UDP is recommended, but you can also select TCP if you need to.

▶ **Target Audience Settings**—This menu item (found under the Options menu) features a submenu with three choices that let you tweak the encoder settings for RealVideo, RealAudio, and MP3 files. When you're tweaking Target Audience Settings for RealAudio, you use a dialog that lets you specifically set the actual bit rate settings for the various categories of audio for each specific connection rate (see Figure 12.13). For the most part, you should not change these settings. If you do change them and you don't get good results, you can click on the Restore Defaults button to set everything back to their original settings.

Figure 12.13
In this dialog, you can tweak Target Audience Settings for RealAudio encoding.

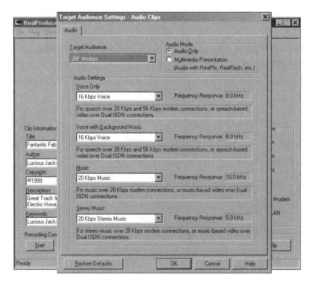

▶ **Audio Settings**—Found under the options menu, this dialog lets you work with the audio settings for MP3 files created by RealProducer by manipulating the settings in the Audio Settings dialog, as shown in Figure 12.14. For example, you can set the bit rate for various connection targets and turn off or on the Force Mono setting. You also can decide whether the Original Bit and Copyright Bits are set. In addition, you can set it to encode high frequencies (good for live music) if you need to avoid the normal discarding of such frequencies.

Figure 12.14
If you plan to use RealProducer for encoding to the MP3 format, be sure to configure the MP3 settings for the encoder.

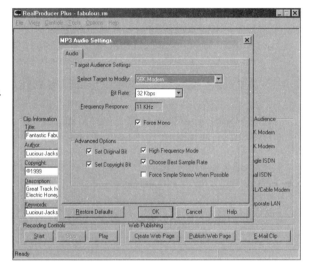

▶ **Choose Best Sample Size**—This setting in the Audio Settings dialog forces the encoder to match up the best sample rate for the final file based on the source file's original sample rate and the bit rate you have selected for the resulting file. The Force Simple Stereo When Possible option forces the encoder to make any mono file a simple stereo file when the target bit rate is 128kbps or higher.

TIP

Although the RealProducer product supports MP3 encoding, you can find much better options for creating quality MP3 files than the Producer program (see the next section). We don't recommend it for anything but casual needs for MP3 encoding.

Encoding for MP3

When you want to encode MP3 files, you can choose from a number of tools on the market. In fact, everywhere you look, someone seems to be offering some form of MP3 encoding as a feature of audio or MP3-oriented software. As we discussed earlier, though, we feel that three major products are worth covering. AudioCatalyst from Xing Technologies (a subsidiary of RealNetworks) is a solid CD Ripper/Encoder product for Macintosh, Linux, and Windows users. Although some people aren't as satisfied with the encoder as they are with AudioActive's or Opticom's, it is a solid product for under $30 that's easy to use. AudioActive 2.0 is a much improved product that matches some good features with a well-respected MP3 encoder, and Opticom's product, which costs a bit more, is considered by many to be the best-sounding codec.

Who Is and What Is Best for MP3 Encoding?

Graham Spice is an active member of the online SHOUTcast community and is a member of the GSBE (The Guy Smiley Blues Exchange), a local band based in Nashville, Tennessee. He's done his fair share of encoding for MP3 files as part of his continuing efforts to promote his band online and through GSBE Radio. The following is his professional take on the various encoding tools and techniques for MP3 encoding:

"After doing a fairly extensive survey of all the encoders available, I've determined that the only one that produces substantially better results at the MP3 standard of 128K are ones based on the original Fraunhofer codec (which include Opticom's and AudioActive's products), but only the professional version.

The Fraunhofer codec is the best sounding encoder, though it is one of the slowest. There were some significant upgrades to the speed of the encoder, but they are parts of illegally produced software.

When you're determining which codec to use, you have to think about how you're going to use it. If you're moving your entire CD collection to MP3s, don't use the slowest codec. I've found the Xing codec (as have many others) to be acceptable in quality and fantastic in speed for applications that demand quick turn-around.

All of my MP3 encoding work is for musicians that demand the highest quality sound. For that, the Fraunhofer professional codec is a must. As bitrates begin to increase above 128K, the differences between codecs don't seem to be as acute. Since 128K is still the standard on the net, I think that you'll find a need for using a product that uses the professional Fraunhofer codec.

A comment closer to home here for Internet radio DJs is that if you're going to pre-encode your music, have your source files be quality MP3s.There's no reason to start with something that has glitches or digital artifacts in your source due to a poor encoder. Therefore, I try to encode all my source files to 128K or 160K MP3s using the professional codec."

Graham Spice
http://www.GSBE.com/shoutcast.asp

Using AudioCatalyst

AudioCatalyst combines the best of the AudioGrabber application with Xing's own MP3 encoder product. You can download a trial version of AudioCatalyst from Xing's site, or you can buy the full version for $29.95 directly from the **www.xingtech.com** Web site.

The trial version limits you to six tracks, which you convert off the CD with the tracks randomly determined at runtime. However, the trial version doesn't support .WAV file encoding of MP3 files.

Using AudioCatalyst is a fairly easy process—although you must deal with a number of options and other configurations beyond selecting tracks from your CDs and then converting them to MP3.

The main AudioCatalyst window consists of a track-listing window and a menu bar composed of seven key function icons, as you can see in Figure 12.15. The menu bar also shows fields in which you can type the artist and album name. Whenever you pop in a CD, you can request that the program connect the CD database (**www.cddb.com**) and search for the CD's album information, including track listings, artist information, and album name. The CDDB has a very updated and broad listing of tracks, so you don't have to manually enter this information. If the program doesn't automatically offer this search, click on the CDDB icon on the menu bar or choose Get From CDDB from the CD menu.

Figure 12.15
The main AudioCatalyst program screen shows CD information.

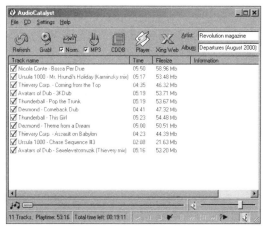

Part III Preparing Content

You can begin creating an MP3 file when you have your track listing information. Notice that each track listing has a check box next to it. You can just check the tracks you want to convert (see Figure 12.16).

Figure 12.16
You can check the tracks on the CD you want to encode.

You first must deal with some critical configuration dialogs. The settings in the MP3 Encoder Settings, Advanced Settings, and Normalizing dialogs control most of the key output issues you need to deal with when you're constructing an MP3 file using AudioCatalyst.

The MP3 Encoder Settings Dialog

You open the MP3 Encoder Settings dialog, as shown in Figure 12.17, by clicking on the MP3 icon on the menu bar or by choosing MP3 Options from the Settings menu.

Figure 12.17
You can change the encoder settings in the MP3 Encoder Settings dialog.

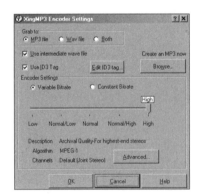

You can choose from the Grab To section to convert the CD tracks straight to the MP3 format, to a .WAV file, or to both. Just beneath these options is the Use Intermediate Wave File check box. During the construction of an MP3 file, if you choose to have AudioCatalyst first convert the CD track to an intermediate .WAV file, you also can enable the program to run a normalization routine on the .WAV file. Choosing this option helps to better enhance the volume settings within the song to bring out the fullest sound prior to encoding. If you don't check this option, you can have AudioCatalyst skip this step to speed the creation of your MP3 files.

The next option in this dialog is Use ID3 Tag. If you select this option, at the end of the encoding process, AudioCatalyst will append an ID3 tag to the MP3 file. Clicking on the Edit ID3 Tag button brings up an ID3 Tag Editor dialog in which you can edit the specifics of the ID3 Tag that each file will have written in with it.

TIP

The Create an MP3 Now Browse button opens a dialog box from which you can select .WAV files for encoding into MP3 files. This option is not available in the demonstration version.

By choosing the Encoder Settings in the MP3 Encoder Settings dialog, you can set the quality of the resulting MP3 file as well as the method used to encode the file itself. The two major choices in this section are constant bitrate and variable bitrate.

Constant Bit Rate Encoding

Constant Bit Rate Encoding (CBR) means that the bit rate setting you choose is maintained throughout the length of the file. This is done regardless of the specific needs of any portion of the song, whether it's a very noisy and dynamic section or a period of complete silence. The result is twofold: Parts of the song that could use extra bits don't get them, and areas of the song might include bits that are essentially unused.

The benefit of CBR is that you can consistently guess the resulting file size because it is an exact outcome of this formula:

bit rate per second $\times$ duration of file

Part III Preparing Content

When you choose the Constant Bitrate option for your encoding process, the slider bar changes, as shown in Figure 12.18, to let you select an exact bit rate for the file to use. You can select the actual bit rate you want to use from the bar from 16 up to 320kbps.

Figure 12.18
When you choose the Constant Bitrate option for the encoding process, the slider bar changes so that you can select an exact bit rate to use.

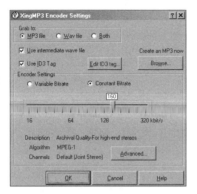

Variable Bit Rate Encoding

Variable Bit Rate Encoding (VBR) differs from CBR because it intelligently applies the bits in the file based on the needs of the audio at any moment in the file. This feature is useful, especially when you're encoding music that has wide variances between stereo channels. For example, if one portion of the stereo channel could benefit from extra bits allocated beyond the 64kbps it has, then Variable Bit Rate Encoding allocates that channel more bits to render the overall file better. Meanwhile, the other channel that might need fewer bits to render properly is given less. Overall, the 128bps never changes; just the amount allocated to each stereo channel changes relative to the needs of the audio source.

VBR files can be smaller and provide a higher-quality sounding file as a result of the encoding process. However, because the bit rate varies throughout the file, predicting the overall size of the file is nearly impossible. In addition, not all MP3 players can accurately determine the timing of a file as it plays; thus, seeking may also be difficult. (It is worth noting, however, that Winamp supports these files perfectly.)

When you use the Variable Bitrate option, you need to set the sliding scale from Low to High. When the scale is set to Low, you get a file that usually averages 96kbps; Normal represents 128kbps, and High represents 192kbps. The scale sets the highest range that the file will go to when encoding any section of the song; sections that can get by with lower bit rates are subsequently encoded at the lower bit rates.

The Advanced Options Dialog

Clicking on the Advanced button in the MP3 Encoder Setting dialog brings up the Advanced Options dialog. This dialog contains several options you can check on or off to further refine the resulting MP3 files you are creating for your broadcast.

▶ **Set Copyright Bit**—This selection adds a small piece of information into the ID3 tag area of an MP3 to define it as copyrighted information. If a user pulls up information about this MP3 in a player which supports the copyright bit, it will display it as Copyrighted. This doesn't prevent copying—it just denotes whether you want to explicitly state a file contains copyrighted material.

▶ **Set Original Bit**—This selection is similar to the Copyright Bit selection. If you select it, you are asking the encoder to set a bit in the ID3 tag area of an MP3 file to denote it was an MP3 developed from the original source material or source owner. As with the Copyright Bit feature, it will display this information only when asked for by a user of a compatible player. Using the Original Bit option is a way to tell more educated MP3 fanatics that your file is not a copy of a copy and that its quality is derived from the best original source material.

▶ **High Frequency Mode**—This is a selection that tells the encoder to increase the range of frequencies it encodes on the high end of the frequency spectrum (20kHz) and works only on CBR bit rates of 112kbps and VBR settings of Low/Normal and higher. This can improve the quality of files with lots of high frequencies in them (say live recordings), but as noted in the documentation provided with AudioCatalyst, only some users have the hardware and hearing to be able to see the difference this effect can produce.

▶ **Choose Best Sample Rate**—When selected, this entitles the encoder to makes its own best choice about the sample rate it will use to create your MP3 file. It does this by evaluating the file's original sample rate and your target bit rate for encoding. The rate also results in the type of MPEG file it will create, which can allow for some backwards compatibility with older MPEG playback software (really old, if you realize that it can result in the creation of MPEG 1 files). According to Xing's help file: "sample rates determine the type of MPEG file that can be created. Samples rates of 32kHz, 44.1kHz, and 48kHz create MPEG-1 files. Sample rates of 16kHz, 22.05kHz, and 24kHz create MPEG-2 files. Using MPEG-1 files is best when you're creating files for higher bit rates (above 80kbps). Using MPEG-2 files is best when you're creating files for lower bit rates (such as 32 to 80kbps)." This can help the encoder take your incoming source file and choose a selected output that offers enhanced quality by choosing a different sample rate and MPEG format. This option is best used when you aren't entirely sure about the source files' dynamics. If you're ripping from CD, you can stay with the 44.1kHz sample rate.

▶ **Force Simple Stereo When Possible**—This is an option that will create stereo MP3 files even when the source isn't a stereo file itself. This doesn't always provide the best quality however. Before you select this option, see "Understanding Stereo Channel Modes" in the Help file for important Stereo Channel Mode information.

▶ **Default for the Bitrate/Filetype**—This will tell the XingMP3 Encoder to make its own choice, when selected, for the best Channel mode for the bit rate and file type you are encoding to.

▶ **Always Mono**—This will force the encoder to always create a mono MP3 file, regardless of the source file's original channel format.

▶ **Restore Defaults**—This will reset the Advanced Options dialog back to the default settings.

The Normalizing Dialog

When you choose to have a file normalize, you ask that AudioCatalyst convert the track to a .WAV file first (a setting offered in the previously discussed MP3 Encoder Settings dialog), after which it normalizes the file prior to encoding it to an MP3 file. Clicking the Normalize icon brings up the Normalizing dialog shown in Figure 12.19.

Figure 12.19
You can set a normalization rate in the Normalizing dialog.

In this dialog, you can select Use Normalizing and then set a normalization rate (most people use the default 98 percent setting), or you can select this option to use normalizing if the track itself is lower or higher than a specific range. If you want to normalize an existing .WAV file right away, choose the Browse button and select a file from the resulting dialog. (This option is available for registered users only.)

For the most part, the track-to-track volume settings on a CD or any good record are the same because they've been engineered and mastered as such. All CDs, LPs, and tapes are not recorded at the same levels, however; thus, if you are encoding from a mixed group of CDs, normalization in AudioCatalyst can help you create a more even flow of volume between tracks.

Most CD levels are set from 95 to 99 percent of the recording level. Tracks from most CDs have the same level of loudness when you set the normalization routine in AudioCatalyst just below the 95 to 99 percent level (91 to 92 percent, for instance). A normalization setting just below 95 percent is recommended; otherwise, you might lose some of the inherent loudness that a track should have.

The Settings Dialog

Choosing General Settings from the Settings menu brings up the Settings
dialog, as shown in Figure 12.20. Here, you can ignore most of the settings
that pertain to the CD-ROM access method used to rip tracks. The two
most common CD-ROM control technologies are ASPI, a newer and more
advanced system, and MSCDEX (Microsoft CD Extensions), an older
technology that debuted alongside CD-ROMs in the earlier days of DOS.
AudioCatalyst most often attempts to autoconfigure your CD. If you
experience problems accessing your CD tracks, you might need to switch
from the ASPI to the MSCDEX system, tweak either settings, or update
your drivers. The Help file included with AudioCatalyst goes into detail
about this process.

Figure 12.20
You can tweak settings
in tho othor Sottingc
dialog for
AudioCatalyst.

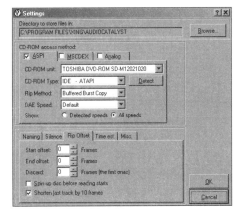

Part III Preparing Content

The second group included in the Settings dialog is a series of tabs that manage track naming, song silence trimming, some ripping and track time-estimating functions (which, for the most part, should be left alone), and the Miscellaneous tab, which lets you turn on or off some features concerning track playback and the encoding process. The Naming tab is the one you might want to give some attention to. You can turn on or off the various information you want included in the MP3's filename and use the arrows to the left to set the field order.

Performing the Encoding

With your settings taken care of, you can now begin grabbing and converting the tracks. Again, you should make sure the tracks you convert are checked. To get started, click the Grab icon; AudioCatalyst instantly displays a status dialog, like the one shown in Figure 12.21, as it goes about ripping and converting the tracks.

Figure 12.21
AudioCatalyst displays a detailed status dialog while ripping a CD file.

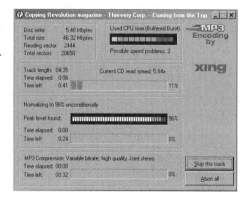

AudioCatalyst couldn't be much easier to use. Its rip-and-go process and decent encoding speed make it a great MP3 tool to own. If you have a few (or more) CDs you want converted to MP3, AudioCatalyst is the way to go.

Using AudioGrabber

AudioGrabber, which is a shareware utility that is the basis of Xing's own AudioCatalyst program, works nearly the same way as does AudioCatalyst—with a few notable exceptions.

The big differences between AudioGrabber and AudioCatalyst are the MP3 settings and the support for Windows Media Audio. AudioGrabber doesn't include the Xing MP3 encoder; instead, it uses any internal codecs that are installed or an encoder such as the Opticom Encoder or the BladeEnc encoder, which can be run via a command line.

You can find the configuration of the MP3 encoding system on AudioGrabber's MP3 Settings dialog, shown in Figure 12.22 (note that this dialog is different from the dialog of the same name found in AudioCatalyst).

Fig 12.22
AudioGrabber's MP3 Settings dialog has a different set of options than does its cousin, Xing's AudioCatalyst.

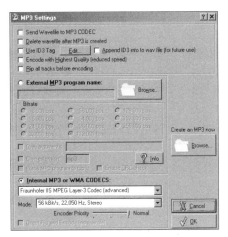

At the top of the dialog box are six check boxes. The first check box, Send Wavefile to MP3 CODEC, is unavailable unless you are using the Internal MP3 or WMA Codecs option (located near the bottom of the dialog). If you are using that option, click the Send Wavefile to MP3 CODEC check box. AudioGrabber automatically sends the completed .WAV file to the codec for compression into the MP3 format after the .WAV file has been grabbed.

The next check box, Delete Wavefile After MP3 Is Created, deletes the .WAV file after the resulting MP3 file is created. The Use ID3 Tag option and the accompanying Edit button bring up the ID3 tag editor for the files.

You can also choose the Append ID3 Info to WAV File option. The Encode with Highest Quality (Reduced Speed) check box tells the program to take more time to analyze the .WAV file and produce a higher-quality sounding MP3.

By clicking on the final check box, you can choose to rip all tracks before encoding.

The next major choices in this dialog concern what third-party system you're going to use to encode your MP3 files. Two choices are offered: using an external MP3 program (including a DOS command-line encoder) and using an internally installed Windows MP3 codec.

Part III Preparing Content

External MP3 Program Name Option

When you use this external method of interfacing to the encoding system, you must provide a path to an external program that encodes your MP3 files. By clicking on the Browse button, you can wade through your computer directories to find an installed system. After that, you need to go through a series of buttons and check boxes with which you can set the bit rate or offer various command-line arguments to the program you want to use. Of course, you must be familiar with the program to know what to do here. Either consult the Help file, Readme documents, and manual that come with the encoder you want to use, or use the Internal MP3 or WMA CODECS option.

Internal MP3 or WMA CODECS Option

Instead of switching from one program to the other, setting an automatic internal MP3 encoder to use is a much more elegant solution to encoding your MP3 files with AudioGrabber. The program interfaces with an installed .DLL or ACM codec to create your MP3 files. Installed codecs appear in the Internal MP3 or WMA CODECS option drop-down list; below that list are the various MP3 encoding modes each particular codec supports. You can make the choices from either list for the codec and MP3 quality you want.

If you've installed the Windows Media Player version 6.0 or the Net Show development from Microsoft, you should have the advanced Fraunhofer IIS MPEG Layer-3 Codec available on your system as well as the latest WMA codec. This codec, which can decode 128-bit or better MP3 files, supports encoding only up to 56kbps at 22,050Hz, stereo. To get the Advanced Plus codec that supports 128 bits, you need to purchase it from Opticom Solutions (**www.opticom.de**) for $49.00. A separate Professional MP3 Encoder codec, which supports a wider variety of methods plus better than 128-bit encoding, runs $199.00. You can also download the freely available BladeEnc (**http://www.bladeenc.cjb.net**), which works through the internal method (though our experiences with BladeEnc give mixed results in terms of quality).

Other encoder choices include the previously mentioned AudioCatalyst, which combines AudioGrabber with Xing's MP3 encoder (which is very good) for $29.95. You can also get the separate standalone Xing MP3 Encoder for $19.95.

AudioGrabber or AudioCatalyst?

Other than some icon differences and the way the MP3 encoding options are set, AudioGrabber and AudioCatalyst are identical. The big reason to use AudioGrabber instead of Xing's AudioCatalyst is if you want to use an encoder other than Xing's MP3 encoder.

Using Audioactive Production Studio 2.0

Audioactive Production Studio from Audioactive (a division of Telos Systems) is a well-known and respected encoder used by a number of professionals in the digital audio industry. It is available for sale at **www.audioactive.com** in both a Pro and Lite versions. The Pro, which gives you access to special features and higher-bitrates, sells for $269, while the Lite version (perfect for most radioheads) sells for $59. The software also works well with Telos' hardware encoder systems. For more on these systems, see Audioactive's Web site.

Audioactive 2.0's main interface has four tabbed interfaces—Encode, Decode, MP3 Convert, and CD Copy. There is also a menu at the top, and each tab will have some buttons of its own for that section of the program. The first place to focus on are the tabs, which give you a direct interface into each feature of the program.

Encode

The Encode tab (Figure 12.23) features four buttons and basically lets you queue up encoding commands. Clicking the Add Files button will bring up a dialog where you can select any .WAV files for encoding, into MP3 files. Once you've selected any number of files for encoding they will be listed in the table on the tab. This table shows you key attributes for each file you are going to encode, including source file, resample (yes/no), output format (with bitrate), the format extension, and the destination file name.

Figure 12.23
The Encode Tab is where you set any .WAV to MP3 encoding processes.

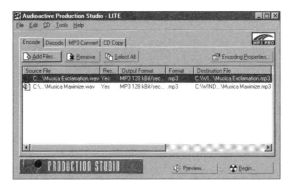

If you'd like to change any settings concerning the encoding process for each file, select the file in question from the list and click on the Encoding Properties button. Clicking on the Encoding Properties button will bring up the Encoding Properties dialog. This dialog lets you tweak some of the options of the individual file that was selected.

Part III Preparing Content

The Encoding Properties Dialog has three major tabs—General, MP3, and FTP. On the General tab (Figure 12.24) you can see key descriptions of the source file. A checkbox lets you tell the encoder if it should delete the source file after it creates the encoded version.

Figure 12.24

The Encoding Properties Dialog focused on the General Tab.

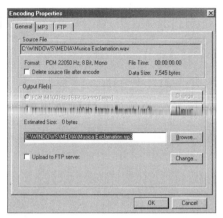

Below the Source File section of the General Tab is the Output File(s) section. Here you can change the attributes of the resulting MP3 file. Two options for output file will be given—PCM and MP3—but only the MP3 will be available since it's assumed you don't want to encode a .WAV file into another .WAV file. By clicking on the Change… button that sits to the right of the MP3 choice, you can switch views to the MP3 Tab (Figure 12.25), which lets you set the characteristics of the resulting MP3 file.

Figure 12.25

The MP3 Tab lets you set the MP3 bitrate and other attributes you want each file to have.

On the MP3 Tab you can choose the output format for the encoded file. This by default is .MP3 but can also be .ASF (which will wrap the MP3 format into an .ASF file but does not create a .WMA file—although this may be a feature when 2.0 ships or in a future version). You can also choose the compression level, which means choosing from any of the outputs MP3 allows for and you have installed codecs for. Finally, in the Optimization section, you can choose from Faster encode for speed or Higher quality encode to instruct the encoder to take its time and create a file with the best sound (only available to users of the Pro version of Audioactive.)

The final tab is the FTP tab, which is reachable by clicking on the FTP tab (Figure 12.26) or by clicking on the Change button to the right of the Upload to FTP server: checkbox found on the General tab (Figure 12.24). This feature lets the Encoder automatically FTP finished encoded files to whichever server you want to send them to. To enable this feature for a file, check the Upload to FTP server box on the General Tab and then fill out the needed information on the Encoding Properties Tab, which includes the server's name (or IP address), the port for the FTP server, a user name, password, and default initial directory. The Connection Test button will let you quickly test the connection right there in the dialog; but don't expect it to offer too much help if you have the information wrong.

Figure 12.26
The FTP Tab of the Encoding Properties dialog.

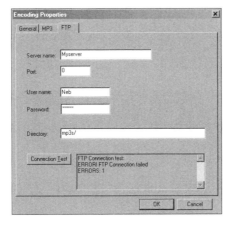

TIP
The port is usually 21 for most FTP servers. If yours is different, check with your IT department or the tech support of the hosting provider or server provider you have. You might also test the connection information with an FTP program like CUTEftp (**www.cuteftp.com**) or Fetch for the Mac to further troubleshoot FTP connection issues that occur with AudioActive.

Part III Preparing Content

Decode

The Decode tab lets you list source .MP3 files and have them decoded back into .WAV files. This tab works almost identically to the encoding process. Click on the Add Files button to add .MP3 files to decode. Then click on each file in the list (or multiple ones) and click the Decoding Properties button, which will pull up the Decoding Properties dialog (which was still titled Encoding Properties when we used a beta version of the software). This dialog is nearly identical to the previously mentioned Encoding Properties dialog that you activate when encoding .WAV files to the .MP3 format.

The differences with the Decoding Properties dialog this time around is that on General Tab the MP3 output choice will be ghosted and you must choose the resulting PCM file characteristics you want each file to have. You also should see that the MP3 Tab will now be titled the PCM tab (Figure 12.27) and you may choose only the .WAV file format as the Output File Format.

Figure 12.27
When Using Audioactive to decode instead of encode, the MP3 Tab will now be titled the PCM tab.

Every other function in the Encoding Properties dialog works the same way as previously presented.

MP3 Convert

This section of Audioactive lets you list files and then convert them to other MP3 files with different characteristics (e.g. lower bitrates). It and the associated Encoding Properties dialog (found by clicking the Conversion Properties button) work identically to the Encode section of Audioactive.

CD Copy

This tab lets you access Audioactive's built in CD-Ripper. Clicking on this tab will cause Audioactive to check your CD for viable files to rip and encode. Those files will list themselves in the listing box featured on the Tab. You can click Scan CD if you want to refresh the listing.

Clicking on CDDB will cause Audioactive (if you're connected to the Internet) to scan the CD Database for track listing and artist information to create automatic .ID3 tags. Clicking on the Encoding Properties button will bring up the associated Encode Properties dialog. This dialog, shown in Figure 12.28, has four tabs. You'll also note that the General Tab (featured in Figure 12.28) lets you select either PCM or MP3 as the output file and, depending on the output type you choose, you will want to visit its associated tab (which work as described earlier) and further define the output file.

Figure 12.28
When using the CD Copy function of Audioactive 2.0, clicking on the Encoding Properties button will bring up the associated Encode Properties dialog that, unlike the previous instances, has four tabs.

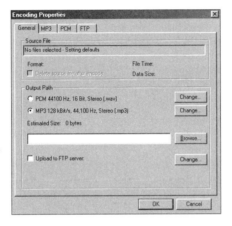

Audioactive Menu Features

The Audioactive drop-down menu contains a few sections that are worth documenting:

Encoding Options (Edit > Options)

Found under the Edit menu, the Options item will bring up the Encoding Options dialog shown in Figure 12.29. This dialog lets you set three options (two of which are accessible only by users of the Pro version).

Figure 12.29
The Encoding Options dialog.

Part III Preparing Content

> ▶ **Execute after each file**—Lets you provide a command line that executes after each file is processed. This can be used to do something to the file, such as send a copy to another directory or run a program that might do further processing on it.

> ▶ **Execute after all files are encoded**—Same as above but activates only after all files listed are processed.

> ▶ **Processing Priority**—Available in both versions, this option lets you set the level of CPU power devoted to the encoding of files. One neat feature is to set it to Idle time processing only. This will let your computer only do encoding when the processor isn't otherwise occupied. Even a low setting will work well if you want to have most of your computer's efforts focused not on encoding, but on foreground activity, like finishing your latest online broadcasting book.

CD Options (CD > Options)

Found under the CD menu, the Options item will bring up the CD Options dialog, which is shown in Figure 12.30. This dialog lets you set a number of options relative to the CD Copy functions of Audioactive. This dialog has a number of tabs and options which are summarized as follows:

Figure 12.30
The CD Options dialog focused on the Device tab.

> ▶ **Device**—This tab (see Figure 12.30) lets you set options and configuration items related to the type of CD player you are running. If you are having trouble getting the CD Copy function to work with your CD drive, consult your CD drive's manual and the Audioactive help file for more information on setting some of these features to make CD Copy with your drive. Most basic current CD drives should work without any further changes to the default settings on this Tab.

▶ **General**—This tab, shown in Figure 12.31, lets you decide how the CD Copy section of Audioactive responds when you rescan a CD that has been in the drive. These options are all self-explanatory. Note the fourth option lets you optionally eject the CD from the drive after it is has completed ripping—a nice way to let you know when the encoder has finished if it is running in the background under a mountain of other open applications.

Figure 12.31
The General Tab of the CD Options dialog

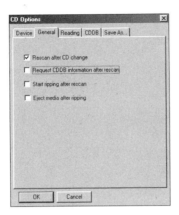

▶ **Reading**—This tab, shown in Figure 12.32, lets you set some characteristics related to buffered reading of the CD drive (to avoid errors in encoding if the machine is kicked or jolted and the drive skips) and if the encoder should stop encoding if it encounters hard errors on the CD.

Figure 12.32
The Reading Tab of the CD Options dialog helps you prevent files encoded with skips and other errors.

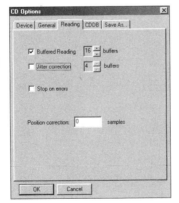

Part III Preparing Content

▶ **CDDB**—This tab, shown in Figure 12.33, lets you denote which CDDB Server you draw information from or whether you use a local database for it. Note that the various CDDB sites go down from time to time, so if the CDDB function on the CD Copy tag isn't working, check this dialog to choose another location. The Write ID3 info tag to MP3 files denotes the version of the ID3 format it will append to the MP3 files it creates.

Figure 12.33
The CDDB Tab of the CD Options dialog lets you configure the built-in CDDB features of Audioactive.

▶ **Save As**—This tab, shown in Figure 12.34, enables you to detail how track names on a CD influence the automatic filename Audioactive creates for the file. You can choose from three templates or use the Custom template feature to create your own (an example of which is shown in Figure 12.34) Below the custom template section is a checkbox that lets you optionally replace spaces in track listing with a special character used for the filename (this is highly recommended and most people use the underscore character _). Below that item is a field where you can denote a special character to be used instead of any number of special characters such as \ * and ? that could trip up a Web or audio server trying to broadcast the file. Finally, the Ask before creating folder checkbox prevents Audioactive from creating new folders without your permission during CD Copy.

Figure 12.34
The Save As Tab of the CD Options dialog enables you to detail how each encoded file ripped from a CD is written.

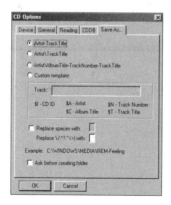

Create Playlist (Tools > Playlist)

This menu item is active only if you are on a tab whose associated file list has some.MP3 files (just encoded or original) presently listed. If so, choosing this menu item will bring up a common Windows File Save dialog where you can choose a file name and Audioactive will write to that file a standard .M3U compliant playlist.

Calculator (Tools > Calculator)

The calculator feature of Audioactive is found under the Tools menu. This dialog (Figure 12.35) helps you calculate characteristics of encoded files. Each of three key characteristics (Data Rate, Time, and Size) can be calculated. To calculate any one, depress the button for it, supply values for the other two items, and hit the "Click Here to Computer" button.

Figure 12.35
The calculator tool.

Previewing and Initiating Encoding

Choosing the Preview button will force Audioactive to quickly encode, decode, or convert a small snippet of the selected files.

Once you've set and/or previewed those settings and you wish to encode, decode, convert, or copy from a CD, you can choose Begin to process the files. A processing dialog will then begin showing the status of processing for each file in the queue and the entire list as a whole (Figure 12.36). Press Skip File if you wish to interrupt the list and have Audioactive move automatically to the next file on the list. You can press details to see a real-time log of the processing functions as well. When it is completed, you must press done to return to the main Audioactive program.

Figure 12.36
The Encoding/Encode Complete dialog shows you the status and log of your encoding process.

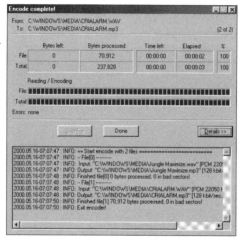

TIP

If you try to re-process files previously processed, Audioactive will respond with a special dialog (Figure 12.37) that gives you three choices. Make name unique will reprocess all the files but give them each slightly changed filenames to ensure not overwriting previous work. Overwrite existing file will do just that, and skip file will move it on to other files on the list and not overwrite or create a new file. Checking the apply to all files box will apply your choice automatically to all remaining files listed for processing.

Figure 12.37
You are given a special warning if you try to reprocess files already created from previous efforts.

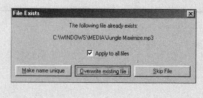

Encoding for WMA

When it comes to encoding for the WMA format, you can use any number of compatible tools, including Stream Anywhere and Sound Forge from Sonic Foundry. However, you can also use the Windows Media Encoder provided as part of the Windows Media Tools 4.X that Microsoft offers for free from its Web site.

> **TIP**
>
> You also can use the Windows Media On-Demand Producer, which is a Sonic Foundry-authored tool that offers an alternative to the freely available Windows Media Encoder.

Using Windows Media Encoder

The basic Windows Media Encoder tool you can download from the Web can convert both .WAV and .MP3 files to the Windows Media Format, which itself is stored as an .ASF file type. (For more on why .ASF is the resulting format, see Chapter 7.)

The encoder is found by downloading it from Microsoft's Web site. The encoder is part of a package of tools called the Windows Media Tools. To download this package go to **http://www.microsoft.com/windows/ windowsmedia/** and click on the download button found along the top of the Web page. This will take you to a download page that features a list to download the Windows Media Tools and Services. Choose from the Windows Media Tools and Services list the Windows Media Tools option and click download now.

Once downloaded, run the wmtools.exe program file; this will install the tools (which includes the encoder) to your system.

When you first load or start a new encoding session with the Windows Media Encoder, you can choose one of three configuration processes: QuickStart, Template with I/O Options, and Custom Settings (see Figure 12.38). The QuickStart feature is good if you want to quickly send a live stream out to a server. You can just choose the type of outgoing stream properties you want and choose Encode, and you're off to the races (see Chapter 14 for more details).

Part III Preparing Content

Figure 12.38
The first thing you must do with the Windows Media Encoder is decide on the wizard process you want to step through to configure the encoding process.

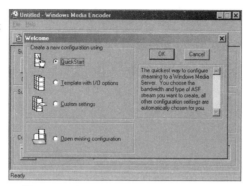

Template with I/O Options is the most useful choice for a quick encoding process. After you select this option, you are greeted with the first configuration dialog, as shown in Figure 12.39. Here, you can choose the basic stream format you want to end up with. Scroll through the list and choose the configuration that best fits your broadcast needs; for most people, the best configuration is the 28.8 FM Radio Stereo setting. Just click on Next to continue.

Figure 12.39
You can start the encoding process by choosing the desired bit rate format of the resulting file.

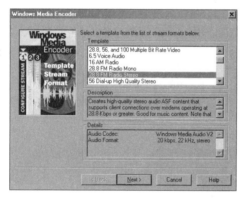

In the next dialog, as shown in Figure 12.40, you can choose whether the encoding is from a live source or from an existing .AVI, .WAV, or .MP3 file. For purposes of this demonstration, we're going to use an .MP3 file. You just click on Next to continue.

Figure 12.40
In this dialog, you can choose whether you want to use a live or prerecorded file.

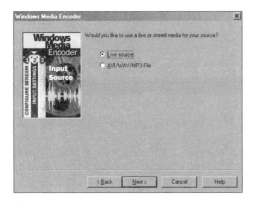

If you've chosen to convert from a pre-existing file, you need to provide the filename of the source file in the next dialog, as shown in Figure 12.41. To do so, either type the filename and path, or click on the Browse button to find the file on your computer or network. After you have set the filename, click on Next to continue.

Figure 12.41
In this dialog, you can tell the encoder the name and location of the source file.

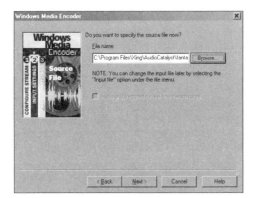

In the next dialog, as shown in Figure 12.42, you need to set the filename and location of the resulting .ASF file as well as define any further characteristics, including the maximum size or duration the file. These settings are important if you're trying to cap the file size or the duration, regardless of the result. When you're encoding music files or some other segment that has its own set duration, you can leave these options alone.

The Automatic Indexing option provides indexing information within the .ASF file that allows users accessing the entire file to fast-forward and rewind while viewing the content. This capability isn't as important for radio as it is for other situations, because listeners aren't given this option, but if you want to be able to quickly skip around an individual file on your end, you should check this option. However, turning off indexing can improve the encoder's speed. Click on Next to move to the next screen in the Wizard.

Part III Preparing Content

Figure 12.42
In this dialog, you can set the output filename and other file characteristics.

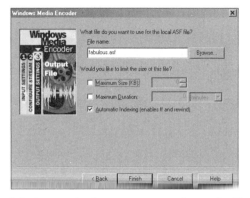

Moving on, in the next screen, shown in Figure 12.43, you can tell the encoder where to send the resulting file. You can have it automatically sent to a Windows Media Server over your network, to a local file, or both.

Figure 12.43
Here, you can tell the encoder where to store the resulting file.

If you choose to store the file locally, you are taken back to the output file name dialog shown in Figure 12.44, where you can check the settings for output and choose Finish to go to the main encoder screen. If you choose to send output to an active Windows Media Server, you are greeted with a screen of further settings, as shown in Figure 12.44.

On this screen, you must first choose a method to transfer the encoded file to the server. For this very server-specific process, you must tell it either a direct IP port or HTTP port to access and send the file through. If you're using the Windows Media Service for broadcasting your files, you'll have this information and be able to use it. Otherwise, you should just store the file locally.

Figure 12.44
With the Windows
Media Encoder, you can
remotely transfer files to
a Windows Media
Server after you tune
the settings accordingly.

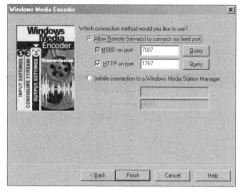

After you've stepped through all the basic queries, your settings are given
to the encoder, and you are sent to the main screen. From this screen, you
can go back through the menus and buttons on the toolbar access
configuration dialogs and tweak any settings as you see fit. If the settings
you entered during the wizard process were fine, you can click on the
Play button, and the encoding process will take place.

Viewing the Encoding Statistics

The Windows Media Encoder includes a couple of other features worth
being familiar with. The Statistics dialog, shown in Figure 12.45, shows
encoding statistics during the encoding process.

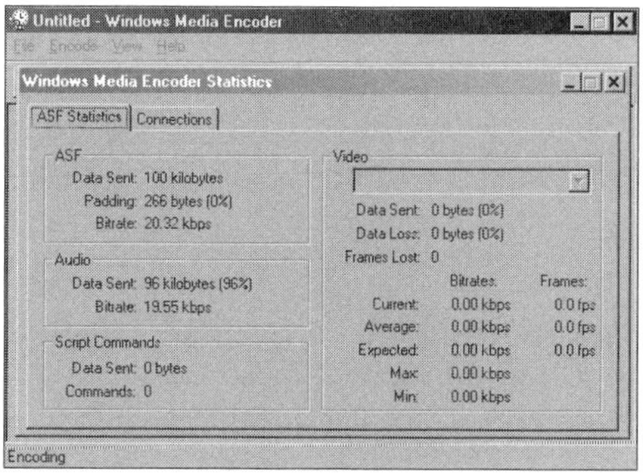

Figure 12.45
You can view statistics
during the encoding
process to get a quick
glimpse of the quality
of the process.

The other items to be aware of is that by choosing Properties from the
Encode menu (Encode > Properties), you are given a dialog with two tabs
that let you expertly set all the of variables that the wizard system steps
you through. As you become familiar enough with the encoder, this can
be a quicker, useful way to setup a session.

Part III Preparing Content

Overall there are a number of packages that now support Windows Media Audio encoding. However, the free encoder included with Windows Media Tools 4.1 and higher provides you a simple, elegant way to encode your Windows Media content for broadcast on-demand or live. Its only drawback is that it doesn't support CD copying or some other batch-oriented conversion features. However, for most radio-oriented broadcasting and especially for those of you smaller personal broadcasters, you don't need a whole bunch of bells and whistles that other Windows Media encoding packages offer (95 percent most of which are video-oriented anyway), so in the end it's worth using the Windows Media Encoder.

Encoding Services

For most radio stations, encoding the audio you play on your station is the best solution, but if you have a ton of content stored in some form other than the encoded form you broadcast in—whether it's reel-to-reel, DAT, CD, vinyl, or unencoded .WAV or AIFF files—you might not want to deal with the chore of encoding. In this case, you might want to turn to a service bureau and outsource your encoding needs. These types of companies take all your content and, as rapidly and perfectly as possible, convert and encode it into the format(s) you want. This is the perfect solution for current radio broadcasters, record companies, or corporations with a backlog of content they want to begin broadcasting on their stations or shows.

Two major encoding service companies exist on the Web today: Loudeye (originally Encoding.com) and Sonic Foundry Media Services. With a little searching, you can find other, lesser-known companies, but these two are well-known and respected encoding bureaus.

Loudeye

If you're looking for the hot Internet startup in the streaming media space, Loudeye is it. This company is basically working on becoming the place you go when you want to automate the encoding of media in large or even small amounts. One of its coolest features for people not encoding hundreds of hours of content at once is its Web-based MediaUpgrade encoding service.

MediaUpgrade.com

MediaUpgrade.com, which is a Web-based encoding solution from Loudeye, enables you to upload media files to an online vault. Then, through a Web-based interface, you can take any file in your online vault and have the file encoded in whatever format you choose. To use this service, follow the steps outlined in the next few sections.

Step 1: Register for Service

To use MediaUpgrade, you first must register on the site (see Figure 12.46). After you register, you go to a page where you can upload files to your online vault and select files for encoding.

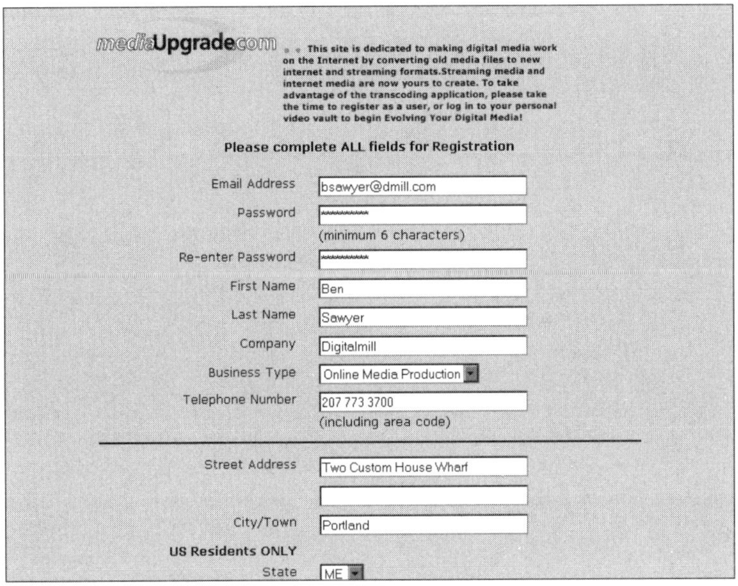

Figure 12.46
Registration is required to use MediaUpgrade.com.

http://www.muskalipman.com

Part III Preparing Content

Step 2: Submit an Original File

Submitting a file is a fairly easy process. At this time, MediaUpgrade accepts only .WAV and .AVI files as original source files. When you upload a file, you also tell MediaUpgrade what format(s) you want it converted to. You are limited to 25MB of space (at the time of this writing), but that space is for final encoded files—meaning you can upload files that are very large but after compression don't take up to 25MB of space. MediaUpgrade also destroys the original file after the encoding process is finished.

Next, you need to fill out the upload form like the one shown in Figure 12.47, choose your codec, and then click on the Upload button when you're finished. When the upload is finished, MediaUpgrade will give you a confirmation screen and eventually send you e-mail when your file has been transcoded.

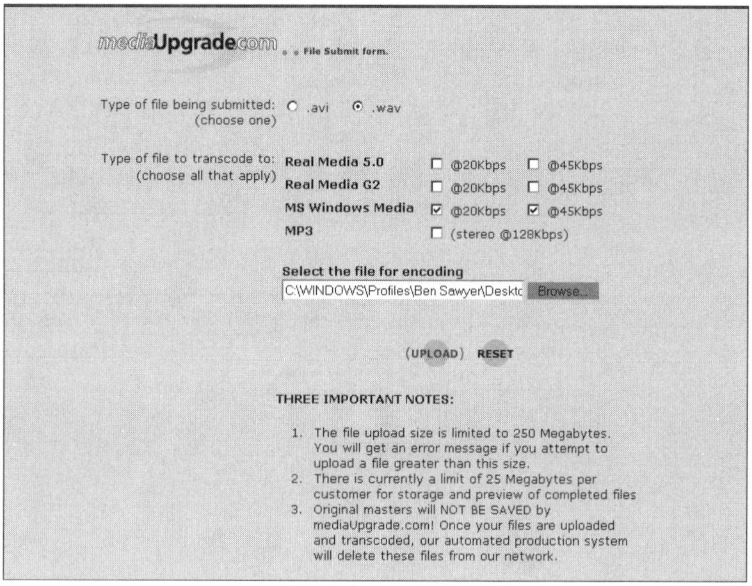

Figure 12.47

Here, you can upload your file and tell MediaUpgrade what formats you want your content encoded to.

Step 3: Retrieve the File

When you return to the main vault screen, you see a listing of files with buttons indicating if they are available for download or still being encoded (see Figure 12.48). When a file is ready for download, you are given up to four choices for it. Click on the View icon if you want to view the file right off the Web site, choose Download to retrieve a file to your PC, or choose Host if you want the file permanently hosted on the Web. If you want to delete a file from your vault, click on the Trashcan icon.

Figure 12.48
When you return to the main vault screen, you see a listing of files with buttons indicating if they are available for download or still being encoded.

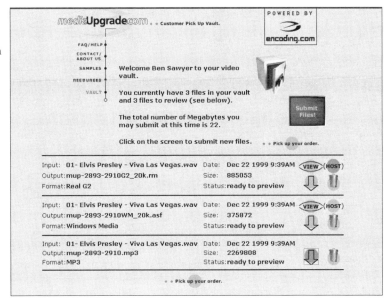

When you first choose an icon, it changes to green. To initiate the work order, click on the Pick Up Your Order icon at the bottom of the vault page. Clicking on this icon takes you to another screen where you can do the actual downloading or present hosting information.

Each item may have a fee listed next to it that will be charged to your account/credit card when MediaUpgrade charges for its use (at the time of this writing, the service is free). To download a file, click on the download link for each item you want. To initiate hosting of a file on MediaUpgrade's hosting partner, InterVU, you first click on the Hosting button, which takes you to a screen where you must agree to the terms and conditions of InterVU's user agreement. After you accept that agreement, MediaUpgrade will send you e-mail that gives you a specific link you can post on your Web site that will initiate download or playback of the encoded file.

For most radio station operators, MediaUpgrade isn't of much use, especially if you're constantly encoding a lot of material. However, for casual users and people who have fast connections to the Internet, MediaUpgrade is a nice tool; it shows the future of encoding as an online-based application. Additionally, if you're a complete neophyte who wants an easy way to take recorded .WAV files and convert them to files for your radio station or show, MediaUpgrade is perhaps the easiest way for you to accomplish your task.

Part III Preparing Content

Sonic Foundry Media Services

When a company makes some of the world's most respected audio editing and encoding software tools, offering encoding services as well should be a no-brainer. Following on the success of Loudeye, Sonic Foundry recently launched its own streaming media service bureau, which you can find on its Web site at **http://www.sonicfoundry.com/mediaservices/**.

Look Both Ways Before You Encode a Beat

Now that you know how to encode your content into whatever format(s) you're choosing to broadcast in, you're probably going to dive in and begin ripping away and encoding all the content you ever dreamed of broadcasting. However, before you begin to encode every song or other content you can think of, you should consider how you plan to organize your entire encoding process. Aside from the basic encoding process and program you choose, you should also make decisions about the following:

▶ **What form will you keep the original recording in?**

Unless you are doing a live broadcast, all recordings must be recorded prior to being encoded, and they must be converted to an unencoded digital format (for example, .WAV or .AIFF). This means that you will most likely be developing lots of unencoded original recordings. If you're very serious about your broadcasting and keeping up with new formats, you might want to back up and store the originally digitized raw files. This way, as new formats and bit rates emerge, you can re-encode from the perfect originals because decoding and re-encoding from previously encoded material degrades the quality of the file. Not everyone can afford to decode and re-encode or do it for every file, but before you encode lots of formats, you need to make a decision about how and whether you want to archive original digitizations for later use.

▶ **Will you encode to multiple formats and bit rates?**

Many broadcasters should consider the implications of encoding to multiple formats and bit rates for their stations. Before beginning the encoding process, you should consider whether you feel that offering your station in various formats (.WMA, .MP3, or RealAudio) will actually benefit you through increased listenership. Certainly, .MP3 is a very popular format, and people who favor it will favor stations that broadcast in it, yet at the same time much of the greater Internet population favors RealAudio simply because these users have player applications that support it. If you're going to encode to multiple formats, then you must decide whether you will use a program that automates multiple formats (such as Streaming Anywhere) or whether you will go with a specialized encoder for each format. Services such as Loudeye and Sonic Foundry Media Services can be a boon for large encoding jobs.

▶ **How will you organize your files?**

The more you encode, the more your hard drives are going to fill up with content. And not every format supports robust metadata either. Thus, you should consider file-naming conventions and file organization processes ahead of the encoding process. Using a media organization program is also a useful idea; we outlined a couple of them in Chapter 4. For a naming process, you have two issues to consider. First, you need to consider what format you will use for the actual filename you choose for your media. We suggest that you use something similar to the following example:

Recording Name - Date of Recording - Subject - (Album Name/Keyword) . Format Extension

You essentially give the first part of the filename a simple name; then you follow it with the date of recording (for example, 10-10-1999), which may be different from the actual date tagged to the file by the operating system. This date is the date the file itself was encoded. Follow this information with the subject of the recording (name of interviewee, artist if it's an album, event name, and so on), and then optionally include the name of the album or a keyword (for example, interview, concert, speech, and so on), followed by the actual extension of the format (for example, .MP3, .WMA, .ASF). This file-naming convention will make managing the files for your station much easier. An example might look like this:

ChuckDInterview-10-10-1999-RapHistory-Interview.MP3

Second, you should always take advantage of any meta information an encoded format offers you. Don't leave these information fields blank, because adding this information can be a key way to organize and build playlists in the future.

In short, encoding involves more than just clicking on the magical Encode button. As you can see, for many of the major programs, you must set a lot of options and do a great deal of work before you actually encode any content. Even before you take these steps, as discussed in the preceding chapter, you have a lot to do to tweak an original recording as well. Finally, before you do anything, you need to establish some rules about how you will store, encode, and organize all your content.

If you don't take these steps, your station—however small and personal or large and commercial—will be harder to run and will feature content that doesn't sound as good as it could.

13

Programming: Doing Talk, Booking Guests, Making Playlists, and Setting Up A Show

Although this book focuses specifically on Internet broadcasting (hence the title), many issues relate to traditional radio as well. You can have all your technological ducks in a row, but if you don't broadcast something worth listening to, you'll be doing all that work for an audience of one—you.

This chapter deals with those content-related issues that help set your station apart. We'll cover all the details that make a radio program worth listening to, whether it is developing a music format and an exciting playlist, creating interesting talk radio programs and interviews, or obtaining free or licensed content. And we'll include some details on show pacing, bumpers, station identifications, and more.

Music Programming

Many of you—probably most of you—will use the Internet as a way to broadcast music. Whether you are a commercial broadcaster or just someone with a passion for music and an interest in spreading your taste, chances are you became interested in Internet broadcasting because you have an interest in music. Or maybe you think all your local stations are terrible and you can do better. Whatever your motivation for broadcasting music, we'll give you some ideas to think about.

Developing a Station Format

Commercial radio has become so beholden to strict formatting that it has grown generally stale and stagnant. Playlists are determined solely by market research, and disc jockeys at all but a handful of stations have lost any power that their counterparts might have had in the Sixties and Seventies. This is your opportunity as the programmer of your own station to seize that power for yourself. That freedom and flexibility can be liberating. For example, an eclectic station that isn't afraid to follow Miles

Davis with Lauryn Hill or Nine Inch Nails can be exciting to some listeners. However, it can also be annoying for jazz fans who gag at the thought of NIN's industrial noisescapes or edgy alt-rockers who can't stand hip-hop. Unless you clearly establish that your station plays everything from jazz to blues to rap to metal to techno, you run the risk of losing all your listeners as soon as a genre they don't like is dropped into the stew.

We don't mean there isn't space for such a station. We can only hope that people haven't become so predictable that they want to hear only one type of music. However, finding the right balance of music and the audience that actually wants to hear everything from Wynton Marsalis to Pearl Jam to Elvis Costello to Korn can be difficult. If you can do it, great!

A more sound idea—and an easier one—is to develop a format for your station. Some Internet stations offer several streams or channels that have a very specific target audience: punk, alternative rock, techno, blues, jazz, and so on. This type of station is attractive to the listener who wants to listen to, for example, punk rock for a long stretch. It is particularly attractive to those who favor a genre of music such as techno that receives little or no commercial radio airplay. Again, in this arena, Internet broadcasting and its lower cost of entry as compared to traditional commercial radio can be extremely powerful—by offering music for a very specific audience.

However, this type of station can be somewhat limiting to a listener who doesn't mind hearing some Bjork along with Fugazi and who doesn't want to spend time hopping from channel to channel. With musical genres becoming as splintered as they have, you can also develop a format based on one relatively broad genre, such as alternative rock (although we're not sure what "alternative" means at this point) and still have the flexibility to cover a variety of music rather than becoming one of those deathly boring radio stations many Internet broadcasters are rebelling against in the first place. And you are not beholden to playing just the hits. If, for example, you think the new Filter record has stronger tracks than the single that gets all the commercial airplay, you, as an Internet broadcaster, have the freedom to play those other tracks, because that's what many of your listeners will be looking for. Or if you think your audience is more interested in hearing an old Nirvana B-side rather than "Smells Like Teen Spirit" for the 15,000th time, you can play those songs, too.

Clock Format

Formatting your station—which not only includes songs but might also include audio advertisements, station identification, bumpers, and more—takes organization and planning. One method of designing a program is to use a one-hour clock. This approach enables you to balance the time allotted to types of music (current hits, album tracks, older hits, rare songs, and so on), speech, advertising, and other aspects of your broadcast.

As you begin developing your program, you must, of course, consider your audience. Will the music come first and thus naturally attract a certain audience? Or are you hoping to attract a particular demographic group and thus select a certain type of music based on that desired demographic? As we stated earlier, if you have high commercial aspirations, it is important to play music that can attract a large or wide audience. At the same time, the variety should not be so wide that it pleases no one.

After you have established a major format type (that is, classic rock, modern rock, jazz, R&B, electronica, and so on), you can then select sub-genres that provide variety. This step involves choosing songs that vary in sound, tempo, era, and so on. In other words, a rock station needn't be limited to up-tempo, hard rock. You can mix the fast with the mid-tempo and slower songs, the heavy with the light, the noisy with the melodic. The key is to present a program that is satisfying from start to finish, no matter how long the time period within which you are working. Keeping the interest of the listeners is far more important than starting off with a bang only to lose that momentum and, along with it, your listeners. You also need to consider how long most of your listeners will stay tuned. Traditional radio has to deal with morning and afternoon drive times, when much of the audience will be listening only for the duration of the work commute. But because listeners generally tune in to Internet radio through a stationary output—their computers—you don't have to be concerned with listeners turning off the broadcast when they get out of their cars. Therefore, if you can establish a show that maintains momentum for an hour or two or even more, you have a better chance of holding on to those listeners. If your program becomes boring or repetitive in its sound or tempo, you will lose that opportunity.

The following programming and scheduling guidelines can help:

▶ If you plan to have speech, station identifications, bumpers, commercials, and other elements between songs, space the non-musical elements wisely so that you don't fall into the repetitive trap of song-element-song-element. Break this repetition by playing two or three songs without interruption.

▶ Space these other elements throughout the hour. Don't cram all your station identifications into the first fifteen minutes and all your commercials into the last fifteen minutes.

▶ If elements vary in length, mix the length wisely—the shorter ones followed by the longer ones and vice versa.

▶ When you're playing new or relatively obscure songs, sandwich them between more well-known tracks to avoid turning off people who don't want to hear three new songs without hearing something more familiar. If you are interested in breaking new songs or artists, you can also establish a program at a regular time each day or week dedicated to just that idea. It can be a popular feature for listeners who want to hear fresh, new music.

▶ If you have repeat features, schedule them for the same time during the program. For example, schedule a news break at the top of each hour or a Top 5 songs feature at the same time each day.

Tips on Making a Good Song Playlist

How you create your playlist depends on how much of a commercial entity you intend your station to be. Commercial stations track songs very closely, playing certain songs and styles at certain times, keeping close track of their playlist so as not to repeat some songs too often and, on the other hand, play popular songs at regular intervals (some would argue those songs are played far too regularly).

How much freedom you allow over your programming depends on how much control you want to have personally over what is played. If it's just you creating the playlist—well, you have all the power! If you have people working or volunteering for you, you can give them total control (maybe not a wise choice unless you have the utmost confidence in them), no control (in which case they might not stick around for long), or some control (which can be a good alternative). Many college stations use a bin system in which disc jockeys are given some, but not total, control of what they play. The station categorizes records in bins, and the DJ is allowed to pick any song from Bin A, then Bin B, then Bin C, and so on. This system gives the program director, who fills the bins, some control over the music while also allowing the DJ to pick specific songs from those bins at the prescribed time.

Although an Internet station won't have records or CDs stacked in bins, you can set up a similar computerized filing system and use it yourself or have your virtual DJs do the same. For example, you can set the pacing of the show by rolling through your virtual bins (folders on your hard drive) that contain similar types of music. That way, the songs change from time period to time period, but the pacing of the time periods remains consistent. This bin system, of course, takes plenty of planning and should follow the ideas mentioned in the preceding section (that is, new music sandwiched between current or known hits). You also should consider your available hard drive space when creating a huge catalogue of files to broadcast. Some people even buy second drives completely devoted to the storage of audio files. With prices falling constantly, you can get some huge multi-gigabyte drives for relatively little money. The key, however, is to organize well by using folders and subfolders and by using a playlist editor like those mentioned in Chapter 4. Finally, you might consider encoding only at the bitrate you'll broadcast at; if that's below 128 bits, it will certainly save room on your drive.

At this point, the clock format comes in handy. You can start the programming time frame with an established older song, followed by a current popular song, followed by a new song, followed by a lesser known song by an established artist, and so on. And if you file your songs in this manner, you can breeze through the various folders and set up your program.

Of course, as the broadcaster, you are responsible for organizing the program as you see fit. Following some established guidelines is necessary to build a quality program, but you should not feel chained to those guidelines. You should allow yourself some freedom while still considering what your audience wants. After all, it's your station!

Talk Programming

The best radio talk shows sound very natural, almost as if the host is simply talking to the audience and any guests are engaged in a conversation. The reason for this is not luck; it is preparation. Even the programs that seem to be the loosest and least scripted follow a predetermined course. If you are interested in creating a talk radio broadcast, you must realize that the least amount of work will be spent actually on the air. Your most important efforts involve creating timely topics for your audience, writing scripts, organizing your program, finding and booking guests, conducting pre-interviews of your guests, writing scripts, and more. If this work is done with care and effort, your talk show will be the payoff.

Setting Up a Script

You might think you can roll through your talk radio program by just winging it or by using notes as aids. This approach might work to some extent; however, the more information you have in front of you, the less stress you will encounter and the less likely you are to get confused, lose your train of thought, or end up with too little or too much to say within the specified time frame.

The key is to be thoroughly prepared while still sounding natural. If you are going to follow a script, you must sound like you are talking to the listeners, not reading aloud. How detailed your script is depends largely on who is reading the script. If you are writing for yourself, an outline with some notes and prompts might be sufficient. If you arc writing for someone else, a better choice is a script that will be rehearsed, possibly modified by the reader, and followed fairly closely.

Using an Outline or Notes

As you begin writing your script, you must first know what points you want to make and how those points make the transition into one another. As you write down the main points, you might need to rearrange the order so that each point flows smoothly into the next. As you organize the order of your thoughts, keep your listeners in mind. Does the move from one point to the next make you scratch your head and ask "where did that come from?" If so, you need to reconsider the order.

As you put your main points in order, you will likely be thinking about what you will say to support those points. Begin jotting down these supporting ideas under each main idea, and your outline will begin to take shape. Of course, you should be sure that each main point is supported by facts or anecdotes.

When you're writing for yourself, especially as you gain experience as an on-air speaker, you might find that you needn't write down every word you want to say. Instead, you can simply use the outline and anecdotal prompts to remind you where you want to go next. In other words, under your first main point, you might have notes such as "mention last winter's trip to Hawaii." If someone else were to read that, that person might have no idea what it meant. However, that simple phrase could lead to two minutes' worth of information from you.

When it comes to facts, such as statistics or studies, using such vague prompts is unwise. Rather than a note such as "mention related statistics," you should have the specific numbers written neatly in your outline. Remembering exact statistics is more difficult than recalling a story. Citing incorrect numbers or rough numbers like "I think somewhere around 35 percent said they favored this" when the actual number is available will undermine your credibility, especially if someone calls you on the inaccuracy. Also, remember to credit the source of the statistics, which adds strength to your facts. Rather than say something like "some survey said…" you should say "according to a study by Jupiter Communications…"

You should write your introduction precisely, either before or after you have completed your outline. Often you might write an introduction before you begin the outline and then, upon reviewing the outline, slightly rewrite the introduction. Writing your complete introduction rather than some rough notes helps solidify your thoughts and gives you a smooth start when it is more likely you might be a bit nervous. When you are through your introduction, those nerves should be fading, and you can cruise through your outline. It is also important to have a very strong introduction to keep people from immediately growing disinterested and turning off your program. Writing and rehearsing your introduction will improve it and get you off on the right foot with your listeners.

The physical appearance of your outline is also important. It must be neat (preferably typed), easy to read and follow, and not covered with cross-outs, arrows, and other notations. Otherwise, you run the risk of getting midway into your monologue and suddenly finding yourself lost. And when panic sets in, you will really be lost.

Completing the Script

As we mentioned in the preceding section, the introduction is extremely important to both capture the interest of the audience and to inform them about what is to come.

Speaking on the air should be conversational but not sloppy. That means avoiding the "ums," "ahs," and "you knows" that sometimes slip into casual conversation. At this point, a tight script that has been rehearsed can come in handy. Having the words in front of you will keep you from using those pauses that naturally occur when you are speaking and thinking at roughly the same pace. A script can lessen the effort spent thinking and allow you to focus on speaking. Although there will be instances when you must think on your feet (technical difficulties, responding to live callers, and more), you will have already done much of the thinking when preparing the script.

The level of casualness also depends on what type of spoken word you are broadcasting. Something as serious as news should be formal, and the script should be followed exactly. But a spoken broadcast that is intended to provoke discussion (either from listeners who call to join the discussion on air or from in-studio guests) can be more conversational.

A good way to write a script is to speak the words out loud, write them down as you do, and then go back and polish the script. This way, the script is based on the spoken word rather than the written word, and the spoken word can than be formalized a bit if needed. This method also keeps your sentences and phrases shorter and simpler and thus easier both for you to speak and for the audience to follow. Written sentences tend to be naturally more complex, which is something you want to avoid.

For example, you might write the following completely understandable sentence:

> Kobe Bryant, after skipping college to go straight into the NBA, struggled to adjust during his first season but has since blossomed into one of basketball's best young players.

However, speaking this information, and therefore writing it into a script, might look and sound more like this:

> Kobe Bryant skipped college to go straight into the NBA. His first season was a struggle. But since then he has blossomed into one of basketball's best young players.

When you're writing a script, write what you speak.

Booking Guests

Because your talk radio program will focus on a certain general subject (politics, music, technology, and so on), you will likely develop contacts and know who the important players are within that area. As you meet these people, it is important for you to let them know if you are interested in having them as guests, whether it is in the near future or down the road a bit. Although you will certainly want to book guests cold (in other words, your first contact is asking them to appear on your broadcast), it is much easier to book people you have met or established a relationship with. As you become known through your broadcasting efforts, booking guests will become much easier as many people will look forward to being asked.

Finding Interesting Guests

Interesting guests are timely guests—people who are in the news and can offer insight on a topic that is relevant to your broadcast and of interest to your listeners. Although many of these people will be in demand, working to get the best guests possible will distinguish your show. As an extreme example, who do you think would make a more interesting guest, Steve Jobs or Steve Jobs' gardener?

This example, of course, raises the question of what to do when the equivalent of Steve Jobs either can't or won't appear on your show. Don't despair—rare is the topic that doesn't have more than a handful of experts. The trick is distinguishing the true experts from the people who *think* they are experts. This ability should come naturally if you are passionate about the topics you cover on your broadcast. You will be involved in the particular area and will have a good idea who you want to interview and who will provide interesting commentary.

Two groups of people worth keeping in mind are reporters and analysts covering the particular topic or industry. Not only are they informed on current events, but they are also less likely to have an agenda (such as promoting their own company) and, having been on the other side of many interviews, can provide thoughtful but concise answers.

The key to finding good guests is to simply be involved with the topic you are covering. Be active online, attend events and trade shows, get to know people, and tell them exactly what you do. In short, learn to schmooze! Not only will this approach lead directly to finding future guests, but you never know when someone you meet will be able to set up a meeting between you and one of his or her colleagues. Going back to our Steve Jobs example—you don't have to be tight with him, you just have to be tight with someone who is tight with him.

Making a Good Pitch and a Flexible Schedule

If you get to know enough people, the pitch will be easy. And when you become more well known, attracting guests for your Internet broadcasts will also be easier. In fact, if your reputation is strong enough, there will come a time when guests even ask to be on your show. However, some guests you will have to convince.

Skeptical guests will want to know a few facts. How large is your listenership? Who listens to your program? What is the tone of the program? What topics will be covered? Will I be able to discuss my latest project?

You need to make your potential guest feel like he or she will benefit from the appearance. Don't be afraid to flatter the person as long as you don't go overboard. It is perfectly acceptable to tell the person how important for your listeners it is to make an appearance. In the end, assuming your interview will not be aggressive and their schedule isn't too overloaded, most people will be happy to appear if it means a reasonable amount of exposure for their interests. And many will do it just out of their commitment to or interest in the topic.

Being flexible in scheduling your guests can be helpful. As you plan future shows, try not to lock a particular topic into a specific day until you have a commitment from your guest or guests. And always have a backup plan available should a guest cancel at the last minute. With any luck, cancellations will happen infrequently, but if they do, don't be caught trying to wing it through your show. Either have a potential backup guest, a different show that doesn't involve guests or, if all else fails, an archived show you can rerun. However, constantly rerunning old shows will not endear you to your listeners and will eventually cause them to jump ship.

Interviewing

On-air interviewing must not only provide answers and information about the particular topic (or about the interviewee), it must also flow smoothly enough so that it is entertaining for the listeners. However, the on-air interview should not answer the most basic questions, such as what the person's position is, how long he or she has been doing what it is he or she does, and so on. Those questions should be answered in the pre-interview and through research. For any interview, preparation is the key.

Research

Because you have booked a particular guest, it goes without saying that you should know something about the person. It is this knowledge that compelled you to book the guest in the first place, right? However, do you know *everything* about the person? And by that, we don't mean the name of the person's dog and the ages of his or her children. You must know everything about the person and, if applicable, his or her organization that is relevant to the interview before you go on the air. The interview is not the time for *you* to find out what you need to know; it's the time for *your listeners* to find out what they want to know.

Whatever basic information led you to book a guest is a good place to start your research. You can learn more about the person through the source that directed you to him or her, through newspaper articles, Web research—wherever you can get your hands on it. Make sure you have the very basic information down first—the correct pronunciation of the person's name, his or her specific title, and what he or she does—and make sure this person is relevant to the topic you are discussing. For instance, if you want to do a show about the MP3 explosion, make sure the guest is qualified to talk about that subject.

Your research will certainly provide you with plenty of information and will lead to several questions that you can ask in the pre-interview. Being fully prepared for the on-air interview will give you credibility; being unprepared will give the listeners the impression that you are either careless or clueless, neither of which is good.

Pre-interview

The pre-interview is just a standard interview between you and your upcoming guest that is not heard by anyone other than you. For example, when a print journalist writes a story, much of the interview process does not result in the quotes that are used in the story but in the background information upon which the story is built. This type of information is what you get in the pre-interview—answers to those questions your listeners don't need to hear, such as "How do you pronounce your last name? How long have you been at Company X?" and more.

The pre-interview is not a rehearsal of the on-air interview. However, the tone of the interview must be considered during the pre-interview. If the on-air interview is going to be controversial or include tough questions for the guest (such as in the case of interviewing a politician), you should absolutely not tell the guest what questions you will ask. These types of guests should be prepared for difficult questions. If they aren't, that is their fault. Their inability to answer these questions will reveal more about them than if they have a day or two to craft answers to your probing questions.

If your interview is on a topic that does not involve controversy, such as interviewing an artist about a new CD or an author about a new book, you can give the guest a rough idea about what topics you want to cover. However, presenting the guest with a list of questions before the interview will rob the interview of the spontaneity that makes talk radio so interesting.

The following are some basic questions to consider during the pre-interview:

▶ How do you pronounce your name?

▶ What is your exact professional title?

▶ Where is your business/organization located?

▶ How long has your business/organization been in existence?

▶ How long have you been involved in that business/organization?

▶ What is the background of the business/organization?

▶ How did the project to be discussed (if there is one) develop?

▶ How does the current topic of discussion relate to the listeners?

The pre-interview will also help you anticipate some likely answers and follow-up questions to those answers.

The information you gather during the pre-interview will enable you to introduce the guest properly before starting the interview. The introduction should include any information about the guest that is relevant to the discussion, the guest's relevant professional background, and any current happenings, such as the guest's relevant recent work (new book, new project, new piece of software developed, and so on).

On-air Interview

The tone of your interview and the types of questions you ask will depend on what type of station you have, what the topic is, and who the guest is. No matter what type of guest, you have to enter the interview prepared (which will be the case assuming you do solid research and a pre-interview as described previously) and know what type of information you want the listeners to gain.

Your research and pre-interview will also give you an idea of how much time you need to give the subject. This point is extremely important because you neither want to be forced to end the interview without covering the subject sufficiently nor do you want the interview to reach its natural conclusion and be left with 5 to 10 minutes to fill.

The following questions will help you create an interesting interview:

▶ Who? For example, "Who is involved in this project?" or "Who will this project affect?"

▶ What? For example, "What has made this project successful?" or "What kind of impact will this project have?"

▶ Where? For example, "Where will the impact of this project be felt?"

▶ When? For example, "When will this project be complete?"

▶ Why? For example, "Why is this project important?"

▶ How? For example, "How did this project come together?" or "How will this project affect people?"

Part III Preparing Content

These types of open-ended questions allow the guest to give answers that are more than "yes" or "no" but offer information to the listeners. That is not to say that you should never ask a question that elicits either a "yes" or "no" answer. Often you can lead into a more open-ended question by getting a "yes" or "no" answer to a preliminary question. Consider this example:

> Q: "Do you think this will have far-reaching effects on American consumers?"
>
> A: "Yes."
>
> Q: "What will those effects be?"

This technique also keeps you from asking two questions at once. If you are totally committed to avoiding any "yes" or "no" answers, you might end up asking something like "Do you think this will have far-reaching effects on American consumers? If so, what will those effects be? And if not, why not?" Cramming multiple questions into one is confusing for the guest and the audience. Also, if your guest is well prepared and has experience being interviewed, he or she will most likely save you the need for a follow-up question by naturally expanding on the "yes" or "no" answer.

It's Not About You

One critical mistake many interviewers make is talking too much. Either because they are used to doing most of the talking as a host of a show, or they are trying to impress their guest and audience with their grasp of the topic, or because they simply are a bit too fond of the sound of their own voice, interviewers sometimes forget that the point of having a guest is so that the guest can provide insight on a topic. Don't make this mistake.

An interview is not even a 50-50 conversation. The guest should do the majority of the speaking. This will happen assuming you are prepared with good questions, can keep your ego in check, and you have booked a good guest (which we discussed previously).

The time you spend talking should generally be limited to introducing the guest, asking questions, clarifying cloudy answers either with statements or follow-up questions, and taking the interview in a different direction with a transitional statement. This way, you have plenty of control over the interview without dominating it.

One other reason to allow the guest to speak is to ensure that the guest will have an enjoyable experience and be happy to return if you want him or her back. If a guest has to fight to get a word in edgewise, it is unlikely he or she will return. A couple of good talks shows that are broadcast on the Internet are Computer Beat with Andy Graham (a Internet simulcast of his local broadcast in Kansas City) and TechTalk Radio (**www.techtalkradio.com**), another Internet/technology-oriented show, originating from Palm Springs, California.

Getting Content for Your Station

What's a broadcast without content? Dead air or, in this case, empty bandwidth. Content—whether it is music, talk, or even the station identifications and bumpers we mentioned earlier in this chapter—is what makes your broadcast. Some content you can create on your own; some you will have to obtain.

Free Versus Licensed Content

Licensed content costs money and includes most music, syndicated music, talk shows, and just about everything else you hear on commercial radio. However, depending on what you want to broadcast, you can find plenty of free content, such as old time radio shows and even some music (unsigned artists are often thrilled for the exposure and don't worry about collecting the relatively small rights fees to which they are entitled each time a song is played). You can also create your own free content.

Creating Free Content

Creating content takes a bit of time and effort but can be worthwhile both in terms of saving money and in getting something on the air that is your own, whether it is your own music or your own talk show.

The following are some examples of free content you might consider creating:

- ▶ Monologues
- ▶ Interviews
- ▶ News programs
- ▶ Call-in shows
- ▶ Talk shows
- ▶ Event coverage
- ▶ Event interviews
- ▶ Song parodies
- ▶ Your own music

Part III Preparing Content

Finding Free Content

You can find free content out there as well, although music is the most difficult to obtain without paying the appropriate licensing fees (see Chapter 16). However, many old radio shows fall under copyright laws that make them part of the public domain, which means you can obtain and broadcast them without any fees.

One outstanding source you might want to check when you're beginning your search for free content is the Free Audio Content Broadcasters Association (**www.facba.org**), which was formed to promote freely available audio content. This group is the relaunch of the former FABCA (Free Audio Broadcasters Association) which was a group listing bands that allowed their songs to be played for free.

For potentially free music, you can turn either to local artists in your area or the Internet's largest collection of unsigned and generally unknown bands at MP3.com (**www.mp3.com**). Wading through the thousands of artists to find what you want can be a time-consuming task. However, MP3.com offers lists of its most popular songs to make the search a bit easier. When you find what you like, you can contact the artists to see whether they would be interested in the free exposure that your broadcast can provide.

When you contact artists, be sure to provide them with all the information necessary to make an informed decision about allowing you to play their music. Tell them about your station (format, number of listeners, where to find it on the Web, how long you've been operating), yourself, why you want to play their music, how it would be beneficial to them, and how and when they can most easily contact you.

The Call-In Show:
Taking Calls and Talking It Up

When it comes to generating content for your radio station or show, nothing is cheaper or easier to produce than a call-in show; it's also free of copyright. That doesn't mean doing one is the best idea. Some talent is required to host a call-in show well, and you're at the mercy of callers. But producing a call-in show is a great way to create attractive original content in an inexpensive manner.

The first issue to be concerned about is being able to take calls. This process can be easy or more complex depending on how important it is to you to screen calls and host multiple callers at the same time.

Screening Calls

Regular radio stations that take on-air calls try to screen their calls to prevent the callers from disrupting a program and to get interesting callers on the air as much as possible. Screening is usually done by someone (usually a producer or assistant producer of the show) taking the initial call and talking to the caller to determine whether he or she is worth putting through. If so, the caller is put on hold, and the host can eventually take the call. High-end stations and programs even have a computer system that allows the producer to log the call and type out who the caller is and what he or she plans to ask. With this system, the host can announce the caller's name and know what direction the call will take the program.

When a call is on the air, to prevent a caller from using profanity, there is usually a three-to-five second delay on the call. This time delay allows the host or producer to press a button that can mute the caller for a few seconds. Part of the reason for this delay is that the FCC (Federal Communications Commission) requires that profane and obscene language not be broadcast over public airwaves. However, the Internet is not covered by that restriction, so building a digital delay into your broadcast isn't required (although you might decide to have it anyway).

The bigger problem for the Internet broadcaster is screening initial calls. Many broadcasters, especially personal broadcasters, do not have the ability to screen calls during a show. If you have someone who can do that and help, all the better, but what can you do if you're producing just a one-person show?

You might want to consider these tips on screening calls:

▶ **Hook up caller ID to your system.** This way, you can note phone numbers that could indicate past callers or troublemakers. Don't take calls from people who block their numbers from caller ID.

▶ **When you screen a call, have the caller state his or her full name, reason for calling, and phone number.** From there, you can quickly ask the caller what he or she wants to talk about or ask when on the air. From this information, you'll have to use your best judgment if the caller is trying to con you into putting him or her onto the air or if he or she is legitimate.

▶ **Set up multiple lines to take calls if you can, and provide a means for people to hear the show while they're on hold.** (See the sidebar, "Enabling Callers to Hear the Show While on Hold.")

▶ **Give your best callers and regulars a private line on which they can call in.** Providing this line makes it easy to get especially good and loyal callers on the air faster.

Part III Preparing Content

▶ **Be patient when taking calls from people with speech patterns or accents that will be hard for listeners to understand.** Be prepared to repeat what they say or ask for listeners who couldn't understand. It would be a rare and extreme case that a caller would be totally unintelligible.

Using Voicemail and the Net

One way for a one-person show to take calls is to use a voicemail system. People leave calls on your voicemail, and then you can screen them during breaks in the program or even beforehand, selecting the best questions and playing them back over the air. The drawback to this approach is that you cannot ask follow-up questions or have a conversation.

You can also make use of the Internet itself by using voice-chat tools and by letting people submit recorded questions via e-mail.

Building Prerecorded Blocks of Content

If you are doing a show yourself and want to do some basic screening of calls, you should plan on running three to five minutes' worth of music or other content so that you can answer the phone and set up the next batch of calls.

Connecting Phones to Your Show

To take calls on your show, you need a way to patch the call in to your outgoing feed. You can do so in a couple of ways. The cheapest way is to purchase a phone-recording patch box for about $30 and then feed it into your sound card. The drawbacks of using this inexpensive device are that the sound quality isn't very great, and it patches in on the incoming phone line and not the handset. Therefore, taking calls from multiple lines is impossible. Using this device also prevents you from doing three-way calls—say between you and two callers; or between you, a guest on the show, and another caller. However, as an inexpensive and quick means to put phone calls on the air, it can't be beat.

The other option is to purchase higher-end equipment that connects to the handset cord of the phone system. This approach will give you much greater capabilities both in terms of what types of phone situations you can set up and in terms of sound quality. You can choose from several devices for improved phone systems. Genter (**www.gentner.com**) is one company that makes some excellent equipment for radio call-in systems. Broadcast Supply Warehouse (**www.bws-usa.com**) is a dealer for Genter's equipment as well as some other capable devices. Table 13.1 includes some suggested products, with ballpark pricing, that you can use for phone in systems.

Table 13.1
Phone Equipment

Product Name	Manufacturer	Price	Features
TS612 v. 2.5	Gentner	~$4200	This product is a good example of high-end call-in show hardware. This rack mount system and phone can handle multiple lines and has high-quality audio output.
Telehybrid	Gentner	~$750	This nice mid-range device gives you excellent audio out of a single phone station (which itself may handle multiple lines).
SPH10	Gentner	~$500	This lower-end rack mount system provides clear caller audio with some simple mixing options.
230- 1x6 Telephone System	Telos	~$2200	The One-x-Six (as it is known) is a rack mount unit that includes a six-line phone system with keypads. The console lets you move around caller, control delays, and other key features. Optional software can be used for call-screening management.
Microtel1	Gentner	~$275	Portable and battery operated, this simple phone interface includes plugs for a handset, your headset, audio in and out, as well as an XLR plug for a microphone. Simple mixing options are also included.
THAT-1	JKAudio	~$150	This simple phone interface includes simple volume control and audio in and out.
THAT-2	JKAudio	~$225	A step up from the THAT-1, this interface also features XLR input/outputs.

Assuming you have the hardware to get audio out of your phone system, you need to decide how you will interface it into your broadcast. This decision is made a bit more difficult by the fact that you also want to route your microphone (headset or otherwise) into the mix and get a single point of audio going into your sound card. In some cases—as with the SoundBlaster Live, Aureal Vortex, and other higher-end sound cards—you will have multiple inputs into your card, usually a microphone in and a line-in. This makes it easier to set up your system, plug your microphone in, and then get a single in-point from your phone system and use your sound card's mixer to set levels. You can also optionally run everything through an outside mixer and then into your sound card. An outside mixer will give you a bit more control over a software-based mixer, and you can have even more inputs. Figure 13.1 shows an outline of a couple of phone system setups to use.

Figure 13.1
Possible phone
system setups.

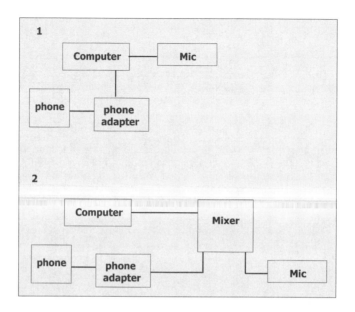

From there, you'll need to have a server system that puts your feed out over the Internet. Check back with each server system detailed in Chapters 5 through 9 for more information on how you can broadcast line-in audio. In some cases, as with SHOUTcast, you can cross-fade and mix locally pre-encoded material with live, line-in content. With other systems, doing so will be more difficult. Some sound cards may not support multiple streams and the capability to play out audio while taking in audio. You'll need to upgrade if that's the case.

Further Tech Issues: Lines

If you're going to do a well-honed talk show on the Internet, you need to further define your telephone side. One line won't cut it, even for a reasonable hobbyist. Having two lines is a useful minimum, and you should ideally have two lines plus a private line for guests and outgoing calls. If you're not using a higher-end call-in system, you'll need to use a basic headset system to output your audio to your broadcast. That means the phone connected to that device needs to give you access to all incoming lines to the show. It should feature some capability to conference callers as well.

The phone line setup is also an important consideration. If you're setting up multiple lines for your call-in show/station, you should order groups of lines that all use the same incoming number. You might want to set up a private line with a separate number that is unpublished. You also might want to consider having a toll-free number. Toll-free service can be added to your regular phone bill for between $5 and $10 a month. Although this service can add to your phone costs, it can be important for national audiences who might not want to be on hold for a half hour on their nickel.

Enabling Callers to Hear the Show While on Hold

One important part of talk radio is that, because of the delay (either planned or inherent given the latency of Web broadcasts), you don't want callers calling in with their radios turned up in the background. Additionally, many callers might not be near their radios when they call in (guests especially). This means you want guests and callers to hear the show as it's being broadcast (or recorded) while they're on hold awaiting their on-air turn. You therefore must set up your phone system so that callers can hear the output from your show while they're on hold. This type of setup requires a piece of hardware that allows the interface of audio with the phone system and probably some sort of splitter that splits the outgoing sound card audio between your headphones and the phone system.

The best, reasonably priced piece of hardware to use for your on-hold system is from On-Hold Plus (**www.onholdplus.com**). This vendor's MOH 400 music-on-hold adapter, which sells for $89.95, lets you pump audio into any ordinary phone line up to four lines. (The company also has higher-end models for those of you with more lines or PBX-style systems.) When a listener calls in and is to be put on hold, you press the star (ᐱ) key on your telephone (not the hold button!), and the system takes over the line and plays whatever incoming audio source is attached to the box.

TIP

On-Hold Plus also sells optional Handset Hold remotes that plug into your handset's cord and allow you to activate the MOH 400's on-hold feature silently by using the * key on the telephone keypad. A two-pack sells for $19.95.

Running Your Show

When you're doing a call-in show, it is important to keep in mind that you are the host, and you have the ultimate responsibility to set the agenda for the show and keep it interesting. One of the best ways to do so is to have an agenda and opening monologue set up for your show. The purpose of an opening monologue is simple: You provide enough fodder and direction to the show at the outset so that your listeners will have something to call in about. It also dictates what you want to talk about. This opening gives you a way to politely turn down calls that you consider off topic.

When you're up and going, you'll want to take calls from listeners as well as calls from predetermined guests. The rest will be up to you, but you should consider the following:

▶ **Keep the program flowing.** Don't spend too much time with one guest or caller unless that person is extremely interesting. If you keep a guest on longer than a half hour, open up the show to calls for a change of pace.

▶ **Don't argue with rude or prankster callers.** Just get them off the air and get on to more legitimate callers.

▶ **If someone is calling from a cell phone, move that person up on the queue as a courtesy.**

▶ **Let non-callers get in on the action through e-mail, ICQ, and live chat rooms.** Mix it up; the Internet makes more than just voice communications possible, and not everyone can hang on hold.

▶ **If opposite sides of an issue are being debated, break down incoming calls between those for and against.** Some shows do so by having two separate numbers to call—one for each side—making it easy to go back and forth between people.

▶ **Don't hit the same topics every show or time period.** Move on to new guests and topics. At the same time, topics and guests that were interesting or especially popular should be revisited at reasonable intervals.

Bumpers, Voice-Overs, and Station Identifications

You might or might not want to include a number of items that go along with your main content. These items include bumpers (the short clips between songs or other content), station identifications, and voice-overs.

One of the leading suppliers of audio content such as bumpers and station identifications is J.J. McKay Productions (**www.jjmckay.com**). McKay has provided voice-over services for nearly twenty years and offers MP3 digital delivery of material.

Some other sites worth checking for bumpers, sound effects, and other audio content include the following:

▶ **Radio Mall (www.radio-mall.com)**—This service sells products such as production effects, sound effects, production music, hit music libraries, and written comedy.

▶ **RadioActive Noise (www.radioactivenoise.com)**—On this site, you can find sound effects for promos, bumpers, and so on. One CD includes 555 original effects for $150.

▶ **Sound Ideas (www.sound-ideas.com)**—This service is one of the largest publishers of professional sound effects. This site offers an extensive collection of music production elements and sound effects on CD. Costs run from about $100 to $4,000.

▶ **CyberSounds Custom Web Site Audio (www.cybersounds.net)**—This service provides professional voice talents and script writers; it also provides fully licensed music in nine styles.

▶ **Hollywood Edge (www.hollywoodedge.com)**—This site has an extensive collection of sounds used in motion pictures. It includes 90 free samples in MP3 format.

▶ **Nash Music Library (http://www.nash.co.jp/nml/)**—This site is a royalty-free production music library.

▶ **Edge City Sound Vault (www.novia.net/~ejanders/sndvault.html)**—At this site, you can find a handful of loops, percussion, turntable noise, and sound effects for download in .WAV format.

▶ **AudioPros.com (www.audiopros.com)**—This service provides professional audio for the Web, radio, and television, including voice-overs, jingles, commercials, copywriting, and song parodies.

No Content, No Show

We hate to state the obvious, but without good content, you won't have a good show. It's as simple as that. Although music is the reason many people get into Web broadcasting, music is not the only content out there; in fact, it can be the most expensive and difficult to obtain and program. However, it can also be the most fun.

Programming your station is more than just playing one song after another. We hope that this chapter has shed some light on how much work and thought is required to create a program that is not only fun for you but will attract and hold an audience.

Keep in mind that all content needn't be created indoors; sometimes the most fun occurs when you pack up your gear and head out into the field to do a remote broadcast. For more details on remotes, move on to Chapter 14.

Part III Preparing Content

14

Doing Remotes and Live Broadcasts

An important part of radio broadcasting is the remote. No one likes to be stuck in the studio the entire time, and sometimes events worth covering are best covered on site. When that's the case, your ability to go into the field and broadcast remotely is one of the more enticing parts of being a radio show or station host.

This chapter covers the ins and outs of going into the field to generate content and broadcast it onto the Web from remote locations.

Types of Remote Broadcasting

You can do the following types of remote broadcasting:

▶ Recorded interviews and reporting from the field

▶ Live, on-site reporting and broadcasting from the field

▶ Mobile broadcasting

The recorded remote is, of course, the simplest method of remote broadcasting, because you simply go out on remote, record your content, and bring it back in-house for broadcasting. If you plan to broadcast this way, you need to get a good recording while you're in the field. We recommend that you use a DAT or MiniDisc recorder and a good microphone. These formats will give you incredibly clear recording and fidelity when later digitized for transmission over the Internet.

The live, on-site remote is the most traditional form people think of when they think of *remote broadcasting*. In today's age of Webcasting, almost everyone has come across a remote Webcast setup at a sporting event or trade show. In this type of broadcast, the interviewers sit on site and originate the broadcast with interviews and guests on site. In this form, the content is captured live and sent back either as unencoded audio or as a single-encoded stream; then it is broadcast to the Web from the broadcaster's server facility.

Part III Preparing Content

The mobile broadcast is a twist that cellular phones have made possible for broadcasters and Webcasters alike. With a quality cell phone in hand, a broadcaster can venture into the field to do live on-air interviews and more directly approach people in crowds at events because they aren't anchored down by the need to be near land-locked telephone lines.

Key Issue: Getting Good Fidelity

No matter what form your remote takes, the key issue that affects any remote broadcast, traditional or Internet-based, is getting an acceptable level of audio fidelity. As anyone who has listened to radio knows, a reporter or DJ on the other end of a phone line, live from an event, doesn't sound nearly as good as one in the studio. At the same time, you can't expect to broadcast a concert by just holding up a phone in the crowd.

The goal of most remotes is to set up the proper equipment on site to get the best-sounding audio back to your server for broadcast. At the same time, the secondary goal is to get this audio in such a way as to minimize setup and the amount of equipment you need to bring with you. By minimizing your equipment, you reduce the chances something will go wrong technically with the remote, and, most of all, you reduce the chance something will get stolen or damaged.

Doing a remote broadcast involves two distinct issues: the technical issue of how to develop an audio stream at a remote location and broadcast it over the Internet and the logistical issue of content development outside your normal studio location. Neither is a terribly difficult issue to solve, but you can take a few different approaches to each one, and you can keep a good checklist to help make remotes go over easier.

Get Back to Where You Once Belonged

When you broadcast from a remote location, the first concern you have to face is how to get your audio back to the facility where your servers are located so that you can broadcast. You either can send back a raw audio feed to the location, or you can encode it on site and send back the encoded stream.

When you send back raw audio, you can send it via ISDN, plain old telephone line, or satellite. Most people choose ISDN, because it provides very good audio quality and the hardware to facilitate that remote feed is readily available. Plain old telephone lines can work as well, but the audio quality isn't as great as ISDN. However, some of the more recent hardware products for sending audio feeds back through telephone lines promise very good audio quality. Satellite is useful in situations in which ISDN access may not be possible, but audio quality still needs to be high.

Planning a Remote Setup

The key to having a successful remote setup is planning. You should not go blindly to any remote thinking you'll be able to broadcast easily. Not every trade show or club facility is easy to broadcast from; not every hotel will have techs available to run phone lines and so on. You should phone the site ahead of time to verify location details and check all your technical needs before even thinking of finalizing a remote broadcast.

The most critical item to check is the availability of ISDN access. This step includes not only getting phone lines run to a facility but also making sure that ISDN service can be enabled for that line. Many nightclubs and trade show facilities—because of the rise in Webcasting over the last few years—have ISDN lines available for Webcasters. If ISDN access is not available, you can try to order it in time from the local telephone company, but you should beware that, in many parts of the country, getting ISDN lines dropped in isn't always a timely experience. On parts of the West Coast, getting an ISDN line installed can take as much as six months. Also, check on cost issues and make sure you're clear who is paying for access. Some facilities will just comp you the line as part of the facilities fee you pay, while others will ask you to pay a bill. Certainly, if you are dropping in a line, you will probably see that as a special charge.

Setting up a phone line or an ISDN line to transmit audio back to a server facility works roughly the same way. On each end of the line, you need an adapter to plug a standard audio in (XLR or RCA plugs) and that also features audio out. Several companies make devices that let you plug in this way, and some of the fancier devices (especially for ISDN) include mixers and other features to tweak the feeds. Some even work by compressing audio, which ensures greater sound quality.

No matter how you plan to broadcast your remote—ISDN or plain old telephone line—you need to patch systems on both ends of the line to send back your audio. On the outgoing side, you'll also optionally want some level of mixing ability to tweak the signal; on the receiving side, you'll just want to grab the audio off the line and get it into the encoding computer.

Part III Preparing Content

The quality of hardware and lines you use should depend mostly on the type of broadcasting you plan to do. If you're broadcasting a concert, then ISDN lines and a system that offers good dynamic range would be best. If you plan to broadcast just news, talk, or a press conference, you can make do with a regular phone line and a good patching system.

Finding the Equipment

Several companies make patching equipment for sending back remote audio. The two biggest companies are JK Audio (**www.jkaudio.com**) and Comrex (**www.comrex.com**). Telos Systems (**www.telos.com**) also makes a great product, the Zephyr, which is an all-in-one mixer/remote broadcasting ISDN system. Table 14.1 covers the major products offered by these companies that enable remote audio connections via phone lines.

Table 14.1
Remote Setup Products

Device	Manufacturer	Comments
THAT-1	JK Audio	Low-cost product that offers RCA in and out and a handset connection.
THAT-2	JK Audio	Similar to THAT-1 except that it features XLR-styled plugs.
Remote Mix C+	JK Audio	Multiple mics and RCA jacks with balances, headphone jacks, and dialpad.
Remote Mix 3 Remote Mix 3.m	JK Audio	Similar to Remote Mix C+ but includes a few extra features, including an on-board VU meter to monitor levels. The 3.m model includes a clean mixer output for use with audio compressor/decompressor (codec) for higher-end transmissions.
TCB-1 TCB-2 Couplers	Comrex	A device that hooks up to telephone lines and translates the incoming signal to audio out XLR plugs.
Nexus	Comrex	Complete ISDN audio adapter available in portable or rackmount versions.
The Hotline	Comrex	A device that gives you very good audio quality over a traditional phone line. It uses a built-in modem and a digital audio codec to produce up to 10kHz audio from a standard line. It is an ideal product when ISDN lines aren't available.
Vector POTs	Comrex	A device that combines a mixer and a plain old telephone audio feed in one box. A built-in codec enables audio up to 15kHz in quality.
Envoy ISDN	Comrex	High-end ISDN audio adapter with built-in mixer.
Zephyr	Telos Systems	Portable ISDN audio adapter with built-in mixer, preamp, and more.

When you use ISDN or a telephone system that uses a compression factor, you need doubles of your equipment—one for each end. Having two of everything doubles the cost for equipment that isn't necessarily cheap (especially for the small business or hobbyist-oriented broadcaster). The solution is renting. You can rent most of the equipment listed in Table 14.1 through various dealers for a fraction of the cost. Contact the manufacturers by phone or look on their Web sites to find recommended dealers near you. If you outsource your broadcast, the outsourcer can also help supply equipment.

Encoding Onsite

Some people may choose to encode on site and send the signal remotely back to their servers for retransmission. This approach is useful if you have the computer equipment on site and an Internet connection fast enough to send the resulting stream back to your server. It also may be cheaper in that you avoid having to purchase the equipment to do a live audio feed over a phone line. Although setting up all that computer equipment on site is more complex, some people prefer to broadcast this way.

TIP

Another option some Webcasters employ is setting up an on-site wireless LAN. By doing so, you can easily locate equipment in your space. You also can use the wireless LAN to send your signal back to a location on site that may be closer to the phone lines you're using to send your broadcast back on. You'll also have an area in which it is easier to set up the PC equipment you intend to use.

When you're encoding on site, another option is to use a hardware encoder like the ones from Audioactive. The Audioactive MPEG RealTime Encoder includes a built-in 10BaseT TCP/IP interface. You can even configure it with its own IP address and adjust bit rates and other settings remotely via a Telnet interface. With its compact size and easy installation, this device is much easier to transport, install, and operate onsite versus a traditional PC setup. However, to send its information back to your broadcast facility, you need to be able to support it with a fast enough Internet connection onsite.

TIP

If Telnet is still an arcane technology for you, check with your ISP and see if it has a document or FAQ you can read. Telnet terminals are built into Windows and other operating systems but can be hidden, because they aren't used by many basic customers.

Part III Preparing Content

Setting Up Your Remote

When you're setting up a remote, you first should go over a basic checklist of items that you either need to know or need to have available. For example, you need to note the position and availability of electrical outlets, ensure that you have an adequate number of phone lines, and make sure you have a quiet enough location or proximity to the audio feeds that will make up your broadcast.

TIP

One phone line sometimes isn't enough to set up a remote broadcast. You should always have a second line available to be able to coordinate back to the server facility. Also, you should make sure you do a good walk-through of the location before even considering doing your Webcast from that site. A critical item to consider during walk-throughs that is often overlooked is electrical power. Make sure there are outlets where you need them and that there is enough power coming to take care of all your equipment. We've seen several instances in hotels and other non-traditional event sites where a fuse has been blown at the worst possible minute.

Finally, make sure there is proper information available to facilitate how computers are connected to internal networks that connect you within the facility to the Internet. Get all that IP address, gateway, and DNS server information that you need to connect on site up front from the local tech contact, or risk not having it when you arrive.

Remote Outsourcing

One of the easiest ways to successfully organize a remote Webcast is to turn to an outsourcer. Dozens of companies around the world can show up on site with all the audio equipment and expertise necessary to set up and remotely broadcast a concert, press conference, or other event onto the Web. Many of these businesses can handle the Internet serving portion of your remote broadcast as well.

When you choose a remote outsourcer, be sure to ask about previous events the service has broadcast and what types of remote feeds it can develop for you. When you're doing a truly remote feed, finding outsourcers who have experience with satellite feeds is especially important. The process of renting and facilitating a satellite truck-based feed is not a light undertaking.

Also, you should consider dealing with local outsourcers who may have experience with the facilities and area from which you're doing the remote. At conventions and other event-oriented facilities, having partners who can deal with local facilities' managers and workers (many of whom are unionized and have strict rules about who lays down wiring and cabling in a center) could be good (especially given that these people may have dealt with these workers previously).

For more details on remote outsourcing, you can read up on outsourcing in general in Chapter 9.

Going Mobile

Perhaps the most difficult form of remote broadcasting is the mobile broadcast. Most remotes require little more than setting up a temporary but stationary link back to your broadcast facility, but these remotes don't always offer the best opportunities for broadcasting. For example, at sporting events, it might be cool to be able to roam through the crowd and talk to spectators.

The easiest way to enable a mobile broadcast is to use cellular phones and connect back to the broadcast facility, which can then encode the signal for broadcast. However, to go a step further, a better approach is to patch the cell phone to a traditional microphone setup that enables you to capture a better range of audio than you can through a cellular headset.

The best way to enable a cellular feed is to get a fax/modem adapter or data interface for your current cell phone. This device plugs into the bottom of the cell phone and gives it an RJ-11 jack. With this jack, you can plug into it any of the normal patch devices you would use with a regular phone. At the time of this writing, these devices tend to run between $60 and $300. JK Audio (**www.jkaudio.com**) itself recommends its RemoteMix C+, RemoteMix 3, or RemoteMix 3x4.

TIP

According to JK Audio, older bag-type phones are the best for remote cellular feeds. The extra power gives them a clearer signal, and they have a lower cost interface and longer battery life.

Part III Preparing Content

Using a Satellite Feed

You'll need satellite feeds on those remotes where nothing else is possible. Most of the time, a satellite truck is needed only for video, given that phone lines are usually available to you. Other times, phone lines won't be available, or a facility may offer you a satellite uplink feature. In both cases, using a satellite feed is a great idea for your remote broadcasts. A satellite feed can range from someone on a satellite phone calling into a facility (not always the best approach, but possible) to renting a satellite truck or using a facility's uplink capability, buying time, and doing a professional feed back to your facility. Satellite trucks and services are usually locally and regionally sourced, so beware that if your plans require their use, you might need to build in time for the truck to drive from a nearby city and set itself up. Also, such trucks can be scarce in remote areas, so if the event is very big, you might have to go further to find an available truck.

Whether you use a truck or a facility's uplink for satellite transmission, you first need to book time and be able to pull the transmission back down at your server facility. Many big-time outsource server facilities (such as Real Broadcast Network and Yahoo! Broadcast Services) have tons of satellite reception capability. Booking time involves working with a satellite time service broker. The broker determines where you're broadcast is, finds an available channel on a satellite for your time frame, figures the costs, sells it, and books it for you. You can then coordinate that information with your on-site managers for your uplink and, more or less, you're good to go.

This is the basic sketch of a remote satellite feed. In general, as a broadcaster, you won't ever actually do any of this work yourself. You can hire a satellite company (usually the same people who hire the truck) or a recommended group if you're doing a facility uplink. That company will set up everything and coordinate to feed your audio out of your local setup and get it going. On the other broadcast end, you need to have a reception satellite, and, in most cases, you might be working with the previously mentioned service companies.

Using satellites is obviously not feasible for the small broadcaster. However, radio on the Internet is growing, and many big stations are gaining audiences large enough to justify the use of satellite time to get a useful broadcast on the Net. Overall costs can reach the thousands of dollars to pull off a satellite-associated broadcast, but this price is not so high that having even a small audience of 10,000 or more expected listeners couldn't justify the expense, especially if you have some sort of associated marketing or business reason for the broadcast.

There's a Whole World Out There to Broadcast From

Using remotes, however well technically pulled off, is a great way to produce interesting content for little money. Crowds, events, and location broadcasts give you attractions that just sitting back and letting a playlist loop will never do. In terms of the expense, consider that the hosts of the *Don & Mike Show*, one of the most popular syndicated radio shows in the United States, get some of their best content by simply taking a tape recorder with them to various events. The hosts of the show (or one of their cast of characters) merely record the happenings and interviews and then, after a bit of editing, play them back on a future show. Getting out of the studio or out of the normal rut of your day-to-day broadcast keeps things fresh. Going the extra step to do the live remote only increases the rush your listeners will feel, knowing that the event you're broadcasting is actually happening wherever you are.

Remotes make the world, especially the Internet, seem less remote.

Part IV

Managing Your Internet Radio Station

15

Promoting Your Station and Broadcast

If you're going to do the work to broadcast over the Internet what you think is important, outstanding, or just plain fun music or content, you might as well have some listeners. Although some of you might be happy to broadcast to a small group of friends or people with the same musical interests, others will want to attract as many listeners as possible. You therefore need to spend some time and effort and, if you have commercial aspirations, money to promote your station.

This chapter covers the basics of Web promotion and also focuses on ways the Internet allows you to specifically promote your Webcast.

Basics of Web Promotion

Online and traditional magazines—both trade and mass market—cover the music industry in general, genres of music, talk radio, broadcasting/radio, the Web, and more issues that might relate to your station and its programming. You can find resources all the way from major music magazines such as *Rolling Stone* and *Spin* (which is interested only in covering major stations) down to regional, music-related, or other publications. Some of them are on the Web and can be found using any number of common search engines. Others are magazines or newspapers.

Online promotion is particularly important because all of your listeners will, by definition, have Web access. That doesn't mean you should ignore traditional publications, though. In fact, many people find Web sites through mentions in more traditional media.

Public and Media Relations

Because a positive review or feature story about your station has more impact than a paid advertisement, public and media relations are very important. People are more likely to be influenced by a third-party endorsement than an advertisement.

Some stations aren't newsworthy on any level, others are newsworthy only on a small level, and yet others—the largest, most extensive stations—make attractive stories. Reporters probably won't just come looking for your station; you'll have to pitch an interesting story to them. Hiring a professional public relations firm can cost hundreds or thousands of dollars per month with no guarantee of results. However, if you have the room in your budget, hiring professionals is usually well worth the money. If not, you can save money by doing the work yourself, although the results are likely to be less stellar.

The Angle

What is it about your station that makes it worthy of coverage? The fact that it exists and you think it's cool isn't enough for reporters to take an interest. However, if your station plays a particular type of music, you can almost certainly find a publication dedicated to that type of music that may be interested in your story. You also might use a unique bit of technology or offer certain features that make your site stand out. A huge listenership is also worthy of coverage in many cases. Think of what makes your station different or better than the rest. If you, or anyone you ask, can't come up with anything, then you will have a hard time gaining coverage.

The Media

Before you contact a particular media outlet, you should do some research about it. Make sure it is appropriate for you to contact. A magazine dedicated to rap music won't be interested in your jazz station. And *Rolling Stone* probably won't be beating down your door to do a story on a station that has only a couple of hundred listeners, even if it plays the most fantastic, eclectic mix of music in the world. (If that's the case, we hope you'll have more than a couple of hundred listeners!)

You should also know to whom you should send your pitch. Contact the relevant reporter directly if you can. If you can't, you can send your information to an editor.

The following are a few tips for putting together and sending an inexpensive media kit. This information is geared toward those of you who have commercial aspirations.

▶ Your company letterhead should include your company's name, logo (if you have one), mailing address, e-mail address, phone number, fax number, and Web address. Your pitch letter should include the name of a contact person and a time to call.

▶ Tell your contact about your station: what kind of music you play, what makes your site and station unique, how long your station has been operating, how much your listenership has grown, and so on. Make sure you show the reporter why his or her readers will be interested in this story. Reporters are interested in who, what, where, when, and why.

▶ Be confident about your station's newsworthiness, but don't go overboard and don't use empty phrases like "By far the best station on the Web." If you think your station is the best, show your contact why you think that; don't just make the statement.

▶ Read, re-read, and then have a friend who writes well edit your materials. No mistakes, no typos. And don't sell it too hard. Reporters hate to see sloppy releases that indicate a lack of care, and they don't want advertising copy.

▶ Without being overzealous, don't be afraid to sell your station. Present a package that will draw interest without being overly self-congratulatory.

▶ Don't mail extensive, expensive press kits to every publication that might have a passing interest in your site. Research the publications and focus your attention on the ones most likely to write about your site and the ones with the biggest potential impact.

▶ If possible, send the information to a specific person—the *correct* specific person. If you don't know who that person is, make a phone call.

▶ Don't contact the media until your station is in excellent shape. You want the story to be positive, and if your site is still encountering problems or is poorly run, the story will reflect those problems. Don't expect a reporter to say your station is great if it's not.

▶ Send your package so that it arrives early in the week. Then you can make your follow-up contact later in the same week.

▶ Make your follow-up phone call a day or so after you think the package has arrived. It's easier to throw a letter in the trash than it is to tell a person to get lost. If an editor or reporter thinks your online store is unworthy of a mention in his or her magazine, make him or her tell you so.

▶ If the reporter doesn't feel your station is worth a story, respond with maturity and respect. If you say something like "Your magazine stinks anyway," you can forget about ever getting any coverage in the future. Ask what would make your station newsworthy in the future.

▶ If the answer is yes, be helpful. Answer interview questions thoughtfully but without rambling. Offer information you think is relevant even if the reporter doesn't ask about it. After the story runs, send a thank-you note.

Online Press Release Outlets

You can have your press release posted by a number of online outlets. However, using them is feasible only for commercial stations, because they can be somewhat pricey. PR Newswire (**www.prnewswire.com**) and Business Wire (**www.businesswire.com**) are two examples. Internet Wire (**www.internetwire.com**) is a bit more affordable and offers services such as Daily Debuts (announcements of new sites).

Listing with Search Engines

Several search engines and directories cater specifically to Web broadcasters. However, you should also pay attention to the more general search engines and directories. Web surfers use search engines and directories when they can't find what they're looking for on the Web. Knowing how to maximize your rankings is essential.

The following sections offer some background on search engines, how to help them work for your site and station, and where to get your station or broadcast event listed with similar sites. Another good resource for search engine information is Search Engine Watch (**www.searchenginewatch.com**).

Automatic Submission

You can choose from hundreds of search engines; however, most people stick to a handful of the most popular. A number of automatic submission sites can also help you save time when you're submitting your site to these directories and engines. However, different search engines use different methods of ranking sites, and automatic submission does not always allow you to tweak your submission to meet the quirks of each particular engine.

If you really don't have the time to submit to individual engines and want to get your site listed by a large number of engines and directories, automatic submission does work well. However, when submitting to directories, which use human editors, make sure you are submitting a site that is ready to be seen and judged by those editors. Don't submit too soon, because you may never get a second chance.

Submit-It

www.submit-it.com

Submit-It is the most popular automatic submission service on the Web, helping you submit your site to more than 400 search engines, directories, announce sites, and award sites. You enter your information once, and Submit-It automates the process. It cuts the submission process from days to about an hour, because all you have to do beyond filling out the form is to decide which engines and directories you want to be listed in. The cost is $30 for one URL. If you like, you also can use a number of fee-based services.

Submission Tips

Although most search engines can find your site without your help, you should find the ones you most want to target and submit information to them. You can easily submit URLs to most of them.

Some search engines have automated information retrievers (often called *spiders*) that follow links through your site and index every page. Others index only the main page or go one level deeper. Although we've included some basic information on some of the top search engines in this chapter, you should visit their Web sites to find more details.

Maximizing Your Ranking

Search engines have their own quirks and change constantly. And no matter how good the engines and how careful you are about your submissions, they are all dependent on the searcher and which keywords he or she chooses. You might have the best jazz station on the Web but wind up with a low ranking because of the engine's imperfections. However, if you work hard enough and are smart enough, you can increase the chances of getting a high ranking.

In the following sections, we'll cover some of the factors that can help maximize your ranking.

META Tags

META tags are pieces of information placed in the head of an HTML document. The META tag information is not displayed by the browser, but it is recognized by some (not all) search engines and is used to rank sites. One place to visit for information on writing effective META tags is the Virtual Library META Tagging for Search Engines page, located at **www.wdvl.com/Location/Meta/Tag.html**.

Two types of META tags can be important in your search engine ranking: keywords and description. Using a "description" META tag, you can include a brief description of your site that will appear when your site is the result of a search. If you fail to include a META tag description, the first portion of text on the page will appear as the description. Engines that don't recognize META tags also use the first portion of text. For this reason, that early text should be able to function as an understandable description.

Keyword and description META tags look like this:

```
<META NAME="KEYWORDS" CONTENT="KEYWORDS">
<META NAME="DESCRIPTION" CONTENT="DESCRIPTION">
```

Now, look at a couple of examples:

```
<META NAME="Keywords" CONTENT="WebROK, hard rock, rock, music,
    radio, alternative, Korn, Limp Bizkit, Rage Against The
    Machine, Pearl Jam, Kid Rock">
<META NAME="Description" CONTENT="WebROK internet radio plays
    the best hard and alternative rock on the Web.">
```

For help writing META tags, you can visit the Meta Tag Builder Site at **http://vancouver-webpages.com/META/mk-metas.html**.

Keywords

People use keywords when searching for something on the Web. You need to come up with the words people are most likely to use when looking for your site. Those words are not necessarily the ones you would use. Try having a group of friends, colleagues, and potential site visitors generate a list of keywords for your site. Consider variations of these words and rank them in order of importance and descriptiveness. Then use the best in your title, headings, text, and META tags.

TIP

One way to help maximize your rankings is to type some of the keywords you might use into a search engine, see which sites are ranked highly, and see how they are optimizing their pages for submission.

Title

Most search engines display the title of the page in the results and use the title words heavily in their ranking of sites. Having an accurate, descriptive title for all pages is important.

Word Repetition

Originally, repeating words was an easy way to increase your site's ranking. Now, though, many search engines have actually begun penalizing sites that have flagrantly unnecessary word repetition. Still, others use word repetition as a criterion for high ranking.

Word Placement

Word selection in the title is essential. Many search engines place a greater emphasis on words located near the beginning of the page.

Text and Page Design

If you don't include any text on a page or embed all the text in a graphic, the spiders won't have anything to read. As we mentioned earlier, some search engines don't recognize META tags and instead take the early part of a page's text for the summary. You should make sure that text can work as a summary.

Number of External Links

Some search engines, most notably Google, use the number of links from other sites to yours to determine your site's popularity and then use popularity as part of the ranking process. Therefore, obtaining links to your site is even more advantageous.

What's Most Important?

In order of importance, search engines and directories consider the following items to be crucial:

▶ **Title**—This is a critical item and must be descriptive and accurate. First twenty-five words on the page. Optimize them for keywords and make sure the keywords are accurate.

▶ **META tags**—Always use them but don't depend totally on them.

Monitoring Your Ranking

PositionAgent (**www.positionagent.com**) monitors your site's rankings in ten top search engines and provides weekly reports on your site's position. PositionAgent monitors AltaVista, Excite, Galaxy, HotBot, Infoseek, Lycos, Magellan, OpenText, WebCrawler, and Yahoo!. The cost is $60 for five URLs and six months of reports.

General Search Engines

Next, we'll cover some of the top search engines and some keys to submitting your site to them. Most of the sites make submitting your site easy.

AltaVista

www.altavista.com

AltaVista not only has general search capability but also offers an MP3/Audio search center. To submit a site to AltaVista, click on Add a Page and submit just the main page of your site. AltaVista's spider follows links through the entire site, and it should be available within two days. You can use the description META tags to control the summary served back with your page. However, do not submit a description or keywords. AltaVista will most likely find your site if it has external links.

Ask Jeeves

www.askjeeves.com

Ask Jeeves allows users to ask questions rather than enter keywords. It uses language-processing technology to determine the meaning of the words and grammar.

Ask Jeeves's human editors consider, but do not include, all submissions. Among the criteria are site performance (load time, ease of navigation, regularity of updates) and editorial content (thorough information). Also, the site must not require users to register to access the site.

Open Directory Project

www.dmoz.org

The Open Directory Project relies on a large number of volunteer editors with the goal of providing a comprehensive Web directory. To get your site listed, find the appropriate category, click on Add URL, and submit your site's URL, title, and description.

Excite

www.excite.com

Excite uses artificial intelligence to discern your site's dominant theme. If your site has not yet been found by Excite's spider, you can click on Add URL. Excite usually recognizes only description META tags, so be sure to use descriptive phrases near the top of your pages.

FAST Search
www.alltheweb.com

FAST Search is an outstanding new search engine that searches 300 million Web pages. It offers both a fast search and an advanced search, which includes language, word, and domain filters. To submit a site, click on Submit Your Site and enter your URL.

Google
www.google.com

To submit a URL to Google, click on About Google and then Add Your URL. Then simply enter your URL and include comments or keywords that describe the content of your page. Enter only your main URL, and Google's spider will do the rest. The process takes from one to four weeks.

GoTo.com
www.goto.com

GoTo.com is one directory that allows you to guarantee a high ranking by paying for it. You can select the search terms that are relevant to your site and decide how much you are willing to pay on a per-click basis for those terms. The more you pay, the higher your ranking.

HotBot
www.hotbot.com

To submit a site to HotBot, you need to find the most appropriate category and click on Add URL. You can submit each page's URL once, and you must limit submissions from the same domain to fifty in a 24-hour period. HotBot now uses human editors to maintain its directories. This service supports META tags and focuses first on keywords in the title, followed by keywords in META tags, and then frequency of keywords in the text.

Infoseek/Go Network
www.go.com

To submit a site to Infoseek, you need to click on Add URL and enter your URL in the box provided. You should allow one week or more for new pages or updates to appear. Infoseek does not accept automatic submissions, and you must submit each page of your site separately. If you want to submit more than fifty pages, you should send them through e-mail rather than submit them directly on the site.

The editors at Infoseek say they choose only the most relevant and valuable sites. Infoseek Select sites are chosen from the index by Infoseek's editors based on editorial value, traffic, and the number of external links to the site.

Lycos
www.lycos.com

Lycos ranks sites based on keywords used in the title, in high-level headings, and in text near the top of the page. Page popularity also improves the ranking. Unnecessary word repetition is penalized.

To submit a site to Lycos, click on Add Your Site To Lycos and use the Site Finder to see whether your page has already been registered. If not, you can enter the URL and your e-mail address. The Lycos spider will dig through your entire site, and your page should show up on a Lycos search two to four weeks after submission. You should definitely use META tags with Lycos.

Netscape Netcenter
www.netscape.com

Using Netscape Netcenter, you can register your Web site with eleven search engines for free. Be sure to visit Netscape's Web site and click on Add Site for information and instructions.

Northern Light Search
www.northernlight.com

Northern Light combines information from premium material in one search. Results are organized into folders that help narrow searches. To use it, click on Register URL and fill in the required information. If you submit only your main page, Northern Light's crawler will index your entire site.

WebCrawler
www.webcrawler.com

WebCrawler indexes every word on your site up to 1MB of text. The keywords under which a page will be found in a search are the words on a page.

WebCrawler suggests using a descriptive title, because it gives slightly more weight to titles than text or META tags. You should use short META tags for keywords and a description/summary but avoid repetition. Also, make sure the main page describes the site fully. *Spamdexing* (using keywords that don't match your site's content) could get your site eliminated from WebCrawler.

Yahoo!

www.yahoo.com

Submissions to Yahoo! are controlled by people. To submit a site, you select a category, narrow it down to a specific subcategory, and click on Add URL. If you have already submitted a site and want to make a change, select Change Form.

Yahoo! suggests you read its information on how to suggest a site and its detailed explanation about how to find a category for your site. You then are asked to provide a title, URL, and brief description (twenty-five words or fewer) of your site. META tags are ignored, and Yahoo! asks that you do not use phrases like "The best site on the Internet" in your description.

You are then given the option to provide other category suggestions and time-sensitive information (if your site is going up or coming down on a particular date).

More Information About Search Engines

As search engines continue to evolve, you can stay on top of developments by checking Search Engine Watch (**www.searchenginewatch.com**). Search Engine Watch includes a number of categories. The most useful for you is the Search Engines Submission Tips. This guide explains how search engines find and rank Web pages with an emphasis on what Webmasters can do to improve how search engines list sites.

The Search Engine Watch's section on Reviews, Ratings, and Tests provides insight on how search engines perform in different areas and gives choices based on popularity and technical performance. The Search Engine Resources section provides a collection of links to search engine-related sources.

You might also check out the book *Search Engines for the World Wide Web,* 2nd Edition: Visual QuickStart Guide by Alfred and Emily Glossbrenner (Peachpit Press, 1998, ISBN: 0201353857).

Broadcast-Specific Directories and Search Engines

Although submitting your site to the general search engines and directories is a good idea, an immense number of engines and directories focus on Web radio stations. The following sections provide information on some that you should consider getting your site and station listed on.

BroadcastLive

www.broadcast-live.com

BroadcastLive allows users to find Webcasts from around the world that are categorized by country and type of broadcast.

To submit your station, click on the Add URL link and fill out the form. You need to provide information on broadcast type, stream type, and genre.

ChannelSEEK

www.channelseek.com

ChannelSEEK lists events and broadcasts of all kinds, including Web radio. Each day includes a featured site and special events, and users can opt for an e-mail reminder of certain events. ChannelSEEK, shown in Figure 15.1, also ranks its top fifty sites.

Figure 15.1
ChannelSEEK includes a list of its top fifty sites and allows you to browse fourteen channels and numerous subcategories.

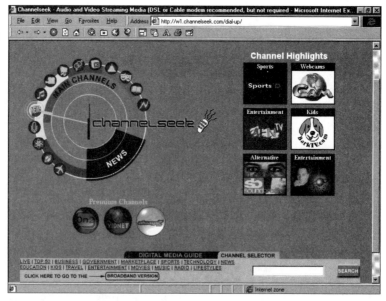

You can submit a site or an event by clicking on the appropriate link and completing the form. Only streaming audio (or video) is listed, and all entries are reviewed by the ChannelSEEK staff. Information you must provide includes file type, content rating (all audiences, some discretion, or for adults), content language, and site classification.

EarthTuner

www.earthtuner.com

EarthTuner is an application that allows listeners to hear Internet media from around the globe. It supports RealAudio and RealVideo, has a 1,400-station database, allows browsing by format, and includes an integrated RealAudio search engine. Macintosh users use MacTuner.com. This service has a one-time charge of $22.95.

To submit your site for inclusion, send the site/station name, Web page URL, stream address, and type of programming to stations@EarthTuner.com.

GlobalStreams

www.globalstreams.com

GlobalStreams allows users to search for radio stations streaming over the Internet from around the world by genre, location, or call letters.

By registering for MyStreams.com, users can program their own radio dials. Each time users return to the GlobalStreams network of sites (see Figure 15.2), those stations are saved in their personal radio dials.

Figure 15.2
GlobalStreams.com spotlights a Station of the Week and highlights Webcast events.

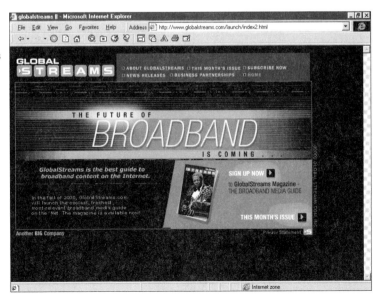

GlobalStreams offers the following categories:

▶ **NetStreams**—Web-only stations, highlighting some of the best

▶ **CitiStreams**—Stations listed by city

▶ **International**—World music

▶ **CollegeStreams**—College music

▶ **ArtistStreams**—MP3 search

GlobalStreams also offers an affiliate program for companies, and its music store partners with Liquid Audio to offer digital downloads in Liquid or G2.

To have your station included, click on Suggest A Station and follow the directions.

OnTheAir.com
www.ontheair.com

OnTheAir allows users to browse stations by format and location and also features "SpotLight" sites and provides Webcasting news. Visitor Links lists stations submitted by visitors and is also where you should submit your site.

Real.com Guide
http://realguide.real.com/

The radio and television area of the Real.com Guide, shown in Figure 15.3, lists stations under the categories of Entertainment, Kids, Money, Music (by far the most stations, with more than 1,100), News, Sci-Tech, Society, Spirituality, and Sports. Each category has numerous subcategories. Users can find a station by format, country, U.S. state, U.S. city, language, or type (television, radio, Web only). This service also features stations.

Figure 15.3
The Real.com Guide is the official guide to RealAudio broadcasts on the Web.

Users can create their own Real.com Guide that allows them to narrow their choices by topic and bandwidth.

To add your site or event, click on Add Your Site/Event and fill out the form. Information you must provide includes a description of your site or event, the media type (RealAudio, RealVideo, SMIL, RMJ/MP3), the content type (site, event, radio station), the target audience (28K modem, 56K modem, single ISDN, and so on), the codec version (G2 Multi-rate SureStream, G2 Single-rate, and so on), and the appropriate category and subcategories.

Scour

www.scour.net

Scour is a search engine that "scours" the Web and Windows Shares for audio and video content. Users can also narrow the search by genre, Webcaster (Spinner, ImagineRadio, SonicNet FlashRadio, or independent), or search for streaming MP3 stations.

Scour's spider does the work, so you don't need to submit your station.

VirtualTuner.com

www.virtualtuner.com

VirtualTuner.com offers more than 5,500 streaming links in more than fifty different languages. Broadcasts are classified by location (Europe, U.S., The World) and content type.

To get your station listed, click on the Add URL link and fill out the form. To be listed in the VirtualTuner database, your station must fit the live or on-demand format and be updated at least once a week.

vTuner

www.vtuner.com

vTuner not only offers the vTuner Player for users, but also has a large directory and rating system for Web radio stations. Stations are rated for best overall sound, speed, and Web site (content of broadcast is not included in the ratings). vTuner also lists new, popular, and unpopular stations (determined by the number of vTuner visitors).

vTuner, shown in Figure 15.4, lists thousands of stations from more than 100 countries. To submit your site, click on the Suggest A Station link and fill out the form.

Figure 15.4
vTuner offers its own player and also rankings of sites and stations.

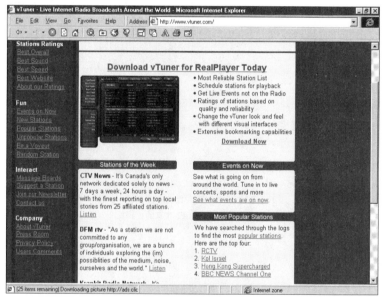

WindowsMedia.com Radio Station Guide

http://windowsmedia.microsoft.com/radio/Radio5.asp

Not surprisingly, WindowsMedia.com is a guide to Internet stations that can be heard in Windows Media Player. Users can browse for and listen to radio stations by state, format, or on an international level or they can enter their U.S. zip code for personalization. Users also can subscribe to a newsletter that lets them know about new stations.

To suggest a site, you can send e-mail to **WEFEED@Microsoft.com**.

Yahoo! Broadcast

www.broadcast.com

Yahoo! Broadcast is a portal for Web audio that lists and broadcasts Internet-only radio and Webcasts what numerous stations are playing over the air. This service also highlights various events.

Getting your station listed on Yahoo! Broadcast offers exposure to Yahoo!'s 1.1 million visitors a day and to Yahoo!'s distribution network, which supports a large number of simultaneous listeners. According to Yahoo!, more than 60 percent of listeners are local to your station if you also have an over-the-air presence. Yahoo! can also consult with you about selling banner ads on your site and can help you collect demographics of your listeners. It provides an entirely turnkey broadcast. For information on getting your station on Yahoo!, go to **www.broadcast.com/about/broadcast_radio.html**.

For Even More Information

As Webcasting grows, so, too, does the number of Webcast directories. There are far too many to list here, but two places to check to find more directories are the Open Directory (**http://dmoz.org/Arts/Radio/RadioGuides**) and Radio Networks and Internet Broadcasters (**http://www.radiospace.com/networks.htm#Internet**).

Some of these additional directories are listed in Table 15.1.

Table 15.1
More Webcasting Directories and Search Engines

Directory/Search Engine	URL	Description
AudioCast.net	www.audiocast.net	Webcaster of talk shows and events in VivoActive
AudioCasting.com	www.audiocasting.com	Webcaster of programs in RealMedia G2
Bandlink.net	www.bandlink.net/radio.html	List of links to stations in various genres
BRS Web Radio	www.web-radio.com	List of audio Webcasters (primarily radio stations)
CBLive	www.cblive.com	List of nearly 2,000 links by location
Flip2it	www.flip2it.com	Portal with links to live Webcasts
Internet Radio List	www.internetradiolist.com	Extensive directory
i-probe Internet Radio List	www.i-probe.com/i-probe/ip_radio.html	List of more than 1,800 stations
Jazzstations.com	www.jazzstations.com	Directory of jazz radio stations on the Web
KR's Radioworld	www.krs-radioworld.com	Comprehensive directory by location
4Radio.com	www.4radio.com	Direct links to broadcasts
2000Radios.com	www.2000radios.com	The name says it—links to more than 2,000 stations
RadioX.com	www.radiox.com	Internet-only radio directory
UBL Radio List	www.ubl.com/fp.asp?layout=main_rs_page	A directory by the famed UBL.com
RadioTower	www.radiotower.com	Service that categorizes and links to Webcasters worldwide
SHOUTcast Directory	http://yp.shoutcast.com	List of servers using MP3-based streaming system

Event Directories

Numerous directories list specific Webcast events. They are useful when you are Webcasting a live concert or some other special event, such as an interview. The following sections describe some of these directories.

OnNow

www.onnow.com

OnNow is a guide to more than 2,000 events, including audio broadcasts, each month on the Internet, AOL, CompuServe, Prodigy, and MSN. To have your event listed, click on the Submitting Events button. You should submit your event at least two or three days ahead of time to give OnNow time to review your submission.

USA Today Cyberlistings

The USA Today newspaper offers cyberlistings for Webcasts, similar to television listings. A listing here means potential access to more than 1 million readers.

Web Times

www.webtimes.com

Although most directories have massive numbers of stations and streams listed, Web Times lists only what it considers to be the best, so that users don't have to wade through an endless number of choices. Web Times, shown in Figure 15.5, also offers Webcasting news and features daily picks.

Figure 15.5
Web Times is a guide to the top Webcasts.

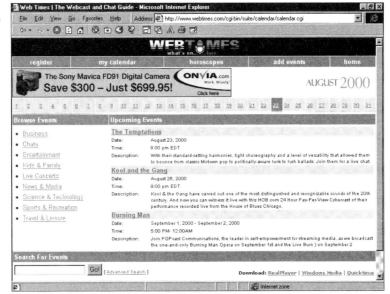

To submit your event, you can click on the Submit Events link, complete the form, and hope that Web Times deems your event worth listing.

Yahoo! Net Events

http://events.yahoo.com/

Yahoo! Net Events lists individual events in the same manner that Yahoo classifies and organizes all its directory subjects. You click on the Suggest an Event link to submit your Webcast event. Then you can fill out the form, which not only includes the standard information but also date, start and end time, and time zone.

RadioSpy

RadioSpy (for more information, see Appendix C) locates, sorts, and connects users to hundreds of audio feeds and also provides free DJ Tools for people to broadcast their own music. Non-commercial broadcasters can also have banners placed in RadioSpy and on the RadioSpy home page.

RadioSpy (**www.radiospy.com**) locates all the SHOUTcast, Windows Media, and RealAudio streaming audio servers on the Internet and sorts them by genre, number of listeners, bandwidth, and other information (see Figure 15.6). Users therefore can not only find the type of music they want but also avoid overloading their Internet connection by selecting the desired bandwidth level.

Figure 15.6
RadioSpy cruises the Internet in search of streaming Webcasts and sorts them for users.

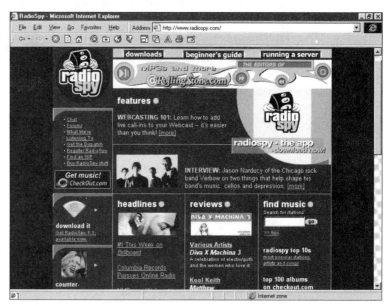

RadioSpy sorts stations using a variety of criteria, including a station's playlist, how often it features the users' favorite artists, and more. Built-in chat and bulletin boards help users and broadcasters interact with each other.

The RadioSpy site also attracts users with news, reviews, interviews, polls, contests, chats and forums, and recommendations from the RadioSpy staff.

For specific instructions on how to broadcast and have your station show up in RadioSpy, go to **www.radiospy.com/running.shtml**.

Link Swapping

Not everyone will find your site through search engines and directories. Even the Webcast-specific directories are becoming crowded with thousands of Web stations. Another way for people to find your site is through a link on another site. You can pursue links through exchanges and other incentives.

You can get links from other sites that are likely to be visited by potential listeners of your station, such as fan sites of bands that your station plays or other music-oriented sites. You might also try to obtain links from the sites of your listeners, award sites, or announce sites. Some people prefer to get just a few potentially valuable links, whereas others shoot for any link they can get. And if your site is more fun than commercial, you might be able to swap links with stations that share a similar attitude.

Linking Far and Wide

The more links you have out there, the more likely someone will stumble across your site. Getting links from a wide variety of sites works if you believe that people have a wide enough, yet defined, range of interests. For example, a visitor to a skateboarding Web site might follow a link to a punk Web station (though unlikely to a classical music station).

The broader the appeal of your station, the more likely you are to benefit from widespread linking. That doesn't mean you have to play everything from death metal to Celine Dion; it just means you have to offer more than the music of a single band.

Usually, people want you to reciprocate with a link to their sites. If you have many links, you should organize them on a links page.

Staying Specific

You might be better off finding a smaller number of links, all of which are likely to lead to visitors. This approach takes a little more research. In the following sections, we'll help you find solid links.

Contacting Similar Sites

As you work at setting up your own station and affiliated Web site, you will almost certainly visit many similar sites and stations. You should bookmark the sites and stations you like and, when you're up and running, contact those sites with which you would like to link.

The best way to contact a prospective site is through e-mail. Use the word *link* in the subject line to differentiate your e-mail. Keep your message brief. Tell the recipient what your station is like and offer the URL so that he or she can check out your site for himself or herself.

Making Link Exchanges

Link exchanges can be done on a barter system with similar sites. Make sure you can convince that site's creator that your site and station are worth swapping links with.

If you can't get someone to link to your site, you might still want to link to others for the benefit of your listeners, assuming those sites contain some useful information. Although it's not required, you might want to let the sites' creators know out of courtesy.

Checking Award Sites

Award sites can be useful for two reasons. Getting honored or obtaining a link from one of the award sites should help increase traffic and listeners. And even if you never receive an award, just looking through an award site for other stations can help you find interesting ideas.

The following are some top award sites:

▶ Cool Site of the Day (**http://cool.infi.net**)

▶ TooCool (**www.toocool.com**)

▶ ProjectCool (**www.projectcool.com**)

▶ Netscape What's Cool
(**www.netscape.com/netcenter/cool.html?cp=hom09cnw1**)

Using Announce Sites

Announce sites are directories of new Web sites. Using them is yet another way to get your site noticed. These sites provide only temporary listings:

▶ Netscape's What's New
(**www.netscape.com/netcenter/new.html?cp=hom09cnew**)

▶ What's New Too (**http://newtoo.manifest.com**)

▶ Nerd World What's New (**www.nerdworld.com/whatsnew.html**)

Using Link Pages and Directories

Like award sites, link pages and directories are not only good places to be linked from but also valuable searching grounds for potential links. You might want to check out the following pages and directories.

InfoSpace

www.infospace.com

InfoSpace offers three options for listing, including one free. The Hot Sites, the first ones listed, are limited to just ten per category and cost $95 per month. The Priority Sites are listed next and cost $99 a year. Free Sites are shown after sites in the top two levels and include a brief description and a link to your site.

Webscout

www.webscout.com

Webscout asks you to select a category and then a subcategory. Each subcategory has fifteen or twenty links with a short review of the site. You can also search the reviews for a particular subject.

Webscout's SuperSearch allows you to select a search engine from a floating window and search by keywords. You can also nominate a site for inclusion, but the folks at Webscout say they are "extremely selective," so be sure your site is in top shape before submitting.

Beaucoup

www.beaucoup.com

Beaucoup can help you find a search engine, directory, or index for your specific needs. Pick a category, and you'll get a list of links to a number of topic-specific search engines or informational sites. Beaucoup's Super Search allows users to query ten engines at once.

Banner Exchange Services

Banner exchange services allow you to display banner advertising for your site on other sites in exchange for displaying banner ads for other sites on your site. This allows you to get your banner ads out there without paying for ad space.

LinkExchange (**www.linkexchange.com**) works as a free advertising exchange agent between sites. LinkExchange members display banner ads for other members. Members determine where they want their banner to be shown by selecting the appropriate categories. A rating system and filtering technology ensure that banners displayed on your site are appropriate for your audience and that your banner is displayed on sites that will provide the most traffic.

Surf Point is the LinkExchange directory. There, you simply categorize your site for inclusion. Friends and sponsors receive additional services for a fee. Surf Point lists more than 100,000 sites.

Beseen's 1-for-1 Banner Exchange, called LookSmart Clicks (**www.looksmartclicks.com**), offers free targeted advertising for your site and ad effectiveness reporting. For every banner you show on your site, you receive a banner on another member's site. This service differs from some banner exchanges, which show your banner only once for every two ads your site displays. The Smart Targeting feature automatically sends your ads where you get the best click-through.

With BannerSwap (**www.bannerswap.com**), you receive one-half credit for every ad shown on your site. You receive an additional half credit each time someone clicks through an ad on your site.

The Benefits of Promotion

How much time, effort, and money you spend promoting your station depends on how much of a commercial endeavor it is. You can draw listeners to your station in plenty of ways, as described in this chapter, without spending a lot of money. However, if you are creating a professional station that you want to turn a profit, having a professional public relations campaign is unavoidable and definitely necessary.

16

The Legalities of Running Your Station

Broadcasting audio files is easy. Broadcasting audio files legally can mean a little more work. And with the recording industry paying closer attention than ever to music on the Internet and even prosecuting copyright violators, it is worth your while to make sure you adhere to the various licensing guidelines. Following these guidelines includes, but is not limited to, paying licensing fees that eventually wind up with the artists and the copyright holders of the music you broadcast.

Although the chances are slim of being prosecuted for failing to meet guidelines if you are simply playing some of your favorite songs via SHOUTcast, do you really want to take that chance? And if you plan to broadcast on more than a private or semi-private scale, you must absolutely know what guidelines apply and stick to them. If you don't, and you wind up on the wrong end of a copyright violation judgment, you'll have no one to blame but yourself.

CAUTION

Although we have researched these issues diligently, we are not lawyers, and the information here is *not* professional legal advice. All rules and regulations are subject to change. You should research the issues yourself and, when in doubt, consult a lawyer. This is especially true for people operating outside the United States., where the laws and our research are even less defined.

General Copyright Law

Before we get started, let's cover some basic information about copyright law. First and foremost, most countries in the world recognize copyrights, even if the copyright for a particular work is not registered in their home country. This isn't 100 percent per se, but more or less when it comes to recordings, songs, art, and other original expression, you can bet that something created in the United States and copyrighted will find protection in the U.K., Japan, or Germany, because each of those countries works hard to recognize the others' copyrights.

A work doesn't have to be explicitly copyrighted to be protected by copyright (as long as it is a type of work that can be copyrighted, it is copyrighted unless you explicitly determine otherwise). In the United States, a work that isn't copyrighted is considered in the public domain and is free to be used. This principle includes works placed on purpose in the public domain and works for which a copyright has expired. In the United States, many changes have been made to the rules regarding expiration of copyright. It's tough, therefore, to make blanket statements about public domain, but we can make a few points that are useful to know:

▶ Works created by the U.S. federal government are in the public domain.

▶ Works are deemed in the United States to be in the public domain if they were created before January 1, 1925 (as of January 1, 2000), because, for the most part, upon publication most copyrights last seventy-five years (2000 - 75 is 1925).

▶ Works which the copyright holder has explicitly made a part of the public domain are usable. However, make sure you find out this information from the genuine copyright holder who has the rights to place the work in the public domain.

▶ Copyrights for works created in 1978 or later last for fifty years beyond the life of the work's author, after which the work lapses into the public domain. If the work is a joint work, prepared by more than one author, its copyright lasts for fifty years after the last surviving author dies.

▶ For works published in the years 1964 through 1977, copyright lasts for seventy-five years from the date of publication.

▶ Before 1964, copyrights for works lasted only twenty-eight years, but authors could get a renewal (which many did) for an additional forty-seven years of protection. So many got renewals that the law was simply changed to a standard seventy-five years with no renewal.

▶ Copyrights secured in the period 1926 through 1949 continue to exist only if they were renewed, and they will expire in the period 1999 through 2024.

▶ If a work was created but never published (rare in the context of music) prior to 1978, its copyright duration is calculated as if it had been created on January 1, 1978, and lasts as long as that calculation specifies or through 2002, whichever is later.

Any later generation music will almost certainly not be in the public domain. However, many older radio shows and songs are entering the public domain every day. Additionally, some people have organized the Free Audio Content Broadcasters Association (FACBA), which is getting acts and other copyright holders to sign off on letting broadcasters use their works without repercussion. See Chapter 13 for more details on this organization.

Most of this information covers U.S. law. Your home country may have different timeout dates and protections, so be sure to consult a local lawyer.

TIP

The Copyright FAQ is located on the Web at **www.aimnet.com/~carroll/copyright/faq-home.html**.

U.S. Webcasting Law Basics

When Webcasting was in its infancy, the law covering it was similarly immature and insufficient. In October 1998, Congress passed the Digital Millennium Copyright Act (DMCA). The act amended U.S. copyright law to cover Internet licensing of radio stations. It also brought the U.S. two new World Intellectual Property Organization (WIPO) treaties that cover international copyright issues in respect to the Internet.

TIP

You can read the full text of the DMCA at **ftp://ftp.aimnet.com/pub/users/carroll/law/copyright/h2281enr.txt**, and you can find the Copyright Office's summary in PDF format at **ftp://ftp.aimnet.com/pub/users/carroll/law/copyright/dmca-summ.pdf**.

Although larger stations and other Webcasting entities must enter specific agreements with various rights organizations, the act does outline a type of license known as a *statutory license*. This type of license guarantees Webcasters a license to broadcast sound recordings as long as these stations and their broadcasts meet certain conditions.

A statutory license is provided by the law rather than specifically granted by individual copyright owners. This process not only makes it easier for people to broadcast legally over the Internet, but it is also an efficient way for rights holders to have their rights protected and managed. With a statutory license, the licensing agencies aren't overwhelmed by the hundreds of thousands of Internet radio stations that will eventually exist.

A station must meet the following conditions to receive a statutory license:

▶ In a given three-hour period, Webcasters cannot do the following:

Play more than three songs from a particular album, including no more than two consecutively.

Play four songs by a particular artist or from a boxed set, including no more than three consecutively.

Pre-announce songs that will be played or provide advance song or artist playlists. (Webcasters can name one or two featured artists as a means of illustrating the type of music they play. DJ "teaser" announcements using artists' names are also permitted, but those promos can't name a specific time they will be played.)

▶ Stations that play a set list of songs in an archived format cannot do so for less than five hours. Playlists that are five hours or more in length can reside on a Web site for no more than two weeks. Changing one or two songs does not constitute a new playlist.

▶ Looped or continuous programs must be at least three hours in duration. As with the previously mentioned condition on archived sets, changing one or two songs does not change this requirement.

▶ Special programs of less than one hour in duration that are performed at scheduled times cannot be broadcast more than three times in any two-week period. If the program is one hour or more, the limit is four times.

▶ Webcasters are obligated to identify the song, artist, and album they are playing if receivers of the service are capable of displaying this information. Tools such as the MP3Spy DJ Plug-in and SHOUTpager (**http://www.gcs.co.za/mbs/shoutpager/**) enable Webcasters to broadcast this information to users via the Web or MP3Spy. It's expected that a future version of SHOUTcast will also build in stronger support for this requirement.

▶ Webcasters are prohibited from falsely suggesting a link between recordings or artists and advertisements for products or services. For example, Webcasters cannot tie the broadcast of a song to a particular product they're trying to sell or an ad the person should see.

▶ Webcasters are obligated to take steps to defeat copying of their streams by recipients, but only if they have the means to do so. Webcasters must accommodate any measures widely used by sound recording copyright owners to identify or protect copyrighted works if it is feasible to do so without hindering the ability to transmit their shows.

▶ Webcasters are also obligated to help defeat scanning by services or people that helps Web surfers specifically tune into particular artists or recordings.

▶ The transmission of bootleg recordings is not covered by the license. The statutory license is limited to transmissions made from lawful copies of sound recordings. This doesn't give Webcasters implicit permission to broadcast bootleg or pre-released records, unless they otherwise receive permission from the rights holder.

▶ Webcasters must not automatically and intentionally cause a device receiving their transmission to switch from one program they offer to another.

▶ Webcasters must transmit copyright management information if feasible. This information is encoded in the sound recording by the copyright owner to identify the title of the song, the featured artist, and other related information (if any).

International Webcasting Laws

The United States has one of the faster acting legislative bodies around, and even then the law pertaining to broadcasting is still nascent and slow to develop. Although the Digital Millennium Copyright Act did a great deal to create Webcasting-specific law, it's still not all there. And in other countries, the situation is even worse.

Where law is undefined, governments tend either to apply old media rules to new ones, regulate the industry heavily (if possible) until a law can be passed, or do nothing. Although explaining the U.S. legal issues that Webcasters need to be aware of is not incredibly difficult, explaining each specific country's laws pertaining to Internet radio is another game entirely.

We can, however, cover some generalities that can help you if you're operating a station outside U.S. borders.

Most countries have strict copyright laws, and treaties are in place allowing copyright holders from one country to sue those violating copyright in another. Even if no licensing issues or other streaming audio-specific laws are on the books in your country, if the issue respects copyright law, you can expect to come under fire from copyright holders or their legal agents should you violate their rights. We suggest, in the absence of any specific laws about Webcasting in your home country, that you follow the statutory licensing rules laid out in the United States as a general precaution.

If you plan to broadcast in your host country, consult a lawyer or check on the Web to see whether any specific legal rules are applicable to Internet radio in your country. Consulting with a lawyer shouldn't take very long, and if you're serious about Webcasting, it's worth the time.

Look for local licensing agents in your country. Although ASCAP, BMI, and others have worldwide affiliates, local artists in your home country may use a local rights organization or rights agencies that represent or connect with ASCAP, et al. For example, the Performance Rights Society (**www.prs.co.uk**) is a local rights agency in the U.K., as is the Mechanical Copyright Protection Society (**www.mcps.co.uk**). Your country should have similar licensing agencies.

Getting the License

If you think you are running a station that meets all the conditions of a statutory license in the United States, you need to file an "Initial Notice" with the Copyright Office in Washington, D.C. This notice should include your full legal name, mailing address, phone and fax numbers, and the date of the first transmission qualifying for the statutory license.

You send this "Initial Notice" with a $20 filing fee to the following address:

> Library of Congress, Copyright Office
> Licensing Division
> 101 Independence Avenue, S.E.
> Washington, D.C. 20559-6000

Files Created for Webcasting

Copies are sometimes referred to as *ephemeral recordings*. The new law grants an exemption for ephemeral recordings if the Webcasting service making those ephemeral recordings is licensed to transmit them (that is, it has a statutory license to transmit the recordings), and it meets the conditions of the exemption.

The following conditions apply to the exemption for ephemeral recordings:

▶ The copy of the recording must be used only by the Webcaster.

▶ The copy must be destroyed within six months, unless preserved exclusively for archival purposes.

▶ Only one ephemeral copy of the recording can be made, and no further copies of the recording can be made from that ephemeral copy.

▶ The copy must be used only for transmissions in the Webcaster's local service area.

A statutory license is available for Webcasters who want to make more than one copy (for example, to transmit sound recordings at different bit rates for different listeners), therefore disqualifying them from the ephemeral recording exemption. The statutory license for ephemeral recordings operates like the one for public performances. The royalty rate is set through negotiation or, if necessary, arbitration, and is effective for two years. The conditions of the ephemeral recordings statutory license are similar to those for the exemption. However, the terms of the statutory license may allow Webcasters to make more than one copy of a recording.

Royalty Payments

At this point, details about royalty payments for the statutory license are a bit sketchy. The DMCA law doesn't set a royalty rate for the statutory license. Instead, sound recording copyright owners can negotiate with Webcasters to set that rate during the six-month negotiation period that started in December 1998. The law requires that the rates be what a "willing buyer and willing seller would agree to in a marketplace." If Webcasters and sound recording copyright owners do not agree on a rate, an arbitration proceeding will take place to determine rates.

After the statutory license royalty rate is set, it applies to all Webcasting that has taken place since the new law became effective (October 28, 1998). Therefore, Webcasters who qualify for the statutory license must pay royalties for all transmissions made since October 28, 1998. The royalty rate was to remain in effect until December 31, 2000.

If a Webcaster does not qualify for the statutory license, he or she must obtain licenses from each of the copyright owners of the sound recordings that he or she wishes to transmit. Unfortunately, no group or organization grants licenses on behalf of copyright owners to Webcasting services that do not qualify for the statutory license. Therefore, the Webcaster must contact each copyright owner individually. Webcasters who do not qualify for the statutory license or do not obtain licenses directly from sound recording copyright owners risk infringement liability.

Dealing with Licensing Agencies

Compliance with the guidelines outlined in the statutory license doesn't guarantee you, as a Webcaster, the right to broadcast whatever you want on your station. You must also potentially pay license fees to ASCAP (American Society of Composers, Authors, and Publishers), BMI (Broadcast Music, Inc.), and SESAC (Society of European Stage Authors and Composers)—the major licensing authorities for music. These authorities are the means that artists and publishers use to get compensation for broadcasting of their work.

You might also have to pay a fee to the RIAA (Recording Industry Association of America), although there is some dispute about whether this is absolutely necessary. Plus, RIAA hasn't made pricing information available on its site. You also might have to pay individuals or smaller rights groups, but with the big three, you'll be very well covered. If you use work that isn't covered by these agencies, is out of the range of copyright, or you have some direct form of permission (for example, it's your own music), then you don't need to pay licensing fees.

Some people might not like the idea of paying a licensing fee to offer, in a non-commercial sense, what is essentially free publicity for an artist. However, the licensing fees aren't particularly high. If you're a non-commercial Webcaster, you most likely qualify for the lowest annual rate from each of the big three licensing firms. These rates are outlined in Table 16.1.

Table 16.1
Licensing Information for ASCAP, BMI, and SESAC

Licensing Agency	Minimum Fee	URL for Licensing Page/Contract
ASCAP	$250/yr	Contract: **http://www.ascap.com/weblicense/ascap.pdf** More info: **http://www.ascap.com/weblicense/webfaq.html**
BMI	$500/yr	Contract: **http://www.bmi.com/about/library/forms/website98.pdf** More info: **http://www.bmi.com/iama/webcaster/index.asp**
SESAC	$100/yr	Contract: **http://www.sesac.com/SESACNetLic.pdf** More info: **http://www.sesac.com/web.htm**

Currently, the licensing fees being charged by the major licensing organizations are considered "experimental," which means they're subject to change at any moment while the agencies experiment with various licensing schemes.

BMI

BMI provides unlimited access to more than 3 million musical works from approximately 180,000 BMI-affiliated composers, songwriters, and publishers. More than half of the music played on commercial radio is BMI-affiliated music. BMI artists include Elvis Presley, The Beatles, Miles Davis, The Rolling Stones, Sheryl Crow, Michael Jackson, and more. BMI songwriters make up 75 percent of the Rock & Roll Hall of Fame, 82 percent of the Country Music Hall of Fame, and 90 percent of the Pioneer Awards for R&B.

BMI offers a variety of licensing options depending on your needs. You can choose a *Web site license*, which enables a site to play unlimited amounts of BMI music without the need to report traffic to music pages. Or you can choose the *Web site music area license*, which requires you to pay based on music impressions (calculated on traffic to the music pages on your site). You can change your agreement each quarter depending on what works best for you.

Before choosing a license, you should calculate which fee makes the most sense. The Web site license fee is 1.75 percent of your gross revenue. The Web site music area fee is 2.5 percent of music area revenue. To determine your music area revenue, divide your music impressions by your total page impressions. Then multiply this fraction by your gross revenue to determine your music area revenue. This amount is subject to the 2.5 percent fee. You should compare the fees to see which works best for you.

To download the BMI Web Site Music Performance Agreement, go to **http://www.bmi.com/about/library/forms/website98.pdf**.

ASCAP

ASCAP has a membership of more than 80,000 composers, songwriters, lyricists, and music publishers. You can search ASCAP's index of artists at **http://www.ascap.com/ace/ACE.html**.

Rate Schedule A is available to all Web site operators, but it was designed primarily for Web sites that are focused on music, such as Internet radio stations. It is the only rate schedule available to sites that do not employ technology generally to track and compile online music performance data.

The minimum Schedule A rate is $250; the maximum rate is $140,000. Your Schedule A rate is 1.615 percent of the amount subject to the fee. This amount is either your operating expenditures (all expenditures made in connection with the operation of your site including, but not limited to, salaries, supplies, lease payments, payments to ISPs, payment to Internet access providers, and depreciation) or Web site revenue.

ASCAP defines total Web site revenue as Web site user revenue (payments made on behalf of site users to access transmission), plus net sponsor revenue (sponsor revenue such as payments by sponsors, advertisers, program suppliers, content providers, and so on minus advertising agency commissions). ASCAP even provides a fee calculator for you, as shown in Figure 16.1.

Figure 16.1
ASCAP has an interactive rate calculator on its Web site. Just answer the questions and click Calculate to see your potential fee.

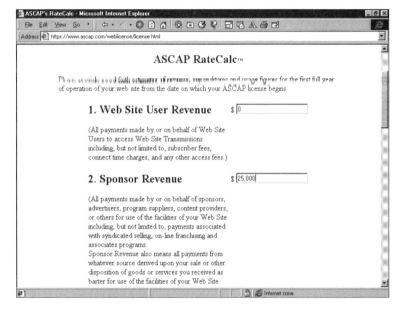

Sites that use limited music and/or employ technology to track that usage are eligible for Rate Schedule B, which bases the fee only on value derived from performances of music on the site.

The annual license fee under Rate Schedule B is 2.42 percent of your base (the greater of Web site revenue or annual operating expenditures) reduced by the relative number of your Web site users who access any performances of music during their sessions on your site.

To qualify for Rate Schedule B, you must employ technology to track and compile data showing your total number of Web site sessions and your total number of sessions during which any performances of music are accessed.

Some sites track their usage of ASCAP music in particular. These sites can use Rate Schedule C. The annual license fee under Rate Schedule C is 4.46 percent of your base (the greater of Web site revenue or annual operating expenditures) minus two fractions. The first fraction is the relative number of your site users who access any performances of music during their sessions on your site, and the second is the relative number of performances of all music on your site that are ASCAP music.

To qualify for Rate Schedule C, you must employ technology to track and compile data showing your total number of Web site sessions, your total number of sessions during which any performances of music are accessed, and your total number of performances and performances of works in the ASCAP repertory. You can change your rate schedule from year to year.

You can download an ASCAP Webcasting license from **http://www.ascap.com/weblicense/ascap.pdf**.

SESAC

Among the many SESAC artists are Garth Brooks, U2, Eric Clapton, Luciano Pavorotti, Mariah Carey, Hanson, and more.

SESAC licensing fees are calculated on the following formulas. If you have no advertising on your site, your license fee is calculated on the average number of monthly page requests multiplied by .005. The minimum fee is $50 per six months, and the maximum fee is $1,250 per six months. If you do have advertising on your site, your fee is calculated on the average number of page requests times .005 times 1.3. The minimum fee is also $50 per six months, and the maximum fee is $1,625 per six months.

You can download the SESAC agreement from **http://www.sesac.com/SESACNetLic.pdf**.

The RIAA

The Recording Industry Association of America, which was founded in 1952, is a trade group that represents American record companies. The RIAA has played a visible role in the recent MP3-related issues facing the recording industry and continues to play a role in Internet-related radio. The RIAA is understandably concerned with the unlicensed use of music on the Internet, which takes money away from artists and specifically the record labels it represents.

It is in the RIAA's interest to eliminate the kind of free trading of copyrighted, unlicensed music that has unfortunately proliferated on the Internet in recent years. The RIAA helped design the legislation that has led to the statutory license. However, there is considerable dispute as to whether an Internet radio station has to pay fees to the RIAA for broadcasting over the Web.

The basic issue between the RIAA and those who say it doesn't have the right to collect fees for Internet broadcasts has to do with how the law is written concerning copyright and performance rights under U.S. law. Recording companies had been previously left out of broadcast rights of music. However, on the Web, many radio services might actually be a bit different than those found in traditional radio. Thus, some of the laws concerning transmission of music have been amended somewhat. As part of those amendments in addition to the rights holders of music (that is, the publisher of the song and a specific artist performing it) who have always had rights, the recording companies also were granted some rights. What is in dispute is where those rights begin and end. The RIAA's point of view is that most Internet broadcasting falls under its right to collect fees. However, others such as Bob Kohn (see the last section in this chapter) argue that only in situations in which users are paying subscription fees to a station or in which the station is interactive or on demand (that is, users can, at any time, request a specific song) can the recording companies get a fee. If you don't charge a subscription fee or provide a request-oriented or on-demand-oriented radio show that plays music from a label represented by the RIAA, you should be off the hook, according to some people's interpretation of the current United States law. You can read Kohn's article on this topic at **www.mp3.com/news/060.html**.

Obviously, before you decide which side you're on, you should consult your own legal experts. In addition, the law as it pertains to the U.S. is just that—U.S. law—and your country may have a different set of laws.

For more information, look at the RIAA's Web licensing FAQ at **www.riaa.com/weblic/wl_faq.htm**.

Get Legit?

You might be wondering why you should pay anywhere from a few hundred to a few thousand dollars every year to broadcast music over the Internet. Why not wait until one of these groups sends you a cease-and-desist order or maybe even brings a lawsuit against you and your site? That's like saying you're going to drive around and not buy insurance until after you have an accident. It's a little late then, isn't it? Paying the fee is also the ethical thing to do. Although putting money in the coffers of major record companies might not seem like a particularly high calling, remember that some of that money eventually makes its way to the artists who absolutely deserve it.

Truth be told, there is a good chance that many small Webcasts will slip under the radar of the various licensing firms. When your station becomes commercial, that is far less likely to happen. However, the law is new, enforcement hasn't been worked out perfectly, and you can hide your broadcasts to avoid getting snared by the lawyers. Just because you can do it doesn't mean you should do it. You shouldn't.

The solution is twofold. First, either you should pay for the right to broadcast music, or you should develop content for your station that doesn't require you to pay a fee. Second, small, non-commercial Webcasters need to communicate with the various rights organizations and the governments of the world to help create law and licensing agreements that make it easy for people to legitimately broadcast music and create their own stations on the Internet at a cost that isn't prohibitive. This pressure isn't created by not paying, but by paying and pushing on lawmakers and rights givers to make it easier and less expensive. Imagine a world in which 10 million small broadcasters each pay $100 a year (less than $10 a month) to broadcast music on the Internet. The organizations that grant rights will understand that, by making it too expensive for people to broadcast on the Internet, they will lose hundreds of millions of dollars annually in rights fees.

With some effort, the laws and the fees will become affordable for everyone. For this reason, it is important for smaller broadcasters to follow the rules. Being a responsible, paying broadcaster gives you leverage.

More Rights Questions? What to Do?

As much as we've tried to cover legal issues and rights involved in running your own Webcast, you probably still have more questions. If you want to double-check issues concerning your own situation or get even more information on Webcasting rights issues, check out the following information.

If you're serious about being compliant, and you should be, we strongly suggest you consult with a lawyer. The rules for Webcasting are changing daily. Also, not all music and material are licensed by ASCAP, BMI, SESAC, and the RIAA (although most is). You might need to deal with smaller and more local organizations. An attorney can help you comply and keep you up to date and better prepared.

Additionally, you might want to check out the following books by Bob Kohn, the CEO of EMusic (**www.emusic.com**). These books and his companion site (**www.kohnmusic.com**) are amazing sources of good information from an expert in the field.

> *Kohn on Music Licensing 2nd Edition* by Bob Kohn
> (Aspen Law & Business, 1996, ISBN: 156706289X)

> *Kohn on Music Licensing 1998 Supplement* by Bob Kohn
> (Aspen Law & Business, 1998, ISBN: 1567068081)

Both books are extremely comprehensive but a bit pricey for the small user. Thankfully, you can find lots of Webcast-specific information on the site.

Do the Rights Thing

The legal issues surrounding Internet radio are not trivial. Although these issues started out completely ambiguous, recent changes in the United States and the professionalism of broadcasters in general are making the situation better. Overall, if you plan to build an Internet radio station that will play copyrighted material—especially music—you need to pay fees and conform to the statutory licensing rules if you want to stay on the good side of the law. If you choose to ignore these rules, laws, or fees, you do so at great risk to yourself. If you're lucky, you might just get a nasty e-mail or letter in the mail. However, that's if you're lucky. If you're unlucky, you could be in big trouble.

So, in the end, the question comes down to whether you should you do the "rights" thing. This question can be answered in two ways:

▶ If you want to broadcast copyright music, you should follow the rules and pay the fees as outlined by the agencies in this chapter.

▶ If you want to avoid the fees, you should look for music or other types of programming that doesn't fall under the jurisdiction of the law or that has someone wanting to collect a fee for it. You can create or even find plenty of free content that doesn't ever come close to putting you in jeopardy over it being played on your Internet radio station or show.

17

Commercializing Your Station

Although some broadcasters are in the business simply for the fun of broadcasting particular content to a small audience, others want to turn their broadcasting passion into a profitable business. You can create such a business on a small, medium, or large scale, depending on the amount of money you're willing to invest and the extent of your goals. This chapter covers various ways to earn revenue, either by selling advertising, selling products as an affiliate store, or through other means. This chapter also describes RealServer's new Advertising Extension, which you can use to insert banner ads in the RealPlayer G2, as well as add audio or video ads into your broadcast stream. This chapter also describes some other third-party tools for commercial broadcasters. Finally, the chapter covers the use of banner ads to attract traffic to your station.

Selling Advertising on Your Site and Station

Selling advertising on your site is generally a task that you should outsource to an Internet advertising service or network. Although using full-fledged advertising services can be pricey, working with a banner advertising network can help you save money if you display ads for other network sites on your site. Many banner advertising networks allow you to advertise your site without paying for ad space, and some offer both cost-per-click (CPC) and cost-per-impression (CPM) pricing.

CPM stands for cost per thousand (M is the Roman numeral for 1,000). Major banner advertising prices are based on a specific price per 1,000 unique impressions (that is, displays) of a banner. When you're buying advertisements, the average price is between $20 and $30 CPM, though the range can be anywhere from $2 to $70 or more, depending on the type of ad, the site, its customer base, and the location of the ad. Prices are often higher for services that deliver a narrower target audience that can improve the response rate to your ad. In general, the more specifically you target your ad, the more you pay per thousand impressions.

The CPC method, on the other hand, charges only for click-throughs.

The biggest problem with selling banner ad space is that people often listen to your station and don't pay attention to banners on the station's accompanying site. Although placing banners on your site can lead to a simple source of revenue (and some Internet radio operators such as Spinner have specialized Web-based players that can help emphasize banner ads), the real draws for advertising and Internet radio are audio-based ads. However, banner advertising is worth understanding, and many of the major banner ad networks may eventually add audio ads to their offerings.

The Keys to Advertising Commercialization

Any station that seeks to commercialize itself through advertising has two key needs. The first is interested advertisers, either through sales efforts you make (which is difficult to do) or through signing on with an ad sales service (many of which require clients to be qualified in some way).

The second is the ability to track listening statistics and other characteristics for your station. No companies will advertise with you if you can't tell them about your station's listening patterns and how many people will see or hear their ads.

Banner Advertising Networks

As an online broadcaster, you are in the position both to buy and sell advertising. Selling advertising could be your primary means of income, whereas buying advertising elsewhere on the Web or being involved in banner swap networks can help attract visitors. The more visitors your site has, the more advertising you can sell.

Advertising and banner exchange services and networks can help you on both ends of the equation. The following sections provide some information on some of the networks and companies worth looking into.

Flycast (www.flycast.com)

Flycast provides direct-response advertising solutions. You work with a personal media consultant and can choose from a number of different programs, depending on which work best for you.

▶ The Flycast Network has 1,575 sites and 23 million viewers. The network is organized into twenty-five content categories, which can be targeted, or you can aim across the entire network.

▶ Flycast CPCnet is a cost-per-click network that delivers the same online reporting and customer service available with all of Flycast's products.

► Flycast eDispatch offers what you need for advertising in e-mail newsletters and managing e-mail content and subscribers.

► Flycast MediaNet is a full-service solution that includes a personal adviser who studies your campaign data for potentially strong relationships. Your adviser implements and tunes your campaigns and presents regular reports with recommendations for improving response rates.

Flycast helps you sell advertising as a Flycast affiliate publisher. The Flycast Network is for sites with 250,000 or more monthly impressions. Flycast CPCnet is for sites with 20,000 to 250,00 monthly impressions.

DoubleClick (www.doubleclick.com)

The core of the DoubleClick Network is DoubleClick Select, a collection of sites represented exclusively and available for custom ad buys and sponsorships. The DoubleClick Network has six categories: auto, business, entertainment, technology, travel, and women/health. DoubleClick's programs allow you to customize your solution to meet your needs.

► DoubleClick DART is ad-serving technology that allows advertisers to deliver their own advertising and measure long-term results.

► DoubleClick Local is geared toward regional and local businesses, allowing you to target advertising toward your local market.

► DoubleClick International goes in the other direction, allowing you to run a global advertising campaign.

DoubleClick can also help you sell advertising by outsourcing ad management, sales, and technology.

ContentZone Network (www.contentzone.com)

ContentZone has a network of more than 2,500 small- to medium-sized sites. You can earn revenue from the ads it delivers to your site while it also helps increase your traffic. Upon acceptance to the ContentZone network, you, as a publisher, can submit as many pages for banner coding to receive ads as you would like. The ContentZone Portfolio Editor helps with page placement and presentation and works to ensure that your registered pages are equipped with proper banner coding.

You can also use the ContentZone's network to increase your audience. You can run your ads throughout the entire network or choose channels that are most relevant for your needs.

ValueClick (www.valueclick.com)

ValueClick provides sites of all sizes with paying advertisers utilizing the cost-per-click model. Advertisers are charged for visitors who click through to their sites, not for impressions or page views. ValueClick hosts are paid each time one of your site's users clicks on one of the ValueClick advertisers' banners. ValueClick pays between 12 and 25 cents per click-through and offers dynamic targeting tailored to your users. There is no commitment or exclusivity required and no fee to join. ValueClick manages the sales, the billing, and the risk.

Advertisers take no risk because they pay only for click-throughs.

Datacom Ad Network (www.datais.com)

The Datacom Ad Network manages advertising for more than 3,500 sites and has relationships with dozens of advertisers and agencies in the United States, Europe, and Asia. Datacom offers programs on a cost-per-click and cost-per-impression basis. It is a network of small- to mid-sized sites and includes twenty-two content channels and numerous targeting options.

Checks are paid when you have a balance of $50 or more, and detailed reports are available 24 hours a day. No exclusivity required.

Click2Net (www.click2net.com)

Click2Net offers a pay-per-click and a Banner Exchange program for advertisers and Web publishers. Click2Net pays publishers for each unique banner click your site generates. It also handles the ad serving, tracking, and reporting. You can sign up for the program for free, and it pays 6 to 10 cents per click, depending on your traffic flow. You can select the ads that appear on your site, and you have access to real-time statistics. Payment is calculated on the tenth of each month and pays out a minimum of $30 per check. If you earn less than $30 in a month, the money is carried over to the next month.

The Banner Exchange program allows you to display ten different banners on other network sites in exchange for showing banners on yours. Members earn a half credit each time a banner appears on your site and three credits when a visitor clicks through. Your banner is displayed once for every full credit. Click2Net allows animated banners that must be 468×60 pixels.

Statistics Packages

Good advertising networks, which are primarily banner-oriented at this time, always keep track of your ad statistics. They can tell when, where, and how many ads they served through your outlet. However, you still should track your listenership as closely as possible. Statistics tell you what times are most valuable during the day, how long people listen, and more.

Traditional Web statistic packages such as WebTrends track many Web page-related statistics, including any media files that are specifically requested from your site. But this type of package is not the same as a statistics package that works directly with your streaming audio server and is specifically tailored for such tracking.

At the time of this book's writing, several processes or programs were available to help you with tracking usage and other station statistics. They're described in the following sections.

MediaReports 1.5

If you're running RealServers or Windows Media Audio servers, you can use Lariat Software's MediaReports (**www.lariat.com**), a well-known package that specifically offers statistics and usage tracking. QuickTime support is expected soon.

SnapShot 2.5

For smaller stations, Lariat offers SnapShot 2.5, an application that can capture and report basic statistics for RealServer 3.0 (or higher) or Windows Media Server. This product is designed specifically for small broadcasters and hobbyists. The package provides real-time information on traffic over a seven-day period, and the summary can track total file accesses, average number of requests per day, and domains served. SnapShot also offers a report that contains statistics on customer operating systems, file requests (including codec selections), the top ten domains used by your customers, connection times, and file usage rates.

SAM

If you use icecast and SHOUTcast servers, SAM (a product from Spacial Audio Solutions) is a useful program that not only gives you improved statistics reporting and log analysis beyond what those systems currently offer but also includes ad insertion help and the ability to sign up with an ad sharing service that lets you earn revenue. For more details on SAM, see Chapter 5.

Creating Audio Ads

When it comes to advertising on the Internet, banners still rule the day despite the huge growth that Internet radio has experienced thus far. As Internet radio begins to grow, however, you can expect audio-based advertising to be a growing component of it.

Today, most Internet audio advertising is run at the beginning of a program. Running these ads is easy, and because they precede the program, you can be sure almost every listener will listen to the ads beforehand. Broadcast.com and others have used this ad format for some time. Most of these ads last about ten to fifteen seconds and introduce sponsors or other audio ads.

Implementing the pre-show ads is also easy. You can set up Real and Windows Media to play an intro file or two. Then, using SHOUTcast, you can create a pre-playlist file, defined in its server.ini file, to be played before joining the broadcast.

To some extent recently, and more so in the future, radio software will make it much easier for you to insert ads at any point into your stream. Moreover, those ads will be pulled intelligently and targeted from an ad server that can track the number of times an ad was sent and handle other tracking and targeting—much like most major banner ad servers do today. Already, RealNetworks has introduced an ad server extension, and with SAM you can insert ads into your SHOUTcast and icecast broadcasts as you run your station.

Streaming Media Ads
with RealServer Advertising Extensions

RealServer 7.0 has introduced an advertising extension that enables you to add streaming media advertising or traditional banner ads in any streaming media presentation. It offers integration with existing ad-serving software and services to allow complete tracking, thus targeting administration.

You can place and play targeted ads within RealPlayer G2 using the same information as traditional Web browser ads. Streaming-media ads can be played before or in between your programming. Each ad provides interactivity, including support for click-throughs to promotional URLs. The program also works with all popular ad networks.

According to the Millward Brown Interactive Report, click-through rates for streaming media ads are five times higher than that of static banners, and after consumers were exposed to a streaming media ad, they were 160 percent more aware of the advertiser's brand name. Millward Brown International is a major advertising research firm.

The Advertising Extension supports standard browser and RealPlayer cookies that uniquely identify the users and direct the appropriate ads to them. This information allows broadcasters to send targeted ads to each user and ensure that the impression count and click-throughs are reported and tracked by their ad-serving system.

By using lead-in advertisements, you can begin your program with a RealAudio, RealVideo, or Flash ad. When the ad is played, your content begins streaming. You can also include interstitial video ads, which allow you to integrate video ads into the streaming presentation much like television ads.

Using parallel banners, you can place a persistent banner in the RealPlayer window so that the users are presented with new ads each time they press Play. Your ad-serving software or network handles the demographic checking, scheduling, and impression count.

Automated rotating banner ads can be scheduled to refresh at specific intervals during your presentation, which is a good way to present ads during live broadcasts.

For more information on the RealServer Advertising Extension, go to **www.realnetworks.com/products/update/advertising.html.**

Creating Associate Stores

As we mentioned briefly in Chapter 10, one way to make your station's Web site a source of revenue is to create an associate store. You can allow visitors to click through to products that are mentioned or featured during your broadcast. Many Web retailers offer you a percentage of any sales generated when someone clicks from your site to theirs and makes a purchase.

Links to Record Stores

The most obvious place to start, assuming you broadcast music rather than talk radio, is to offer links to various online music stores. You can offer direct links to artists' pages on those sites or even to specific albums. Depending on the extent of the technology, some stations offer links to currently playing artists, whereas others offer a list of the station's popular artists and link to online music stores from there.

You can also offer album reviews or recommendations and link to those albums. If you do decide to review or recommend albums, you should be honest. Reviews obviously involve opinion, but you should not try to pass off a piece of garbage as a brilliant record. Doing so might get you a sale or two, but in the long run, dishonesty will destroy your credibility and cost you listeners. Make sure the readers know what type of music you're reviewing; in other words, don't try to pass off Britney Spears as a cutting-edge rocker or convince visitors that the new Nine Inch Nails CD is a great gift for mom (unless you have a *really* cool mom).

To make money this way, you can sign up with the various online music retailers to participate in their affiliate programs. However, you need to check with the various licensing agencies such as ASCAP and BMI concerning how this relationship affects your station's licensing needs. For more details on legal issues and how to work with the various agencies, refer to Chapter 16.

Before you join an affiliate program, you should be sure that the particular retailing site is a good one, with extensive inventory or at least inventory that will satisfy your type of listenership. It should also be a site that offers excellent customer service. These factors not only increase the chances that sales will be made and you will make money from these sales, but they also will reflect well on you, your station, and your site. Poor customer service or weak inventory will reflect poorly on you. Unfortunately, some music Web stores such as CDPoint (**www.cdpoint.com**) and CheckOut.com (**www.checkout.com**) don't offer affiliate programs.

Most affiliate programs work similarly. You register your home page with the stores and receive pieces of HTML code to embed in any URL that links to their sites. This way, the stores can keep track of the customers you send to the store. Most affiliate programs offer between 10 and 15 percent of the sale, but often they do not send a check until you have earned a certain amount of money in a given time period (for example, $25 a month).

The following sections describe some affiliate programs worth considering.

Amazon.com (www.amazon.com)

Amazon.com, originally an online bookstore, is now a major e-commerce site offering music, DVD and video, electronics and software, toys and video games, and home improvement. Depending on the type of station you operate, any or all of these categories might offer profitable affiliate opportunities. Currently, more than 350,000 sites of all sizes are participating in Amazon's Associates Program.

Amazon handles all the customer service, fulfillment, shipping, and tracking of sales. You can link to Amazon by recommending specific products, by placing an Amazon search box on your site, or by just linking to the Amazon home page. At the time of this writing, there is no charge, and you can earn up to 15 percent on books featured on your site and 5 percent on all other items. You can check you earnings and traffic reports online at any time and benefit from Amazon's customer service.

For extensive information about Amazon's Associates Program, click on the Join Associates link on the home page.

CDNow (www.cdnow.com)

CDNow offers music and videos for sale and offers two types of affiliate programs.

The first program, Cosmic Credit, is geared toward fan sites, home pages, and others. Cosmic Credit members earn up to 15 percent of purchases made through your links. When you accumulate $100 of credit, CDNow will send you a check. The percentage you earn is based on how much you sell. Less than $500 of sales in a month earns you 7 percent of those sales. The percentage climbs incrementally, with only those sites generating more than $17,000 in sales earning 15 percent. You can check your credit by logging in to the members area of the site.

The second program, C2, is a business network that also allows you to earn a percentage of sales generated through your site and allows you to co-brand with CDNow, link to its content, and receive special promotions, sales, and contests. It also allows your visitors to return to your site with just one click. There is no cost to join C2, and you can link to specific artists and albums.

For information on CDNow's programs, click on the Sell Music link on the home page.

Tower Records (www.towerrecords.com)

Tower Records is one of the largest record chains in the country. Tower does not require its affiliates to meet sales quotas, and it pays 4 percent on sales—about 50 cents for an average title. You can recommend specific titles, add a Tower search box to your site, or use a Tower banner to link directly to its home page.

For more information on its affiliate program, click on the Affiliate Program link on the home page. Contact Tower for information on corporate affiliate accounts.

Borders (www.borders.com)

Borders allows you to help sell music, books, and videos. Up to 7 percent of sales is possible, depending on your sales. In the beginning, Borders pays 5 percent of the net sales amount. When you earn $20,000 in total sales, the percentage increases to 6 percent. Not until you have sold $1,000,000 does the percentage increase to 7 percent. You begin receiving checks after your commissions exceed $50.

For more information, click on the Join Friends & Associates link on the home page.

Barnes & Noble (www.bn.com)

Barnes & Noble sells music, books, posters, software, and magazines. It offers 5 percent on music, software, videos, and gift certificates and up to 7 percent on books and magazines. You can link to the Barnes & Noble home page, featured subject areas, Bargain Book Store, Music Store, best-seller lists, and specific title pages, or you can put a Barnes & Noble search box on your site.

Barnes & Noble also offers tips about online selling and provides news about hot products in addition to sending out a monthly e-mail newsletter. It offers eighteen online reports that enable you to track impressions, click-throughs, orders, shipments, and commissions earned.

For more information, click on the Affiliate Network link on the home page.

Links to Non-Music Stores

Although music stores are the most obvious potential affiliate partners, some others are worth considering. Books and videos are also great sources of affiliate links because many musicians also have complementary books and videos. You also might find other products that listeners to your station's particular genre of music would be interested in. For example, if you play hardcore and punk music, you might consider an affiliation with a skate or surf shop, because some fans of that music are also interested in those activities. Talk-oriented stations can link to relevant books and movies as well.

Also worth linking to are software and hardware stores so that you can link to portable MP3 players, sound cards, and various audio software.

Buying Advertising

If you plan for your station to become commercial, which generally includes selling advertising, you also need to generate traffic to make those ad buys worthwhile to potential advertisers. Chapter 16 covers some ways to promote your site without buying advertising. Here, we'll dig more deeply into details about purchasing advertising that can create traffic.

Creating Banner Ads

Before you start buying banner advertising, you need to have some banner ads. Banner ads can be a great source of traffic for your station. Although you can hire a designer to create your banners, if you have some Web skills, creating your own banners isn't exceptionally difficult. Doing so can save you money that you can put toward buying ad placement.

Many ad creation packages make it easy to create banners even if you're not artistic. If you prefer to hire a professional graphic artist or Web designer, you can expect to pay between $100 and $500 per banner.

You can create many different types of banners, but they all have standard sizes, as shown in Table 17.1.

Table 17.1
Standard Banner Sizes

Banner Type	Pixel Size
Full Banner (most common format)	468×60
Full Banner with vertical navigation bar	392×72
Half Banner	234×60
Square Button	125×125
Button Style 1	120×90
Button Style 2	120×60
Micro Button	88×31
Vertical Banner	120×240

Banners also must conform to some basic technical aspects. They must be stored in the .GIF file format, should generally be no larger than 17KB (some sites require smaller sizes), and cannot be transparent. Some services also limit the amount of time a banner's animation, if any, can last.

NOTE

Some banner exchange services may use different sizes or have different rules. Check with them before submitting a banner.

What Makes a Good Banner Ad?

A good banner ad should have a "hook" to attract users to click through. For example, you can feature some of the artists that your station plays. The banner can just be well-positioned text with a simple, colored background. You can also have multiple frames that cycle through, pausing to offer key information at the right moments to impress the readers.

You might consider some of the following tips as well:

▶ Get a good banner ad/animated GIF-creating software such as Ulead's GIF Animator (Windows), Adobe ImageReady (Mac, Windows), or MetaCreation's Headline Studio (Mac, Windows).

▶ Use interesting but legible fonts that contrast well with the background.

▶ Always feature your URL in the ad in case the readers don't click through immediately.

▶ Create two or three ads. A fresh ad can breathe life into your campaign.

▶ If you have an interesting event or show to broadcast, focus on it.

▶ Learn good banner ad techniques by looking at several existing ads on major sites.

▶ Have both an animated and static version, because some sites don't accept animated ads.

▶ Keep your ad text simple, to the point, and interesting.

Purchasing Ad Space

Building a good ad campaign can take some testing to find the right demographic and site-specific mix that offers a good return on your advertising dollars. The effort involved in testing, coupled with the need to spend a lot of money on ads to get a large amount of traffic, can make banner advertising too expensive to be worthwhile for some stations.

As we mentioned earlier in this chapter when covering the sale of advertising space, banner exchange services can help you advertise without the cost risk involved in purchasing banner ad space. Yahoo! has a good list of banner exchanges, including the ones mentioned earlier in this chapter. You can find it at **http://dir.yahoo.com/Computers_and_Internet/ Internet/World_Wide_Web/Announcement_Services/Banner_Exchanges/**.

You can also look for inexpensive banner space on small- to mid-sized sites that might be happy to take any money you can offer. They might even offer you banner space in exchange for a link or banner on your site. Look for small- to mid-sized quality sites that have visitors who would be interested in what your station offers.

On the more expensive side, many search engines and directories such as Yahoo! and Excite let you purchase specific keywords or phrases that trigger your ad's appearance on their site. In other words, if someone begins a search for "internet hip-hop radio," your station's banner will appear along with the search results.

It is important to test and understand the effectiveness of your ads. Ad services provide you with information about your ad's response rate and more. It is a good idea to first purchase a small amount of ad space and target it toward certain demographics. Then you can check the results and, if they are effective, increase your spending in those areas. If the ad buys are ineffective, you have risked only a small amount of money.

Justifying the Expense

Banner ads have become such a standard part of many sites that they are becoming increasingly ignored, or at least left unclicked. That doesn't mean they can't be effective. However, you need to create an appealing ad, place it in the right spots, buy enough impressions, and more.

When you're justifying your advertising costs, remember that your ad might not generate a 1:1 response. Approximately 1 to 2 percent of viewers will actually click on a banner ad. As you learned in Chapter 16, an offline advertising and PR-focused approach can prove to be very effective in the early going. However, you should include some form of banner advertising as part of your overall advertising mix.

Internet Advertising Agencies

The companies described in the following sections offer a variety of advertising services and are geared toward larger sites and stations looking to buy advertising on the Web.

AdForce (www.adforce.com)

AdForce's strategic partners include many of the biggest names in Web publishing and networking, new media, and direct marketing. AdForce offers point-and-click software to schedule your campaign, or you can rely on its client services team.

AdForce allows you to target the people your advertisers want to reach by serving ads from a central point and by using criteria such as domain, content area, keywords, geography, and more. AdForce also has an automated advertising inventory management system that allows you to gain insight into your current and future space.

AdForce offers dozens of reports and analysis and three levels of service, depending on how much you require.

Avenue A (www.avenuea.com)

Avenue A offers strategic planning, media planning, and buying services along with a centralized ad-serving system. Among Avenue A's clients are Eddie Bauer, Ticketmaster Online, and Gateway.

Avenue A is a good option for a commercial stations looking to buy advertising.

Engage (www.engage.com)

Engage offers a number of solutions, such as AudienceNet, AdManager, and Knowledge. AudienceNet offers customer profiles to allow identification and targeting of a precise audience. AdManager allows you to manage your advertising investment. Knowledge is a database of 35 million anonymous user profiles based on demographic and geographic data and more than 800 interest categories.

Funding Your Hobby– and Maybe More

In the future, commercialization will become a key component of Internet radio. Although this chapter covers some of the basics, you can take a few steps today to earn revenue from your station; then the real revenue will flow when you can dynamically add audio ads throughout a broadcast to target users. Although everyone loves the mostly commercial-free nature of Internet radio today, without commercialization, it will be hard for it to grow from its current small size.

Even as ads return to radio as it exists on the Internet, the targeted nature of ads and the decreasing need to have so many of them should keep Internet radio superior to the advertising-saturated nature of today's traditional radio.

For small and hobbyist broadcasters, commercialization promises to add some additional fun to broadcasting because, with ad networks and sharing of revenues, even the smallest broadcaster who can provide twenty to fifty listeners over the course of a year might earn enough back in shared ad revenue to cover their own costs. The concept of Internet radio commercialization needs a bit of work. The largest commercial concerns can obtain software and custom development to improve their ability to make money. The rest of us must wait for those tools and services that have enabled us to easily create banner advertising to add support for Internet audio ads.

Appendices

Appendix A
Multicasting Your Broadcast

Multicasting is the act of casting one signal that itself is repeated and broadcast many times over as it goes out to listeners. Unlike repeater services that take a single stream and then split and repeat it into many more unicasted streams, multicasting is actually a low-level network protocol that, when built in and followed by compliant networks, network hardware, and listening clients, can automatically split and repeat one stream to as many as needed—thus enabling thousands or even millions of people to listen to a broadcast.

The problem with multicasting today is that it's still a nascent technology. As we explained in Chapter 3, multicasting is still being developed as a universal Internet technology. It's part of IPv6, which itself is just being rolled out by Internet companies. Today, multicasting is possible, but only through special sections of the Internet and to those listeners running compliant hardware. Thus, you can use it, but you just need to know a bit more than what you know to send out a stream via unicast today.

Today's Multicasting Options

Today, most multicasting is done through the mBone, a specialized section of the Internet that is multicast-compliant. Table A.1 provides a list of useful links and books about the mBone. If you want to experiment with multicasting via the mBone, check into these sources to learn more details.

APPENDICES

Table A.1
Useful Multicast Resources

Links

MBONE: Multicasting Tomorrow's Internet
http://www.savetz.com/mbone/
Complete text of a book that was previously published about the mBone.

MBONE FAQ
http://www.cs.columbia.edu/~hgs/internet/mbone-faq.html

Dan's Quick and Dirty Guide to Getting Connected to the MBONE
ftp://genome-ftp.stanford.edu/pub/mbone/mbone-connect

Books

mBone: Multicast Multimedia for the Internet
by Vinay Kumar (New Riders Publishing, 1996, ISBN: 1578700191)

Multicasting on the Internet and Its Applications
by Sanjoy Paul (Kluwer Academic Publishers, 1998, ISBN: 0792382005)

The Basics of Multicasting Your Audio Today

To multicast on the Internet today, you need to send out a session on the Multicast Internet, which is also known as the mBone. A typical multicast session involves announcing the multicast and then sending it. A multicasted stream is always a live stream; it's never an on-demand stream. You use separate protocols and processes for both the announcement and then for the broadcast. Using them requires a little learning on your part, and that means some additional reading. The following two documents are helpful:

▶ "How to Connect to the mBone," by Ross Finlayson (**http://www.livecaster.com/mbone/**)

▶ "Streaming MP3 via IP Multicast," a PowerPoint presentation given at the MP3 Summit by Ross Finlayson in 1999 (**http://www.livecaster.com/mbone/mp3summit1999.ppt**)

Who Is Compliant?

The big question to ask yourself is what software you need to start learning and experimenting with multicasting. Eventually, everyone will be multicasting-capable. Already, all the major servers described in this book are either semi-capable, entirely capable, or currently planning multicasting capability. If anything, people are waiting until the entire Internet is multicast-compliant rather than just the mBone section. Still, what you can learn today will help you even more when this capability is widespread tomorrow.

Both Windows Media Server and RealServer 7 are multicast-compliant. However, the free Basic Server version is not; you need to upgrade to a paid version of the software to gain access to multicasting capabilities. Also, RealServer 7's much superior administration interface and documentation make it much easier to work with than Windows Media Server for multicasting.

For MP3 servers such as SHOUTcast and icecast, you need to work with a separate third-party system known as LiveCaster (developed by Ross Finlayson), which can work with those systems or as a standalone system to help you build MP3-based multicasted broadcasts.

Introducing LiveCaster

Because many MP3 fans are broadcasting fans, and several major technologies for broadcasting such as SHOUTcast use MP3 as the broadcast format, it seems appropriate to talk about technologies conducive to multicasting MP3 streams.

One of the main products available today for multicasting MP3 files is LiveCaster (**www.live.com**). Developed by Ross Finlayson, LiveCaster is available for Windows 95/98/NT, Linux, Solaris, and FreeBSD platforms.

Broadcasting with LiveCaster

LiveCaster is fairly straightforward to use, and a good set of step-by-step instructions is included on the Live.com Web site. To start, download the LiveCaster software, and read the installation instructions on the download page located at **http://www.livecaster.com/liveCaster/ downloading.html**. If you're a Windows user, you should pay particular attention to the notes concerning the Windows version of LiveCaster and make sure you follow them; otherwise, you may induce unnecessary problems with your multicast.

After you install LiveCaster, you can find comprehensive instructions for its use at **http://www.livecaster.com/liveCaster/gui.html**.

LiveCaster can stream MP3 files stored in a directory, or you can supply it a live stream to multicast. That option is useful because you can stream out using a typical SHOUTcast server and then connect LiveCaster to one of those streams and use it as a multicasting solution.

LiveCaster has special documentation for live input located at **http://www.livecaster.com/liveCaster/liveInput.html**.

Helping Users Receive Your Multicast

A few tricks are required to enable a multicast broadcast; a few tricks are also required to receive one. Until the entire world is multicast-compliant, it's going to take some specialized instructions to get a product to work with multicasting.

Fortunately, you can find some documentation covering how to connect popular MP3 players to a multicast broadcast on the Live.com Web site located at **http://www.livecaster.com/liveCaster/receiving.html**.

Some Basic Information on Popular Players

FreeAmp (version 1.3 or higher), which is available for Linux and UNIX systems, has built-in support for RTP. To listen to an MP3/RTP stream, you need to use the rtp:// header when opening a file in the following format:

rtp://<multicast-address>:<port>

The AudioActive MP3 player, which is available for Windows, can play RTP streams as well, using the same rtp:// header style FreeAmp uses.

If you use Winamp, you need to install a plug-in to enable RTP streams. Live.com offers a plug-in for the Winamp player at **http://www.livecaster.com/multikit/winamp-plugin.html**. That page also includes installation and usage instructions.

Waiting and Not Waiting for a Multicast World

In general, the world that multicast offers broadcasters is amazing. Thousands, even hundreds of thousands or millions, of users the world over can repeatedly connect to one upstream broadcast. With the growth of multicasting, the need for large amounts of outgoing bandwidth will be reduced greatly, and even the smallest garage broadcaster could capture the world's attention with just a simple modem line and a great broadcast. However, we must wait for that day.

In the meantime, savvy broadcasters can use the Multicast Internet, or the mBone, to join and experiment with multicasting. Using it takes a bit of work, and it's a fun thing to experiment with. You can just dive into it with the leads provided here and see where you get. When you're up and running with multicasting, you'll find a vibrant community of listeners and multicasters. As multicast hits the rest of the Web, it will bring a big change. Why not get out in front today?

Appendix B
DJ Tools for Live Mixing

The term *DJ* can mean many things, but in this case, we're talking about DJs who mix up their music in clubs using turntables. If you've ever dreamed of being the next Paul Oakenfeld, DJ Spooky, or DJ Red Alert, then you've come to the right place.

Many people in the Internet radio movement are fans of electronica, hip-hop, club, house, acid, and every other form of techno music. So, it's no wonder then that some of the programmers out there have created specific programs that might be of interest to those people who want to mix it up live on the air. In this appendix, we'll look at some of the cool tools that are available for the professional DJ and wannabe DJ who want to cut it up live on their Internet radio station or show.

Setting Up for Mixing

Essentially, you can mix live music for your Internet radio station in two ways. The first way is to set up a regular, real-world mixing setup and encode it live for broadcast. This method is the best if you're skilled in the realm of beatmixing and using turntables. Each of the chapters about servers in Part II covered live encoding, so by now you should know how to set up encoding and go to work.

The second way to do beatmixing is to run specialized software that lets you mix together multiple MP3 files. Although this method isn't nearly as hardcore as traditional turntable-based mixing, it's a bit cheaper for hobbyists, and it lets you create mixable broadcasts right from your computer. The three most often-used products—PCDJ, Pitchfork, and Virtual TurnTables—are all MP3-based.

If you want to use these products as radio tools, the key is to be able to rebroadcast the resulting stream from these programs back out over your station. You can do so by using the linerec:// method in SHOUTcast to broadcast the mix. You can find out more details about the linerec:// method in Chapter 5.

APPENDICES

PCDJ

Visionic is a company that specializes in software and hardware specifically for digital music DJs. One of the many products it makes is PCDJ (shown in Figure B.1), an MP3-based DJ tool that enables you to mix two MP3s together. To find it, you can visit **www.pcdj.com**.

Figure B.1
PCDJ in action.

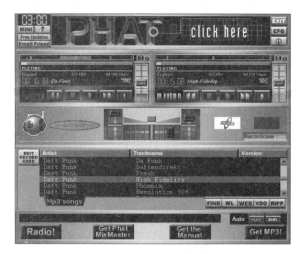

Visionic actually makes several PCDJ programs, which include the following:

▶ **PCDJ PHAT**—Visonic's lowest end product is available for free. Using this product, you can play two simultaneous MP3 files, sync them, and easily cross-fade between the two songs.

▶ **PCDJ Mixmaster**—The next step up from the free version of PCDJ offers beatmatching and cue-point setting.

▶ **PCDJ Digital 1200SL**—This $499 package is aimed at "professional" DJs. It features loads of beatmatching tools, pitchmatching, cue points, and more.

Pitchfork

Pitchfork (shown in Figure B.2) is a Winamp plug-in that enables you to pitchshift and nudge a song position so that you can sync two different MP3 streams in real-time to do classic DJ beatmixing. You can download the plug-in from Winamp.com's Plug-ins page (**www.winamp.com/customize/**) or directly from **http://users.one.se/liket/mp3stock/pitchfork.htm**.

Figure B.2
Pitchfork is a Winamp plug-in that allows you to do classic DJ beatmixing with two MP3 streams being played back by Winamp.

Pitchfork's author, Leif "Liket" Claesson, recommends you have two sound cards and a mixer table to use it to its peak capability. You then can set up two instances of Winamp, each feeding into the mixer that lets you set the output to either card. Pitchfork lets you adjust the feed of the MP3s coming out so that you can sync them together to the same beat. You do so by changing the pitch of one song to fit the pitch of another song. After you sync one song via its pitch, you can use Pitchfork's nudge controls to sync the actual set of beats so they match perfectly. Then you can use the mixer from the two cards to shift between channels and generally cut it up.

According to Pitchfork's documentation, you'll need a somewhat speedy computer so that it can decompress two simultaneous streams. (Claesson says that he's had good results on a K6-2 300 or better machine.) You also have to configure Winamp specially. First, you need to disable the buffering in Winamp by going to the WaveOut Plug-in Configuration and setting the buffer length slider to 0. You should also set the thread priority to Maximum. On the General tab of the Nullsoft Nitrane Preferences dialog, make sure that Decode Thread Priority is set to Highest. Claesson also recommends making sure you are using the best graphics drivers that you have on your system. Using good drivers reduces interference from display adapters, which can cause Winamp to skip.

When you have Pitchfork set up, using it is fairly self-explanatory. You adjust the pitch of a song by sliding the pitch up or down using the pitch slider located on the left side of the screen. You also can use a variety of buttons to nudge the pitch into place for your liking. You have to do so by listening via headphones in one ear while the speakers blare the song currently fed out to them. When you have the pitch to your liking, click on the = button to lock it into place. The documentation notes that, as a rule of thumb, if you have to slide the pitch higher than 8 percent or lower than -4 percent, the songs are, for all intents and purposes, incompatible.

APPENDICES

After you sync the beat, you need to get the beats to hit together at the same time. They may be hitting at the same rate but not hitting at the same time. Using the nudge buttons located in the lower-left corner of the screen, you can nudge the two beats together so they are hitting at the same time. As Pitchfork's documentation says, "Doing that by ear is supposedly easy for an experienced DJ," but novices will need a good amount of practice to do it right.

To help with matching the beats, Pitchfork offers a cueing feature, which enables you to set the position of one song a second earlier and then pause at just the right time. This way, you can wait until you hear the other song in place and then press the Cue button. This feature can help drastically reduce the time it takes to get beats hitting in sync.

You can find complete documentation and explanations of how to set cues in memory and use the nudge controls in the documentation file that comes with Pitchfork.

Virtual Turntables

Unlike Pitchfork, Virtual Turntables by Carrot Innovations (**http://carrot.prohosting.com/**), as shown in Figure B.3, is not a plug-in for Winamp. Instead, Virtual Turntables is a complete standalone DJ mixing program that includes support for MP3 files.

Figure B.3
Virtual Turntables from Carrot Innovations was one of the first standalone MP3-related DJ programs.

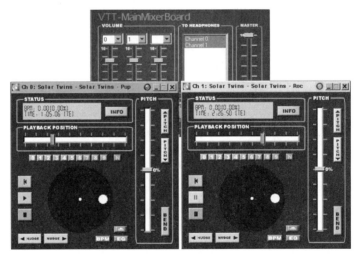

The program enables you to set up two complete MP3 streams (or .WAV files) and work with them to first pitch them into place and then to nudge the beats into place so that two songs are in sync with each other. The latest version offers a virtual "Jog Wheel," which you can use to help tweak pitch and bend positions. Virtual Turntables also lets you save settings for each song, which makes subsequent beatmixing sessions much easier once you've tweaked them the first time. The program also supports some Winamp plug-ins. Virtual Turntables is also shareware. You can use the free version for 40-minute segments but then must restart the product. A registered version is $42.00 and includes discounted upgrades and more.

With Pitchfork, you need two sound cards and a mixer to be able to cross-fade the streams together. Virtual Turntables, however, includes a virtual mixer console that lets you control all the mixing of the two streams right within the computer. Therefore, you don't need an outside mixer. The downside to this is that streams aren't separate, so you can't listen in your headphones to one while the other goes out to speakers. You also don't have visualization and other features Winamp offers to you while using Pitchfork.

In order to broadcast Virtual Turntables mixed music, you'll need to broadcast out the audio stream it creates, because it won't automatically output through to the SHOUTcast server. To do this, you'll need a soundcard like the SBLive that lets you broadcast out what is playing through the soundcard (aka the "what u hear" setting) and then use the Winamp linerec:// broadcasting method described in Chapter 5.

APPENDICES

Appendix C
Using RadioSpy

Formerly known as MP3Spy, RadioSpy (**www.radiospy.com**) locates, sorts, and connects users to hundreds of audio feeds and also provides free DJ tools for people to broadcast their own music. Noncommercial broadcasters can also have banners placed in RadioSpy and on the RadioSpy home page. RadioSpy is the creation of GameSpy Industries (**www.gamespyindustries.com**). GameSpy Industries is well known among game players as the creator of GameSpy (**www.gamespy.com**). GameSpy helps players locate game servers on the Internet, check various characteristics of the servers such as response time and number of players, and then connect to them.

RadioSpy is similar in that it locates all the SHOUTcast, Windows Media, and RealAudio streaming audio servers on the Internet and sorts them by genre, number of listeners, bandwidth, and other information. Users therefore can not only find the type of music they want but also avoid overloading their Internet connection by selecting the desired bandwidth level.

RadioSpy sorts stations using a variety of criteria, including a station's playlist, how often it features the users' favorite artists, and more. Built-in chat and bulletin boards help users and broadcasters interact with each other.

The RadioSpy site (shown in Figure C.1) also attracts users with news, reviews, interviews, polls, contests, chats, forums, and recommendations from the RadioSpy staff.

APPENDICES

Figure C.1

RadioSpy organizes and
helps you listen to the
hundreds of active radio
stations on the Internet.

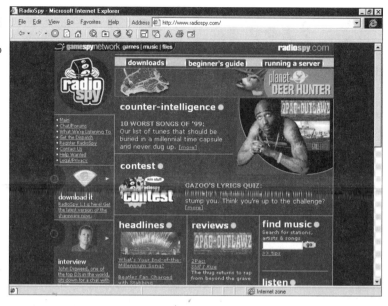

Future versions of RadioSpy will include more ways to interact with
station operators, playlists, and other station information. If RadioSpy
catches on, you can expect it to become the central way to find and listen
to radio stations around the world. As the program expands to track and
help people organize all kinds and styles of radio broadcasts happening
around the world, this program should evolve to become a major software
product used by the growing legions of hardcore Internet radio fans.

Using the full registered version of RadioSpy, you can turn off ad
banners, obtain free lifetime updates, and access special sneak previews
of new versions.

For RadioSpy to work, you must download RadioSpy and an MP3 player
that supports streaming audio such as Winamp, UltraPlayer or Sonique.
RadioSpy also supports linking to RealAudio-powered broadcasts and
Windows Media Audio, so you will have to have a player that supports
those formats (which for RealAudio is basically the RealPlayer). To
download RadioSpy, click on the Downloads link on the home page
(**www.radiospy.com/download.shtml**), and follow the directions.

Using RadioSpy Step-by-Step

The RadioSpy screen is divided into three major windows and one main menu. As you can see in Figure C.2, the three windows consist of the Server List window, a chat area below, and a window that lists the people who are in your current chat area. Each chat area is directly related to the same station you are listening to and may include the actual DJ of the station itself.

Figure C.2
The RadioSpy program in action.

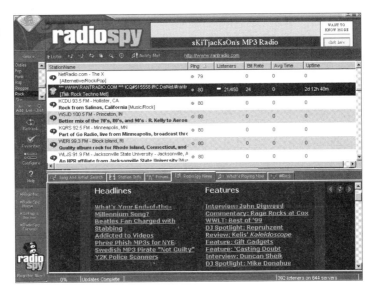

When you are not chatting, you can check out the music news stories RadioSpy has collected.

On the left side of the screen is the main menu for RadioSpy. Using this menu, you can refresh the server list, look at favorite stations, change configurations, or tune to different channels of music. At the bottom of the screen is the status bar, where you can see update messages scroll through, followed by the address of the server you're currently listening to and then the total number of listeners and servers active for that musical genre.

Configuring RadioSpy

When you first install RadioSpy—and at any later time—you can configure your RadioSpy settings. Choosing Configure from the menu brings up the Configuration dialog box. The Winamp Directory field lists the directory in which you installed Winamp. Clicking the Find button (which looks like a magnifying glass and a folder and is located to the right of this field) causes RadioSpy to attempt to locate your Winamp directory automatically.

APPENDICES

In the General configuration area of the dialog, the Chat Nick field is the place where you set the name you will display to others in RadioSpy chat rooms. Next to that field is the Net Connection drop-down list. From this list, you can select your connection speed—from 28.8K modem to T1 or greater.

Below the Net Connection list is the Stream Buffer list, which runs from 16K to 256K. Below the Chat Nick box is a check box labeled Disable Banners, which lets you turn off the banner ads associated with RadioSpy. This option is available only for registered users. Below that is a check box labeled Show RadioSpy in System Tray.

You can then choose Basic or Advanced Interface Style.

GameSpy Industries also asks for some basic personal information (name, age, e-mail address, and zip code). Because the top of the RadioSpy window includes ads, having demographic information on users helps GameSpy sell those ads. If you don't care whether the company sell ads, consider this: The advertising revenue supports further development and covers costs. And the company promises not to resell your information. If you want to avoid the ads, you can always register the product.

If you click on the Notify Me When a New Version Comes Out check box, the RadioSpy developers will e-mail you right away when a new version or update becomes available.

Next is the chat configuration; you can choose Connect to Chat on Startup (the default), Hide Join/Parts in Chat, or Don't Set Auto-Away. Then you can add your home channel to the appropriate box.

The third part of the dialog is the firewall/proxy configuration. You need it only if you are running behind a firewall or proxy server. If you are, you can use the fields for Proxy Address, Port, Username and Password to configure RadioSpy to work in a proxy situation. If you work in a company and need help, you should contact your Web or network help desk. However, we're not sure that admitting to running RadioSpy on your corporate desktop is such a good idea. You can also use a SOCKS Proxy for chat.

The Skins configuration allows you to use the default skins or click on Get Skins Here.

When you're done, click the OK button to close the Configuration dialog box and save your settings.

Connecting to a Server

To connect to a server, you first must connect to the Internet and then start RadioSpy. After it has started, you can select one of the thirty-two genres in the top-left corner, and RadioSpy will build a new server list.

The server list is divided into six columns: StationName, Ping, Listeners, Bit Rate, Avg. Time, and Uptime. An icon to the left of the station name indicates whether the station is a RealAudio station, a SHOUTcast station, or a Windows Media station. To add a server to your Favorites list, right-click on it, and select Add To Favorites. To access those Favorites later, just click on the Favorites button in the left column of the RadioSpy window.

TIP

If the server name column or any column isn't wide enough for you to read all the information, you can widen it by dragging the right side of the column header further to the right. Place the mouse cursor right on the border line, and it will change shape to denote that you are in position to widen or contract the column size.

In the StationName column, some stations include an ICQ number or Web page address where you can contact the DJ for requests, view the playlists, and find out more details about the station.

Ping rates, in the second column, vary from server to server. The lower the rate, the more quickly data travels to you from that server. Very long ping rates can even denote the server being down. To sort servers based on their ping rates, simply click on the Ping column header, and RadioSpy will automatically rank all the servers in ascending or descending order. The green, yellow, and red spots next to the ping rates indicate short (green), medium (yellow), and long (red) rates. Yellow stations could be having problems, whereas red stations are almost surely having skipping problems and may even be down entirely.

Following the Ping column is the Listeners column. Here, you can see whether a particular SHOUTcast station is full. This column is irrelevant for RealAudio or Windows Media stations, but SHOUTcast stations have a maximum number of listeners they can support. RadioSpy lists the number of current listeners followed by the maximum number of listeners. Clicking on the Listeners column header lets you quickly rank the stations in the list by the number of listeners they currently have.

TIP

Remember to refresh by pressing the refresh button every once in a while to make sure you have the latest data when looking for stations with lots of listeners.

After the Listeners column comes the Bit Rate column. The bit rate denotes what the quality of the stream will be. The higher the bit rate, the higher the quality. Bit rates range between 16 and 128, with 128 being equal to most of the regular MP3 files you download from the Web. To rank SHOUTcast stations by their bit rates, simply click on the Bit Rate column header.

The final column, Uptime, lets you know how long the station has been broadcasting since it was last launched. It's not uncommon for DJs to take their SHOUTcast servers down from time to time to install new software because of bandwidth issues or simply to take a break or make other changes. Clicking on the column header to rank stations for Uptime lets you find stations that have been running strong for several days or more.

At any point, you can double-click on any station, and RadioSpy will launch the correct player and tune you to the desired station.

Chatting with RadioSpy

With RadioSpy, each station is also effectively its own chat room, where you can chat with other station listeners or the station staff if they're present.

All chat takes place on the lower part of the RadioSpy program window. Using the graphical icons displayed as a menu between the main chat window and the list of chat room occupants, you can control all chat functions. The first icon, the plug icon, controls whether you are connected to the chat network to begin with. If you don't see any chat activity, click on this icon to connect.

When you connect to any SHOUTcast station, you are automatically transferred to that station's associated chat room. If you want to just chat on another station's chat room but not listen to it, simply click once on any station in the station list, and then click on the Door icon to connect to that station's chat room.

The next icon provides a Channel List, and the fourth icon allows you to send a private message to a selected recipient.

Next, the File Transfer icon lets you send files to anyone you've selected from the chat room occupant list. Using this option can be a great way to transfer MP3 files you want to share with other listeners you meet in chat rooms.

Clicking on the Lock icon keeps you in any currently active chat room even when you change genres or tune to a different SHOUTcast station. MP3Spy has its own specific chat channel, which you can get to by clicking the RadioSpy icon.

Other Features

RadioSpy includes a handful of other features located in the bar between the station window and the lower news and chat window.

Song and Artist Search

Using the Song and Artist Search feature, you can find stations playing your favorite songs and artists by searching the playlists.

Station Info

Highlighting a station and clicking on Station Info gives you an expanded idea of what the station is all about. Information available includes Web address, IP address, genre, number of current listeners, number of maximum listeners, bit rate, and last ten songs played.

Forums

RadioSpy's forums allow you to start a new discussion or add to an existing thread.

RadioSpy News

Choosing RadioSpy News shows you the music news and features currently on the RadioSpy Web site as well as community news and more.

What's Playing Now

The What's Playing Now feature helps you browse the songs playing in the selected genre and tells you how long ago they started playing. You can also click the song notification message to be alerted when a particular song or artist is playing.

A Note For DJs

RadioSpy is mainly a tool for listeners, but DJs should be aware of the special DJ features that RadioSpy offers. For more on these, check out the DJ Tools (which were in version 1.5 as we wrote this). The DJ tools replace the DJ tools provided by the SHOUTcast Source DSP plug-in created by Nullsoft and provide voice over and chat functionality as well.

Most importantly, you will ensure your radio station or show is listed in the RadioSpy directory (which used to be automatic if it was listed in SHOUTcast.com but isn't automatic now). Since you can gain listeners by listing on RadioSpy, it can be a useful addition to your promotional mix. To list with RadioSpy without running the plug-in, or if your broadcast isn't a SHOUTcast-based broadcast, visit their promotion form at **www.radiospy.com/promote.asp**.

RadioSpy also sports banners which you can submit to them for cycling among the other banner advertisements shown in their program. To find out instructions on creating and submitting a banner visit **www.radiospy.com/banners.shtml**.

Instructions on the DJ Tools are available on RadioSpy's Web site at **www.radiospy.com/running.shtml**.

Seek and RadioSpy Shall Find

Finding audio content used to be difficult, and most of what you could find was illegally pirated tracks. As the MP3 scene has grown and the tools have matured, many new bands and other musicians have embraced MP3 for Internet distribution of their music. This growth was only enhanced by the invention of SHOUTcast. And as Internet radio has grown, RadioSpy has expanded its scope to cover not only SHOUTcast stations but also RealAudio and Windows Media.

The trick is to know where to find all this content and how to separate the good from the bad. RadioSpy helps you do just that.

Appendix D
Streaming Audio Master

Streaming Audio Master (SAM) is a program that helps you in many ways to produce, manage, and track your personal radio station or show. Created in 1999 by Louis Louw, the software began life as a dynamic helper application for Winamp that let people track their streams, maintain connections to servers, and generally ensure a better broadcast.

Since its birth, SAM has rapidly grown to include a host of features—many of them aimed at people running dynamic broadcasts, not just a repetitive slate of their favorite eighty songs over and over.

Today SAM works with a number of major streaming audio servers, including Winamp and icecast, and services like Live365.com. It allows you to truly manage a broadcast—drop in commercials, ensure good connections and resets to your broadcast server, offer chat and DJ requests, and get statistics on your listeners, such as how and from where they are connecting to you.

Most radio servers do one thing great—stream audio out to listeners. However, many don't do much more than that. That's where SAM comes in—it fills in all the gaps to broadcasting online and enhances many of the major radio station software products and services we've covered in this book.

In this appendix, which we've worked on in conjunction with Spacial Audio Solutions (the developers of SAM), we've documented the latest version of SAM. After you've learned the basics of either SHOUTcast or icecast, go to the master level and add SAM to the mix.

Installing SAM

New users of SAM should download the full installation. This includes a lot of things you might want to use later, such as the default Web output template.

To install SAM, download the full installation and run Sam.exe program file which will run an automatic installer for the program. The installer offers complete, minimal and custom installations. Note that there are many different aspects to the latest SAM complete package, including an executable version of the icecast server (see Chapter 6 for more on icecast). If you already have icecast, you may want to skip installing this version unless you know it to be an update.

Updating from Previous Versions of SAM

If you already have downloaded the full installation of SAM, you might want to download new SAM versions periodically. The installer now allows it to automatically update only those files that have changed. Updates can also be found on the **www.spacialaudio.com** Web site. Different components and extensions are updated over time, so be sure to check back often.

Configuring SAM

The SAM Setup Wizard will help you through different sections of the SAM setup.

To configure SAM using the Wizard:

1.   Open SAM.

2.   Click on the Config button at the top of the screen. The Configuration screen will appear.

3.   The first screen features a button titled Run Wizard. Click on this button to start the Wizard.

Getting SAM Broadcast Ready

Here are the fields that you need to complete while preparing your SAM broadcast.

▶   **Station Name**—This is your station name as it would appear on a service such as Live365 or AudioRealm.com. You can also include a short comment or description after the station name—for example, "OldRock—We play only the best in classic rock!"

▶   **Genre**—The genre of music you play on your station. You can include a few different genres by separating them with commas.

▶   **Homepage**—If you have a Web site for your station, you can enter the URL for it in this field. Do not just enter "www.mystation.com"; enter the full URL including "http://".

▶   **Server Type**—SAM can be used with various broadcasting methods, including SHOUTcast, icecast, Live365.com, and Windows Media Audio. However, SAM needs to know which type of server or service you are broadcasting to or with, otherwise it won't be able to retrieve the correct statistics for you during broadcast.

Additional SAM Configuration Notes

SAM now has a built in SAMamp player. Winamp is no longer required to send SAM any signal, although you can still use Winamp if you want to. To use SAMamp, choose the SAMamp option over Winamp in Step 5 of the SAM Setup Wizard. The configuration button for SAMamp will bring you into the SAMamp configuration interface, which works quite similar to Winamp's own configuration interface.

SAM now has support to make it more friendly for Blind users. On Step 7 of 8 of the SAM setup wizard, you'll find a checkbox to enable Blind accessibility settings.

Also on Step 7 of 8 there is now a DMCA complience button. It will make sure your playlist and requests are set up to the minimum required by DMCA. Be sure to load a playlist prior to clicking this button for maximum impact.

SAM now supports delay requests. In Step 3 of the overall setup system, which controls request properties, you can set the time delay between a request and fulfillment of it. This is to ensure stronger compliance with the DMCA.

Setting Broadcast Details

The following options allow you to set broadcast details.

▶ **Host (IP)**—The IP or DNS name of the server you are broadcasting to. Avoid using "localhost" or "127.0.0.1" here. If you do, SAM will try to resolve your IP address, and if you have multiple IP addresses this might fail.

▶ **Port**—The port on which you are broadcasting. For SHOUTcast and icecast, the default is usually 8000. For a Windows Media server, however, this will actually be the publishing point root. Use the dropdown list to select the root rather than typing it into the port field.

▶ **NB**—Icecast users also need to add their mount point to the end of the port if it is required by the icecast server.

APPENDICES

► **Show my details on the public list**—If you check this box, your station will be listed on AudioRealm.com. This is a great way for potential listeners to find you.

► **Auto Songname**—On the public list, the current song that you are playing can also be automatically shown. If you do not wish to have the current playing song listed, you may uncheck this box and type in your own static message, which will be shown instead of the current song playing.

► **Link override**—On AudioRealm.com, there is an automatically calculated link on which listeners can click to tune into your station. This doesn't work for Windows Media users, however. Windows Media users are required to override the link and supply an URL to an ASX file or something similar that will result in users tuning into the station.

NOTE

SHOUTcast and icecast users may also override the "Listen To" link if they wish to do so.

Statistics and Graphs

Here are some statistics and graphs you will have available:

Statistics

► **Auto connect at startup**—If checked, SAM will automatically try to connect to your broadcast server to gather real-time statistics for you.

► **Show line on graph**—If checked, this server will show up on the graph. This can be turned on/off at any time using the Relays screen on the DJ-Tools/Statistics screen.

► **Line color**—The color of the line on the graph.

► **Server location**—The physical location of the server. This is to guide people in choosing relays closest to them. A good format might be Country, State. Example: USA, TX (AudioRealm servers).

The following fields may or may not be visible on your screen. If these are not visible, it means that they do not apply to the type of server you specified for SAM.

► **Password**—(SHOUTcast) Password to connect to the broadcasting server. Please make sure you enter this correctly.

▶ **Live365 username**—(Live365 members only) If you are using Live365 to broadcast, you can enter your username here. This is also used in the auto-error recovery routine.

▶ **Start tailing log on connect**—(icecast) Tailing the log means the server will send events to SAM. This is required for SAM to be able to keep real-time statistics.

▶ **Admin password**—(icecast) This is the administrator password for icecast. Please refer to the icecast documentation for more details on the different types of icecast passwords.

▶ **Operator password**—(icecast) The operator password is optional. This will give you the power to do things like shut down the icecast server and more using the icecast console in SAM.

▶ **WMA publishing point**—(Windows Media) This is the Windows Media Unicast publishing point. By clicking on the drop-down list, you can select a valid registered publishing point from the list. The value of the virtual root will be stored in the port field.

▶ **Bitrate**—(Windows Media) Unfortunately, SAM cannot detect the bitrate for a Windows Media Unicast stream. Thus, you have to manually enter the correct bitrate into the bitrate box.

Graphs

▶ **Interval xx minutes**—The interval on which the graphs are updated.

▶ **Visible history xx minutes**—This is how "wide" the graph must be in minutes. For example, a value of 45 will result in the graph showing the statistics for the last 45 minutes.

▶ **Total history xx minutes**—This is the total amount of minutes to keep in the graph. You can "pan" to the history by holding the Ctrl key down while dragging your left mouse button on the graph. Holding down the Shift key with a left-click on the graph will restore the graph. Shift plus a left mouse drag will zoom into the box drawn by the mouse. Shift-click restores the graph again.

Relays

SAM has the ability to get statistics from several relay sources. These relays might be of any supported server type and of any bitrate. This allows broadcasters to get global statistics for advertisement and station listings. Also, on the AudioRealm.com station list, each relay will be shown so a user can easily select to which relay he or she wants to connect.

APPENDICES

To add a new relay, simply click on the Add Relay button. A new relay will be inserted. Now complete the fields.

To delete a relay:

1. Scroll to the correct relay using the grid on the bottom.

2. Make sure the correct relay is selected.

3. Click on the Delete relay button.

4. Choose Yes to delete the currently selected relay.

To edit a relay, scroll to the correct relay using the grid on the bottom. Then type the correct values into the fields. You can also edit most fields directly in the Grid, but this is not recommended because it is "unguided."

► **Server Type**—The type of relay in use.

> **NOTE**
>
> If you are using the latest version of SHOUTcast, you should select SHOUTcast v1.5b+ from the list.

► **Host (IP)**—The host/IP address where the server is located.

► **Port**—The port the server is listening on for connections. For Windows Media servers, this will contain the publishing point virtual root.

► **Show line on graph**—If checked, this relay server will show up on the graph. This can be turned on/off at any time using the Relays screen on the DJ-Tools/Statistics screen.

Remote Relays

You can download another application called SAMRelay which can report statistics to the main SAM from a remote location. The SAMRelay application is usually run close to the actual relay server, which then reports statistics to the main SAM. This way the relay-owner can also view statistics about the relay server in use.

The main reason SAMRelay was created was to implement support for new types of servers more easily.

► **Allow SAM relay connections**—If checked, SAM will allow SAMRelay applications to connect to SAM.

► **Username**—The relay username. Make sure you use the same username in the SAMRelay application.

▶ **Very important**—The relay username and password must be different from the admin username and password.

▶ **Password**—The relay password. Make sure you use the same password in the SAMRelay application.

Request Policy

Here are some request-related items:

▶ **Automatically handle requests**—If checked, SAM will automatically insert song requests from a Web site or chat room into your quelist. The exact details on how the request should be handled are then specified below.

▶ **Add requested song to**—When a song is requested, this option specifies where it will be inserted.

—**Next to play**—Will insert the song directly into Winamp and it will play next.

—**Top of que**—Will insert the song in the queue at the top position, thus the song will play directly after the next song.

Bottom of que   Will play the song after all songs in the queue have played. This is the recommended setting.

▶ **When it is requested xx times**—If this value is greater than 1, SAM will wait until the song is requested xx times before it actually inserts the song into the queue. You can view the songs requested on the main DJ-Tools window by clicking on the Requests button located just below the playlist.

▶ **Same IP may vote xx times in mm minutes**—This will limit a user to the amount of songs for which he or she can vote in a certain time frame. It is recommended that you set it to two songs per 20 minutes to prevent one user from "controlling" your broadcast.

▶ **Prevent users from requesting the same or recently played songs**—This is highly recommended. It will prevent users from requesting the same song twice and also preventing the same popular songs from being requested too often in a short period of time.

NOTE
SAM's request feature will also allow only valid songs to be accepted. Requests sent via a Web page will arrive on the same port used for the Remote Administration of SAM. The default for this port is usually 1221.

▶ **Log request to file**—Optionally, requests can be logged to a file to keep track of the most popular songs. If you wish to log requests, check this box and choose your log filename.

▶ **Comma delimited format**—If checked, SAM will output the log in comma delimited format. This data can be imported into most spreadsheet programs to generate statistics or graphs.

▶ **Log only valid songs**—Some requests fail for various reasons, such as the song having been recently played, invalid song, and more. If you check this option, only requests that were actually executed are logged.

Input/Output files

▶ **HTML output enabled**—Turns HTML output on or off. HTML output is the dynamic creation of HTML files that is populated with song information according to tags in an HTML template. The full version of SAM comes with a default HTML template you can modify to your needs. Please refer to the section explaining the template tags for more information.

▶ **Source file > Destination file**—In this grid you can enter the source HTML files that act as the templates and then where the generated files will be written to. In the "U" column, a "Y" means that this file will automatically be uploaded using FTP. You can easily add, edit, or delete files by clicking on the corresponding buttons on the right. The "up-arrow" and "down-arrow" buttons will move the selected row up or down.

▶ **Playlist output**—Because the playlist HTML file can become pretty big (more than 500Kb), it must be handled in a different way than the other HTML files. This HTML file is created and uploaded only if the playlist changes. You can optionally split the playlist up in different pages so that a user won't have to download the full playlist.

▶ **Playlist output style**—You can choose between two different output styles:

—**Normal**—The playlist is created as one big HTML file. Only use this option if your playlist is less than 200 songs big.

—**Split pages, order by Artist**—The recommended setting. This will first sort the playlist by artist name and then output the playlist to twenty-seven different pages. Each page will only contain the artists that start with a certain letter. The first page will contain all those with non-alphabetic names, i.e. "2Pac." The second to last page will contain all the alphabetic letters from "A" to "Z." The filenames of each HTML page will also be accordingly named, i.e. "0_9Playlist.htm" to "Zplaylist.htm."

▶ **Playlist source file**—The location of the template file for the playlist. If you downloaded the full version of SAM, you can find the default template in the webinput directory on the SAM directory.

▶ **Playlist destination file**—The location where the generated file(s) must be written.

▶ **Automatically upload**—If checked, SAM will automatically use FTP to upload it to your Web site.

Output tags

On this page, you can specify a few "special" tags that can automatically be inserted into generated HTML files.

▶ **"On Air" picture**—This can be text or a picture. If Winamp is playing and the DSP plugin is connected, then this text will be inserted into the *OnAir* tag. This can be used to display a status picture or use it plainly to announce the online status of your station with normal text.

▶ **"Offline" picture**—This can be text or a picture. If Winamp is not playing or the DSP plugin is disconnected, then this text will be inserted into the *OnAir* tag. This can be used to display an "offline" status message.

▶ **Custom01-Custom04**—In these tags, you can place any text you would like to have dynamically inserted into generated HTML pages. These values will be inserted into the *Customxx* tags, where the xx is the number of the tag, i.e. *Custom01* for the first tag.

Potential uses include:

▶ Stations with multiple DJs and programs use these tags to announce the current active DJ and program playing.

▶ If you don't have banner rotation code, you can easily use this to rotate banners.

AAT

AAT (Advanced Audio Tags) are external MP3 tags containing extra song information like pictures, text, links and even sounds. These can be created using the AAT editor that comes with the full download of SAM.

▶ **Use AAT tags**—If you don't use any AAT tags, you might still want to check this. AAT default tags can come in handy.

APPENDICES

▶ **AAT depository directory**—The directory where all of your AAT files are located. This should be the same directory to which your AAT Editor is set. (Refer to the AAT Editor help for more information.)

▶ **First look in local path**—If chosen, SAM will first look for an AAT file in the same directory as the MP3 file. If no matching AAT file is found in the local path, SAM will look for one in the depository path.

▶ **First look in depository**—If chosen, SAM will first look in the depository directory specified above. If no matching AAT is found, it will then continue to look in the local path in which the MP3 is located.

AAT Defaults

The AAT default values are used when no AAT tag for a file can be found. It also is used in cases where the AAT tag doesn't contain this specific "chunk." A chunk is a sub-part of the AAT tag containing a specific type of data, i.e. the album cover. In this case the Description (chunk) would typically be "Cover" and the Value (data) will typically be either the raw image data itself or just a link to the image location. Only text-type data can be entered into the default AAT tags section below.

AAT defaults can also be used in basically the same way as the Customxx tags were used earlier. For instance, in the default setup, SAM is set up to replace the *BuyCD* AAT tag with a default link which will search for the CD on CDNow. If you had an AAT tag for a specific song, you could use the AAT editor to supply a direct link to purchasing the CD. This is great for independent artists who would like to sell their own CDs.

Other tags can also be used inside AAT tags. As in the CD search we described, the #Artist# or #Album# tag can be included and when the HTML file is created these tags will be replaced by the actual song information. The "#" specifies that the tag must be URL encoded for the Web server to correctly decode the parameters.

▶ **AAT defaults grid**—In the grid you can simply type in the AAT descriptions and values.

▶ **Description**—This is actually the name of the AAT chunk. This will typically be words like "BuyCD," "Cover,""Lyrics," and so on as used in the AAT files.

▶ **Value**—This is the value that will be inserted into the HTML file. Typical values will be "No lyrics available" or "No band info available."

Uploading

SAM can automatically recover from various errors. These include bad or invalid songs, a lost server connection, network errors, and more.

▶ **Auto upload to webserver**—If checked, SAM will automatically upload all HTML files created to the specified FTP server.

▶ **Show upload status**—This will pop up a window displaying the upload status of the files every time the files are uploaded. The main purpose of this window is to check if your files get successfully uploaded and, if not, to show what error has occurred. Once you know everything is working, you can turn this off.

▶ **Compress files before uploading**—This option is useful only for the FTP server running on the AudioRealm servers. AudioRealm runs a specially written FTP server that was optimized for use with SAM. This FTP server accepts Zip compressed files and will automatically uncompress these files.

SAM will compress all files and send it in Zip format, and the server will then uncompress it. This turns a 200Kb download into a 30Kb download, saving bandwidth for both you and AudioRealm!

▶ **Username**—This is your FTP username. Contact your FTP administrator if you are unsure of your username. If you signed up for your free Web space at AudioRealm, you can easily view your username under the Web hosting page in the member section.

▶ **Password**—This is your FTP access password. Contact your FTP administrator if you are unsure of your password. If you signed up for your free Web space at AudioRealm, you can easily view your password under the Web hosting page in the member section.

▶ **Host**—The DNS or IP address of the server on which the FTP server is located. The AudioRealm FTP server is located on **ftp.audiorealm.com**.

▶ **Port**—The FTP port. The default for FTP is usually port 21. If you unsure about this value, use 21.

▶ **Directory on FTP server**—This can be a relative or fully qualified path to the directory into which you wish to upload your files. If you are using your own private server, in most cases you will leave this edit field blank. AudioRealm users should use upload in this field. All files uploaded to the upload directory are handled in a special way by the SAM-optimized FTP server of AudioRealm. It is recommended you upload all files to this directory.

APPENDICES

Proxy & Firewall settings

SAM offers some basic support for users behind proxy or firewall support. This is basically used only for touches to AudioRealm and also for FTP server connections. The main use is for the connection to your streaming server for gathering statistics if you are located behind a proxy.

► **Proxy Host**—The IP or DNS name of the proxy server. You can obtain this address from your network administrator.

► **Proxy Port**—Most proxy servers will use the default port of 80, but in some cases you might be using another port. If you are unsure, leave this value at 80.

► **Username**—Very few proxy servers require a username. In most cases, you can just leave this field blank.

► **Password**—Very few proxy servers require a password. In most cases, you can just leave this field blank.

► **Use proxy for FTP**—Check this box if you also need to go through a proxy server to use FTP.

Remote Administration

Most of SAM's features can also be remotely controlled via the Remote Administration tool provided with SAM. You can connect to SAM from anywhere in the world and control almost any aspect of your broadcast.

SAM currently allows for only one admin to be connected at a time. This avoids confusion caused by two people trying to use SAM at the same time. If two admins connect, the one that connects last will become the admin. The old admin will get a message that it is no longer the admin.

► **Allow administration**—If you turn this on, you absolutely must also change your admin password or risk somebody else remotely controlling your station.

► **Username**—You can use any username. Remember to use the same one in the Remote Admin application.

► **Password**—You can also use any password. Remember to use the same one in the Remote Admin application.

► **Port to listen on**—This is the port on which all incoming admins must connect. Use the same port in the Remote Admin application.

NOTE

This port is also the port on which all other clients connect. This includes the delivery of requests from a Web page. If you change the port away from the default (1221), you also need to change the tags in your HTML code to reflect the port change, i.e. add '&port=1221' replacing '1221' with your new port to the request URL. You will need to change the port only if you want to run multiple instances of SAM on the same computer.

AudioRealm Revenue service

If you are running a commercial station or want to earn some extra cash, AudioRealm's Revenue service can help. AudioRealm will get the advertisers, SAM will automatically download the audio ads and automatically schedule them into your broadcast. However, you will have full control over this process and can schedule ads with an ASQ script.

After signing up to become an AudioRealm member, set SAM up to play AudioRealm ads:

▶ **Automatically use AudioRealm advertisements**—When checked, this will automatically schedule ads into your broadcast according to the details below.

▶ **Hide advertisements and promos from history list**—When checked, this will hide AudioRealm ads, in-house ads, and promos and jingles from the history list. These files won't show up in the HTML, chat rooms, etc. but will still be shown in the history logs.

▶ **Adserver Host (IP)**—The DNS name or the IP of the server that is actually serving the ads. At the moment the only server doing this is the AudioRealm server located at **www.audiorealm.com**.

▶ **Member ID number**—Your member ID you received when you signed up with AudioRealm. If you have not yet signed up, you can do so at **www.audiorealm.com/samdb/join.php3**. Very few proxy servers require a username or password. In most cases you can just leave this field blank.

▶ **Insert xx advertisement unit(s) every mm minutes**—This specifies how many advertisements you want inserted. At the moment each unit is set at 15 seconds each. We recommend placing two to three units every 15 to 20 minutes. There are rules in the member section about guidelines for placing audio ads.

▶ **Directory to store ads in**—SAM automatically downloads advertisements, but it needs to save them somewhere. Here you can specify where advertisements are stored. You should use fully qualified directory names, i.e. "c:\program files\spacialaudio\sam\promos".

APPENDICES

SAM Plug-ins

Via the SAM API, programmers can develop plug-ins for SAM to extend its functionality.

Plug-ins include:

▶ Multiple bitrate streaming
▶ PHP/SQL song handling
▶ Custom request handling
▶ Custom advertising modules

You can download the latest plug-ins from the SAM Web page.

Setting up the plug-ins

At Step 8 you will activate your plug-ins. This is very simple to do. You simply check all the plug-ins that you want to use. You might also have to focus a plug-in by clicking on it in the list and then clicking on the Configure Plugin button. (You can also double click on the plug-in in the list.) This will bring up the plug-in's own configuration screen if it has one.

NOTE
Only valid plug-ins will show up in the list. Only plug-ins located in the ./plugins/ directory will be included in the list.

You can get the latest plug-ins from the SAM Web page. Please refer to the SAM API for details on writing your own plug-ins.

Basic Playlist Usage

After you have configured SAM correctly, the next step is to add some songs to your playlist.

NOTE
SAM doesn't have to handle the playlist. Winamp can still continue to handle the playlist, but then you'll lose the best functions of SAM. To turn off SAM's playlist, you can uncheck the little white checkbox on the right-hand top corner of the playlist.

Make sure you check that Winamp is on Shuffle & Repeat mode, or Auto recovery will kick in after each song.

How to add songs to the playlist

Adding songs to your playlist is easy. Click on the [+] button to bring up a popup menu. There you may choose how to add songs to the playlist. These methods are very similar to Winamp's, so we won't discuss them here in any more detail. You can also drag songs from Windows Explorer into the playlist.

Another way to add songs to your playlist is to click on the [<] button. This will import the current Winamp playlist into SAM. However, sometimes Winamp uses relative paths in its playlists and this might cause SAM to interpret these songs as invalid.

A quick rundown of the other buttons:

> [ ] (Top checkbox)—Turns the SAM playlist Off or On
>
> [S]—Shuffle button
>
> [R]—Repeat button
>
> [2]—If this is down, SAM will try not to play the same song twice
>
> [+]—Will add songs to your playlist
>
> [-] Will remove files from the playlist
>
> [<]—Will move all the files in the current Winamp playlist into SAM
>
> [>]—Will move SAM's playlist into Winamp
>
> [sel]—Selection options
>
> [misc]—Various functions including Sort of playlist, Save & Load of playlist, Generation of Playlist HTML

Playlist shortcuts

You can drag songs into a new position in the playlist. You can select multiple songs by holding down Shift or Ctrl.

> **Enter or Double-click**—Adds a song to the Que (You can also drag songs into the Quelist!)
>
> **Ctrl+A**—Selects all songs
>
> **Del**—Removes selected song(s)

Right-click on playlist also pops up a menu with a few options.

Searching for a Song

SAM makes it real easy to find a song. There are basically two ways to search for a song—Quick Search and Advanced Search.

APPENDICES

Quick Search

Right beneath the playlist there is an edit box. You can type your search in there and either click on the Go! button or press Enter to start the search. SAM will then highlight the first matching song. To find the next matching song click on the [>>] button or press Enter again.

Advanced Search

Click on the Advanced button or use the keyboard shortcut Ctrl+F. A screen will pop up. Enter your search string and, if you wish, you can change the details through which SAM searches to make a match. Now click the Go! button or press Enter.

On the right hand panel, you will see a list of all the matching songs. You can double-click, press Enter, or drag a song onto the quelist to add that song to the que. Right-clicking on a song also pops up a menu with a few more options.

Another way to bring up the advanced search screen is to start typing your search while the playlist is focused.

Basic Quelist Usage

The quelist is used to play songs in a certain order. When a song changes or the user clicks on the [>>] button of the que, SAM will insert the top song in the que into Winamp to play next. Songs are added to the quelist from many different sources, i.e. requests, playlist, advanced search, jingles, promos, and advertisements.

You can also drag songs from Windows Explorer into the quelist. The total duration of the songs in the que are displayed in the top right-hand corner of the que. This time includes the song next to play.

Removing songs from que

Pressing Del will remove all the selected songs from the que. You can also click on the scissors icon and choose a deletion option, or right-click on the quelist to get a popup menu.

Moving order of songs

To change the order of the songs in which they will play, you can move the songs up or down in the que. Select the songs you want to move and click on the red arrows to move the selected songs up or down in the que. You can also right-click on a song and then choose an option from the popup menu to move the song to the top or bottom of the quelist.

Choosing next song to play

SAM will automatically insert the top most song in the que to play next. You can also click on the [>>] button above the quelist to move the top song into Winamp to play next (or use the keyboard shortcut Ctrl+N).

The song whose title is listed in the "Next To play" box will play right after the current song has finished playing. This allows you to view all songs that will be played before they are actually played. This also applies to songs randomly inserted into next to play from sources like the playlist.

General Use

The Mini-Winamp is the "Winamp controls" located at the top middle of the DJ-tools section. The buttons located on the mini-Winamp corresponds to Winamp's own controls. Here follows a short description of each button:

I<—Previous button*

> —Play

I I—pause

[]—Stop

>I—Next*

[EQ]—Shows/Hides Winamp's Equalizer

[PL]—Show/Hides Winamp's Playlist

[PR]—Shows/Hides Winamp's Preferences box (Setup screen)

[Linerec]—Starts LineRec plugin

Note that if SAM is handling the playlist, pressing this will only cause the "Next to play" song to be played.

The following functions are only available with DSP plugin v1.5b or later with the advanced mode selected:

[Push to Talk]—When you press this button, the music will fade out to the level you selected and then you can talk over the music. When you release this button the music will fade back to its original level.

[Lock]—Locks the [Push to talk] button into the "talk" position.

On the top-right hand corner there are also two buttons. The first button ([^]) will show or minimize Winamp. The second button will either close Winamp ([x]) or start Winamp ([+]).

Also located in the mini-Winamp is the time display and volume control. To change the volume, just drag the green bar to a new position.

NOTE

When using the directsound plug-in, the volume might not display the correct value. It will always display the WAV volume settings, and DX sounds also have an internal volume setting SAM doesn't recognize.

Time display

SAM shows the time of the currently playing song in the mini-Winamp window. SAM can either show the time remaining or the time elapsed. To change it, click on the time box.

Linerec button

As of this writing, SAM has no built-in support for live mixing, but it is expected to be added soon. The SHOUTcast DSP plugin v1.5b introduced a new advanced mode where you can talk over music. SAM now fully supports this functionality from the mini-Winamp screen. Also, check out the keyboard shortcuts—spacebar and Ctrl+T.

For now you can use the LineRec plugin to stream data directly from a Mic or Line-in. The [Linerec] button (or the keyboard shortcut Ctrl+L) will only que the linerec plugin. This means that only once Winamp actually starts the next song will the LineRec plugin kick in.

Here's a popular way of using the [live] button:

Step 1: Click on the [Live] button.

Step 2: Click on the [>>] button of the quelist to que the linerec plugin to play next.

Step 3: Now, you can either wait for the currently playing song to finish or press the play ([>]) button whenever you are ready to start using the LineRec plugin.

HTML Output

One of the primary functions of SAM is to produce HTML files populated with song information. SAM parses template HTML files. In these template files are tags which are replaced with the correct song information. For example, the tag *artist00* will be replaced with the artist name of the song currently playing. This approach makes it easy to produce highly customizable templates.

Having your Web site output current song information has many advantages:

▶ Keeps visitors longer on your site

▶ You help promote artists and CD/MP3 sale

▶ You can sell CDs/MP3s on your site

▶ Visitors will come back for more

With AAT, you can also provide information like lyrics, band picture, album cover, BuyCd links, and so on.

Setting it up

Setting this up is simple. You specify which source file will be parsed and then to what file name the completed file will be written. We suggest using full paths when doing this.

The only file that's handled a bit differently is the Playlist HTML file. Here you also have the option of splitting up the playlist into smaller files. This is useful for broadcasters with a lot of songs in their playlist. The Playlist HTML file also is created only when the playlist actually changes. You can always force an HTML creation using the [misc] button and then choosing Generate HTML playlist.

All HTML files created can also optionally be uploaded to a Web server using FTP. AudioRealm runs a specially modified FTP server which allows you to compress the files before uploading it. This greatly improves bandwidth usage and speed. You can sign up for your own free 15MB Web site at AudioRealm if you wish to make use of this service. The FTP upload works with any standard FTP server if you do not use compression.

For more information about the HTML tags supported, please refer to the HTM Tags.txt document in your ../sam/docs directory. Also take a look at the demo Web page template provided with the full download of SAM.

Take special note that PlayList and QueList tags are handled in a special way, which is not obvious if you don't look at the actual HTML code.

This should be enough to get you started. If you need more detailed help, please ask your questions in the forum.

Setting up the Request Function

Certainly one of the most popular reasons to use SAM is the automated requests. SAM can automatically insert requests into your quelist to be played. Requests can currently be made via a Web site or IRC chat.

▶ **Web site**—You can place a link on your Web site for each song. When this link is clicked upon, it will contact the AudioRealm request service, which will try and deliver the request to your SAM.

▶ **IRC chat**—The user can enter !req <song number> to request a certain song.

The first step is to enable requests in your SAM setup and optionally select to port where requests are received. In the SAM configuration, go to the Request policy page. Check the Automatically handle requests checkbox. You can change the default port where requests are received at the Remote Admin panel. The default is port 1221.

The last step is to create the HTML links. Most people use the SAM HTML output for this—more specifically, the HTML playlist output. The Web template provided with the full version of SAM demonstrates this very clearly.

The URL looks like this:

http://www.audiorealm.com/req/req.php3?host=*ip*&port= 1221&dir=mydir&file=#filefull#

▶ **Host**—The IP/host where your SAM is located. If parsed by SAM, *ip* will be replaced with the correct IP. Please note that people with multiple IPs might have to make use of the *ip00*,*ip01*, etc. tags or just enter the IP if they have a static IP.

▶ **Port**—The port as specified under the "Remote admin" setup. Default is 1221.

▶ **Dir**—If you have submitted your own custom request pages, this field will contain the directory where they are stored on the server.

▶ **File**—URL encoded filename (with full path) to the song to be requested. SAM will parse the #filefull# tag and insert the correct filename URL encoded if the HTML output is used. Again, please refer to the web template provided with the full version of SAM.

▶ **Requests through IRC Chat**—To turn requests through IRC chat on, simply click on the "Allow requests in this channel" button in the chat room.

NOTE

Only do this in your own private channel dedicated to your broadcast. In public rooms, this might upset other people not interested in your station.

All requests can be logged to a log file. For more information on this, please refer to the documentation for Step 3.

Also, you can get some basic statistics of your requests by going to this page: **http://www.audiorealm.com/req/stats.php3.**

Additional functions

▶ **[Announce song names in this channel]**—If this button is down, song titles will be announced in this channel.

NOTE

Only do this in a private channel dedicated to your broadcast.

▶ **[Allow requests through this channel]**—If this button is down, SAM will accept requests made in this channel.

NOTE

Once again, only do this in a private channel dedicated to your broadcast.

You can also [dock]/[undock] the chat as well as hide the chat window. Clicking on the lock icon will dock/undock the chat window. The [X] button will hide the chat window.

Statistics

Once the main server is set up, the statistics should function without any further intervention. SAM collects the global statistics from the main server, as well as from all the relay servers, and reports the combined statistics to the graph.

Selecting a relay

To view more information about a specific relay, go to the Relays tab and click on that relay in the relay list. On the right panel you should now see various information about the relay, i.e. Host:Port, server type, and so on. Once selected, you can also change a few settings on the fly.

Graphing functions

Each server can also be individually graphed by checking the Show line on graph checkbox on the Relays tab. You can also change the color of the line by clicking on the line color box and choosing the new color.

NOTE

These changes are not permanent; you have to configure permanent changes in the SAM configuration.

With Shift-drag left mouse you can drag a box. The graph will then zoom to that box. Shift-click on the graph to restore the graph to normal size.

With Ctrl-drag you can pan the view of the graph. This can be used to browse back into history. Shift-click once again restores the graph to normal.

Special functions

▶ **[Restart All Relays]**—This button will close all current relays, and refresh the current relay list. Use this button if you change some of the relay stuff in the configuration.

Most relay connections will have the following buttons:

▶ **[Connect]**—Connect to the relay server and start collecting statistics

▶ **[Disconnect]**—Disconnect from server

Icecast

SAM has a special built-in front end for use with icecast. Most of the major icecast commands are only a button click away.

To use the icecast console, click on the icecast button to get to the icecast console screen. Select the icecast server you want to work with. This can be done by selecting the correct one from the drop-down list on the top right-hand corner of the screen.

If the icecast relay is not connected to the server, click on the connect button.

Entering commands

You can enter icecast commands in the command line editor on the bottom of the screen. To get help on commands, just type "help <command>". To get a list of all available commands, type "help".

Using the command buttons

A much faster way to enter commands is simply to click on the command buttons.

To find out what a button does, click on the Help on button and click on the button in question. Icecast will display some help on that command.

Operator login

Some commands are available for use only by an operator. If you have entered the operator password in the SAM config, you can now click on the Login as operator button to login as an operator. You should now be able to use commands like Shutdown and Touch that can be used only by operators.

ASQ (Auto Song Queing)

ASQ allows you to program your playlist to play music without having to be in front of your computer 24/7. You can use it to:

▶ Schedule in-house advertisements

▶ Schedule AudioRealm advertisements

▶ Schedule promos and jingles

▶ Rotate your playlist

▶ Program a "format" for your station.

▶ Schedule different playlists for DJs

▶ Schedule music programs

ASQ Editor

The ASQ editor can be found on the DJ-tools screen. Click on the tab saying Playlist Automation (ASQ). The [>] button will start the script; the [| |] button will pause the script; the stop button will stop the script; and the [>|] button will fast forward to the next command. The [>>|] button will:

▶ pause your script

▶ skip to the next command without executing the current command.

Use this to "jump" over loops. Also, try double-clicking on the ASQ script while it is running. You can now change the execution point to the new line. This is great for skipping code to test long ASQ scripts. However, this might cause some loops to function badly the first round. Avoid skipping into a Repeat..Until loop.

The ASQ scripts can also be Loaded or Saved. ASQ scripts are normal txt-formatted files and can easily be edited using Notepad or something similar.

ASQ can be in two modes—Edit and Run. If you wish to edit the script, first click on the Edit button. You can now simply type your ASQ commands into the window. After you are done entering your commands, click on the Run button. Then, to start executing the script, click on the [>] (play) button.

How ASQ works

ASQ is basically a programming language. You enter the commands and then SAM follows these instructions to manipulate the playlist. ASQ is started as soon as Winamp is loaded. Every second thereafter it will check, interpret, and execute the next command until the end of the script ("program") is reached.

Basic structure information

Please refer to the ASQ.txt file in SAM's doc directory for a complete list of ASQ commands. ASQ is quite sensitive to syntax, so make sure you type commands exactly as they appear in the ASQ.txt file. You can put spaces in front of commands, but there should be no extra spaces within the command itself, i.e. ^^^AmpLoadDir^c:\music\ is correct, but ^^^AmpLoadDir^c:\music\^^ won't work (where ^ = space). However, ASQ is case-insensitive.

Each command should be on a new line and all unrecognized commands are simply ignored. Comments start with {, [, or //.

ASQ currently only supports Repeat. Until loops, and also supports nested loops up to six levels deep.

Events

ASQ can be considered as a primitive event-driven programming language because it spends most of its time waiting for events to happen. Events can be used to pause execution of the script until the event occurs. It can also be used to loop the script until the event occurs.

Here are a few brief examples on how to use events.

OnTime hh:mm:ss—Waits until the specified time
    Example:
    {—Start—}
    { Loads a new playlist at 6:30am }
    { Note the '0' in front of '6' is required }
    OnTime 06:30:00
    LoadPlaylist c:\music\morning.m3u
    { Loads a new playlist at 5:30pm }
    OnTime 17:30:00
    LoadPlaylist c:\music\afternoon.m3u
    {— END —}
OnTime Now+hh:mm:ss—Waits until Now + hh:mm:ss later
    Example:
    {—Start—}
    { Inserts an advertisement every 15 minutes }

OnTime Now+00:15:00
InsertAdd
{Restart from top!}
Restart
{— END —}

OnAfter xx—Waits for xx songs to be played
Example:
{—Start—}
{ Inserts an advertisement every 5 songs }
OnAfter 5
InsertAdd
{Restart from top!}
Restart
{— END —}

OnQueEmpty—Waits for the que to become empty
Example:
{—Start—}
{ Inserts 5 new random songs if que is empty }
{ This is only done during 1pm and 5pm }
OnTime 13:00:00
Repeat
OnQueEmpty
{ Insert 5 random songs into the top of the que from the specified directory }
LoadRndSubDir 5,QueTop,c:\music\rock\
Until OnTime 17:00:00
{Restart from top!}
Restart
{— END —}

More examples

A simple promo scheduler

{This simple example will insert a song from the promo list every 10 minutes}
OnTime Now+00:10:00
Insert Promo
OnQueEmpty
Restart

Complete schedule by Tabasco from http://riograndemud.com/radio

(This example will insert jingles, promos, and advertisements on a fixed schedule. In this case, the promos were used for running the station IDs and Jingles were used to run sound bites from movies, TV, comedy, and so on.)

```
OnTime Now+00:08:00
InsertPromo 1,1
OnQueEmpty
OnTime Now+00:04:00
InsertAdd 1,1
InsertJingle 1,1
InsertPromo 1,1
OnQueEmpty
OnTime Now+00:06:00
InsertPromo 1,1
OnQueEmpty
OnTime Now+00.00.00
InsertAdd 1,1
InsertJingle 1,1
OnQueEmpty
OnTime Now+00:12:00
InsertPromo 1,1
InsertAdd 1,1
InsertJingle 1,1
OnQueEmpty
OnTime Now+00:06:00
InsertPromo 1,1
OnTime Now+00:03:00
InsertJingle 1,1
OnQueEmpty
OnTime Now+00:03:00
InsertAdd 1,1
InsertPromo 1,1
InsertJingle 1,1
OnQueEmpty
Restart
```

Using the 'Jingles, Promos and Ads' section

This section was provided for Station IDs, promos, jingles, advertisements, and other content that can give a station a professional feel. The Jingles, Promos and Ads are best used when called by an ASQ script. The high level of customization ASQ offers will make running your station professionally very easy.

When clicking on the Jingles, Promos & Ads tab, you get a screen with a "treeview" box listing all the types of Playlists, i.e. AudioRealm ads, Jingles, and so on.

AudioRealm.com offers a revenue service where it will pay you to play ads on your station. When this page is selected, it will show you all the ads available for playing. You won't have control over which ads are inserted, but you have full control over when the ads are inserted. Also, since the ads are added to the queue, you also have the power to move, cancel, or remove ads that you don't want to play.

This function is very much automated either by selecting an insertion schedule of xx minutes in the SAM setup or by using an ASQ script to insert the Advertisements. You can also click on the AudioRealm ad button to insert an advertisement manually.

This process is fully automated: SAM will automatically download new advertisements, delete old ones, and choose which ads to play. It also automatically registers Advertisement impressions to the AudioRealm server, where your account will be increased with the value of the advertisement.

NOTE

You can manually download, insert, and remove advertisements if you wish. AudioRealm will still keep track of impressions if the ads are copied to the .../promos directory or the directory you specified as the advertisement's storage directory in your SAM configuration.

Jingles, Promos, Advertisements

All three of these function in exactly the same way, thus we will cover only the usage of Jingles. Jingles, Promos and Advertisements can also optionally be removed from the history list so that it doesn't show up on your HTML output.

Select the Jingles tree node by clicking on it. The music notes icon should change into a red arrow and on the right there should be a listbox with the caption *Jingles*.

All the functions mentioned below work exactly the same as with the main playlist.

Clicking on [+] will allow you to add files, whole directories or M3U playlists to the current list.

Clicking on the [-] button will allow you to remove files from the Jingle list.

▶ **[sel]**—Selection functions
▶ **[misc]**—Miscellaneous functions like loading and saving the jingle list

You can drag songs into a new position in the playlist and you can select multiple songs by holding down Shift or Ctrl.

> **Enter** or **Double-click**—Adds a song to the Que. You can also drag songs into the Quelist!)
> **Ctrl+A**—Selects all songs
> **Del**—Removes selected song(s)

Right-clicking on playlist also pops up a menu with a few options. You can click on the Insert Jingle button to insert a random jingle from the jingle list. You can also quickly do this by pressing F1, F2, F3, or F4 to insert an AudioRealm ad, Jingle, Promo, or In-House ad respectively. Alternatively you can double-click on a Jingle in the list to add it to the list

You can also make use of ASQ scripts to insert these types of songs. Please refer to the ASQ section for more details.

Running Multiple Instances of SAM

You can run more than one instance of SAM on the same computer to allow you to run multiple stations from the same machine. For each station, create a directory to hold Winamp, SAM, and the server (if applicable). This is done to create a unique setup for each station so you don't have to re-configure everything every time you start the station.

Now set up Winamp and server as needed. In the SAM setup, you need to first give each SAM a unique port. The default is 1221. Make sure the ports are at least two apart—if Station1 is port 1221, then the port for Station2 should start at port 1223, or anything above that. The port setup can be found under the Remote admin tab in the SAM setup.

In the General tab in the SAM setup, you need to specify the path to Winamp for that station. The last step is to select the correct Winamp instance each time SAM loads. This can easily be done with the drop-down menu located on the Winamp page. (Click on the Winamp button left of the DJ-tools button.)

Remember to specify the correct port in the HTML for requests, i.e. **http://www.audiorealm.com/req/req.php3?host=*ip*&port=1221&dir=my dir&file=#filefull#**

Controlling SAM from a Remote Location

You can control SAM from any location connected to the Internet or over a network running TCP/IP via the SAM_Remote application. This will allow you to monitor and operate your broadcast from anywhere in the world.

Setting up the remote application

The remote application is distributed together with the full installation of SAM, and is also available as a separate download. Click on the SAM Remote Admin icon or locate and run the SAM_Remote.exe to start up the application. Make sure you have set up SAM correctly to allow Remote Administration before continuing.

In the Remote Admin app, the configuration has three screens—Remote Admin, Chat, and Graph. We discuss only Remote Admin since the other two are basically the same as they are for SAM.

▶ **Username**—Enter username as specified in SAM

▶ **Password**—Enter password as specified in SAM

▶ **SAM Host**—Host or IP where SAM is located. You may use a local LAN IP or an Internet IP or a DNS name if available

▶ **SAM Port**—This is usually 1221 except if specified as different in SAM

Using the remote application

The first step is to connect to SAM. You can click on the Connect button to do this. If there is only a Disconnect button, then you are already connected. After connecting, the Playlist should be downloaded automatically. At any time, you can re-download the playlist play clicking on the [<<<] button in the playlist window. Clicking the [>>>] button will upload the current playlist.

On each song, change the QueList and NextToPlay song will automatically be refreshed. Adding songs to the PlayList or QueList will automatically be uploaded to the master SAM. Deleting songs from them will NOT be updated automatically. You have to click the [>>>] button to upload the changes.

The [+] box on the mini-Winamp screen will start Winamp and the [X] screen will close Winamp.

NOTE
If auto-recovery is on, SAM will automatically start Winamp, even if you close Winamp.

The rest of the functions are basically the same as in SAM and should be self-explanatory.

SAM Troubleshooting and FAQs

Here are some frequently asked questions and troubleshooting tips for SAM.

Can SAM handle huge playlists (10,000+ songs)?

Yes. It has been tested with 10,000 songs. It should be able to go to an unlimited amount, depending on the resources of your computer.

Can I have my own custom request pages?

Yes. You can download the request.zip file from the SAM download section. It contains full instructions of what needs to be done to have your own custom request pages show up after a request has been made.

How can I view the songs most requested?

SAM allows you to log all requests to a file. You can parse this file to get the statistics. The file can optionally be written in comma-delimited format, which can easily be read by a spreadsheet. This should simplify the parsing process.

Alternatively, and this might be more convenient, you can go to **http://www.audiorealm.com/req/stats.php3** where you can get detailed stats in summary form of requests made to your specific SAM.

SAM's auto error recovery pops up every other song—how do I fix this?

Turn on Shuffle and Repeat on Winamp.

SAM keeps scrolling songs every second.

The problem you have is that Song Title scrolling is turned on, which will interfere with SAM's detection of the song changing. To fix this, in Winamp, go to the Preferences > Options > Display menu and uncheck the Scroll song title in Windows taskbar option.

My stats connect—but then just garbage shows in the log screen.

If you are you using Live365, you must select Live365 as your server type. Slow connections can cause SAM to not send the login password fast enough, and subsequently the server detects you as a listener and not a broadcaster. To fix this problem, which happens only on rare occasions, go to the Relays tab on the DJ-tools screen and click on the Disconnect button. Then click the Connect button to initiate a re-connect to the server.

My stats connect—but don't
show a listener count or bitrate.

Ensure you specified the correct type of server, as well as the correct port. Make sure you entered the correct password. If you are using SHOUTcast v1.1 or earlier, or SHOUTcast v1.3x, upgrade to version 1.5b or later.

Be patient—with most types of servers, SAM will start showing stats only as soon as a listener connects/disconnects. If you have no listeners right away, you won't have the stats. On some servers, SAM polls the server for stats every minute or so. Try to connect to your own stream and wait approximately five minutes. If no stats show up, then you probably have a problem in your setup.

My HTML output shows
the same song in all the fields.

You have the wrong Winamp directory specified in your SAM setup. In the SAM configuration, go to the General tab. Enter the complete path to the version of Winamp you are using on your system. The button with the red arrow will also automatically insert the default path to Winamp as registered in your registry.

Songs and promos less than five seconds in length
seem to loop a few times before the next song plays.

With short songs, SAM sometimes cannot get everything done in time to detect the next song change. This causes short promos to loop a few times. Fixes for this are a bit harder. First, make sure that there is always a song queued in the Queue List after a short song/promo, which is a good use of ASQ. Second, merge some short songs together to make a slightly longer song in the form of a single file that stitches short clips together. Finally, avoid songs or audio clips less than 5 seconds in length. A clip of 10 seconds as the minimum should be a safe length.

Winamp plays the currently queued song,
but then stops after the song is done.

Turn on Repeat on Winamp. You might also want to turn on SAM's auto error recovery feature.

Index

Index

INDEX

D

INDEX

INDEX

J

K

L

INDEX

M

INDEX

O

P

INDEX

MUSKA&LIPMAN

Order our free catalog by visiting
http://www.muskalipman.com

Order Form

Postal Orders:
  Muska & Lipman Publishing
  P.O. Box 8225
  Cincinnati, Ohio 45208

Online Orders or more information:
  http://www.muskalipman.com
Fax Orders:
  (513) 924-9333

Title/ISBN	Price/Cost
Online Broadcasting Power! 0-966288-98-X	
Quantity _____	
	× $29.95
Total Cost _____	

Title/ISBN	Price/Cost
Sound Forge Power! 1-929685-10-6	
Quantity _____	
	× $29.95
Total Cost _____	

Cakewalk Power!
1-929685-02-5
  Quantity _____
  × $29.95
  Total Cost _____

Ship to:

  Company _____

  Name _____

  Address _____

  City _____ State _____ Zip _____ Country _____

  E-mail _____

Educational facilities, companies, and organizations
interested in multiple copies of these books should
contact the publisher for quantity discount information.
Training manuals, CD-ROMs, electronic versions, and
portions of these books are also available individually
or can be tailored for specific needs.

Subtotal _____

Sales Tax _____
(please add 6% for books shipped to Ohio addresses)

Shipping _____
($5.00 for US and Canada $10.00 other countries)

TOTAL PAYMENT ENCLOSED _____

Thank you for your order.